W. C. PRIVY

"Bathroom reading: It's your right ...
and your responsibility."

W. C. Privy's
Original
Bathroom
Companion

W. C. PRIVY

EDITED BY ERIN BARRETT & JACK MINGO

St. Martin's Griffin / New York

W. C. Privy's Original Bathroom Companion. Copyright © 2003 by Erin Barrett and Jack Mingo. All rights reserved. No part of this book may be used or reproduced in any manner whatsoever without written permission, except in the case of brief quotations in critical articles or reviews. For information, contact St. Martin's Press, 175 Fifth Avenue, New York, N.Y. 10010

www.stmartins.com

Designed, packaged, and produced by the Univark Deconstructionists

ISBN 0-312-28750-X

First edition: April 2003

10 9 8 7 6 5 4 3 2 1

Acknowledgments

To the *Bathroom Companion* staff members, our family and friends, thank you for helping us keep W. C. Privy's dream alive.

Heather Jackson Silverman
Lindy Settevendemie
Pam Suwinsky and Thalia Publishing Services
Kathie Meyer
Susan Shipman
Chris McLaughlin
Mary-Nell Bockman
Michele Montez
Oilville Goochland
Louisa Fernside
Georgia Hamner
Elana Mingo
Jackson Hamner
Eric "Stumpy Joe" Childs
Vera Mingo

Jerry & Lynn Barrett
Powell Hamner
Everyone at St. Martin's Press
The Honorable Mr. Doo-Wop
Ms. Deborah
Mark Hardin
Ray Davies
The BCOMPs (members of the W. C. Privy fan club—p. 478)
"Big Bob"
Ms. Fawcett
Shirley & Nigel Jest
Joe Mugs
Ed Zorn
Roxanne Barrett
The Univark Truckers

"Bugs: Everything You Wanted to Know About Insects," adapted from *Just Curious About Animals and Nature, Jeeves,* by Erin Barrett and Jack Mingo, Pocket Books, 2002. Adapted with permission by authors.

"Between Courses: Tricks for the Dinner Table," originally published in *How To Spit Nickels,* by Jack Mingo, McGraw Hill, 1993. Adapted with permission by author.

"Doctor Riots: The Mobs That Smashed Medical Schools," adapted from *Doctors Killed George Washington,* by Erin Barrett and Jack Mingo, Conari Press, 2002. Adapted with permission by authors.

"A Toast to Toasters: Bred for Bread ... and So Much More," "Full Metal Lunch Jacket: The Birth of the Cool Lunch Boxes," and "Anty Matters: How Uncle Milton Put the Ant in Ant Farm," "Toaster Foods: The Best Thing Since Sliced Bread," adapted from the *Whole Pop Magazine Online.* With permission from the editors.

Excerpts taken from *Just Curious, Jeeves* (Ask Jeeves, Inc., 2000) and *Just Curious About History, Jeeves* (Pocket Books, 2002) for "Presidential Trivia I & II: Presidents & Their Vices." With permission from authors.

Excerpts from *Cats Don't Always Land on Their Feet,* Conari Press, 2002, for "Cat Lovers: From the Ailurophiles," and "Cat Haters: Real-Life Ailurophobes." Permission granted by authors.

Excerpts from *Not Another Apple for the Teacher!,* Conari Press, 2002, for "More Deskware Trivia." Permission granted by authors.

Some images © 2001–2002 www.arttoday.com.

W. C. PRIVY

Genius!
MR. PRIVY, THE ORIGINAL

"There will be imitators, but no matter: 'Imitation is the sincerest form of plagiarism.' They can be nothing but pale counterfeits of the genuine Privy." —W. C. Privy

EXACTLY ONE CENTURY AGO, a remarkable thing happened in bathrooms across America. In the spring of 1903, W. C. Privy published *W. C. Privy's Original Bathroom Companion*, making him the foreflusher of bathroom reading. Composed of jokes, stories, quotations, facts, and other brief articles, the *Companion* made a big splash in the smallest room of the house.

And none too soon. For eons, the world had been waiting for bathroom reading. Reading, of course, had been around since 8000 B.C.; however, the real problem had been the bathroom. Before the approach of the twentieth century, bathrooms were not clean, well-lighted places suitable for reading. Instead, they were dark, smelly, uncomfortably hot or cold, and invariably infested with mosquitoes, horseflies, bats, and vermin. "Anyone who lingered to read in an outhouse was likely demented, addlepated, insensate, or drunk," Privy noted.

The simple fact was that bathroom reading required indoor plumbing, electric lights, a sturdy, locking bathroom door ... and a visionary like W. C. Privy.

EARLY HISTORY

Admittedly it's not much, but here's what little we know about Mr. Privy. He was born in 1875 in either Cincinnati, Ohio, or the Szechwan Province of China. He spent the bulk of his childhood either studying in the Toledo (Ohio) Academy for Boys or working in a bootblack factory outside of London, England.

In 1893, Privy visited an elderly aunt in Iowa and experienced indoor plumbing for the first time in his life. According to the proud aunt's memoirs, Privy spent many long hours locked in her bathroom "with a book or magazine, and he wouldn't come out no matter how much I knocked." One such day, she heard splashes followed by her teenage nephew shouting "Eureka!" Seconds later, W. C. burst out of the bathroom.

W. C. told his aunt that he'd had a revelation about the importance of bathroom reading to digestion, health, happiness, and life in general. The 1890s were a time of many emerging beliefs about diet, meditation, sex, and self-improvement; even a young man of Privy's temperament was not immune. Privy began formulating a philosophy about the benefits of "filling the mind while evacuating the body." (Alas, his seven volumes of detailed philosophical observations have been apparently lost to time. No doubt they would have made fascinating reading.)

THE BOOK THAT LAUNCHED 2000 FLUSHES

"Bathroom reading: It's your right ... and your responsibility!"
—*W. C. Privy*

Philosophy aside, it's sufficient to say that the *Bathroom Companion* was a direct result of Privy's twin obsession with indoor plumbing and good reading. When enough homes had indoor plumbing to make it economically feasible, the twenty-eight-year-old Privy published the first volume of his *W. C. Privy's Original Bathroom Companion*.

Privy had a great deal of humor and curiosity, which he developed in his younger years by writing short books on the fads of the 1860s and the songs of popular stage shows. Neither prudish nor prurient, levelheaded but not unromantic, he had a healthy contempt for the publishers of his day "who issued volume after worthless volume of flowery prose, erroneous facts, and uplifting-sounding pablum." A look at his first *Bathroom*

Companion's Table of Contents shows the sorts of things he believed would transfix and transform his readers: humor, fiction, quizzes, wordplay, explanations of how things work, histories, puzzles, optical illusions, and trivia. He included pictures and rhymes so the young could also experience the joys of bathroom reading. Finally, he offered a limited number of advertisements (some of which are reproduced in this book as a curiosity).

W. C. Privy binding copies of *Bathroom Companion #6*

Privy apparently had a firm grip on what people wanted to read behind closed doors, and soon a grateful world beat a path to his bathroom door. Although some Victorian-era doctors and clergymen warned that bathroom reading was immoral and could lead to insanity, blindness, and unwanted hair growth, the first *Bathroom Companion* went through many printings, and the public began clamoring for more. For the next twelve years, W. C. Privy issued a *Bathroom Companion* annually, each more popular than the previous one. Thanks to his fame, "Going to see Privy" became a euphemism for a bathroom stop in the United States; in England, the phrase became, "Where's the W. C.?"

AFTERMATH

What happened to Privy? After thirteen editions of the *Bathroom Companion*, he was tired ... and rich beyond his dreams. In 1916, as World War I raged in Europe, W. C. Privy announced his retirement and disappeared into obscurity somewhere in the wilds of the Pacific Northwest.

What happened to all the copies of his books? That's the strange thing. Although Privy sold millions of copies of his *Bathroom Companion*, there are no known copies now in existence. All that's left of Privy's bestsellers are thirty-three loose and yellowed pages found in a long-abandoned outhouse near Beaverdam, Virginia, revealing a few articles, Privy's introduction, and the Table of Contents mentioned above.

How could it be that all those books just disappeared? Well, to put it delicately, the concept of store-bought toilet paper had caught on much slower than that of indoor plumbing. People had gotten used to "recycling" newspapers, catalogs, and even pages from books when they'd finished reading them. Under the circumstances, a book designed to reside in the bathroom was both Privy's folly (in that it was used on the posterior instead of saved for posterity) or genius (in that he sold more books that way).

(To save this book from a similar fate, we're depending that readers have an ample supply of store-bought paper ... but just to make sure, we've included an emergency stash in the back to be used only in dire circumstances.)

A HUNDRED YEARS LATER

Thanks to a dissolute Privy descendant and a lucky bar bet, we have obtained the rights to carry on W. C. Privy's formidable tradition. On this hundredth anniversary of its first edition, we're proud to present the rebirth of *W. C. Privy's Original Bathroom Companion*.

While sitting firmly on Privy's oval seat of wisdom and fun, we aim to let fly with all we've got. While we can't possibly hope to be as financially successful as Privy himself was, we'll at least aspire to his high standards in presenting (as he put it) "a mighty fine read." We hope you enjoy leafing through this book as much as we enjoyed putting it together. And W. C., wherever you are, we hope we've done you proud.

Jack Mingo
Jack Mingo

Erin Barrett
Erin Barrett

ABOUT BARRETT & MINGO
Erin Barrett and Jack Mingo are particularly well-suited for the task of reviving the *Bathroom Companion*, having written dozens of entertaining books including *Just Curious, Jeeves, Doctors Killed George Washington, Cats Don't Always Land On Their Feet, The Whole Pop Catalog,* and *How the Cadillac Got Its Fins.* Their fun fact column appears daily in newspapers around the country.

What's Inside...

Monopoly!

THE WORLD'S FAVORITE REAL ESTATE GAME

Who came up with the idea for a game about buying and developing prime property? And how did a game like this become so popular? With a little digging, here's what we found.

ACCORDING TO PARKER BROTHERS, Monopoly was invented by an out-of-work heating engineer named Charles Darrow. During the Great Depression, his family could no longer afford their trips to Atlantic City, so Darrow created the game to remind them all of happier times.

There's no doubt that Darrow created a game, but there's great controversy over how much of it was his original idea. At the time, there were at least eight similar real estate oriented games, including a popular one at Harvard Law School. There's evidence that Charles Darrow learned the game from a group of Quakers while in Atlantic City but that he added Chance cards and the Railroads before pitching his game to gaming companies.

Parker Brothers originally turned the game down. The company listed several reasons why the game was a failure: The rules were too complicated, the concept was too dull, the game was too long, and the players went around and around the board instead trying to reach a destination. When Darrow took his game to market on his own, though, it was a huge and instant success. Parker Brothers ate crow and bought the game. The company quickly snatched up earlier versions of the game and spread the Darrow-as-sole-inventor story.

The game has changed little over the years. The minor differences are in the game pieces. The original line up in 1935: race car, flat iron, cannon, pocketbook, lantern, baby shoe, top hat, racehorse, battleship and thimble

with "For a Good Girl" engraved on it. The hotels were made of wood instead of plastic and had "Grand Hotel" written on them. In 2002, a brand new token—the first one in over 40 years—was added to the line up. It's a sack full of money.

The streets in the game are real streets in Atlantic City. At least they were when the game was put out. You may be a little disappointed if you trek to see them today, though. All of the upscale places in the game are pretty run-down and seedy, and some, like Pacific Avenue, are hang-outs for hookers. Kentucky Avenue is lined with greasy burger joints. Marven Gardens, misspelled on the game board, is located

so far out of town the trains don't even stop there anymore, and St. Charles Place is completely gone—wiped out by a parking lot for a casino. But one thing remains the same: there's always plenty of free parking at the jail.

Monopoly has continued to be a top seller over the years. It's published in over 23 languages, including Japanese, Russian, German, French, Chinese, and Spanish. The games are slightly changed to reflect the cultures of the people playing them. For instance, Boardwalk is "Rue de la Paix" in the French version, and different according to locale in other versions, like "Mayfair" (UK), "Kalverstraat" (Netherlands), and "Schlossallee" (Germany).

Over the years there have been specialty editions of the game. A gold set by Alfred Dunhill was offered in 1974 for $5,000, and Nieman-Marcus sold an all-chocolate set in the 1970s for $600. Other current and more affordable editions include the Braille edition, the Disney edition, the Power Puff girls edition, and the Pokémon Gold & Silver edition.

MONOPOLY FACTS & FIGURES:
• The spaces most frequently

landed on are, in order, Illinois Avenue, GO, B & O Railroad, Free Parking, Tennessee Avenue, New York Avenue, and the Reading Railroad.

• The smallest game of Monopoly ever played had an inch square board. The players looked through magnifying glasses during the 30-hour-long game.

• The longest game played underwater went for fifty days, or 1,200 hours. Divers in wet suits—1,500 of them—took turns playing in shifts.

• The largest outdoor game was larger than a city block—938 feet by 765 feet. Messengers on bicycles relayed plays to the participants.

• During World War II, Parker Brothers claims, "escape maps, compasses, and files were inserted into Monopoly game boards and smuggled into P.O.W. camps. Real money for escapees was slipped into the packs of Monopoly money."

• Parker Brothers annually produces more than twice the amount of money that the U.S. mint puts out each year. Despite this, you may be surprised to learn that a standard Monopoly game comes with a mere $15,140, total.

TIPS & TRICKS:

• Since there are only 32 houses available in each game, if you have low-rent properties, quickly build up four houses on each property to confront your opponents with a housing shortage.

• Jail can be a sanctuary later in the game when traveling around the board becomes monetarily dangerous. Get out of jail quickly early in the game when there's still property up for grabs.

• The rules don't allow for shuffling of the Chance and Community Chest cards. Therefore, remembering the order of the cards can work to your advantage.

• On average, you'll land on four properties each time around the board. To estimate the cost to you, count the unmortgaged properties that are owned by others in the game. Divide that number by 7 to get an estimate of the number of rents you can expect to pay on your next trip around the board.

Potty Pourri
Random Kinds of Factness

• Elvis Presley didn't believe in encores. A few moments after Elvis walked offstage, a voice on the PA would announce to the cheering fans, "Elvis has left the building," and that was that.

• Cats can drive even a genius crazy, what with that out-again, in-again thing they do. Sir Isaac Newton's cat kept interrupting his work on the laws of gravity, so he put his intellect to work. He invented that sanity-saving contraption, the cat door flap.

• Thirty-six dollars an ounce? No, don't call the vice squad, call the spice squad. Pickers pluck the stamens of nearly 5,000 blossoms to get just one ounce of saffron, making it the most expensive spice on your grocer's shelf.

• The Food and Drug Administration allows up to 210 insect fragments and seven rodent hairs in a regular 700-gram jar of peanut butter before considering the product too unsanitary for public consumption. The consuming public may have a differing opinion, of course.

• If you *deliberately* eat bugs, you're an "entomophagist."

• The very first American entrepreneur to be worth a billion dollars? Car mogul Henry Ford.

• That flavor we call "bubblegum" is a mix of vanilla, wintergreen, and cassia (a form of cinnamon).

• Experts say you should scrub with soap and water for at least 20 seconds if you want your hands to be sanitary.

• Douglas Engelbart invented the "X-Y Position Indicator for a Display System" in the late 1960s. "XYPIDS" didn't catch on as a name—early users first called it a "turtle," then a "rodent," then the cuter-sounding "mouse," the name that finally stuck to that computer thing that rolls, points, and clicks.

•When watching TV, you burn 1–2 calories per minute.

Apples & Oranges
JUICY TALES ABOUT FRUIT

Some fruitful incidents, fruitless accidents, and weird fruit facts from *Bathroom Companion* contributor Chris McLaughlin.

LET'S DO LAUNCH
Slipping on banana peels is a staple of silent films and clown acts. But it can really happen, as occasional lawsuits against produce markets show. However, the slippery peel phenomenon can also be a virtue. In 1995, owners wanted to launch the showboat *Branson Belle* into Missouri's Table Rock Lake without polluting the water  with industrial grease. They covered the 160-foot-long launch ramp with 40 crates of unpeeled bananas.

REASON #12 FOR AVOIDING ITALY RIGHT BEFORE LENT
Every February, Ivrea, Italy, holds a Battle of the Oranges where thousands of people team up to lob surplus oranges at one another in mock battle. Although the combatants wear helmets and eyeguards, first-aid workers report hundreds of minor injuries from hard tosses, sprained throwing arms, and orange juice dripping in the eyes.

... BUT SPANISH TOMATOES ARE ANOTHER MATTER
Fewer injuries are reported each year at the Bunol, Spain, Tomato Festival, in which 30,000 partygoers attack each other with truckloads of ripe tomatoes. The tradition started in the

1940s with some teenagers tossing their lunches at each other in the city square. They had so much fun, they agreed to repeat the practice annually. Each year, more people joined in, and the event became one of Spain's most popular festivals.

DOLEFUL POLITICS
In an attempt to punish Senator Bob Dole for trying to block foreign aid to Turkey, the mayor of Izmir banned the sale of Dole bananas within his city. Only one problem with the boycott: the Senator had no connection with the company.

SGT. MANNERS
In San Bernardino, California, the county sheriff's department issued a book of etiquette that included an official way for an officer to eat a banana. No joke: You first must separate it into pieces, and then eat it with a fork.

GLAD TO SEE ME?
Two wild-and-crazy journalists from Slovakia were nabbed by security staff and stripped of potentially dangerous contraband at the 2002 Olympics in Salt Lake. Their offense? They were toting bananas in their pockets.

HAPPY GLOW IN THE DARK
If you ever get shipwrecked on Bikini Atoll, don't eat the fruit. The coconuts, oranges, lemons, bread fruit, and pandanus grow there as part of a United States Department of Energy experiment aimed at reducing radiation in the soil. Atomic testing from 1946 to 1958 left large quantities of radiactive cessium in the soil, and it still leeches into the fruit.

COCONUT CONCUSSION
If life hands you a coconut, look out below. A coconut dropped from 30 feet can cause concussions or more. In fact, beach towns in northern Australia decided to uproot their coconut trees in favor of "safer" fruits.

MORE COCONUT DANGERS

A couple in Albany, Georgia, was scared out of their Buick by a swarm of honeybees that were apparently attracted by a coconut-scented air freshener. An animal control officer said that the scent was so strong that it could be easily smelled by humans outside the car with the doors and windows shut. Bees, with an even stronger sense of smell, apparently found the odor irresistable.

EVEN MORE COCONUT DANGERS

Monkeys in Malaysia have been trained by growers to climb trees and twist the coconuts from them. One monkey in Kuala Lumpur, however, went severely off-task when it leapt onto the shoulders of a person passing by and tried to twist his head off. He was treated at a local hospital for a sprained neck.

DEATH BY DURIAN

People (and orangutans) are passionate about durians, which look like overinflated porcupines. They grow on 100-foot-high trees that bloom only at night and are pollinated by bats and fireflies. Death by randomly falling durian is not uncommon among those who farm them. Then again, you might just want to die when you encounter one: it smells like "civet cat, sewage, stale vomit, gasoline ... onions and moldy cheese." If that doesn't put you off, it tastes (we are told) like "custard, garlic, marshmallows, chicken pudding ... (and) butter-like custard with onion sauce imitations." The quotes are from a food critic, Fredric Paten-

The stinky, sweet durian fruit

Marvels of the Tropics

body parts into a fruitbowl. He's done several for the rich and famous including one of a Hollywood star's rear end. The cost ranges from $1,000 to $4,000.

THIS JUST IN: BANANAS NOT FRUIT
Horticulturally, bananas are not a fruit. They grow on the tallest herb in the world—up to thirty feet high—that has no woody trunks or branches and dies after a growth season.

OUT, OUT, ORANGE SPOT
Orange growers are asking us all to stop using the name "blood oranges" when referring to the red-juiced citrus fruit. They believe that the name is unappetizing to consumers. They'd prefer that we use the term "Moro oranges" instead.

aude, who says, "It is simply the best thing there is!" We'll take his word for it.

CHEEKY LITTLE FRUIT BOWL
Sculptor Mark Maitre, of Woodland Hills, California, can turn castings of your

Type Your Password Here

· While many people use names of their spouses, children, or lovers, "God," "sex," and "money" are among the most popular computer passwords.

· Among middle-aged women, the most popular password is "love."

· About ten percent of male users have passwords that refer to obscenities or their masculinity.

· Younger users use self-laudatory terms more than any other group. Popular passwords among the under-25 crowd were "stud," "goddess," "cutiepie," and "hotbod."

· A surprisingly large number of people, no doubt trying to be clever, use the words "secret" or "password."

Aesop's Odds & Ends
AN ASSORTMENT OF FABLES

Here are some pretty obscure fables featuring stomachs, pots, and clouds, from the legendary Greek slave, Aesop.

THE BELLY AND THE MEMBERS

One fine day it occurred to the Members of the Body that they were doing all the work and the Belly was having all the food. So they held a meeting and, after a long discussion, decided to go on strike until the Belly consented to take its proper share of the work. So for a day or two, the Hands refused to take the food, the Mouth refused to receive it, and the Teeth had no work to do. But after a day or two the Members began to find that they themselves were not in a very active condition: the Hands could hardly move, and the Mouth was all parched and dry, while the Legs were unable to support the rest. So thus they found that even the Belly in its dull quiet way was doing necessary work for the Body, and that:

All must work together or the Body will go to pieces.

THE TREE AND THE REED

"Well, little one," said a Tree to a Reed that was growing at its foot, "why do you not plant your feet deeply in the ground and raise your head boldly in the air as I do?"

"I am contented with my lot," said the Reed. "I may not be so grand, but I think I am safer."

"Safe!" sneered the Tree. "Who shall pluck me up by the roots or bow my head to the ground?" But it soon had to repent of its boasting, for a hurricane arose that tore it up from its roots and cast it a useless log on the ground, while the little Reed, bending to the force of the wind, soon stood upright again when the storm had passed over.

Obscurity often brings safety.

THE TWO POTS

Two Pots had been left on the bank of a river, one of brass and one of earthenware. When the tide rose they both floated off down the stream. Now the earthenware pot tried its best to keep aloof from the brass one, which cried out: "Fear nothing, friend, I will not strike you."

"I am contented with my lot."

"But I may come in contact with you," said the other, "if I come too close; and whether I hit you, or you hit me, I shall suffer for it."

The strong and the weak cannot keep company.

THE WIND AND THE SUN

The Wind and the Sun were disputing which was the stronger. Suddenly they saw a traveler coming down the road, and the Sun said: "I see a way to decide our dispute. Whichever of us can get the cloak off that traveler shall be regarded as the stronger. You begin." So the Sun retired behind a cloud, and the Wind began to blow as hard as it could upon the traveler. But the harder he blew the more closely did the traveller wrap his cloak round him, until at last the Wind had to give up in despair. Then the Sun came out and shone in all his glory upon the traveler, who soon found it too hot to walk with his cloak on.

Kindness has more effect than severity.

THE ROSE AND THE AMARANTH

A Rose and an Amaranth blossomed side by side in a garden, and the Amaranth said to her neighbor, "How I envy you your beauty and your sweet scent! No wonder you are such a universal favorite." But the Rose replied with a shade of sadness in her voice, "Ah, my dear friend, I bloom but for a time: my petals soon wither and fall, and then I die. But your flowers never fade, even if they are cut; for they are everlasting."

Greatness carries its own penalties.

Stately Knowledge

12 REASONS WHY YA GOTTA LOVE ALABAMA

We've searched the vaults and come up with some pretty impressive facts about Alabama. Here are a dozen of our favorites.

1 Although New Orleans gets all the attention, it was Alabama, not Louisiana, that first introduced the Mardi Gras celebration to the Western world.

2 The first open heart surgery in the Western Hemisphere was performed in Montgomery in 1902. Dr. Luther Leonidas Hill sutured a stab wound in a young boy's heart.

3 George Washington Carver conducted most of his research at the Tuskegee Institute in Tuskegee, Alabama. He came up with over 100 new products from the sweet potato, and more than 300 from the peanut.

4 Other famous Alabamians include: home-run king Hank Aaron, actress Tallulah Bankhead, singer Nat King Cole, and author and blind-and-deaf educator Helen Keller.

5 The boll weevil is a terrible crop pest, yet there's a monument to the boll weevil in Enterprise, Alabama. Why? Well, when the boll weevil destroyed cotton crops, farmers in Alabama were forced to diversify into other crops, resulting in increased prosperity. In gratitude, they honored the little bugger with a statue.

6 Montgomery operated the very first electric trolley streetcars in the United States in 1866.

7 If you've ever irretrievably lost your luggage, you might be able to buy it back at the huge Unclaimed Baggage Center in Scottsboro, Alabama. Clothing, cameras, skis, radios, books, and CDs are all for sale, and the center even has a Web site where you can shop online.

8 Workers in Alabama built the first rocket booster that helped shoot man to the moon.

9 An Alabamian was the only American to ever get beaned by a meteorite. Mrs. E. Hulitt Hodge was in her sitting room in Sylacauga, Alabama, in 1954 when a meteorite crashed through the roof and hit her in the hip, bruising her, but otherwise leaving her unharmed. The meteorite is now housed in the Smithsonian in Washington, D.C.

10 A 56-foot statue of Vulcan, the Roman god of fire, stands near Birmingham. It was built in Birmingham as an exhibit for the 1904 World's Fair in St. Louis. It's not just the world's largest cast metal statue, but also the largest statue ever

made in the United States. His hand holds a neon torch that is normally green, but turns red whenever there's a traffic fatality in the Birmingham area.

Vulcan being built in 1903

11 At the Bessemer Hall of History museum in Bessemer, Alabama, you can see a typewriter once owned by Adolf Hitler.

12 In 1864, when the Union Navy tried to enter Mobile Bay to take the city, "torpedoes" (mines) began going off. When Union Admiral David Farragut was warned of their presence, he issued his famous command: "Damn the torpedoes! Full speed ahead!" The Union Navy moved into the Bay, overtaking the Confederates at Mobile.

Slogos!

Try to match the slogan with the logo. This one's all about cereal and Saturday morning commercials. See if you can get them all.
Rated: Easy.

1. Which spokes-cartoon commanded a young television audience to "Follow your nose!"?
A. Sam the Toucan (Froot Loops)
B. L. C. Leprechaun (Lucky Charms)
C. Tony the Tiger (Frosted Flakes)
D. Sugar Bear (Golden Crisps)
E. Sonny the Cuckoo Bird (Cocoa Puffs)

2. "____ are for KIDS!" was always the answer to this poor, starving mascot.
A. Tony the Tiger (Frosted Flakes)
B. Sugar Bear (Golden Crisps)
C. Sonny the Cuckoo Bird (Cocoa Puffs)
D. Dig 'Em Frog (Smacks)
E. Trix Rabbit (Trix cereal)

3. Who claimed to be "Cuckoo for ..." his cereal?
A. Sugar Bear (Golden Crisps)
B. Sonny the Cuckoo Bird (Cocoa Puffs)
C. L. C. Leprechaun (Lucky Charms)
D. Tony the Tiger (Frosted Flakes)
E. Dig 'Em Frog (Smacks)

4. Whose smoky voice sang out "Can't get enough of that ____"?
A. Tony the Tiger (Frosted Flakes)
B. L. C. Leprechaun (Lucky Charms)
C. Sugar Bear (Golden Crisps)

D. Captain Crunch (Captain Crunch)
E. Dig 'Em Frog (Smacks)

5. Which cartoon cereal mascot shouted, "They're gr-r-r-eat!"?
A. Dig 'Em Frog (Smacks)
B. Sonny the Cuckoo Bird (Cocoa Puffs)
C. Captain Crunch (Captain Crunch)
D. Tony the Tiger (Frosted Flakes)
E. L. C. Leprechaun (Lucky Charms)

6. Pick the cartoon logo that croaked "Dig 'Em!"
A. Tony the Tiger (Frosted Flakes)
B. Sonny the Cuckoo Bird (Cocoa Puffs)
C. Trix Rabbit (Trix cereal)
D. Dig 'Em Frog (Smacks)
E. Sam the Toucan (Froot Loops)

7. Who skipped and frolicked, singing "They're magically delicious!"?
A. Captain Crunch (Captain Crunch)
B. L. C. Leprechaun (Lucky Charms)
C. Sam the Toucan (Froot Loops)
D. Sonny the Cuckoo Bird (Cocoa Puffs)
E. Trix Rabbit (Trix cereal)

Answers: 1. A—Before he followed his nose, Toucan Sam talked in pig latin. Commercials got kids asking their moms for "Oot-fray Oops-lay!" 2. E—Trix Rabbit. The Trix Rabbit was allowed to eat Trix cereal just once in 1976 when kids voted (over 99 percent!) to let him indulge. 3. B—Sonny the Cuckoo Bird. 4. C—Sugar Bear. Originally, they were Super Sugar Crisps, but changed when "sugar" became a dirty word to health-conscious moms. 5. D—Tony the Tiger. 6. D—Dig 'Em Frog. Kellogg's Smacks is another cereal that lost its original too-sugary title "Sugar Smacks." 7. B—Lucky the Leprechaun. The little marshmallow shapes, called "marbits," were originally created by one John Holahan who worked for General Mills. Marbits debuted with Lucky Charms in 1963.

Ripe Ol' Corn

"Uncle Josh at the Opera"

"Uncle Josh," Cal Stewart's country bumpkin, had problems figuring out modern city life (circa 1901). Here he visits a metropolitan opera house.

WELL, I SAID TO MOTHER when I left home, "Now mother, when I git down to New York City I'm goin' to see a regular first-class theater. "

We never had many theater doin's down our way. Well, thar was a theater troop come to Punkin Centre along last summer, but we couldn't let 'em have the Opery House to show in 'cause it was summer time and the Opery House was full of hay, and we couldn't let 'em have it 'cause we hadn't any place to put the hay.

An then about a year and a half ago thar was a troop come along that was somethin' about "Uncle Tom's Home"; they left a good many of their things behind 'em when they went away. Ezra Hoskins, he got one of the mules, and he tried to hitch it up one day; Doctor says he thinks Ezra will be around in about six weeks. I traded one of the dogs to Ruben Hendricks fer a shot gun; Rube cum over t'other day, borrowed the gun and shot the dog.

Well, I got into one of your theaters here, got set down and was lookin' at it; and it was a mighty fine lookin' picture with a lot of lights shinin' on it, and I was enjoyin' it fust rate, when a lot of fellers cum out with horns and fiddles, and they all started in to fiddlin' and tootin', end all to once they pulled the the-

ater up, and thar was a lot of folks having a regular family quarrel. I knowed that wasn't any of my business, and I sort of felt uneasy like; but none of the rest of the folks seemed to mind it any, so I calculated I'd see how it come out, though my hands sort of itched to get hold of one feller, 'cause I could see if he would jest go 'way and tend to his own business thar wouldn't be any quarrel.

Well, jest then a young feller handed me a piece of paper what told all about the theater doin's, and I got to lookin' at that and I noticed on it whar it said that five years took place 'tween the fust part and the second part. I knowed durned well I wouldn't have time to wait and see the second part, so I got up and went out.

UNCLE JOSH'S PHILOSOPHY

"Those who hanker fer justice would be generally better off if they didn't git it."

"Suspicion—Consists mainly of thinking what we would do if we wuz in the other feller's place."

"Advice—Advice is somethin' the other feller can't use, so he gives it to you."

"Glory—Gittin' killed and not gittin' paid fer it." —Cal Stewart

Persons of the Tale
WHAT CHARACTERS DO BETWEEN CHAPTERS

Robert Louis Stevenson imagined what his characters did when he wasn't writing about them. Here is his fantasy of two of his characters conversing between chapters of *Treasure Island*.

AFTER THE 32ND chapter of *Treasure Island*, two of the puppets strolled out to have a pipe, and met in an open place not far from the story.

"Good-morning, Cap'n," said the first, with a man-o'-war salute, and a beaming countenance.

"Ah, Silver!" grunted the other. "You're in a bad way, Silver."

"Now, Cap'n Smollett," remonstrated Silver, "dooty is dooty, as I knows, and none better; but we're off dooty now; and I can't see no call to keep up the morality business."

"You're a damned rogue, my man," said the Captain.

"Come, come, Cap'n, be just," returned the other. "There's no call to be angry with me in earnest. I'm on'y a chara'ter in a sea story. I don't really exist."

"Well, I don't really exist either," says the Captain, "which seems to meet that."

"I wouldn't set no limits to what a virtuous chara'ter might consider argument," responded Silver. "But I'm the villain of this tale, I am; and speaking as one sea-faring man to another, what I want to know is, what's the odds?"

"Were you never taught your catechism?" said the Captain. "Don't you know there's such a thing as an Author?"

"Such a thing as a Author?" returned John, derisively. "The p'int is, if the Author made you, he made Long John, and he made Hands, and Pew, and George Merry and Flint; and he made this here mutiny; and he had Tom Redruth shot; and—well, if that's a Author, give me Pew!"

"Don't you believe in a future state?" said Smollett. "Do you think there's nothing but the present story-paper?"

"I don't rightly know for that," said Silver; "and I don't see what it's got to do with it, anyway. What I know is this: if there is sich a thing as a Author, I'm his favorite chara'ter. He does me fathoms better'n he does you—fathoms, he does. And he likes doing me. He keeps me on deck mostly all the time, crutch and all; and he leaves you measling in the hold, where nobody can't see you, nor wants to, and you may lay to that! If there is a Author, by thunder, he's on my side, and you may lay to it!"

"I see he's giving you a long rope," said the Captain. "But that can't change a man's convictions. I know the Author respects me; I feel it in my bones; when you and I had that talk at the blockhouse door, who do you think he was for?"

"And don't he respect me?" cried Silver. "Ah, you shoulda heard me putting down my mutiny, George Merry and Morgan and that lot, no longer ago'n last chapter; you'da seen what the Author thinks o' me! But come now, do you consider yourself a virtuous chara'ter clean through?"

"God forbid!" said Captain Smollett, solemnly. "I am a man that tries to do his duty, and makes a mess of it as often as not. I'm not a very popular man at home, Silver, I'm afraid!" and the Captain sighed.

"Ah," says Silver. "Then how about this sequel of yours? Are you to be Cap'n Smollett just the same as ever, and not very popular at home, says you? And if so, why, it's *Treasure Island* over again, by thunder; and I'll be Long John, and Pew'll be Pew, and we'll have another mutiny, as like as not. Or are you to be somebody else? And if so, why, what the better are you? and what the worse am I?"

"Why, look here, my man," returned the Captain, "I can't understand how this story comes about at all, can I? I can't see how you and I, who don't exist, should get to speaking here, and smoke our pipes for all the world like reality? Very well, then, who am I to pipe up with my opinions? I know the Author's on the side of good; he tells me so, it runs out of his pen as he writes. Well, that's all I need to know; I'll take my chance upon the rest."

"It's a fact he seemed to be against George Merry," Silver admitted, musingly. "But George is little more'n a name at the best of it," he added, brightening. "And to get into soundings for once. What is this good? I made a mutiny, and I been a gentleman o' fortune; well, but by all stories, you ain't no such saint. I'm a man that keeps company very easy; even by your own account, you ain't, and to my certain knowledge you're a devil to haze. Which is which? Which is good, and which bad? You tell me that!"

"We're none of us perfect," replied the Captain. "That's a fact of religion, my man. All I can say is, I try to do my duty; and if you try to do yours, I can't compliment you on your success."

"And so you was the judge, was you?" said Silver, derisively.

"I would be both judge and hangman for you, my man, and never turn a hair," returned the Captain. "But I get beyond that: it mayn't be sound theology, but it's common sense, that what is good is useful too—or there and thereabout, for I don't set up to be a thinker. Now, where would a story go to if there were no virtuous characters?"

"If you go to that," replied Silver, "where would a story be, if there wasn't no villains?"

"Well, that's pretty much my thought," said Captain Smollett. "The Author has to get a story; that's what he wants; and to get a story, and to have a man like the doctor (say) given a proper chance, he has to put in men like you and Hands. But he's on the right side; and you mind your eye! You're not through this story yet; there's trouble coming for you."

"What'll you bet?" asked John.

"Much I care if there ain't," returned the Captain. "I'm glad enough to be Alexander Smollett, bad as he is; and I thank my stars upon my knees that I'm not Silver. But there's the ink-bottle opening. To quarters!"

And indeed the Author was just then beginning to write the words: "CHAPTER XXXIII...."

Word Thieves I

SOME TERMS WE'VE BORROWED FROM THE FRENCH

Some of the world's citizens criticize Americans because we don't know much about other languages. However, it could be said that we speak dozens of languages a day.

barrage: From the French *tir de barrage*, which means "curtain of fire." It entered the English language during World War I.

Baton Rouge: The city in Louisiana got its name from a red marker that defined the boundary between two Native American tribes. It's French for "red stick."

cahoots: While there are other theories, our favorite is that it came from *cahute*, French for "cabin."

camouflage: Another World War I word, from the French *camoufler* ("disguise").

carry-all: It once was *carriole*, a light wagon, but during the 1700s got confused in translation.

clarinet: French word for "little bell." In French, though, the *t* doesn't sound.

Detroit: From *de troit*, "of the strait," describing the river that runs between Lake Erie and Lake St. Clair.

fruit: From *frut*, "means of enjoyment" in French.

mirror: From *mireor*, an old French word for "look at" or "wonder at."

oboe: Anglicized from *hautbois*, French for "high wood" (pronounced "oh-bwah").

pimp: First recorded in the diary of Samuel Pepys in 1666, it came from the French word *pimpant* ("speak seductively").

sashay: Corrupted from the French word *chasse* ("chase"), sashay originally referred to a sideways-shuffling dance step popular in the 1700s.

saloon: From *salon* ("hall").

Terre Haute: French fur traders named the future city after a flood in 1816. It means "high ground."

Hellish Neighbors

THERE GOES THE NEIGHBORHOOD

You think you've got it bad? Take a gander at some of these horror stories about naughty neighbors. This article was written by *Bathroom Companion* friend, Kathie Meyer.

YOUR FACE WILL SURELY SHOW IT
In the booming year of 1999, Denver logged 2,500 complaints against construction commotion, nearly a hundred percent increase from five years earlier. Neighbors understandably tended to get upset over debris, noise, and the steady stream of construction workers needed to complete remodeling projects. One contractor reported that while working on a deck project, a neighbor decided to retaliate. She blasted him with the children's song "When You're Happy and You Know It, Clap Your Hands" played loudly over and over for an entire week. "I asked her to turn it down, but she just said, 'It's my backyard,'" he recalled. "It took me a month to get that song out of my head."

BACK TO CLASS
Richard E. Clear ran a martial arts school in Tampa, Florida, that specialized in helping people effectively deal with stress. That, unfortunately, didn't stop Clear from getting a little overly stressed himself, shooting at a neighbor when the neighbor complained Clear's dog was barking too much.

IT KEEPS GOING, AND GOING, AND GOING....
In April 2002, Bo McCoy and his cousin, Ron McCoy, of Durham, North Carolina, filed suit against Hatfield descendent

John Vance and his wife Barbara. The McCoys complained that the Vances closed the only road to the McCoy family cemetery. The

Vances countered that the road was a private driveway and cited liability concerns as their reason for posting "No Trespassing" signs. Three McCoys buried in the cemetery were killed in a pawpaw patch ambush by Hatfields in August 1882. So are two other McCoys who were killed in another Hatfield-related incident in 1888. At least twelve people died as a result of the famous blood feud that began in 1860 with a fight over a pig. The battle apparently rages on.

NO PORKING ZONE
Neighbors of Ron Ripple in Crystal River, Florida, didn't much like the idea of seeing a mobile home parked in Ripple's yard. As a result, he was denied a permit to park one next to his home. In retaliation, he got permits and set up shop as a pig farmer instead. Lesson learned, we guess.

A LITTLE TO THE LEFT
It cost Stacy Ford of Stanwood, Washington, $40,000 to move her house three feet to the left. She had to either move it or tear it down—the result of complaints by a neighbor who cited an ordinance stating a house must be at least five feet away from property lines. Ford's was only two. She inherited the house from her uncle, Dennis Davis, the person with whom the neighbor was really at odds. The feud had started years earlier when the neighbor felled a tree in the wrong direction and destroyed Davis's storage shed.

CQ, CQ. NO 88 LOST BETWEEN THESE FELLOWS. OVER & OUT.
Charles Kissinger discovered another way to get in touch with his neighbor when he and Woodring Fryer began feuding over interference

from ham radio signals. Since the two neighbors shared a wall between their apartments, Kissinger began early morning short-range broadcasts using a bull horn and a colorful vocabulary. Roger—over and out.

COLOR ME MAD

On the south side of his house, Michael  Glick of Redington Shores, Florida, painted the siding purple and decorated it with yellow frowny faces to indicate his feelings about the neighbors next door. That's not all. He also included a troll in a mooning position and a stuffed pink panther displaying his middle fingers. On the other side lived neighbors who were in Glick's good graces. For them, he painted the side of his house orange with a large yellow smiley face. Glick, who ran an unsuccessful 1998 campaign for mayor, was visited by the police sixty times in in one decade for various complaints regarding actions against people he considers "mean." "There's no law that says I can't paint my house purple, and there's no law that says I

can't have a stuffed animal on my roof," he said. "I'm maybe a little eccentric."

POLLY WANT A DEATH THREAT?

A longstanding feud between two women who lived next door to one another resulted in Maria Bruna Bortlussi laboriously training her blackbird to recite repeatedly, "Norina, I'm going to kill you."

LAY THAT PISTIL DOWN

In Painesville, Ohio, Robert Moore was arrested for taking a potshot at his neighbor Patrick Dial. It seems Dial's young children enjoyed picking the 75-year-old Moore's daffodils. That made Moore very grumpy indeed.

OH, WHAT A TANGLED WEB SITE

A feud between Julie and Keith Conrad and Tim and

Lori Gough of Fishing Creek Farm, a wealthy community near Washington, D.C., became so intense it spawned its own Web site: **www.fishingcreekfarm.com**. The feud began in 1997 when the Goughs received an anonymous letter accusing them of bad parenting. The Goughs believed one of the two Conrads had penned it. With these accusations, the fracas snowballed, sides were taken, and the Conrads were ostracized by the some of the neighbors. After losing a $2 million defamation lawsuit against the Goughs, the Conrads set up the Web site documenting the bickering in an attempt to clear their name. The feud has attracted media attention from as far away as Hong Kong.

NO LAWN ORDER

Kurt King of New Orleans, had pushed his lawn edger about three inches or so into his neighbor, Alfred Abadie's, yard. Abadie shot and killed him.

GOOD OFFENSES

If friends are sick of listening to you vent about your neighbor, you can post your frustrations on a special website set up for that purpose: http://www.youdontwantmyneighbor.com/

Neighborly Lexicon

• The word *neighbor* is a combination of the English words *nigh* or *neah* meaning "near" and *gebur* which means "dweller."

• *Neighborhood* dates from the 15th century, but was not used in the sense of indicating a district until the 17th century.

• The word *feud* originates from the Old French *fede* or *feide* and simply means "hostility."

• While the concept of a suburb seems relatively modern, the word is a derivative of *urban*, coming from the Latin *urbanus*, meaning "city." *Suburb* and *suburban* date back to the 14th and 17th centuries respectively, but *surburbia* did not appear until the 1890s.

In the Cards

A HALLMARK MOMENT

Hallmark has dominated the greeting card market for nearly a century. Mix sweet sentiments with the economy of sending a card instead of a present, and you can see why the company's done so well.

The Hallmark Card style is instantly recognizable. This card inscription, featuring the world's cutest kittens on the front, is one of the company's all-time best sellers, written decades ago by the company's founder, Joyce C. Hall:

"These kittens feel important
Cause here's what they get to do—
They get to bring this birthday wish
Especially 'fur' you."

Hall was the youngest son of a devoutly religious Nebraskan woman who named him after a Methodist bishop, Isaac W. Joyce. Although mercilessly teased about his feminine first name, he didn't use his middle name—Clyde—because he thought it would be even worse. He finally settled on J. C.

Hall's father, a traveling preacher, abandoned his wife and children when J. C. was nine. The boy began taking on odd jobs selling perfume, sandwiches, and lemonade to help support the family. Eventually Hall and his two older brothers found a market in selling imported postcards, which had become popular for correspondence and seasonal greetings.

In 1910, Hall dropped out of high school a semester short of graduation and took a train to Kansas City, where he gambled on a desperate ploy to increase his postcard business. In the YMCA room that was both his home and office, he put together hundred-packs of postcards and mailed them unbidden with invoices to shopkeepers throughout the Midwest.

Some of the dealers sent

"And I Haven't Forgotten a Soul!"

"I HAVE learned my lesson. It is this. The people who always do the right thing at the right time—the people we come to love for their constant acts of kindness—who are always known for their thoughtfulness—these people aren't inspired. They don't act on the impulse of a moment. They simply use forethought. They are always thinking ahead about ways of showing their good will to others.

"It was last Christmas morning that this came over me, when the postman handed me dozens of Christmas cards from friends to whom I had entirely forgotten to send cards. I was so mortified that then and there I made a vow.

"And today, long before Christmas, I have made up my list of friends to send cards to this year. First, everyone who sent one to me last year, for I saved every card I got and on the back I wrote the name and address of the sender.

"Then I got out my old school class book for the friends of long ago. From the church list and the woman's club yearbook I got my acquaintances there, and from the local telephone book the correct addresses of my neighbors.

"I'm sure I haven't forgotten a soul. And what a relief it is to know that it's all done way ahead of time, that all the addresses are right, and that I can go out now and buy just the appropriate card for each person, with plenty of time to choose before the stores are crowded.

"And this year there won't be in my mail any cards from people I forgot to remember."

Send 10c for "Forget-me-nots"—a little book of days to remember

The Greeting Card Association *331 Fourth Ave New York City*

Scatter Sunshine with Christmas Cards

him back his postcards with blistering letters about his shady trick. Others just kept the cards without paying. But about one shopkeeper in three sent him a check, enough to have made the ploy worthwhile. Within a few months, Hall had socked away $200 in a local bank.

J.C. wrote to his brother, Rollie, who joined him in Kansas City. Acting as distributors for other companies' cards, they became successful enough to move out of the Y.

Things went well enough until January 1915, when their warehouse was full of Valentines ready to ship. All those passionate messages in one place apparently caused spontaneous combustion and the building went up in flames, leaving the brothers without inventory and $17,000 in debt.

After the disaster, the Halls decided to change the focus of the company. Rather than merely distribute cards, they were going to start manufacturing them as well. Somehow they convinced a banker to lend them enough money to buy an engraving company from one of their suppliers. They began designing and printing their own cards, shifting away from postcards and into the envelope variety. With syrupy inscriptions and sentimental pictures, they expressed the feelings of a tongue-tied nation. Hall Brothers became the biggest greeting card company in the world.

Today, Hallmark holds a fearsome share of the market, accounting for nearly half of all greeting cards sold in the United States (some are disguised as other lines, like Shoebox and Ambassador). Hallmark produces more than 11 million cards a day in 13,000 different designs (as well as 5,000 non-card products like gift wrap and Christmas decorations). The cards are generated by a staff of 700 writers and illustrators, and helped out by 70,000 unsolicited ideas that pour in from consumers every year.

A Little Latin Quiz

FOOD, LAW, OR AILMENT?

What do they mean? Hey, it's all Greek to us, but maybe you can identify these Latin words and phrases. Circle the category that matches the meaning of the word or phrase.

1. Epistaxis	Food	Law	Ailment
2. Nemo est supra leges	Food	Law	Ailment
3. Kephalalgia	Food	Law	Ailment
4. Onus probandi	Food	Law	Ailment
5. Nolo contendere	Food	Law	Ailment
6. Apium graveolens	Food	Law	Ailment
7. Beta vulgaris cicla	Food	Law	Ailment
8. Aphthous stomatitis	Food	Law	Ailment
9. Habeas corpus	Food	Law	Ailment
10. Sarda ita fit	Food	Law	Ailment
11. Jus sanguinis	Food	Law	Ailment
12. Vulnus sclopeticum	Food	Law	Ailment
13. In vitulinam elixam	Food	Law	Ailment
14. Amicus curiae	Food	Law	Ailment
15. Aliter baedinam sive agninam excaldatam	Food	Law	Ailment

Answers: 1. Ailment: A nose bleed; 2. Law: "No one is above the law"; 3. Ailment: A headache; 4. Law: "The burden of proof"; 5. Law: "No contest"; 6. Food: Celery; 7. Food: Beet greens; 8. Ailment: A big canker sore; 9. Law: "Produce the body"; 10. Food: Tuna; 11. Law: Regarding children inheriting a parent's citizenship; 12. Ailment: A gunshot wound; 13. Food: Boiled veal; 14. Law: "A friend of the court"; 15. Food: Steamed lamb

Unforgettable

DESCRIBING THE FACES OF HISTORY

You'd think big names in history like Anne Boleyn, Joseph Stalin, and Cleopatra would have faces that time could never forget. So much for that theory. Here are firsthand accounts of what these historical bigwigs really looked like.

SUBJECT: Cleopatra, Queen of Egypt
TIME PERIOD: 69–30 B.C.
OBSERVER: Plutarch, Greek biographer
DESCRIPTION: "Her actual beauty was not in itself so remarkable that none could be compared with her, or that no one could see her without being struck by it, but the contact of her presence, if you lived with her, was irresistible; the attraction of her person, joining with the charm of her conversation, and the character that attended all she said or did, was something bewitching."

Cleopatra, temptress of bewitching beauty

SUMMARY: Popularized by Hollywood, the image of Cleopatra as the beautiful temptress may have been far from the truth. At best, accurate depictions of her show an average-looking woman with buck teeth. At worst, she looked alarmingly like Robin Williams in drag. But Cleopatra spoke nine languages and had a way with words, not to mention a much-coveted kingdom. She was, in essence, irresistible.

SUBJECT: Abraham Lincoln, 16th U.S. president, reformer, orator, giver of good speeches
TIME PERIOD: 1861–1865

OBSERVERS: Contemporary writers Joshua Speed, William Herndon, and Abram Bergen

DESCRIPTIONS: "Mr. Lincoln's person was ungainly. He was six feet four inches in height; a little stooped in the shoulders; his legs and arms were long; his feet and hands large; his forehead was high. His head was over the average size. His eyes were gray. His face and forehead were wrinkled even in his youth. They deepened with age, 'as streams their channels deeper wear.'"

"Lincoln's voice was, when he first began speaking, shrill, squeaking, piping, unpleasant; his general look, his form, his pose, the color of his flesh, wrinkled and dry, his sensitiveness, and his momentary diffidence, everything seemed to be against him, but he soon recovered."

"Then involuntarily vanished all thought or consciousness of his uncouth appearance, or awkward manner, or even his high keyed, unpleasant voice."

SUMMARY: Honest Abe was lacking in beauty, but when he spoke, his face came alive and he was extremely animated. As a result, this made it difficult to catch his true "look" in a painting or photograph. Walt Whitman, who wrote "O Captain, My Captain" about the president, had this to say: "Though hundreds of portraits have been made, by painters and photographers (many to pass on, by copies, to future times), I have never seen one yet that in my opinion deserved to be called a perfectly good likeness: nor do I believe there is really such a one in existence."

Hun! I'm home!

SUBJECT: Atilla, powerful and vicious leader of the Huns, noted "Scourge of God"

TIME PERIOD: 5th century A.D., specifically A.D. 448.

OBSERVER: Priscus of Panium, a visiting Goth

DESCRIPTION: "He was haughty in his walk, rolling his eyes hither and thither, so that the power of his proud spirit appeared in the movement of his body.

He was indeed a lover of war, yet restrained in action, mighty in counsel, gracious to suppliants, and lenient to those who were once received into his protection. He was short of stature, with a broad chest and a large head: his eyes were small, his beard thin and sprinkled with gray: and he had a flat nose and a swarthy complexion showing the evidences of his origin."

SUMMARY: Atilla the Hun is a perfect example of the complexity of human beings. He popularized spearing the babies of the folks he was pillaging and plundering, but at the same time adored his youngest son and treated those he considered his friends to the finest food, drink, and entertainment. Not unlike some current world leaders, come to think of it. He died from a nosebleed on his wedding night.

SUBJECT: Alexander the Great, Greek Macedonian ruler and noted pretty boy
TIME PERIOD: 356–323 B.C.
OBSERVER: Plutarch, Greek biographer

Alexander, conqueror of the world

DESCRIPTION: "It is the statues of Lysippos which best convey Alexander's physical appearance (and he himself felt it proper that he should be modeled only by Lysippos). For it was this artist who captured exactly those distinctive features which many of Alexander's successors and friends later tried to imitate, namely the poise of the neck slightly turned to the left and the melting glance of the eyes."

SUMMARY: There are those who believe Alexander's well-known stance of right-tilted head and large-eyed glare were the result of a battle injury. A condition known as Brown's Syndrome causes the tendons in the eye to stiffen as a result of injury, causing a bug-eyed, glaring look. But most historians believe he was very good-looking (soft, curly hair, jutting jaw, fair complexion, perfectly proportioned lips), as well as extremely intelligent (he was educated by Aristotle himself) and charismatic. More than likely, Alexander spent a lot of time, in his youth and beyond, primping and practicing his steely gaze in a mirror.

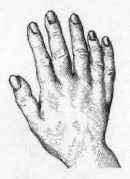

Among other oddities, it was claimed Anne had six fingers.

SUBJECT: Anne Boleyn, second wife of Henry VIII, rumored to be very ugly, and supposed bearer of several physical deformities

TIME PERIOD: Around 1532

OBSERVER: A visiting ambassador from Venice

DESCRIPTION: "[She's] not one of the handsomest women in the world. She is of middling stature, with a swarthy complexion, long neck, wide mouth, bosom not much raised, and in fact has nothing but the King's great appetite, and her eyes, which are black and beautiful."

SUMMARY: Henry VIII's first wife, Catherine of Aragon, had been a popular queen, and the king had managed to get an annulment from her in order to marry the young Anne Boleyn. Needless to say, this made Boleyn's marriage to the king more than a little unwelcomed by the people. As a result, there are no objective descriptions of Anne, and the rumors of her physical oddities are probably a result of the intense dislike the English felt for her. Ironically, it was probably her exotic dark eyes and skin — not a picture of popular beauty during the sixteenth century, when blond hair and fair skin were the epitome of loveliness — that attracted Henry to her. Anne was reportedly godly and fair, and tried hard to be a good queen. Because she didn't bear the king a son, however, she lost her most staunch defender in England — Henry — as well as her head. She did leave behind a daughter, though — Elizabeth, who would later become the famous (supposed) Virgin Queen of England.

SUBJECT: Iosef "Soso" Dzhugashvili, a.k.a. Joseph Stalin, ruthless Bolshevik leader

TIME PERIOD: Early twentieth century

OBSERVER: Tsarist police warrants; similar to modern-day

APBs

DESCRIPTION:

- 5'4" male
- Sunken hazel eyes
- Soft voice
- Birthmark on left ear
- Pockmarked face
- Thick black hair and mustache (but no beard)
- Withered left arm
- Second and third toes of left foot grown together

SUMMARY: "Stalin" means "man of steel" in Russian. His physical description doesn't exactly match the overbearing, paranoid, and ruthless ruler image that his name usually conjures.

Got a favorite historical icon? Let us know and we'll see if we can find the down and dirty on what they really looked like.

Match the writer to the correct *nom de plume*:

1. George Orwell	a. Alissa Rosenbaum
2. Jack London	b. Howard Allen O'Brien
3. John le Carre	c. Charles Ludwidge Dodgson
4. Henry James	d. John Griffith Chaney
5. O. Henry	e. Patricia Neal
6. Ayn Rand	f. L. C. Kellenberger
7. Anne Rice	g. William Sydney Porter
8. Lewis Carroll	h. David Cornwell
9. Fannie Flagg	i. Eric Arthur Blair

Answers: 1. i; 2. d; 3. h; 4. f; 5. g; 6. a; 7. b (Mom and Pop wanted a boy); 8. c; 9. e

Every Picture Tells a Story

Mona Lisa **by Leonardo da Vinci**

• There are only seventeen paintings attributed to Leonardo da Vinci, and about half of those are disputed. Of the few, two of them are big pop-art hits—*Mona Lisa* and *The Last Supper*.

• Da Vinci painted the mysterious portrait on pine wood, not canvas. He worked on it over a four-year period.

• Did you ever notice that Lisa doesn't have eyebrows? The stylish women of Florence in the early 1500s plucked their eyebrows, so Lisa Gherardini, the wife of Francesco Gioconda, was right in fashion.

• *Mona Lisa* was reportedly da Vinci's favorite painting.

• The painting was stolen in 1911 and wasn't found again until 1913. Some claimed afterward that it didn't quite look the same and wondered if maybe forgers had painted a copy and kept the real one. However, x-rays since then have pretty well knocked that theory down, and revealed two other paintings of the same woman underneath the one we see.

• It is the most-viewed painting of all in the Louvre. A few years ago, the museum moved it into its own separate room to better accommodate the crowds.

"Mr. Dullard"

THE QUIRKY LIFE OF ALBERT EINSTEIN

The brainy guys are often a little bit strange. Take Al Einstein, the slow kid who befriended chickens. As a humble patents office clerk, he shook the world of physics.

EINSTEIN WASN'T CLEARLY A GENIUS early in life. As a child, little Albert was slow in learning to talk and walk. As he got older, his large feet made him waddle like a duck. He was extremely introspective, spending long hours watching ant colonies or trying to befriend the family's chickens. Most children in Ulm, Germany found him a dull companion.

• At school, he was inattentive and slow in everything but math and literature. Teachers called him "Herr Langweil," which roughly translates as "Mister Dullard."

• Although Einstein was Jewish, his family wasn't devout. Albert even attended a Catholic school. One traumatic year during Lent, his teacher held up three large rusty nails and told the students, "These were the nails the Jews used to crucify Jesus."

• As he grew up, Einstein was a lousy student who rarely took notes and often cut classes. He also had an attitude problem, preferring to work solutions out for himself instead of accepting the teacher's answer. "The problem is you don't think anyone has anything to tell you," scolded one teacher.

• When his father asked the headmaster what profession Albert should adopt, he got the answer, "It doesn't matter, he'll never make a success of anything."

• Einstein applied to the Polytechnic Academy in Zurich but flunked the entrance exam. One of the examiners noticed his brilliance in mathematics and recommended he go to a small liberal arts school; if he did well he could return to the Polytechnic in a year. Easy enough. A year later Einstein began a four-year course in physics.

• In college, he met Mileva Maric, who became his wife. She was a bright and independent women who was studying to become a math teacher. She and Einstein's best friend Marcel Grossman made sure that Albert, perpetually lost in the world of physics, remembered to take care of basics like eating and going to classes.

• After Einstein graduated in 1902, he couldn't find a teaching job, so he went to work in the Swiss patent office. Yet, he kept working on physics questions. Remarkably, in 1905, he published five papers that shook the physics world by explaining Brownian motion, photons, and relativity. This paved the way for a teaching position in Zurich in 1909.

• Albert and Mileva had two sons, the younger of whom was schizophrenic and spent most of his life living either with his mother or in an institution.

• Einstein's second wife, Elsa also had to protect him from his absentmindedness. Once when Einstein was sick and confined to his bed, Elsa banned paper and pencils from his room to keep him from working. She allowed a small group of students to visit him on the condition they not talk about physics or math. But after the students left, Elsa found equations scrawled all over Einstein's bed sheets.

• Einstein gave his eldest son the fatherly advice, "Don't get married." When his son married shortly after, Einstein warned him, "At

least don't have children."
His son ignored this advice,
too, and had several children
in a very happy marriage.
Einstein grumbled, "I don't
understand it. I don't think
you're my son."

• Einstein charged people a
dollar for his autograph,
which he gave to charity. He
made an exception when he
met Charlie Chaplin, giving
him an autographed photo
for free.

• For many years Einstein
thought of his work in
physics as something of a
hobby. He considered himself
as something of a failure because what he really wanted
to do was play concert violin.

• Einstein was uncharacteris-
tically intense when playing
his violin, cussing a blue
streak whenever he made a
mistake. One evening, while
playing violin duets with
Queen Elizabeth, Einstein
suddenly stopped mid-piece
and unceremoniously told her
she was playing too loudly.

• Einstein was reluctant to
give up his rarely used home
in Germany until a friend
convinced him that the Nazis
would drag him through the
streets by his famous hair if
he returned. Einstein finally

renounced his German citizenship and abandoned the
country of his childhood forever.

• After the war, Einstein used
his fame to support political
ideas he favored, like Zionism
and pacifism. He also re-
mained an eccentric in other
areas as well: For example, he
gave up wearing socks as an
unnecessary complication.

• Meanwhile he continued
with his work. In 1949, at the
age of seventy, he presented
his Generalized Theory of
Gravitation, the product of
half a lifetime's work.
Unfortunately, he had not yet
been able to work all the
mathematical proofs. His
health was failing, and he
knew he wouldn't live long
enough to prove the theory
either true or false.

• When asked about the proofs he would joke weakly, "Come back in twenty years." Four years later, he was dead. Since then his theory of a "unified field" in physics remains unsubstantiated.

• By his request, Einstein's brain was removed before cremation in 1955 so that it could be studied. For unknown reasons it got chopped into pieces and shelved in the study of Dr. Thomas Harvey, the doctor who removed it from Einstein's cranium.

• The brain spent three decades in Weston, Missouri, stored behind a beer cooler in a couple of Mason jars inside a box labeled "Costa Cider." It has since been found and has been made available to other scientists.

The Quotable Dr. Einstein

"Gravitation can not be held responsible for people falling in love."

"If we knew what it was we were doing, it wouldn't be called research."

"Put your hand on a hot stove for a minute, and it seems like an hour. Sit with a pretty girl for an hour, and it seems like a minute. THAT'S relativity."

"I have no particular talent. I am merely inquisitive."

"It's not that I'm so smart , it's just that I stay with problems longer."

"If I had my life to live over again, I'd be a plumber."

"As far as I'm concerned, I prefer silent vice to ostentatious virtue."

"The secret to creativity is knowing how to hide your sources."

"The faster you go, the shorter you are."

"The only reason for time is so that everything doesn't happen at once."

Home Sweet Home

WHO LIVES AT THESE FAMOUS ADDRESSES?

Match the famous address with its most famous inhabitant.
Answers appear below.

A. 1600 Pennsylvania Avenue

B. 221B Baker Street

C. 10 Downing Street

D. 17 Cherry Tree Lane

E. 32 Windsor Gardens

F. Bag End, Hobbiton

G. 1313 Mockingbird Lane

H. 742 Evergreen Terrace

I. 4 Privet Drive

J. 77 Sunset Strip

1. British prime minister

2. Bilbo Baggins

3. The Munsters

4. Gerald "Kookie" Kookson III

5. The Simpsons

6. Mary Poppins

7. Sherlock Holmes

8. Harry Potter

9. U.S. president

10. Paddington Bear

Potty Pourri

RANDOM KINDS OF FACTNESS

• In 1932, Ole Kirk Christiansen needed a name for his new toy company. He took inspiration from *leg godt*, the Danish words for "play well," and called his company LEGO.

• Americans send over 3 billion Christmas cards each year.

• Ancient Egyptian doctors didn't use anesthesia, but they found an effective alternative—before operating, they whacked the patient on the head with a wooden mallet.

• Henry Ford's first car was named "Quadricycle Runabout."

• "The Pill" is known by (almost) the same name in most languages. For example, "la Pilule " (French), "die Pille" (German), "la Pildora" (Spanish), and "la Pillola" (Italian).

• The man who invented the birth control pill—Carl Djerassi—also invented an insect repellent based on similar principles: bug hormones that keep creepy crawlers from developing into mature, reproductive adults.

• Would it be fun to be a funambulist? Well, maybe. A funambulist is a tightrope walker.

• You may have heard of the herbal remedy for depression, St. John's Wort. It was first identified as a cure for the blues in the seventeenth century by a group of lawyers.

• Raisinettes, please! Movie theatre owners make the bulk of their money from selling snacks—more than $650 million in 2001 alone.

• Shoeless Joe Jackson still hasn't made it into baseball's Hall of Fame. However, his shoes are on display there.

• Like Elvis, Liberace had a twin who died during birth.

• In a poll, about half of all American Oreo consumers twist the cookies apart before eating them. Three times as many women as men engage in this twisted practice.

Family Feud

FRANKLIN'S SON: ENEMY OF THE STATES

America's Revolutionary War was supported by far less than a majority of the colonies' population. One of the Loyalists was Ben Franklin's son.

THE STRUGGLE ON THE BATTLEFIELDS of Revolutionary America was also even reflected within households, with Tories and revolutionaries facing off across the dinner table for spirited discussions that, in some cases, ripped families into opposing camps. This was true even among the most famous revolutionaries themselves: John Adams, George Washington, and John Hancock, for example, all had fervently Royalist in-laws. But few saw their families split apart as irrevocably as Benjamin Franklin's estrangement from his once-beloved son, William.

LIKE FATHER, LIKE SON
William Franklin is something of a mystery. Although he was clearly Ben's son, it is still not clear who his mother was. In his lifetime, Ben Franklin was a notorious womanizer—so much so

that throughout much of the nineteenth century it was considered bad taste to mention Franklin's name in the presence of ladies. Although his reputation has been cleaned up and softened over the decades, Franklin was once referred to sarcastically as "the all-embracing Doctor Franklin, America's upstanding genius," grabbing, kissing, and propositioning anything in petticoats.

Despite the scandal behind William's conception, he was Ben's pride and joy. When his son was still a child, Ben provided him with a pony and

plenty of books. As William grew older, he helped his dad with the *Poor Richard's Almanack* and acted as his secretary and assistant. For twenty-five years they were not just father and son, but partners, confidants, and friends. When Ben undertook his most famous scientific experiment with electricity, it was William who raced through cow pastures to get a kite to fly in a lightning storm. Benjamin sat dryly in a nearby shed.

In 1757, Ben went to England to argue tax matters as a representative of the Pennsylvania Assembly. With the idea of saving William from what Ben considered an unfortunate engagement with the daughter of one of Ben's political enemies in Philadelphia, Ben convinced his son to come on the journey. That may have been a mistake.

Benjamin ended up staying for fifteen years, leaving his long-suffering, common-law wife Deborah back in Philadelphia. (She was terrified of transoceanic travel.)

REBEL DAD & ANGLOPHILE SON
In England, William began to emerge from his father's shadow and find an affinity with all things British. He studied law at the Inns of Court, was called to the bar in 1758, and slowly transformed himself from the bastard son of a colonial printer to an English gentleman. His skill at law favorably impressed some of King George's advisors. When Ben was ready to return to Philadelphia in 1762, William announced that he was ready to go, too—as the newly married, newly appointed Royal Governor of New Jersey.

Initially, Benjamin was a proud papa, writing to his sister, "I have no doubt but that he will make as good a Governor as Husband: for he has good principles and good Dispositions, & I think is not deficient in good Understanding." William Franklin at first busied himself with administrative concerns like upgrading roads and improving the debtors' laws, but he soon threw himself into representing the Crown with vigor. Ben worried that his son had become more English than American.

Ben and William in happier days

BEGINNING OF THE END

Meanwhile, Ben had become enough of a revolutionary troublemaker that he was removed from his royal position as colonial Postmaster General. He asked his son to resign his royal appointment, too. William refused, fretting that his aggravating papa was ruining his chance for his hoped-for promotion to Governor of Barbados. "You are a thorough courtier," Ben wrote accusingly, "and see everything with government eyes."

Ben returned to England in 1764, where he badgered William back home with letters demanding payment for a variety of moneys owed, including repeated references to the cost of a small quantity of Lapsang Souchong tea. William, in the meantime, attempted to mediate between the Crown and colonists, but slowly became one of the most vocal critics of American hopes of independence from Britain, even suggesting after the Boston Tea Party that the city's citizens should be heavily taxed to pay for the tea.

When Benjamin returned from England after eleven years in 1775, he found the colonies on the brink of outright revolution. He traveled to the Governor's mansion in Perth Amboy for one last-ditch attempt to convert his son to the rebel cause. The meeting did not go well. "I have lost my son," Ben wrote mournfully to his daughter's husband.

William Franklin, Ben's Tory son

AN ARREST

In June 1776, Ben was in Philadelphia, helping write the Declaration of Independence, when he got word that his monarchist son had been arrested by the New Jersey Assembly as "an enemy to the liberties of this country." It was a fate William might have escaped except for his predisposition, learned from his father, to practice what he believed.

"All over colonial America natural opponents of the rebellion were moving to their country houses and keeping quiet," wrote historian Willard Sterne Randall in *A Little Revenge: Benjamin Franklin & His Son.* "William Franklin might have suffered no worse fate than to sit out the Revolution in elegant comfort had it been his nature to acquiesce." Instead, he convened the loyalist New Jersey Assembly and began sending intelligence reports back to the British Army headquarters. One of his last letters, in fact, was a report on his father's rebellious activities, including the news that Benjamin had traveled to Canada to try to stir up rebellion there as well.

TOUGH LOVE

With his father's blessing William was thrown into a rat-infested hellhole of a jail in Litchfield, Connecticut. The floor was covered with straw, matted with the waste of previous occupants. The date, ironically, was July 4, 1776. Even George Washington urged Congress to have William moved to better quarters, but Ben used his influence to block a transfer. He also prevented William's son from seeing him, successfully working to alienate the boy from his father. He wrote to a friend about his grandson: "I have rescued a valuable young man from the danger of being a Tory...."

Meanwhile, William was discovered writing Tory diatribes that were being smuggled out of his cell, so the authorities confiscated all pen, ink, and paper.

During confinement, William lost his teeth, hair, health, and wife, Deborah. When she was on her deathbed, William sent a message to George Washington, requesting that he be allowed to visit her one last time. Washington was so moved that he wrote to Congress that "humanity and generosity plead powerfully in favor of his application." Congress looked to Ben for a sign of concurrence.

Benjamin Franklin, unforgiving dad

FREE AT LAST

William stayed confined for nearly three years until English authorities, alarmed at his conditions, won William's release in a trade for some rebel prisoners.

Intended lesson unlearned, William traveled to British-held New York, where he worked with new vigor to subvert the revolution, developing a network of informers and planning raids into rebel-held New Jersey. Finally, when it became clear that the cause was lost, he moved to London, never to return to the land of his birth.

Benjamin made an effort to erase all records of his son from his life. He expunged William's name from all diary entries and from his autobiography (the first draft of which had been dedicated to his "beloved son Billy" and had begun, "Dear son,..."). Ben not only disinherited him and forced him to give up his properties in the colonies, he even sent a bill for the "loan" of every farthing Ben had spent raising William from infancy.

ATTEMPT AT RECONCILIATION

The estrangement continued after the war. Finally, in July of 1784, William wrote to his father, who was on diplomatic mission to France: "Dear and Honoured Father, Ever since the Termination of the unhappy Contest between Great Britain and America, I have been anxious to write to you and to endeavor to revive that affectionate Intercourse and Connexion which till the Commencement of the late Troubles had been the Pride and Happiness of my Life.... I have uniformly acted from a sense strong of what I conceived my duty to my king and regard to my Country required....

"On a subject so disagreeable I have no Desire to say more, and I hope everything which has happened relative to it may be mutually forgotten.... I beg you to be assured of my constant Prayers for your Health and Happiness, and that I am, as ever, Your very dutiful and affectionate Son...."

His father's answer came back a month later: "I am glad to find you desire to revive the affectionate intercourse that formerly existed between us. It would be very agreeable to me; indeed, nothing has hurt me so much ... as to find myself deserted in my old age by my only son; and not only deserted, but to find him taking up arms against me in a cause wherein my good fame, fortune, and life were all at stake.

"Yet I ought not to blame you for differing in sentiment with me in public affairs. We are men, all subject to errors. Our opinions are not in our own power; they are formed and governed much by circumstances.... I will be glad to see you when convenient, but would not have you come here at present...."

Benjamin never did invite William to France. A year would pass before the father found it "convenient" to see his son, and only because he would be briefly stopping in England en route home. It was a brief and coolly formal meeting. Ben had spent most of his time in London meeting with old friends and associates, knowing that at near eighty, this was likely his last transatlantic trip. Finally, he arrived at William's door to present some financial documents to sign, and then sailed back to America as soon as a ship would take him away.

In 1788, two years before his death, Franklin wrote, "My son is estranged from me and keeps aloof, residing in England." When Benjamin Franklin died, he left the city of Philadelphia a large quantity of money, but provided little to William: It canceled Ben's claim to the sum that he believed William still owed him (including the cost of raising him) and left him a small parcel of land in Nova Scotia.

"Fish Eyes!"

A Translation of Diner Lingo

Mmm ... nothin' like a meal at an old-fashioned diner. But "nervous pudding"? "Adam and Eve on a raft"? What the heck is the waitress talking about?

BEVERAGES

"Adam's ale" = Water
"A cold spot" = Iced tea
"Mug of murk" = Coffee
"A brunette with sand" = Coffee with sugar
"Cow juice" = Milk
"Belch water" = Soda water
"Sinkers and suds" = Doughnuts and coffee

BREAKFAST

"An order of down with mama" = Toast with marmalade
"A bowl of birdseed" = Cereal

"Adam & Eve on a raft" = Two poached eggs on toast

"Deadeye" = Poached egg

"Wrecked hen fruit" = Scrambled eggs

"Warm a pig" = Ham

"Looseners" = Prunes (they loosen things up a bit)

BLUE PLATE SPECIAL

"Betsy in a bowl with cow feed and mystery in the alley" = Beef stew with salad and hash on the side

ENTREES

"First lady" = Spareribs (Eve was made with Adam's spare rib)

"Bowl of red" = Chili

"Pig between the sheets" = Ham sandwich

"Radio sandwich" = Tuna (a pun on "tuner")

"Burn one" = Grill a burger

"Jack" = spelled "GAC," or Grilled American Cheese sandwich

"Put out the lights and cry" = Liver and onions

"Bun the pup" = Hot dog

"Irish turkey" = Corned beef and cabbage

"Noah's boy" = Ham (in the Bible, Noah had a son named Ham)

EXTRAS

"Mike and Ike, the twins" = Salt and pepper

"Axle grease" = Butter

AS YOU LIKE IT

"Keep off the grass" = No lettuce

"On the hoof" = Rare

"All the way" = With everything

"High and dry" = Plain

"Breath" = With onion

JUST DESSERTS

"Nervous pudding" = Jell-O

"Eve with a lid on" = Apple pie (folklore has Biblical Eve tempted with an apple)

"Fish eyes" = Tapioca pudding

Y'all come back now, y'hear!

Etiquette from 1290 A.D.

While you're out dining, here are a few good rules from an old book of table etiquette. From *Fifty Table Courtesies* by Bonvieino da Riva, written in A.D. 1290.:

• "A number of people gnaw a bone and then put it back in the dish. This is a serious offense."

• "Refrain from falling upon the dish like a swine while eating, snorting disgustingly and smacking the lips."

• "Do not spit over or on the table in the manner of hunters."

• "When you blow your nose or cough, turn round so that nothing you expel falls on the table."

Escape Artist

How To Get Unstuck from a Quicksand Pit

Even though they're the stuff of B-grade movies, quicksand is real and can happen almost anywhere. Don't know what you'd do if you fall into a quicksand pit? Read on ... quickly!

Quicksand is the result when water mixes with sand or any grainy soil. Unless you happen to dive in head first, quicksand doesn't really have to be dangerous:

1. As with any frightening situation, don't panic. Stay calm and use your head. Most quicksand pits are rather shallow, and you probably won't sink over your head.

2. If it is deep, though, don't try to wriggle free or thrash about wildly. Even if it's shallow, it may be difficult to simply pull your feet out if the sand/water mixture is above your knees.

3. You are lighter than quicksand, so you have the capacity to float if you'll stay still. Slowly spread your arms and legs outward. Do not try to pull them up. This will cause a suction that will pull you deeper.

4. Lean backward and try to float on your back. Quicksand is essentially dense water. You'll float pretty easily.

5. Slowly "swim" and inch your way to the edge of the pit, without sudden movements.

6. Follow the slow-and-steady rule while getting out, too. Pulling parts of your body out too fast will create suction that can easily begin to pull you under again. Find some solid ground, and gently—ever so gently—pull each limb out one at a time until you're free.

Write On!

HOW BIC GOT ITS BALL ROLLING

The ballpoint pen seems pretty simple, but it took decades to make it work right. Here's the story of the ballpoint, and why you don't write with a "Bich pen."

LOOK CAREFULLY AT THE POINT of a ballpoint pen. There's a tiny little ball there, of course, which transports the ink from the ink reservoir onto the paper. It looks simple, and in theory it is. But actually developing a usable ballpoint pen was not as easy as it looks. Otherwise the pen in your pocket would be a Loud instead of a Bic, Parker, or Scripto.

John J. Loud of Massachusetts patented a "rolling-pointed fountain marker" on October 30, 1888. It used a tiny, rotating ball bearing that was constantly bathed on one side in ink. Over the next thirty years, 350 similar ballpoint patents were issued by the U.S. Patent Office. But none of the products appeared on the market. The main problem was getting the ink right. If it were too thin, the pens blotched on paper and leaked in pockets. If it were too thick, the pens clogged. Under controlled circumstances, it was sometimes possible to mix up a batch of ink that did what it was supposed to do ... at least until the temperature changed. The best they could do was a ballpoint that would (usually) work fine at 70° F, but would clog at temperatures below 64° and leak, blotch, and smear at temperatures above 77°.

At least that's how it was until the Biro brothers decided to take the challenge on. After World War I, eighteen-year-old Ladislas Biro, newly discharged from the Hungarian Army, tried out a number of career options. He studied medicine, art, and hypnotism, but nothing held his interest long enough to become a career. Eventually, he fell into newspaper work.

In 1935, Biro was editing a small newspaper and found himself cursing his fountain pen. The ink soaked into the paper's newsprint like a sponge, allowing the pen's sharp tip to shred it into soggy pulp. Even when he was working with a decent quality of paper, the ink left smudges on his fingers and clothes—and had to be refilled too often. He recruited his brother Georg, a chemist. The brothers Biro started designing new pens.

After trying dozens of new pen designs and ink formulations, Ladislas and Georg, unaware that it had already been done at least 351 times before, invented the ballpoint pen.

Vacationing at a resort on the shores of the Mediterranean, the two brothers began talking to an elderly gentleman about their new invention. They showed him a working model, and he was suitably impressed. It just so happened that the elderly gentleman was the president of Argentina, Augustine Justo, who suggested that the brothers open a pen factory in his country.

A few years later, World War II began, and the Biros fled Hungary. They remembered their old pal, the president of Argentina, and set sail for South America. They landed in Buenos Aires with $10 between them. Luckily, Justo remembered them. With his help, they lined up some investors. By 1943 had set up their manufacturing plant.

The results were spectacular. A spectacular failure, that is. They had made the mistake that all of their forerunners had made—they depended on gravity to move the ink onto the ball. That meant that the pens had to be held straight up and down at all times. Even then, the ink flow was irregular, leaving heavy globs.

The Biros returned to the lab and came up with a new design. This one depended on capillary action instead of gravity, siphoning the ink toward the point no matter what position it was held in. Within a year, the Biros had brought out their new improved model in Argentina, but the pens didn't sell very well. The Biros ran out of money and stopped production.

However, the U. S. Air Force came to the rescue. American flyers, sent to Argentina during the war, discovered that the ballpoints worked upside-down and at high altitudes without having to be refilled very often. The wartime U.S. Department of State attempted to get American manufacturers to manufacture a similar pen. The Eberhard Faber Company, in an attempt to corner the market, paid $500,000 for the United States rights, yielding the Biro brothers their first profitable year ever.

About this time a Chicago man named Milton Reynolds had seen the Biro pen in Argentina. He came back to the United States and discovered that similar pens had been patented by John J. Loud and other Americans, but that the patents had expired. He therefore figured he could get away with copying the Biro design. He began stamping out pens and sold them for $12.50 each through Gimbels department store in New York City. They were such a novelty that Gimbels sold out its entire stock the first day—a total of 10,000 pens.

Various manufacturers jumped on the bandwagon. Reynolds hired swimming star Esther Williams to show that the pen would write underwater; other manufacturers showed their pens writing upside-down or through stacks of a dozen pieces of carbon paper.

There was one problem, though: Despite the hoopla, the ballpoint pen still didn't work very dependably. They leaked, ruining many a document and good shirt. They plugged up. Sales started falling, as did prices. The item, once an expensive luxury, began selling for as little as 19¢. But even at that price, people bought one, tried it, and—frustrated—vowed never to buy another ballpoint as long as they lived.

The man who eventually change their minds was Marcel Bich from France. As a manufacturer of penholders and cases, he watched with professional interest as the ballpoint industry first took off and then began crashing to the ground. He was interested in the innovative design of the ballpoint pen, but was appalled at the high cost and low quality. He determined that he could take over much of the ballpoint market if he could come up with a dependable pen at a low cost.

The Biro brothers licensed their patents to Bich, who went to work. For two years, he bought every ballpoint pen on the market and systematically tested them, looking for their strengths and weaknesses. In 1952, Bich unveiled his triumph: a six-sided, inexpensive, clear plastic ballpoint pen that wrote smoothly and didn't leak or jam. Looking at the international market, he figured that his name would be a problem in America. Rather than risk having his product referred to as a "Bitch pen," he respelled his name on the pen so it would be pronounced correctly no matter where it was sold—"Bic."

The Bic ballpoint was an immediate hit all over the world. Billions of them, their style essentially unchanged in the years since, have been sold, used, misplaced, disassembled, lost, and disposed of. While Bic has expanded into other pen designs and even diversified into other products, the cheap but dependable Bic pen continues to be responsible for a large chunk of the company's year-

More Deskware Trivia

(From Erin Barrett's and Jack Mingo's book Not Another Apple for the Teacher!)*

• Want to know what that distinctive crayon smell is? Maybe you don't. It's stearic acid, also known as beef fat.

• The first two crayons in a box to be worn down to nubs are usually first the black and then the red.

• The first paper clip was invented in 1899 by a Norwegian patent clerk named Johann Vaaler. A monument to him, shaped like a giant paper clip, stands near Oslo.

• Norwegians take pride in Vaaler and his wiry invention. During the Nazi occupation, Norwegians wore paper clips in their lapels as a sign of nationalism and resistance.

• Then how come we can never find one when we need one? The world generates more than 10 billion pencils every year. Two billion of these come from the United States. No, not all from Pencilvania.

• Pencils are the writing instrument of choice of astronauts, because unlike most pens, they write dependably in zero-gravity.

• Graphite, a carbon compound, has been used for writing since before pencils were invented. In 1789 geologist Abraham Werner named the mineral from a Greek word meaning "to write."

Potty Talk

READING THE WRITING ON THE STALL

Here you sit brokenhearted in a public restroom without your *Bathroom Companion*. What do you do? Well, it may be a poor substitute, but you can always analyze the bathroom graffiti.

WALK INTO ANY PUBLIC RESTROOM and there's a chance you'll be bombarded with hand-written messages, some incoherent, some crude, and some even moderately funny. Believe it or not, scholars have spent time researching the writing on the stall walls, and have even give a name to it: *latrinalia.* Here's what they've found out.

WHERE IT ALL BEGAN

Many of us assume that the scrawlings on public stalls are a modern-day invention, but archeologists have learned that the practice isn't new. It seems even the ancient Romans expressed their ideas while sitting on the throne. When archeologists excavated the ruins of Pompeii that had been buried under ash since the eruption of Mount Vesuvius in A.D. 79, they found a treasure trove of artifacts from everyday life. Brushing ash from the walls of the public toilets, they uncovered a wealth of graffiti:

- *"Apollinaris, doctor to the Emperor Titus, had a crap here"*
- *"Artimetus got me pregnant"*
- *"The risen flesh commands, let there be love!"*
- *"Fortunatus made it with Anthusam"*

- *"Serena hates Isadore"*
- *"Daddy Colepius kisses the ladies where he shouldn't"*
- *"Hello, hello Mago, fare you well, you're obviously castrated"*
- *"Hello! We are wineskins!"*

There was even response graffiti. To the philosophical message, "Lovers, like bees, enjoy a life of honey" was a deflating zinger in a different hand: "Wishful thinking."

GRAFFITI FROM ANCIENT POMPEII. THE DRAW-ING IS A ROMAN SOLDIER. THE INSCRIPTION SAYS, "AUGE LOVES ARABIENUS."

The practice of writing on the walls of stalls didn't stop there, of course. And the study of bathroom graffiti didn't start in our time. *The Merry-Thought or The Glass-Window Bog-House Miscellany* is an 18th-century compilation of the writings from privy walls, put together by an early sociologist named Hurlo Thomas. One example of the earthy compositions he documented is this, which he found at "the bog house at the Nags'-Head in Bradmere":

> *You are eas'd in your Body*
> *and pleas'd in your Mind*
> *That you leave both a Turd*
> *And some Verses behind—*
> *But to me, which is worse,*
> *I can't tell, on my Word:*
> *The reading your Verses*
> *Or smelling your Turd.*

The walls of the Tower of London, too, bear messages, written by political prisoners awaiting execution. The graffiti was written in the only writing medium available— blood. Here's one:

> *Be frend to one*
> *Be ennermye to none.*

GRAFFITI, OR LATRINALIA?

Although all latrinalia is considered bathroom graffiti, not all bathroom graffiti is considered latrinalia (pronounced, in case you want to drop it casually into a conversation, *la-tri-NA-le-ah*). Dr. Alan Dundes at the University of California (Berkeley) was the first sociologist to seriously study the fine art of stall scribbling. In his 1966 seminal thesis, "Here I Sit…." he defines the distinctive characteristic of latrinalia: It is universal enough to be found in many public restrooms. It's a piece of writing that is so memorable and universal that its readers spread it to other restrooms across the world.

For example, the familiar couplet *"Here I sit all broken hearted / Came to shit but only farted"* is classic latrinalia because it's been around since the 1920s. In that time it has spread from its first location to millions across the world (for example, it's been sighted in the girls' bathroom at Hong Kong International School). In contrast, *"Mr. Skinner stinks"* is mere graffiti because it is an individual statement that is specific to the few restrooms where Mr. Skinner would likely be known.

THE VARIATIONS
Dr. Dundes defined five categories of latrinalia:

• **Advertisements or solicitations.** For example: *"For a good time, call* [phone number]." Although the specific names, place, and phone number differ in each location, the phrases are so well known that Dundes includes them as latrinalia.

• **Requests or commands.** *"If you sprinkle when you tinkle, please be neat and wipe the*

seat." Or the less serious request: *"Don't throw your cigarette butts in the urinal — it makes them soggy and hard to light."*

• **Facetious instructions.** *"In case of atomic attack, hide under this urinal. Nobody ever hits it."* Or the one found on a wall at Goddard Space Center: *"Look Up!"* On the ceiling it continued, *"You are now in launch position."*

• **Commentaries.** Above urinal: *"You are holding the future of America in your hands."* Or this three parter:
> To be is to do — Friedrich Nietzsche
> To do is to be — Immanuel Kant
> Do be do be do — Frank Sinatra

• **Introspective musings / Personal laments.** *"Here I sit all tired and dirty, trying to hide until 4:30,"* wrote an employee at a sandwich shop.

THE CULPRITS
Research has shown that most latrinalia writers are men.

However, women write on bathroom walls as much as men or more, but their markings tend to be conversational and situation-specific (*"I'm bored because my friend left me here"*).

So why is there a gender difference? Well, researchers aren't totally sure. Some argue the practice is a leftover from the pre-civilization days of marking territory. Others argue that men are more driven to leave something significant of themselves behind, so are more likely to scribble things in public places. Whatever the reason, though, sociologists say that after the advent of the women's movement in the 1970s, more true latrinalia was found in women's rooms.

We're still a culture that's embarrassed about bodily functions. When that's gone, experts say, much of the writing on the stalls will decrease. We hope we stay uptight, then, because latrinalia makes good reading.

Stalling For Time

• On the stall door: *"Congrats! You've won a free game of Toilet Tennis! Now look left."* On the left wall: *"Look right."* On the right: *"Look left...."*

• *"Please do not throw cigarette butts in our urinal. We don't use your ashtrays as toilets!"*

• *"If PRO is opposite of CON, then what's the opposite of progress? CONGRESS."*

• *"Patrons are requested to remain seated thruout entire performance."*

• On an **Employees Must Wash Hands** sign, some soul scribbled, *"I waited and waited, but I finally gave up and washed them myself."*

• *"My wife follows me everywhere,"* complained one bathroom patron. In a different handwriting below it: *"I do not!"*

• *"Beauty is only a light switch away."*

• *"Fart for Jesus!"*

• *"Make love, not war. Hell, do both – get married."*

• *"Beer: Helping ugly people have sex since 3472 B.C."*

Giving Blood

CENTURIES OF CONFUSION ABOUT TRANSFUSION

Have you given blood? It's an easy way to save lives and be a hero. But it took hundreds of years, many deaths, and a bunch of monkeys before doctors figured out how to do it right.

IT'S A STRANGE THING, if you think about it—taking blood from one person and injecting it into another. Nobody really knows when the first successful blood transfusion took place. Some historians believe that it might've been in the time of the Incas, who were fairly advanced medically. The interesting thing is that transfusions between Incas would've worked out just fine because Incas were all the same blood type (O+).

INNOCENT BLOOD

The first documented attempt at giving a blood transfusion took place in Rome in 1492. Pope Innocent VIII was dying, and his doctor thought giving him some new blood would help. It didn't. This is a 1492 account from *Diareo della Citta 'di Roma* by Stefano Infessua, complete with shades of the antisemitism of the time:

> Three ten-year-old boys, from whose veins a certain Jewish physician (who had promised that the pope would be restored to health) extracted blood, died without delay. The Jew had told them he could heal the pontiff, if only he could have a certain quantity of young human blood. He ordered it to be extracted from the three boys, to whom he gave a ducat for each. Shortly after they died. The Jew fled, and the pope was not healed.

The deaths of the pope and the boys put a damper on further experimentation for a few centuries.

ARTERY & SCIENCE

Finally, in 1665, Dr. Richard Lower of England successfully transfused blood back and forth between two dogs using feather quills as hypodermic needles. It took some trial and error—at first he tried hooking the dogs up vein to vein, but the blood didn't go anywhere; it just clotted in the quills. Finally, Lower figured out that he needed to plug into the artery of the donor and the vein of the donee to set up an imbalance of pressure, and his dog-and-aorta show was off and running.

So far, so good. However, like many scientists, Lower didn't know when to quit. He tried what seemed to be the next logical step—a lamb-to-man transfusion. At about the same time in France, another doctor tried a calf-to-man transfusion. Both patients died. Because of the public outcry, research on blood transfusions again stopped.

In 1818, James Blundell tried a person-to-person transfusion in Guy's Hospital in London. Not only was he successful, but he was able to save his patient's life with the procedure. His success on the first try was a lucky fluke, however, since the mystery of compatible blood types had not yet been figured out. His first smashing success was soon shattered by a string of unexplained sudden deaths, and Blundell abandoned his research.

THANK YOU, RHESUS

Finally in 1900, Dr. Karl Landsteiner discovered the problem. He discovered the A, B, and O blood groups, and further figured out that mixing incompatible blood types creates a curdled mess of small red dumplings floating in yellowish liquid.

Landsteiner discovered, however, that blood within the same blood group could be successfully mixed without getting dumplings. To honor the research monkeys that gave their blood and lives to his research, Landsteiner coined the term *rh factors* — "rh" being short for "rhesus."

The good doctor's discoveries won him a Nobel Prize and led to a quick succession of breakthroughs. As World War I broke out, other doctors learned that sodium citrate kept blood from clotting without harming the blood recipient, allowing the storage of blood outside the donor's body. As a result of this discovery, the first blood bank opened in Chicago in 1937.

DR. DREW BLOOD

Pioneer hematologist Dr. Charles Drew was the first to realize that blood plasma — the straw-colored liquid that remains when you remove the red cells, white cells, and platelets — would store longer than whole blood, yet was just as useful in emergency applications. In 1940, he opened New York's first blood bank and set up a drive to raise 5,000 units of blood plasma for England's fight against the Nazis.

After the United States entered the war, Dr. Drew was offended and exasperated by the U.S. military's

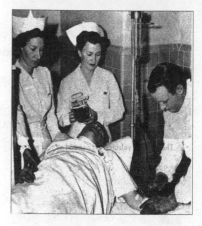

requirement in World War II that blood be sorted by the race of its donors. For one thing, he knew that it didn't make any medical difference and suspected that waiting for the right "race" of blood would result in the unnecessary deaths of countless injured troops. For another, military segregation — even reaching down to blood supplies — must have been personally galling, because Drew was an African American. Eventually, that restriction fell as the army became fully integrated.

Nowadays, there are about 5,000 blood banks in the United States alone. All are regulated by the United States Food and Drug Administration.

Escape Artist

HOW TO EVADE AN ALLIGATOR

We know there aren't many chances to get chased and eaten by an alligator in the U.S., but what about when you visit Papua New Guinea? It's always best to be prepared, to borrow a phrase.

ALMOST ALL ALLIGATOR ATTACKS happen because the alligator's been fed by humans. Rule #1: Don't feed alligators. If you run into one, though, here's what to do:

1. You've probably heard you should run in a zigzag pattern if you find yourself chased by an alligator. This may sound like it makes sense, but trust us: it doesn't. Although an alligator can run up to 30 mph, it can't do so for long. The best escape route you have is running fast; the best way to do that is by running straight ahead.

2. So the above didn't work and the alligator's got your leg, and what you need to do is keep it from rolling you under water or shaking you—these things will cause more damage. Hold the alligator's jaw clamped shut on your limb. This will keep it focused on its jaw, not on pulling you under.

3. If you have access and can do this while in its clutches, cover the alligator's eyes. Reptiles often become docile if the light is blocked from their eyes.

4. Punch its snout. Although alligators have been known to open their mouths when touched lightly, if your leg or arm is in its clutches and you don't have time to spare, punch hard. This should open the alligator's mouth long enough for you to escape.

5. An alternative? Go for its eyes. A quick punch or hard slap to the eyes will often produce a similar jaw-opening reaction.

Ben's Naughty Advice

ON TAKING AN OLDER MISTRESS

Ben Franklin was a brilliant man who didn't hesitate to write about a wide range of subjects. Here he offers a marriage-shy New Yorker named Caldwallader Colden some tongue-in-cheek advice.

June 25, 1745

My Dear Friend:

I know of no Medicine fit to diminish the violent natural inclination you mention; and if I did, I think I should not communicate it to you. Marriage is the proper Remedy. It is the most natural State of Man, and therefore the State in which you will find solid Happiness. Your Reason against entering into it at present appears to be not well founded. The Circumstantial Advantages you have in View by Postponing it, are not only uncertain, but they are small in comparison with the Thing itself, the being married and settled. It is the Man and Woman united that makes the complete Being. Separate she wants his force of Body and Strength of Reason; he her Softness, Sensibility and acute Discernment. Together they are most likely to succeed in the World. A single Man has not nearly the Value he would have in that State of Union. He is an incomplete Animal. He resembles the odd Half of a Pair of Scissors.

If you get a prudent, healthy wife, your Industry in your Profession, with her good Economy, will be a Fortune sufficient.

But if you will not take this Counsel, and persist in thinking a Commerce with the Sex is inevitable, then I repeat my former Advice that in your Amours you should *prefer old Women to young ones*. This you call a Paradox, and demand my reasons.

They are these:

1. Because they have more Knowledge of the world, and their Minds are better stored with Observations; their Conversation is more improving, and more lastingly agreeable.

2. Because when Women cease to be handsome, they study to  be good. To maintain their Influence over Man, they supply the Diminution of Beauty by an Augmentation of Utility. They learn to do a thousand Services, small and great, and are the most tender and useful of all Friends when you are sick. Thus they continue amiable. And hence there is hardly such a thing to be found as an old Woman who is not a good Woman.

3. Because there is no hazard of children, which irregularly produced may be attended with much inconvenience.

4. Because through more Experience they are more prudent and discreet in conducting an Intrigue to prevent Suspicion. The Commerce with them is therefore safer with regard to your reputation; and regard to theirs, if the Affair should happen to be known, considerate People might be inclined to excuse an old Woman, who would kindly take care of a young Man, form his manners by her good Councils, and prevent his ruining his Health and Fortune among mercenary Prostitutes.

5. Because in every Animal that walks upright, the Deficiency of the Fluids that fill the Muscles appears first in the highest Part. The Face first grows lank and wrinkled; then the Neck; then the Breast and Arms; the lower parts continuing to the last as plump as ever; so that covering all above with a Basket, and regarding only what is below the Girdle, it is impossible of two Women to know an old from a young one. And as in the Dark all Cats are gray, the Pleasure of Corporal Enjoyment with an old Woman is at least equal and frequently superior; every Knack being by Practice capable by improvement.

6. Because the sin is less. The Debauching of a Virgin may be her Ruin, and make her for Life unhappy.

7. Because the Compunction is less. The having made a young Girl miserable may give you frequent bitter Reflections none which can attend making an old Woman happy.

8. 8th & lastly. They are so grateful!!!

Thus much for my Paradox. But still I advise you to marry immediately; being sincerely

Your Affectionate Friend,

Benj. Franklin

So You Think Your Child's a Musical Genius?

• **Mozart.** Wolfgang Amadeus Mozart started playing harpsichord at age 4 and a year later was giving concerts for royalty. The first pieces he published at age 6 are still played today.

• **Michael Jackson.** Okay, maybe he hasn't been that great as an adult, but did you know he got his first gold record (for "I Want You Back") at age 11?

• **Chopsticks.** A 16-year-old girl wrote the musical piece that is the one most performed on the piano. Yes, it's "Chopsticks," that percussive little melody that is the bane of piano owners everywhere. Euphonia Allen was an English girl who published her only known musical endeavor under the name of "Arthur de Lulli" in 1877. The title had

nothing to do with Chinese eating utensils, but told how the piece was to be played: "with both hands turned sideways, the little fingers lowest, so that the movement of the hands imitates the chopping from which this waltz gets its name."

• **"Blind Tom."** Thomas Wiggins was born in 1845 with many strikes against him: he was blind, autistic, and a slave. At age 4, he began sneaking to the master's parlor piano and reproducing music he'd heard. He could play any piece after hearing it once. By age 8, he performed all over the world and had a repertoire of 7,000 pieces. As a stage gimmick, he sometimes played with his hands reversed and his back to the piano.

Listen Up

LIFE ADVICE FROM THE RICH AND FAMOUS

"Do not allow children to mix drinks. It is unseemly and they use too much vermouth." — Fran Lebowitz

"First wipe your nose and check your fly." — Alec Guinness

"People disappoint you. Lovers disappoint you. But theatrical memorabilia stays with you, as long as you keep it under clear plastic." — Sylvia Miles

"Don't do anything you wouldn't be willing to explain on television." — Arjay Miller

"If your house is really a mess and a stranger comes to the door, greet him with, 'Who could have done this? We have no enemies!'" — Phyllis Diller

"The hardest years in life are those between ten and seventy." — Helen Hayes

"Brown shoes don't make it." — Frank Zappa

"No day is so bad it can't be fixed with a nap." — Carrie Snow

"Do not use a hatchet to remove a fly from your friend's forehead." — Chinese proverb

"Be honest with yourself until the end of your life. Then listen to the slow movement of the Schubert Quintet and kick the bucket." — Nathan Milstein

"The secret to success is to know something nobody else knows." — Aristotle Onassis

"Success usually comes to those who are too busy to be looking for it." — Henry David Thoreau

Bats, Clubs & Racquets

INVENTING THE WILD WORLD OF SPORTS

Before sports became big business, games were just games, and people invented them and changed them as they saw fit. Here are the stories behind some of our favorite sports.

GOLF

Who invented golf? We could say the Scots, but that wouldn't be telling the whole story. The simple fact is that hitting a rock into a hole in the ground is such an obvious concept for whiling away the hours that the basic game was "invented" in every corner of the world.

The ancient Romans, for instance, played a golf-like game called *paganica*, using a bent stick and a leather ball filled with feathers. The Visigoths—known for their plundering and over-all pillaging—for sure played paganica after they overthrew ancient Rome on August 4, 410, but may have played a golf-like game even before then. It's been documented in writing and art that the Chinese played *Chuiwan* ("hitting ball") as early as the tenth century, but the French swear that golf came from their ancient game *jeu de mail*. Golf also might've come from an early British game called *knur and spell*, Belgium's *chole* that goes back to the 1300s, or the Dutch game of *kolven*.

The truth is that no one knows the origins for sure. Whatever the game's early roots, though, linguists agree that the word "golf" comes from an ancient Scottish word *gowf*, that meant "to strike."

And everyone agrees, as well, that the Scottish did love their golf. In 1744, the Company of Gentlemen Golfers of Leith

81

(Scotland) created the earliest known written golf code, consisting of thirteen rules. Ten years later, Scotland's St. Andrews golf club formed.

At the end of the nineteenth century golf really began to take off. In 1873, the Royal Montreal Golf Club opened, making it the first permanent golfing club in the Western Hemisphere. The first golf book in America, *Golf In America: A Practical Manual*, was published in 1895. Still, most Americans were terribly confused by the game, as evidenced by this explanation in the *Philadelphia Times*:

"It is sometimes agreed that the game shall be won by him who makes the largest number of holes within a given number of minutes, say 20 or 30.... Each player places his ball at the edge of a hole designated as a starting point. He then bats it ... toward the next hole. As soon as it has started he runs forward ... and his servant, who is called 'caddy,' runs after him...."

BASEBALL

Despite a myth spread enthusiastically by early promoters, baseball was not really invented by Abner Doubleday in Cooperstown, New York. In fact, it wasn't exactly invented at all — instead it

TAKE ME OUT TO THE BALLGAME

Vaudevillian Jack Norworth wrote the words to "Take Me Out to the Ballgame" before he'd ever even seen a baseball game. He was inspired to put the new sport fad to verse in 1908 after seeing a sign on a bus advertising "Baseball Today—Polo Grounds." His friend Albert von Tilzer wrote the music. It wasn't until after the song became a hit that either of them actually went to "root root root for the home team."

While almost everybody knows the sing along chorus, almost nobody knows the verses. Here's the one to get you started:

"Katie Casey was baseball mad
Had the fever and had it bad.
Just to root for the hometown crew,
Every sound, Katie blew,
On a Saturday her young beau
Called to see if she'd like to go
To see a show but Miss Kate said, 'No
I'll tell you what you can do—
Take me out to the ball game....'"

evolved from the British games of cricket and rounders which, early on, were sometimes called "base ball."

By the early 1800s, Americans had already begun adapting the games into new variations called "town ball" and "one old cat—two old cat—three old cat." In 1845, Alexander Cartwright drew up some rules for the New York Knickerbocker Base Ball Club, arbitrarily fixing the diamond size at ninety feet square, and putting the batter at home plate instead of in a batters' box nearby. He also ruled out the deadly practice of "plugging" base runners—hitting them with a thrown ball to get them out. But still, the game had quite a bit of evolving to do in the coming years before it became the game we know today.

TENNIS

The French originated tennis during the twelfth century. They called it *jeu de paume*, ("game of the palm") because, in the beginning, players used their hands to bat the ball back and forth over the net. Rackets came later, and the name changed to *tenetz* ("get and hold").

The father of modern tennis is Major Walter Clopton Wingfield of England, who in 1873, introduced the modern sport with the idea of playing it on grass courts. Wingfield wasn't quite as good at coining names—he called the game *sphairistike*, Greek for "playing ball."

Most went back to the French name, and tennis soon replaced croquet as England's most popular outdoor sport, and in 1874, Mary Ewing Outerbridge, an American sportswoman, purchased tennis equipment from British army officers in Bermuda and introduced the sport to America.

BADMINTON

Badminton was invented in the 1860s by the daughters of the Duke of Beaufort. It was based loosely on an ancient game called *battledore and shuttlecock*, and used the same equipment.

They named the game after their dad's Badminton House in Gloustershire, England, where they first played it. The dimension of the modern official badminton court (44 feet long and 17 feet wide) report-

LACROSSE

Native Canadian tribes played a game like lacrosse hundreds of years ago. By the 1800's, French pioneers had begun to play, too. In 1867, Canadian George Beers standardized the game—setting field dimensions, team size, and rules.

JAI ALAI

Jai alai originated in the Basque regions of Spain and France during the 1600s. The name in the Basque language means "merry festival." It may well be the only game in which lefthanders are specifically banned from playing.

edly matches those of the room where the young women developed the game.

Badminton has been an Olympic event since 1992, and it's Malaysia's official national sport.

A Word to the Wise

"The roots of education are bitter, but the fruit is sweet." —Aristotle

"Soap and education are not as sudden as a massacre, but they are more deadly in the long run."—Mark Twain

"No man who worships education has got the best out of education. Without a gentle contempt for education, no man's education is complete." —G.K. Chesterton

"If you think education is expensive, try ignorance." —Derek Bok

"Education is a form of self-delusion." —Elbert Hubbard

"He that increaseth knowledge increaseth sorrow." —Ecclesiastes

"Education is what remains when we have forgotten all that we have been taught."—George Savile

"Education seems to be in America the only commodity of which the customer tried to get as little he can for his money." —Max Forman

"Education is the process of casting false pearls before real swine." —Irwin Edman

Presidential Trivia I

PRESIDENTS & THEIR VICES

From the question-and-answer books *Just Curious, Jeeves* and *Just Curious About History, Jeeves*, by Jack Mingo and Erin Barrett, we found some juicy little bits of gossip on some United States Presidents and Veeps.

How many U.S. presidents have been divorced?

Just one: Ronald Reagan.

Wasn't JFK pretty sick during his presidency?

He was sick. He suffered from two serious problems: Addison's disease, in which the body can't produce sufficient amounts of the crucial hormone cortisol, and a degeneration of the spine, probably due to repeat injuries. He also suffered the physical complications of having contracted malaria during World War II.

During his childhood, back problems, jaundice, and other ails kept Kennedy scrawny and weak. When he was serving in Congress he underwent steroid shots and back surgeries. There were at least four incidents prior to his death in 1963 where he had last rites administered by priests.

During the time of his presidency, though, Kennedy was healthier than he'd been in a while. Because so much of his appeal was based on his boyish good looks and athleticism, he went to great lengths to conceal his illnesses from the public.

Which president said he believed the Earth was flat?

Andrew Jackson. Ol' Andy never did cotton much to book larnin'.

Have there been any unusual pets in the White House?

It hasn't all been just cats and dogs. Calvin Coolidge had a raccoon. Teddy Roosevelt had a badger. Herbert Hoover had a horned toad. Woodrow Wilson had a ram named Old Ike that visitors fed so much chewing tobacco to that it became hopelessly addicted. Tad Lincoln had a pet turkey, and Andrew Jackson had a parrot with language so foul that the bird had to be removed from Jackson's funeral. But probably the most unusual pet was an alligator that John Quincy Adams kept around because he said he enjoyed "the spectacle of guests fleeing from the room in terror."

Were any of the United States presidents gay?

It's impossible to prove for sure. However, our only bachelor president, James Buchanan, had that reputation in his lifetime. His long-time roommate, Senator and later Vice President William Rufus De Vane King of Alabama, also never married. According to historians, the two had an inseparable relationship for nearly twenty-five years until King's death—in fact, King was called "Buchanan's better half," "James's wife," and "Miss Nancy" by some of his colleagues. When the two were temporarily separated after King was appointed minister to France in 1844, King wrote Buchanan, "I am selfish enough to hope you will not be able to procure an

associate who will cause you to feel no regret at our separation." Buchanan wrote to a Mrs. Roosevelt, "I am now 'solitary and alone,' having no companion in the house with me. I have gone a wooing to several gentlemen but have not succeeded with any one of them. I feel that it is not good for man to be alone; and should not be astonished to find myself married to some old maid who can nurse me when I am sick, provide good dinners for me when I am well, and not expect from me any very ardent or romantic affection."

But that's not all. Hang onto your stovepipe hats, because a few rogue historians also claim that Abraham Lincoln was homoerotically involved with a lifelong friend named Joshua Speed. They shared private thoughts, fears, desires, and a bed for four years. Lincoln biographer Carl Sandberg wrote that their relationship had "a streak of lavender and spots soft as May violets."

Were any U.S. presidents not Christians?

If you judge them by their fruits, you could argue a number of them were not. However, Abraham Lincoln was one who specifically rejected Christianity, even writing a pamphlet called "Infidelity" that sought to disprove the Bible generally and the idea of Jesus being the son of God specifically. Later, as a politician, he succumbed to pressure to mention God in speeches but pointedly did not mention Jesus.

Thomas Jefferson attended an Episcopal church, but refused to discuss his religious beliefs during his election campaign and so was accused by rabble-rousing preachers of being ungodly and in league with Satan. Actually, he believed in the moral teachings of Jesus, but not in his divinity.

How old was George Washington when he chopped down the cherry tree?

Sorry to burst your bubble, but the cherry tree story's just a myth. (Where've you been, my friend?) It doesn't mean he wasn't ethical as a child, however. As a matter of fact, there's evidence George was extremely moral in his formative years. As a schoolboy he wrote rules of behavior for himself into his exercise book that still survives today. What's not clear is whether it was his own idea or that of his mother or schoolteacher.

Decide for yourself. Following are some of them (rendered in his own boyhood spelling, capitalization, and punctuation):

- Turn not your Back to others especially in Speaking, Jog not the Table or Desk on which Another reads or writes, lean not upon any one.

- Use no Reproachfull Language against any one neither Curse nor Revile.

- Play not the Peacock, looking every where about you, to See if you be well Deck't, if your Shoes fit well, if your Skokings Sit neatly, and Cloths handsomely.

- While you are talking, Point not with your Finger at him of Whom you Discourse nor Approach too near him to whom you talk especially to his face.

- Be not Curious to Know the Affairs of Others neither approach those that Speak in Private.

- It's unbecoming to Stoop much to ones Meat Keep your Fingers clean & when foul wipe them on a Corner of your Table Napkin.

How many U. S. presidents have resigned from office?

One. Richard Nixon.

How many U.S. vice presidents have resigned from office?

Two: John Calhoun resigned in a policy dispute with the president; Spiro Agnew resigned after it was discovered he'd been taking bribes.

We've Got Your Number

We'll give you a number, abbreviated words, and a clue. Tell us what the famous phrase is. Answers below. (Don't cheat!)

1. 2001 A S O (Apes and spacecraft)
2. A B & T 40 T (Baghdad tale)
3. 1 L T L (Llanview soap opera)
4. 5 L M J O T B (Doc said: no more jumping!)
5. J & T 12 A (Attendees at a final dinner)
6. 3 L F & A M F T (1940s aqueous novelty song)
7. 2 B, 4 B, 6 B, A D (On your feet and cheer)
8. 1 P, 2 P, 3 P, 4 (You're it!)
9. 5 4 3 2 1, W H I, W H L-O (I'm a rocket man)
10. T 2 A & C M I T M (Telephone prescription)
11. 52 P-U (Wanna play a card game?)
12. 4 S & 7 Y A (An address in Pennsylvania)
13. P 6-5000 (Big band hit)
14. I L O A 4-L C (Don't overlook lucky tokens)
15. 1 R T R T A (Makes for a very bad hobbit)
16. 3 S & Y O (Baseball and harsh sentencing)
17. T G O 4 (Chinese clique)
18. 40 D & 40 N (Didn't it rain, children)
19. 88 K O T P (Flats, sharps, and naturals)
20. 99 B O B O T W (Endlessly annoying song)

Answers: 1. *2001: A Space Odyssey;* 2. *Ali Baba & the 40 Thieves;* 3. *One Life to Live;* 4. *5 Little Monkeys, Jumping on the Bed;* 5. *Jesus & the 12 Apostles;* 6. *3 Little Fishes & a Momma Fish Too;* 7. *2 Bits, 4 Bits, 6 Bits, a Dollar;* 8. *1 Potato, 2 Potatoes, 3 Potatoes, 4;* 9. *5-4-3-2-1, We Have Ignition, We Have Lift-off;* 10. *Take 2 Aspirins & Call Me in the Morning;* 11. *52 Pick-up;* 12. *4 Score & 7 Years Ago;* 13. *Pennsylvania 6-5000;* 14. *I'm Looking Over a 4-Leaf Clover;* 15. *1 Ring to Rule Them All;* 16. *3 Strikes & You're Out;* 17. *The Gang of 4;* 18. *40 Days & 40 Nights;* 19. *88 Keys on the Piano;* 20. *99 Bottles of Beer on the Wall*

Myth-Making

HER LIFE ... ACCORDING TO CALAMITY JANE

Martha Canary, known as "Calamity Jane," created quite a legend for herself. Unfortunately, most of it was not true. So, with several grains of salt ready, we present "The Life & Adventures of Calamity Jane by Herself," as published in a promotional pamphlet.

MY MAIDEN NAME was Marthy Cannary. I was born in Princeton, Missouri, May 1st, 1852. As a child I always had a fondness for adventure and out-door exercise and especial fondness for horses which I began to ride at an early age and continued to do so until I able to ride the most vicious and stubborn of horses.

In 1865 we emigrated from our homes in Missouri by the overland route to Virginia City, Montana, taking five months to make the journey. While on the way the greater portion of my time was spent in hunting along with the men and hunters of the party, in fact I was at all times with the men when there was excitement and adventures to be had. By the time we reached Virginia City I was considered a remarkable good shot and a fearless rider for a girl of my age.

Joined General Custer as a scout at Fort Russell, Wyoming, in 1870, and started for Arizona for the Indian Campaign. Up to this time I had always worn the costume of my sex. When I joined Custer I donned the uniform of a soldier. It was a bit awkward at first but I soon got to be perfectly at home in men's clothes.

Was in Arizona up to the winter of 1871 and during that time I had a great many adventures with the Indians, for as a scout I had a great many dangerous missions to perform and while I was in many close places always succeeded in getting away

safely for by this time I was considered the most reckless and daring rider and one of the best shots in the western country.

After that campaign I returned to Fort Sanders, Wyoming, until spring of 1872, when we were ordered out to the Muscle Shell or Nursey Pursey Indian outbreak. In that war Generals Custer, Miles, Terry, and Crook were all engaged. This campaign lasted until fall of 1873.

It was during this campaign that I was christened Calamity Jane. It was on Goose Creek, Wyoming, where the town of Sheridan is now located. Capt. Egan was in command of the Post. We were ordered out to quell an uprising of the Indians, and were out for several days, had numerous skirmishes during which six of the soldiers were killed and several severely wounded. When on returning to the Post we were ambushed about a mile and a half from our destination. When fired upon Capt. Egan was shot. I was riding in advance and on hearing the firing turned in my saddle and saw the Captain reeling in his saddle as though about to fall. I turned my horse and galloped back with all haste to his side and got there in time to catch him as he was falling. I lifted him onto my horse in front of me and succeeded in getting him safely to the Fort. Capt. Egan on recovering, laughingly said: "I name you Calamity Jane, the heroine of the plains." I have borne that name up to the present time.

We were afterwards ordered to Fort Custer, where Custer city now stands, where we arrived in the spring of 1874; remained around Fort Custer all summer and were ordered to Fort Russell in fall of 1874, where we remained until spring of 1875; was then ordered to the Black Hills to protect miners, as that country was controlled by the Sioux Indians and the government had to send the soldiers to protect the lives of the miners and settlers in that section. Remained there until fall of 1875 and wintered at Fort Laramie. In spring of 1876, we were ordered north with General Crook to join Gen'ls Miles, Terry, and Custer at Big Horn river. During this march I swam the Platte river at Fort Fetterman as I was the bearer of important dispatches. I had a ninety mile ride to make, being wet and cold, I contracted a severe illness and was sent back in Gen. Crook's ambulance to Fort Fetterman where I laid in the hospital for fourteen days. When able to ride I started for Fort Laramie where I met Wm. Hickock, better known as Wild Bill, and we started for Deadwood, where we arrived about June.

During the month of June I acted as a pony express rider carrying the U.S. mail between Deadwood and Custer, a distance of fifty miles, over one of the roughest trails in the Black Hills country. As many of the riders before me had been held up and robbed of their packages, mail and money that they carried, for that was the only means of getting mail and money between these points. It was considered the most dangerous route in the Hills, but as my reputation as a rider and quick shot was well known, I was molested very little, for the toll gatherers looked on me as being a good fellow, and they knew that I never missed my mark. I made the round trip every two days which was considered pretty good riding in that country. Remained around Deadwood all that summer visiting all the camps within an area of one hundred miles. My friend, Wild Bill, remained in Deadwood during the summer with the exception of occasional visits to the camps.

On the 2nd of August, while setting at a gambling table in the Bell Union saloon, in Deadwood, he was shot in the back of the head by the notorious Jack McCall, a desperado. I was in Deadwood at the time and on hearing of the killing made my way at once to the scene of the shooting and found that my friend had been killed by McCall. I at once started to look for the assassin and found him at Shurdy's butcher shop and grabbed a meat cleaver and made him throw up his hands; through the excitement on hearing of Bill's death, having left my weapons on the post of my bed. He was then taken to a log cabin and locked up, well secured as every one thought, but he got away and was afterwards caught at Fagan's ranch on Horse

Creek, on the old Cheyenne road and was then taken to Yankton, Dak., where he was tried, sentenced and hung.

I remained around Deadwood locating claims, going from camp to camp until the spring of 1877, where one morning, I saddled my horse and rode towards Crook City. I had gone about twelve miles from Deadwood, at the mouth of Whitewood creek, when I met the overland mail running from Cheyenne to Deadwood. The horses on a run, about two hundred yards from the station; upon looking closely I saw they were pursued by Indians. The horses ran to the barn as was their custom. As the horses stopped I rode along side of the coach and found the driver John Slaughter, lying face downwards, he having been shot by the Indians. When the stage got to the station the Indians hid in the bushes. I immediately removed all baggage from the coach except the mail. I then took the driver's seat and with all haste drove to Deadwood, carrying the six passengers and the dead driver.

I left Deadwood in the fall of 1877, and went to Bear Butte Creek with the 7th Cavalry. During the fall and winter we built Fort Meade and the town of Sturgis. In 1878 I left the command and went to Rapid City and put in the year prospecting.

In 1879 I went to Fort Pierre and drove trains from Rapid City to Fort Pierre for Frank Witc then drove teams from Fort Pierce to Sturgis for Fred Evans. This teaming was done with oxen as they were better fitted for the work than horses, owing to the rough nature of the country.

In 1881 I went to Wyoming and returned in 1882 to Miles City and took up a ranch on the Yellow Stone, raising stock and cattle, also kept a way side inn, where the weary traveler could be accommodated with food, drink, or trouble if he looked for it. Left the ranch in 1883, went to California, going through the States and territories, reached Ogden the latter part of 1883, and San Francisco in 1884. Left San Francisco in the summer of 1884 for Texas, stopping at Fort Yuma, Arizona, the hottest spot in the United States. Stopping at all points of interest until I reached El Paso in the fall. While in El Paso, I met Mr. Clinton Burk, a native of Texas, who I married in August 1885. As I thought I had travelled through life long enough alone and thought it was about time to take a partner for the rest of my days. We remained in Texas leading a quiet home life until

1889. On October 28th, 1887, I became the mother of a girl baby, the very image of its father, at least that is what he said, but who has the temper of its mother.

When we left Texas we went to Boulder, Colorado, where we kept a hotel until 1893, after which we travelled through Wyoming, Montana, Idaho, Washington, Oregon, then back to Montana, then to Dakota, arriving in Deadwood October 9th, 1895, after an absence of seventeen years.

My arrival in Deadwood after an absence of so many years created quite an excitement among my many friends of the past, to such an extent that a vast number of the citizens who had come to Deadwood during my absence who had heard so much of Calamity Jane and her many adventures in former years were anxious to see me. Among the many whom I met were several gentlemen from eastern cities who advised me to allow myself to be placed before the public in such a manner as to give the people of the eastern cities an opportunity of seeing the Woman Scout who was made so famous through her daring career in the West and Black Hill countries.

An agent of Kohl & Middleton, the celebrated Museum men, came to Deadwood, through the solicitation of the gentleman who I had met there and arrangements were made to place me before the public in this manner. My first engagement began at the Palace Museum, Minneapolis, January 20th, 1896, under Kohl and Middleton's management.

Hoping that this little history of my life may interest all readers, I remain as in the older days,

Yours, Mrs. M. BURK

BETTER KNOWN AS CALAMITY JANE

THE TRUTH

The truth of Calamity Jane's life is harder to dig up, in part because she and Wild West writers tirelessly lied about it. She did wander the West working as a cook, dancehall girl, and prostitute. In spring 1876, she drove ox carts to outlying camps. If she ever actually met Wild Bill Hickok, it was only briefly, because he died shortly after her arrival. She didn't capture his killer, never was on the Army's payroll, didn't barely miss being massacred at Little Big Horn, didn't really ride with the Pony Express.... From 1895 on she appeared in Wild West shows and exhibitions, but in 1901 was fired for erratic behavior and alcoholism. She died in poverty in 1903.

Potty Pourri

RANDOM KINDS OF FACTNESS

• A survey in 1978 by PEN, an international literary organization, found that the median annual income earned by published writers was $4,700, with 68 percent making less than $10,000, and 9 percent earning nothing. The results were so depressing to its members that the organization didn't bother updating the survey in subsequent years.

• In the United States, more gold is used to make class rings than any other piece of jewelry.

• How many O's in a can of SpaghettiOs? About 1,750.

• Ever see "carragenan" on an ingredients panel and wonder what it is? It's a thickener used in lots of things like dairy products. It's an extract made from red seaweed.

• What is it called when you're unnaturally afraid of machines? Mechanophobia.

• Wedding cake was originally provided at weddings as something to throw at the new bride and groom. Unfrosted, luckily.

• Why are they called "sardines"? Because the process of canning small herrings was invented on the Italian island of Sardinia.

• Competent writers know that "e.g." means "for example" and "i.e." means "that is" and never confuse the two in their writing. However it's a sure bet that few know that the abbreviations stand for *exempli gratia* and *id est*.

• A researcher asked kids which season is most boring. 53 percent said, "Summer."

• When troublemaker Henry David Thoreau graduated from Harvard, he refused to take his diploma. "It isn't worth five dollars," he said, complaining that Harvard taught "all the branches of learning, but none of the roots."

• Cheetahs are fast, reaching speeds of about 71 miles per hour.

Putting on the Dog
FACTS ABOUT "MAN'S BEST FRIEND"

Groucho Marx said it best when he said, "Outside of a dog, a book is a man's best friend: and inside a dog, it's too dark to read."

• People have been breeding dogs for at least 10,000 years. Evidence of the oldest known breed—the saluki, a Middle Eastern dog—appeared on artifacts from about 7000 B.C. Before 1500 B.C., Egyptians were breeding hunting dogs that resemble large mastiffs. The irresistible, fluffy Maltese also dates back to ancient Egypt, sometime around 500 B.C. Not surprisingly, they were worshiped as gods alongside members of the royal family.

• The American Kennel Club recognizes 150 breeds of dog in seven main categories: sporting dogs, hounds, working dogs, terriers, toy dogs, non-sporting dogs, and herding dogs.

• The American foxhound is descended from English hounds, brought to the United States in 1650, and a French hound that was given as a present to President George Washington. He is credited with introducing this classic hunting dog to the world

• The chihuahua, highly regarded by the Aztecs, was possibly first bred to be a hand warmer for royals in drafty palaces. The little dogs could easily fit inside the sleeves of robes, after all. Priests also used them as afterlife amulets for the dead (believing their presence warded off evil spirits), sacrificing them in burial rituals. Aztec commoners, however, merely kept them as house pets and sometimes for food.

• Jack Russell terriers were bred in the 1800s using fox terriers. They got their names from the man who originally bred them: the Rev. John ("Jack") Russell. As old as this English breed is, it wasn't officially recognized by the AKC until 1997.

• Although it looks nothing like a bull, bulldogs were so named because they were especially bred for bull baiting. This was a "sport" in which a bull was chained to a pole and dogs were let loose to tear the bull to bits while spectators watched and cheered. The sport was made illegal in 1835, and breeders successfully bred the traits of viciousness and fearlessness from these dogs so they could live on as house pets.

•Ever hear of a Staffordshire terrier? That's what the AKC called the American pit bull until 1936.

•The wrinkly skinned sharpei is named with the Chinese word for "sharkskin."

• Great Danes originated in Germany, bred by mixing Irish wolfhounds and English mastiffs. French dog breeders were under the impression that the dog came from Denmark, so they gave the dog its inaccurate name; Germans, however, call them *Deutsche dogges* ("German dogs").

• So what do the Germans call the German shepherd, then? *Deutscher schaferhund,* meaning "German Shepherd hound."

• It's not just in cartoons, St. Bernard dogs really did save lives in the Alps—more than 2,500 over the last 200 years alone. During the Middle Ages, a monk named Bernard founded a travelers' hospice in Valle d'Aosta on the border of Switzerland and Italy. His monks bred and trained the large shaggy dogs for search and rescue missions. The hospice is still operating there, and so are the big furry dogs.

These days, however, they're there more for sentimental reasons than for rescue since technology is more effective at rescuing stranded people than big sloppy dogs. And, yes, the St. Bernards really did wear casks of Brandy on their collars. It helped give rescuees an illusion of being warmer until real help arrived.

• The ten most intelligent breeds are the border collie, poodle, German shepherd, golden retriever, doberman pinscher, Shetland sheepdog, Labrador retriever, papillon, rottweiler, and Australian cattle dog. The ten least intelligent breeds are the shih-tzu, basset hound, mastiff, beagle, Pekingese, bloodhound, borzoi, chow chow, bulldog, basenji, and Afghan hound.

• Forget the "one year equals seven dog years" formula.

Seeing Eye Dogs

After World War I, a school to train guide dogs first opened in Pottsdam, Germany, but closed due to lack of funding. Before it failed, one of its visitors was a wealthy American named Dorothy Harrison Eustis, who wrote about it for the *Saturday Evening Post.*

A blind man named Morris Frank heard about Ms. Eustis's article. Tired of depending on others to get around, the Nashville, Tennessee, native wrote to her that he was eager to see if he could become more self-sufficient by means of a dog companion. Eustis agreed to fund his training with a dog if, in return, Frank would start his own guide dog training school in the United States.

Frank called his school The Seeing Eye, from a Bible verse: "The seeing eye, the hearing ear; The Lord hath made them both." (Prov. 20:12). In its first year, the school graduated seventeen people and dogs. Now, after decades of success (as well as incorporating and having the term "Seeing Eye" trademarked), the school is located in New Jersey and still functions to train dogs and their blind companions.

The first year of a dog's life is equal to about nineteen or twenty human years. In that first year, the dog will go through infancy, young childhood, puberty, and teen rebellion. By the time it hits its second year, it's a young adult. From that point on, you can figure about four dog years for every human year.

• There is a precise word for the poop of domesticated dogs: *scumber*. If you're speaking of wild dog poop, though, the word is *lesses*.

• The main ingredient in chocolate is a caffeine-related chemical called *theobromine*. The better or darker the chocolate, the more theobromine. Because dogs metabolize theobromine more slowly than humans, the chemical can be highly toxic to them. Get your dog medical attention immediately if it gets into your Halloween stash.

• French-speaking trappers and explorers, using sled dogs to make their way across the frozen Canadian tundra, shouted "*Marchons!*" ("Let's go!" in French). English speakers heard it as "Mush on!" Eventually it was shorted to just "Mush!"

• A good sled with six to eight good working dogs should get you blazing through snow in excess of 20 miles per hour.

• Dogs aren't completely colorblind. They can see color, just not all color. Canines have a type of colorblindness called *deuteranopia*, meaning they don't the green spectrum. While they can recognize shades of the red spectrum, they're best at detecting blue.

• According to Disney, animators painted a total of 6,469,952 dog spots in *101 Dalmations*.

Two Little Ones

• Orchids got their name from *orkhis*, the Greek word for "testicles," which is what its root system looks like.

• The word *testimony* comes from the old Roman practice of cupping the genitals when swearing an oath.

Creepy Tales

AESOP FABLES FEATURING INSECTS

What can you learn from a bug? The story of the ant and the grasshopper is as well-known as any fable. Here it is, and several more.

THE ANT AND THE GRASSHOPPER

In a field one summer's day a Grasshopper was hopping about, chirping and singing to its heart's content. An Ant passed by, bearing along with great toil an ear of corn he was taking to the nest.

"Why not come and chat with me," said the Grasshopper, "instead of toiling and moiling in that way?"

"I am helping to lay up food for the winter," said the Ant, "and recommend you to do the same."

"Why bother about winter?" said the Grasshopper; we have got plenty of food at present." But the Ant went on its way and continued its toil. When the winter came the Grasshopper had no food and found itself dying of hunger, while it saw the ants distributing every day corn and grain from the stores they had collected in the summer. Then the Grasshopper knew:

It is best to prepare for the days of necessity.

THE BEE AND JUPITER

A bee from Mount Hymettus, the queen of the hive, ascended to Olympus to present Jupiter some honey fresh from her combs. Jupiter, delighted with the offering of honey, promised to give whatever she should ask. She therefore besought him, saying, "Give me, I pray thee, a sting, that if any mortal shall approach to take my honey, I may kill him." Jupiter was much displeased, for he loved the race of man, but could not refuse the request because of his promise. He thus answered the Bee: "You shall have your request, but it will be at the peril of your own life. For if you use your sting, it shall remain in the wound

"I pray thee, a sting...."

you make, and then you will die from the loss of it."

Evil wishes, like chickens, come home to roost.

THE BALD MAN AND THE FLY

There was once a Bald Man who sat down after work on a hot summer's day. A Fly came up and kept buzzing about his bald pate, and stinging him from time to time. The Man aimed a blow at his little enemy, but WHACK! His palm landed on his head instead; again the Fly tormented him, but this time the Man was wiser and said:

"You will only injure yourself if you take notice of despicable enemies."

THE ANT AND THE CHRYSALIS

An Ant nimbly running about in the sunshine in search of food came across a Chrysalis that was very near its time of change. The Chrysalis moved its tail, and thus attracted the attention of the Ant, who then saw for the first time that it was alive. "Poor, pitiable animal!" cried the Ant disdainfully. "What a sad fate is yours! While I can run hither and thither, at my pleasure, and, if I wish, ascend the tallest tree, you lie imprisoned here in your shell, with power only to move a joint or two of your scaly tail." The Chrysalis heard all this, but did not try to make any reply. A few days after, when the Ant passed that way again, nothing but the shell remained. Wondering what had become of its contents, he felt himself suddenly shaded and fanned by the gorgeous wings of a beautiful Butterfly. "Behold in me," said the Butterfly, "your much-pitied friend! Boast now of your powers to run and climb as long as you can get me to listen." So saying, the Butterfly rose in the air, and, borne along and aloft on the summer breeze, was soon lost to the sight of the Ant forever.

"Appearances are deceptive."

Every Picture Tells a Story

Self-Portrait with Bandaged Ear by Vincent Van Gogh

• Vincent Van Gogh painted sixty-two self-portraits—more than any other major painter. He had good reason: while institutionalized for insanity, he didn't have models or landscapes available.

• He painted *Self-Portrait with Bandaged Ear* while confined after his most notorious bit of performance art. Trying to impress a local prostitute named Rachel, he cut off his ear lobe on Christmas Eve 1888, and presented it to her, telling her, "Guard this object carefully."

• When she unwrapped his lobe offering, she fainted, and the police were called. They found the artist catatonic, lying in a fetal position. It was the first of several attacks of madness until Van Gogh killed himself a year and a half later.

• His loss of sanity was the art world's gain. Of his 850 known works, about two-thirds were painted in the last two years of his life. Unfortunately, he sold only two paintings in his life, in sales arranged by his brother, Theo. Worse, even that degree of success—and a positive review from an influential art journal—seemed to disturb and unhinge him further. He shot himself in 1890.

Foodonyms

ASK FOR IT BY NAME

Ever wonder how some of your favorite snacks or dishes got their names? Was Fig Newton named after Sir Isaac Newton? You might be surprised by some of these origins.

Melba Toast: Named for the Australian operatic singer, Nellie Melba. The dessert Peach Melba was also named for her. Both were invented by the French chef Auguste Escoffier, who seemed to have a little crush on Miss Melba.

Ritz crackers: In 1934, the National Biscuit Company made a cracker with a lot more shortening so it glistened, and shined.The name is glommed from that grand hotel, the Ritz.

Waldorf salad: A famous maitre d' named Oscar Tschirky at New York's Waldorf-Astoria Hotel created this salad of apple, nuts, and mayonnaise sometime around 1900. He named it the Waldorf salad, which was probably wise. It might not have lasted had he called it the Tschirky salad.

Graham crackers: Graham flour is just whole wheat flour. The name comes from the health nut, Rev. Dr. Sylvester Graham, who in the early 1800s preached that eating altered foods was a sin. Graham believed that altered food led to sexual desires.

Chicken à la king: Nobody really knows, but one of more than eight supposed origins for this dish is that King Edward VII really liked the recipe, hence the "à la King."

Fig Newton: Like all of the Boston-based Kennedy Biscuit Company's cookies and crackers, the Fig Newton was named after a nearby town. Other company products like the Beacon Hill, the Brighton, and the Quincy are lost to history, but Newton, Massachusetts, will always be remembered.

Cubical Sounds

HOW MUZAK INVENTED MOOD-ELEVATOR MUSIC

When's the last time you listened to Muzak? Do you remember what song was playing? No? That's good—you're not *supposed* to remember. In fact, if it's working "right," you're not really supposed to notice that it's there at all.

IF YOU WANT TO MAKE Muzak's 174 franchisers and 350,000 subscribers mad, call it "background music" or "elevator music." They call it "environmental music," and it's all tied into a theory called "Stimulus Progression." To quote company literature: "Each segment plays music on an ascending curve during descending periods of the industrial work curve." In other words, they play peppy music at the times when people usually feel fatigued, and relaxing music when people usually feel tense.

ELECTRICITY KILLED THE RADIO STAR

Muzak began with Maj. Gen. George Owen Squier, a retired Army officer born at the end of America's Civil War. He was a pioneer in military radio work, discovering in 1907 that a live tree could be tapped into and used as a radio antenna ("tree telephony" he called it). In 1922 Squier came up with an idea he called "line radio" or "wired wireless," in which music, news, lectures, entertainment, and advertising would be transmitted into homes through power lines, not unlike modern cable.

He pitched the idea to a public utility holding company in New York City. They liked it. Squier always liked the brand name "Kodak." So, to name his product, he wedded "music" and "Kodak," ending up with "Muzak."

Wired Radio first began broadcasting through electrical wires in Cleveland, offering four different channels. With a low-cost receiver, people could listen to music and news by plugging into the electrical outlets that brought their power and light. In 1934, the company switched to telephone lines instead of power lines to transmit the music, but they were losing ground to the radio stations that broadcast over the air for free.

POP (AND JAZZ) PSYCHOLOGY

Finally, Muzak found a reason for existing. Two British industrial psychologists published a study on the benefits of music in the workplace. They said that music programming could increase productivity; and second, that the music must be "rationed" into segments—music played continuously creates as much monotony as having no music at all. Based on this study, Muzak executives decided to begin programming music for the work environment: soothing yet invigorating, and "rationed" into segments. Its sales reps convinced enough business owners to try it out, and Muzak, as we know it, was born.

Success in New York led to a franchise system in other cities, operated under the firm rule that franchises would play, without variation, all programs exactly as they originated from Muzak headquarters.

With technological advances, Muzak began using satellite and radio channels as well as phone lines to get music to its subscribers, which now included hotels, churches, mental institutions, corporate offices, prisons, secret military installations, and even a whorehouse in Germany.

GIVING YOU THE BUSINESS

Here's how it works: The songs come from all over. A repertoire manager listens to the radio to find music to re-record for the channel. At any given time, Muzak has an active library of 5,000 titles.

Every song played on the channel is custom-recorded.

In the 1980s, a Czech radio orchestra recorded 75 percent of their songs, but now Muzak uses a number of instrumental configurations. But the basic workplace package allows no singers.

Voices are eliminated for the same reason Muzak favors violas over violins, French horns over trumpets, and muted percussion over drum solos—because Muzak is to be "felt and heard," but not listened to.

Each song is given a "stimulus value" score which denotes how stimulating it is, determined mathematically by measuring the song's tempo, rhythm, instrumentation, and orchestra size. Muzak arranges the songs into 15 minute sets of five songs each, customized for each specific time of day by a computer. The music reaches peaks of liveliness at 10 A.M. and at 2 P.M.—both lull times for most workers.

MUSIC HATH CHARMS?

Despite claims, "environmental music" doesn't work the same way with everybody. It is supposed to put shoppers in the mood to linger and buy, yet convenience stores in the Northwest began using it for the opposite effect: to chase away loitering teens who couldn't take another strings-and-piano rendition of "You Light Up My Life" or "Killing Me Softly With His Song."

The company dismisses anti-Muzak critics out of hand. "You know," says a spokesperson, "pollsters have done research of the electorate, and they found that there's a certain percentage that is just anti-everything. You have a hard core that's against everything, a vocal 10 percent, and I suspect that we're hearing from that vocal fringe group many times. If a business person is considering Muzak for an office and is going to be swayed by the 10% that always complains about something, then he'll have a big problem running his business."

MUZAK FACTS

• Twice the human voice was heard on the Muzak channel: in 1981, to announce that American hostages had been released from Iran, and Good Friday, 1985, when it joined thousands of radio stations around the world in a broadcast of "We Are the World."

• Muzak now has sixty channels of all musical styles for telephone on-hold music and store ambiance.

Potty Pourri

RANDOM KINDS OF FACTNESS

- Women could not legally practice law in the United States until 1872.
- Ever hear of the "lawyer bird"? The North American black-necked stilt is called that because one of its identifying features is "a big bill."
- Despite the name, a Venus flytrap most often eats ants.
- How's this for election reform? Ancient Athens chose its 500 lawmakers by lottery. They served a year, and then were replaced by the next year's winners.
- Before she was a master chef, Julia Childs was a spy. This was in India and China during World War II.
- The Pentagon has twice as many bathrooms as necessary, because it was built during a time when Virginia law required separate facilities for blacks and whites.
- Sculptor Frédéric-Auguste Bartholdi used his mother as the model for the Statue of Liberty's face and his girlfriend as the model for her body.
- On TV, CPR works most of the time to restart a heart. In real life, alas, it's not that often—only about 15 percent of the people survive.
- Author Anthony Trollope worked for the British post office for thirty-three years. During that time he produced four dozen novels by rising at 5:30 A.M. and writing a thousand words before trudging off to work. Within postal circles his biggest claim to fame is that he invented the street-corner mailbox.
- A good batch of cider will not just contain one kind of apple, but a blend of three to five varieties.
- Where's the much-maligned town of Podunk? Massachusetts.

Stately Knowledge

12 REASONS WHY YA GOTTA LOVE COLORADO

We've searched the vaults and come up with some pretty impressive facts about Colorado. Here are a dozen of our favorites.

1 Colorado means "red colored" in Spanish, referring to its reddish rocks. A reddish-colored marble, dubbed "Beulah red," gives the state Capitol its unique shade. Unfortunately, all of the known Beulah red marble in the world was used during its six-year construction, meaning it can't ever be replaced.

2 Penrose, Colorado, has a rocking chair that's 21 feet high and 14 feet wide, big enough for more than fifty people to rock on at a time.

3 The highest incorporated city in the United States is Leadville, Colorado, standing 10,430 feet above sea level.

4 When Denver was offered a shot at hosting the 1976 Winter Olympics, it became the first city in history to ever turn it down. The voters decided the Olympics would bring unwanted crowds, pollution, and urban growth.

5 Farmers trying to prepare Sunday dinner have long known that chickens can run around without heads for several minutes. But four and a half years? Fruita, Colorado, every year celebrates Mike the Headless Chicken Day to commemorate the bird who lost his head in 1945 but didn't actu-

ally die until he choked on a piece of corn in 1950.

6 How romantic is this? Loveland, Colorado, has such a great name that hundreds of thousands of Valentines are sent to the post office there every year to be remailed with the LOVE-LAND postmark and a cupid. Awwww!

7 The Pinto Bean capital of the world is Dove Creek, Colorado. If you decide to go, be sure to pack a good supply of Bean-o.

8 The largest sand dunes in America are in the Great Sand Dunes National Monument near the town of Alamosa, Colorado. The 700-foot dunes were the result of ocean tides and winds more than a million years ago back when Western states like Utah, Nevada, and California were still part of the ocean floor.

9 Gunslinger Doc Holliday, friend of Wyatt Earp and practicing dentist, is buried in Glenwood Springs, Colorado. The epitaph on his grave? "He Died in Bed." He and Wyatt Earp ended up here for a while when hiding out from an arrest warrant from Arizona. Other Western legends who spent some time in Colorado include Calamity Jane, Bat Masterson, and Frank James.

10 "Rocky Mountain Oysters" came from the Denver area. They're not really from the sea. They go to prove the truism: "If you don't know what they are, don't order them." In case you didn't know, Rocky Mountain Oysters are fried bull testicles. Yum.

11 Alferd Packer was convicted of murder and cannibalism in 1874. He and five others got stuck in the snow and their provisions ran out. When authorities came upon the scene, the five others had been killed and one of them had been partially roasted and eaten. Packer served seventeen years and lived out the rest of his life as a recluse (and, some say, a vegetarian). More than fifty years later, the students at Boulder University voted to name the school cafeteria the "Alferd Packer Memorial Grill." It's most popular dish is the *"El Canibal"* burrito.

12 At the southwest corner of Colorado you'll find the only location in the United States where four states come together in one place. The states are Colorado, Arizona, Utah, and New Mexico.

Cat Haters

REAL-LIFE AILUROPHOBES

An ailurophobe is someone who hates cats, or is frightened by them. Here are a few examples from the book *Cats Don't Always Land on Their Feet*, by Erin Barrett and Jack Mingo.

• In his dictionary, Noah Webster had little good to say about cats, calling them "a deceitful animal and when enraged extremely spiteful."

• Cats were once used as torture devices in eighteenth-century America. Punishment involved the bareback of the accused and a fearful, angry cat dangling by its tail, just within reach of his or her back. The cat was then pulled back by its tail, across the victim's back. Inhumane on both counts, we'd say.

• Ever wonder why a cat plays a fiddle in the old nursery rhyme Hey Diddle Diddle? It's not that cats were thought to be musical—it's a rhyme of mismatches: the heavy cow flying; the tined fork and the bowled spoon, for instance. The word *fiddle* is a variation of the French word *fidele*, or "faithful one." The cat, to the author anyway, was considered the opposite embodiment of faithfulness.

• *"I just spent four hours burying the cat."*
" Four hours to bury a cat?"
"Yes—it wouldn't keep still." —Monty Python's Flying Circus

• Dwight Eisenhower loathed cats. He ordered his staff to shoot any found on the grounds of his Gettysburg home.

• Napoleon was deathly afraid of cats. He was once found cowering in his tent with a little kitty mewing at him. His guards quickly removed little Fluffy for the emperor so he could carry on with his war.

• The spread of the Black Plague in Western Europe can be attributed to a lack of available cats. Eradicated during a witch scare or two, the cat population was so low that rat numbers increased. So did their fleas and with them, the Plague.

• *Larousse Gastronomique,* the authoritative French cookbook, suggests choosing a young cat for cooking, as younger ones tend to be more stringy. It goes on to say that cooking cat like you would rabbit is your best bet: fricasséed or braised.

• Adolf Hitler was a known ailurophobe. Not that he feared them, per se, but he hated them.

• During the European witch hunts from 1560 to 1700, simply owning cats was sometimes enough evidence necessary to burn a person at the stake. This was especially true if you were an older woman who fit the stereotype of being a "witch." For example, in the St. Osyth witch trials of 1582 in Essex, England, one Alice Mansfield was accused of harboring satanic entities named Robin, Jack, William, and Puppet "all like unto black cats." She and the cats were put to death.

• How did lullaby composer Johannes Brahms spend his leisure time away from his keyboard? Sitting at an open window with a bow and arrow, shooting at the neighbors' cats.

• Percy was a homing pigeon that won the France-to-Sheffield race in 1993. Or would have, anyway. The moment Percy landed, a cat attacked and ate him. Percy's owner attempted to retrieve Percy's tag to show the judge, but by the time she could wrench it away from the cat, two other pigeons had flown in ahead. The deceased Percy never got his day, and his owner, now likely an ailurophobe, took home a third place ribbon.

• Ivan the Terrible lived up to his terrible name even as a youngster, throwing cats and other animals out of high windows of the palace for sport.

• In the 1700s, French apprentices, protesting working conditions, hideously tortured and killed their masters' cats "in a mood of great jollity and high good humor," according to one account.

• *"Cats are intended to teach us that not everything in nature has a purpose."* —Garrison Keillor

The Devil's Dictionary: A

Ambrose Bierce mysteriously disappeared in Mexico in 1914. Before that, he wrote a sardonic dictionary that present-day commentators still regularly steal from. We decided to do the same.

ABORIGINES, *n.* Persons of little worth found cumbering the soil of a newly discovered country. They soon cease to cumber; they fertilize.

ABSTAINER, *n.* A weak person who yields to the temptation of denying himself a pleasure.

ABSURDITY, *n.* A statement or belief manifestly inconsistent with one's own opinion.

ACCORDION, *n.* An instrument in harmony with the sentiments of an assassin.

ACQUAINTANCE, *n.* A person whom we know well enough to borrow from, but not well enough to lend to. A degree of friendship called slight when its object is poor or obscure, and intimate when rich or famous.

ADMIRATION, *n.* Our polite recognition of another's resemblance to ourselves.

ADMONITION, *n.* Gentle reproof, as with a meat-axe.

ALLIANCE, *n.* In international politics, the union of two thieves who have their hands so deeply inserted in each other's pockets that they cannot separately plunder a third.

ALONE, *adj.* In bad company.

AMBITION, *n.* An overmastering desire to be vilified by enemies while living and made ridiculous by friends when dead.

AMNESTY, *n.* The state's magnanimity to those offenders whom it would be too expensive to punish.

ANOINT, *v.t.* To grease a king or other great functionary already sufficiently slippery.

ANTIPATHY, *n.* The sentiment inspired by one's friend's friend.

APHORISM, *n.* Predigested wisdom.

APOLOGIZE, *v.i.* To lay the foundation for a future offense.

APPEAL, *v.t.* In law, to put the dice into the box for another throw.

APPLAUSE, *n.* The echo of a platitude.

APRIL FOOL, *n.* The March fool with another month added to his folly.

AUCTIONEER, *n.* The man who proclaims with a hammer that he has picked a pocket with his tongue.

Barrymorisms

The Barrymore dynasty—Ethel, Lionel, John, Drew—is legendary in Hollywood. Here are a few words of wisdom from the late, great actor, John Barrymore.

ON MORALS
"The good die young, because they see it's no use living if you have got to be good."

ON FINANCES
"Why is there so much month left at the end of the money?"

ON WOMEN
"Love is the delightful interval between meeting a beautiful girl and discovering that she looks like a haddock."

ON SEX
"Sex: the thing that takes up the least amount of time and causes the most amount of trouble."

ON MARRIAGE
"In Genesis, it says that it is not good for a man to be alone; but sometimes it is a great relief."

ON DIVORCE
"You never realize how short a month is until you pay alimony."

ON AGING
"A man is not old until regrets take the place of dreams."

ON HAPPINESS
"Happiness sneaks through a door you didn't know that you left open."

DYING WORDS
"Die? I should say not, dear fellow. No Barrymore would allow such a conventional thing to happen to him."

Ripe Ol' Corn

"UNCLE JOSH AND THE LIAR'S CLUB"

"Uncle Josh Weatherby," Cal Stewart's country bumpkin, lived in the bucolic town of Punkin Centre. Here's a scene of classic rural codgerism.

WELL, SOMETIMES A LOT of us old codgers used to git down to Ezra Hoskins' grossery store and we'd set 'round and chaw terbacker and whittle sticks and eat crackers and cheese and prunes and anything Ezra happened to have layin' 'round loose, and then we'd git to spinnin' yarns.

Well, one afternoon we was all settin' 'round spinnin' yarns when Deacon Witherspoon said that echos was mighty peculiar things, 'cause down whar he was born and raised thar was a passell of hills come together and you couldn't git out thar and talk louder 'n a whisper on account of the echo. But one day a summer boarder what was thar remarked as how he wasn't afraid to talk right out in front of any old lot of hills what was ever created; so he went out and hollered jist as loud as he could holler, and he started an echo a-goin' and it flew up against one hill and bounced off onto another one and gittin' bigger and louder all the time 'til it got back whar it started from and hit a stone quarry and knocked off a piece of stone and hit that feller in the head, and he didn't come to fer over three hours.

Well, we thought that was purty good fer a Deacon. None of us said anything fer a right smart spell and then Si Pettingill remarked that he didn't know anything about echos, but he calculated he'd seen some mighty peculiar things; said he guessed

113

he'd seen it rain 'bout as hard as anybody ever seen it rain. Someone said, "Well, Si, how hard did you ever see it rain?" and he said, "Well one day last summer down our way it got to rainin' and it rained so hard that the drops jist rubbed together comin' down, which made them so all-fired hot that they turned into steam; why, it rained so gosh-dinged hard, thar was a cider barrel layin' out in the yard that had both heads out'n it and the bung hole facing up; well, it rained so hard into that bung hole that the water couldn't run out of both ends of the barrel fast enough, and it swelled up and busted."

Well, we all took a fresh chew of terbacker and nudged each other; and Ezra Hoskins said he didn't remember as how he'd ever seen it rain quite so hard as that, but he'd seen some mighty dry weather; he said one time when he was out in Kansas it got so tarnation dry

that fish a-swimmin' up the river left a cloud of dust behind them. And hot, too; why, it got so all-fired hot that one day he tied his mule to a pen full of popcorn out behind the barn, and it got so hot that the corn got to poppin' and flyin' 'round that old mule's ears and he thought it was snow and laid down and froze to death.

Well, about that time old Jim Lawson commenced to show signs of uneasiness, and someone said, "What is it, Jim?" and Jim remarked, as he shifted his terbacker and cut a sliver off from his wooden leg, "I was a-thinkin' about a cold spell we had one winter when we was a-livin' down Nantucket way. It was hog killin' time, if I remember right. Anyhow, we had a kettle of boilin' water settin' on the fire, and we set it out doors to cool off a little, and that water froze so durned quick that the ice was hot."

Ezra said, "Guess it's 'bout shuttin' up time."

Piercing the Veil

OUIJA OR WON'T YA?

Is Ouija an ancient fortune-telling device that will connect you with the Other World or a mirror of your own subconscious mind? Is it (as some psychics and fundamentalist Christians claim) a spiritually dangerous brush with satanic spirits, or a harmless party game? Here's the story; you decide.

OUIJA is not, as some have claimed, an ancient fortune-telling device that was first used thousands of years ago by ancient Egyptians or Sumarians. And while its inventors *might* have believed in its powers, the manufacturer, William Fuld, was by all accounts completely cynical about it.

GHOST WRITERS
The first Ouija rolled off the assembly line a little more than a hundred years ago. Its roots go back a few decades earlier to France, where interest in spiritualism was at the peak of a cyclical revival. In the 1850s, someone in France—tired of depending

on channelers and mediums to supposedly bring forth spirits from the Other World—invented a device that was meant to let anyone have a direct long-distance line. That device was called a *planchette*, which means "little plank" in French. (Legend has it that the inventor's name was also Planchette, but that seems too coincidental to be true.)

The planchette was an easy-rolling, heart-shaped piece of wood with, at the heart's point, a pencil. The way it worked was that one or two people placed their hands on it. When their hands mysteriously moved, the pencil traced the path, handwriting a message from Beyond.

The earliest messages were all in French, but as the device spread to other countries, spirits began speaking other languages, too. When planchettes arrived in the United States in 1868, they became an immediate sensation as a parlor game, and millions were made by toy manufacturers. Many people took their messages seriously, but still complained at the slowness and illegibility of the writing.

Some business partners at the Kennard Novelty Comp-any came up with the idea of a spiritual typewriter from Beyond. Rather than trying to interpret the shaky writing of disembodied hands, they figured that messages would be clearer if you gave the spirits the equivalent of a computer mouse and a menu that they could click-and-point to. The partners kept the planchette, but got rid of the pencil and created a lap tray with a helpful array of preprinted letters, numbers, and common words like *yes* and *no*. Suddenly, the spirits could communicate with speed and clarity. The new board was poised to revolutionize the spiritual medium.

But what to call it? The chief partner, Charles Kennard, came up with the brilliant idea of consulting the board itself for the name. The board gave him "Ouija," which it said was the Egyptian word for "good luck." Even though that turned out to be untrue, the name stuck. However, the Spirits from Beyond played an even worse trick on poor Kennard. Despite his frequent use of the board, they neglected to warn him that his company was about to be taken away from him. His partners suddenly forced him out and turned the company over to his shop foreman, William Fuld.

Fuld immediately began rewriting the history of the Ouija, representing himself as the inventor and claiming that the name actually came from the French and German words for "yes," *oui* and *ja*. Fuld ran the company for thirty-five years, until he was struck by his own unforeseen tragedy—while supervising the replacement of a flagpole at the top of his headquarters, he fell several stories and died.

Fuld's heirs ran the company until 1966, when they sold out to Parker Brothers. Sales continue to hold steady, but the boards sell especially well during times of crisis, especially during wars, when believers are willing to try any method to keep track of loved ones in battle.

TIPS AND TRICKS

So how *do* you tell the future using a Ouija board? A good beginning is the instructions printed on the back of Ouija boards and written by William Fuld in 1902. Those who believe in the Ouija add some more hints. Some are downright scary, depending on how much you believe in the power of the board. Here's a distillation of what they say:

• Why just "channel" spirits of the dead? Some Ouijaists say they also connect with angels and even extraterrestrials.

• If you're afraid of accidentally invoking evil spirits, visualize a protective white light of energy coming from your mind and completely surrounding yourself, the board, and everybody in the room. This will protect you.

• Using the Ouija is like meeting people on the Internet: Get a new entity's name and its reason for coming to talk to you, and check it out carefully before trusting too much. In your session, ask a few simple questions about things you'll know the answer to in the next few days, to determine if your informant is reliable for more important, long-range questions. If it seems that spirits are telling you to do weird things (like send your money to Satan or Jerry Falwell), just walk away from the Ouija and try again later.

• "Don't ask spirits to do harm to others. Do not use the board to control others. Do not let others use your board when you are not using it. Don't get addicted to the board." — Advice from a Ouija Web site.

WHAT DOES IT MEAN?

In the best of all worlds, all good spirits would have good spelling and grammar skills. But despite people who have claimed that spirits dictated entire books to them in perfect English, Ouija doesn't usually work that way.

Let's say you and a friend are using the board and you ask, "Who will I marry?" The indicator starts moving as if by a force from Beyond, and laboriously begins stopping on letters: M R S N O.

"Mrsno"? What the devil does that mean? Before you give up in disgust, look at the letters and try to figure out what a dyslexic spirit might be trying to say. (This, some say, is where the *real* power of the Ouija lies — how you interpret the cryptic message

tells what your unconscious mind is thinking.)

So what are the possibilities?

MRSNO — Is it shorthand for someone you know? Mark Snott? Marsha Nobbins? Are they the first letters of a name? Or (sob!) are the spirits saying you'll never get married ("Mrs? No!")

Mr. SNO — Are they initials (Mr. Scott Nevil Orson)? Or maybe the "snow" indicates someone who has so far treated you coldly.

As you can see, there are a number of ways to interpret a message.

HOW IT WORKS

There are three theories as to why a Ouija board works (when and if it does):

1. The Spiritualist Theory. Forces or spirits from beyond our world are contacted by your use of the board, and they're moving the planchette. *Evidence for:* It sure seems like the thing is moving by itself, sometimes giving answers you don't expect. *Evidence against:* Try using the board with both people blindfolded and see how well the "all-seeing spirits" do.

2. The Ideomotor Theory. You are moving the indicator,

but don't consciously know it. It may be a mild form of self-hypnotism in which your hands move as if they're not in your control. So some say that the Ouija board can be used as a shortcut to knowing your unconscious mind. *Evidence for:* While people are often surprised at what comes from it, they are just as often not at all surprised when they get the message they expected. *Evidence against:* It's hard for people to imagine that you wouldn't "know" you're moving the indicator.

3. The Other Person's A Big Fat Liar Theory. This theory holds that both partners will usually deny manipulating the planchette, and that at least one is lying. *Evidence for:* How many Ouija sessions have ended with the two partners struggling as if arm wrestling to spell out the answer each wants? *Evidence against:* Very trustworthy people have sworn convincingly that they hadn't deliberately cheated, yet still got messages.

STRANGE OUIJA STORIES
• One woman in the early twentieth century claimed that she had contacted the spirit of Mark Twain. Although in his life he pre-ferred a typewriter for writing (in fact, was the first published writer to use one), she said that she wrote a novel that he dictated by Ouija board. However, the book, called *Jap Heron*, was clearly inferior to the mortal Twain's works (one reviewer sniffed that apparently "Twain left more than his body when he passed over to the other side").

• The Ouija has also been tried on the other end of the criminal justice system with equally disastrous results. Four jurors in a murder trial in England allegedly used a Ouija board to ask the victim who had killed him. They convicted the accused murderer ... and their use of the board became the basis for an automatic appeal.

• Although many have tried this with no good results, at least one person, Iris

Maloney, won $1.4 million in a state lottery after consulting a Ouija board.

• Ghosts, high spirits, or mass hysteria came into play when ten Alberta teenagers went berserk while playing with a Ouija board, striking at "something in the air" with their fists. Worried parents called a local minister who performed a "spiritual cleansing" on the teens, and everything returned to normal.

• While most adults believe Ouija to be a harmless game, some fundamentalist Christians believe the Ouija is, as one put it, "the quickest and easiest way to become possessed by demons." One fundamentalist Web page earnestly warns of "spirit possession, insanity, financial ruin, adultery and divorce, criminal acts (including murder),

and other tragedies" from using the Ouija board.

• This sort of fearmongering isn't new. Some mediums— perhaps not wanting the competition—have also issued grave warnings about Ouija dangers. One "Dr. Curry from the State Insane Asylum of New Jersey" was quoted in the 1930s as predicting that "insane asylums will be flooded with patients if interest in Ouija boards continues."

That was seventy years, and millions of boards ago. By some accounts, the Ouija continues to outsell all other games besides Monopoly. Which game is more injurious to mental health and the soul—the ghosts of the Ouija or the unforgiving capitalism of Monopoly—has yet to be determined.

The Last Leaf

A STORY OF LOVE & SACRIFICE BY O. HENRY

After being jailed for embezzling from his employer, William Sydney Porter borrowed the name of a prison guard named Orrin Henry and began writing stories about life in New York. This is one.

In a little district west of Washington Square the streets have run crazy and broken themselves into small strips called "places." So, to quaint old Greenwich Village the art people soon came prowling, hunting for north windows and 18th-century gables and Dutch attics and low rents.

At the top of a squatty, three-story brick Sue and Johnsy had their studio. "Johnsy" was familiar for Joanna. One was from Maine; the other from California. They had met and found their tastes so congenial that the joint studio resulted.

That was in May. In November, Pneumonia stalked about the colony, touching one here and there with his icy fingers. A little woman with blood thinned by California zephyrs was hardly fair game for the old duffer. But Johnsy he smote; and she lay, scarcely moving, on her painted iron bedstead, looking through small Dutch window-panes at the blank side of the next house.

One morning the busy doctor called Sue into the hall. "She has one chance in — let us say, ten," he said, as he shook down the mercury in his clinical thermometer. "And that chance is for her to want to live. Your little lady has made up her mind that she's not going to get well. Has she anything on her mind?"

"She wanted to paint the Bay of Naples some day," said Sue.

"Paint? — bosh! Has she anything on her mind worth thinking about twice — a man, for instance?"

"A man?" said Sue, with a jew's-harp twang in her voice. "Is a man worth—but, no, doctor; there is nothing of the kind."

"Well, it is the weakness, then," said the doctor. "I will do all that science can accomplish. But whenever my patient begins to count carriages in her funeral procession I subtract 50% from the curative power of medicines. If you will get her to ask about the new winter styles I will promise you a one-in-five chance for her, instead of one in ten."

After the doctor had gone Sue went into the workroom and cried a Japanese napkin to a pulp. Then she swaggered into Johnsy's room with her drawing board, whistling ragtime.

Johnsy lay, scarcely making a ripple under the bedclothes, with her face toward the window. Sue stopped whistling, thinking she was asleep. She arranged her board and began a pen-and-ink drawing to illustrate a magazine story. Young artists must pave their way to Art by drawing pictures for magazine stories that young authors write to pave their way to Literature.

As Sue was sketching the figure of the hero, an Idaho cowboy, she heard a low sound, several times repeated. She went quickly to the bedside. Johnsy's eyes were open wide. She was looking out the window and counting—counting backward.

"Twelve," she said, and a little later "eleven"; and then "ten," and "nine"; and then "eight" and "seven," almost together.

Sue looked solicitously out the window. What was there to count? There was only the blank side of the brick house twenty feet away. An old ivy vine climbed half up the brick wall. Its skeleton branches clung, almost bare, to the crumbling bricks.

"What is it, dear?" asked Sue. "Tell your Sudie."

"Leaves. On the ivy vine. When the last one falls I must go, too. I've known that for three days. Didn't the doctor tell you?"

"Oh, I never heard of such nonsense," complained Sue, with magnificent scorn. "Don't be a goosey. Why, the doctor told me this morning that your chances for getting well were ten to one! Why, that's almost as good a chance as when we ride on the street cars. Try to take some broth now, and let Sudie go back to her drawing, so she can buy port wine for her sick child, and pork chops for her greedy self."

"You needn't get any more wine," said Johnsy, keeping her eyes fixed out the window. "There goes another. No, I don't want any broth. That leaves just four. I want to see the last one fall before it gets dark. Then I'll go, too."

"Johnsy, dear," said Sue, bending over her, "will you promise me to not look out the window until I am done working? I don't want you to keep looking at those silly ivy leaves."

"Tell me as soon as you have finished," said Johnsy, lying still as a fallen statue, "because I want to see the last one fall. I went to turn loose my hold on everything, and go sailing down, down, just like one of those poor, tired leaves."

"Try to sleep," said Sue. "I must call Behrman up to be my model for the old hermit miner. I'll not be gone a minute. Don't try to move 'till I come back."

Old Behrman, past sixty and with a Michelangelo's Moses beard, was a failure in art. Forty years he had been always about to paint a masterpiece, but had never yet begun it. For several years he had painted nothing except now and then a daub in the line of commerce or advertising. He earned a little by serving as a model to those young artists in the colony who could not pay the price of a professional. He drank gin to excess, and still talked of his coming masterpiece, and regarded himself as mastiff-in-waiting to protect the two young artists in the studio above.

Sue found Behrman smelling strongly of gin in his dimly lighted den below. In one corner was a blank canvas on an easel that had been waiting there for 25 years to receive the first line of the masterpiece. She told him of Johnsy's fancy, and how she feared she would, indeed, light and fragile as a leaf herself, float away when her slight hold upon the world grew weaker.

Old Behrman, with his red eyes, plainly streaming, shouted his contempt and derision for such idiotic imaginings.

"Vass!" he cried. "Is dere people mit der foolishness to die because leafs dey drop off from a confounded vine? Ach, dot poor lettle Miss Johnsy. No, I will not bose as a model for your fool hermit-dunderhead."

"The fever has left her mind full of strange fancies," said Sue. "Very well, Mr. Behrman, if you do not care to pose, you needn't. But I think you are a horrid old flibbertigibbet."

"You are just like a woman!" yelled Behrman. "Who said I will not bose? Go on. I come mit you. Gott! dis is not any blace in which one so goot as Miss Yohnsy shall lie sick. Some day I vill baint a masterpiece, and ve shall all go away. Gott! yes."

Johnsy was sleeping when they went upstairs. Sue motioned Behrman into the other room. In there they peered out fearfully at the ivy vine. A cold rain was falling, mingled with snow. Then they looked at each other without speaking. Behrman took his seat as the hermit miner on an upturned kettle.

When Sue awoke from an hour's sleep the next morning she found Johnsy with dull, wide-open eyes staring at the drawn green shade. "Pull it up; I want to see," she whispered.

Wearily Sue obeyed. But, lo! after the beating rain and fierce gusts of wind through the night, there yet stood out against the brick wall one ivy leaf. Still dark green near its stem, but with its serrated edges tinted with the yellow of decay, it hung bravely from a branch some twenty feet above the ground.

"It is the last one," said Johnsy. "I thought it would surely fall during the night. It will fall today, and I shall die with it."

"Dear!" said Sue, leaning down to the pillow, "think of me, if you won't think of yourself. What would I do?" But Johnsy did not answer. The lonesomest thing in the world is a soul making ready to go on its mysterious, far journey.

The day wore away, and even through the twilight they could see the lone ivy leaf clinging to its stem against the wall. With the night the north wind was again loosed, while the rain pattered down from the low Dutch eaves. When it was light enough Johnsy commanded that the shade be raised.

The ivy leaf was still there.

Johnsy lay for a long time looking at it. And then she called to Sue, who was stirring her chicken broth over the gas stove.

"I've been a bad girl, Sudie," said Johnsy. "Something has made that last leaf stay there to show me how wicked I was to want to die. You may bring me broth now, and some milk with a little port in it, and I will sit up and watch you cook."

An hour later she said, "Sudie, some day I hope to paint the Bay of Naples."

The doctor came in the afternoon, and Sue had an excuse to go into the hallway as he left.

"Even chances," said the doctor, taking Sue's thin, shaking hand in his. "With good nursing you'll win. And now I must see another case downstairs. Behrman, his name is—some kind of an artist, I believe. Pneumonia, too. He is an old, weak man, and there is no hope for him; but he goes to the hospital today to be made more comfortable."

The next day the doctor said to Sue: "She's out of danger. You've won. Nutrition and care now—that's all."

And that afternoon Sue came to the bed where Johnsy lay, contentedly knitting a very blue and very useless woolen shoulder scarf, and put one arm around her, pillows and all.

"I have something to tell you, white mouse," she said. "Mr. Behrman died of pneumonia today in the hospital. He was ill only two days. The janitor found him on the morning of the first day in his room downstairs helpless with pain. His shoes and clothing were wet through and icy cold. They couldn't imagine where he had been on such a dreadful night. And then they found a lantern, still lighted, and a ladder that had been dragged from its place, and some scattered brushes, and a palette with green and yellow colors mixed on it, and—look out the window, dear, at the last ivy leaf on the wall. Didn't you wonder why it never fluttered or moved when the wind blew? Ah, darling, it's Behrman's masterpiece—he painted it there the night that the last leaf fell."

LOOKING BACK AT GREENWICH VILLAGE

There was a time when Greenwich Village really was a village, back when New York City was just a small city at the southern tip of Manhattan. Once a swamp, Greenwich became first a tobacco farm, then a small town miles from the big city. It became a refuge for the rich, then eventually a writers' and artists' haven as the rich moved to more fashionable parts of the city.

Some literary highlights:

• O. Henry got his inspiration for his story "The Last Leaf" from the gate at 10 Grove Street.

• Louisa May Alcott wrote *Little Women* while living at 130 MacDougal Street.

• Thomas Paine reportedly wrote *Common Sense* at 59 Grove Street.

• Edgar Allen Poe wrote *The Raven* at a club at 83 West 3rd Street while living at 49 East 9th Street.

• The ever-mobile Thomas Wolfe wrote *Look Homeward, Angel* in three different Greenwich Village apartments.

Word Thieves 2

SOME TERMS WE'VE BORROWED FROM THE DUTCH

Here's some confusion: The "Pennsylvania Dutch" were really German ("Deutsch"). However, real Dutch did come to North America, and added some words to our language.

aardvark: Dutch for "earth pig," which is what settlers called any animal that lived in the ground and looked vaguely pig-like. The African animal kept the name; Americans translated *aardvark* into "groundhog."

booze: From the Middle Dutch *busen*, meaning "drink heavily."

boss: From the Dutch *baas*, meaning "master."

cole slaw: It has nothing to do with "cold" or somebody named "Cole." It came from *koolsla*, meaning "cabbage" and "salad."

cookies: From *koekje*, meaning "little cake."

cruller: From *kruller*, meaning "to curl."

dope: From *doop*, which was a Dutch dipping sauce made of suspiciously murky ingredients.

easel: From *ezel*, meaning "ass," as in beast of burden.

hunky-dory: In tag games, Dutch children try to reach what they call *honk*, the safe base where they can't be tagged. So the word came to mean, "safe, fine."

mannequin: From *mannekijn* ("little man").

poppycock: From *pappekak* ("soft dung").

Santa Claus: From *Sinter Klaus* ("Saint Nicholas"), we got both the name and the general idea of what the holiday gift-bringer looks and acts like from the Dutch.

snoop: From the word *snoepen*, which means to secretively eat sweets.

waffle: From the Dutch word *wafel*, which came in turn from the French *gauffre* ("honeycomb"), so named because of the pastry's pattern.

Flornithology I
HOW TO TELL THE BIRDS FROM THE FLOWERS

We now present this helpful field guide by Robert Williams Wood (1868–1955) for those who may have trouble seeing the difference.

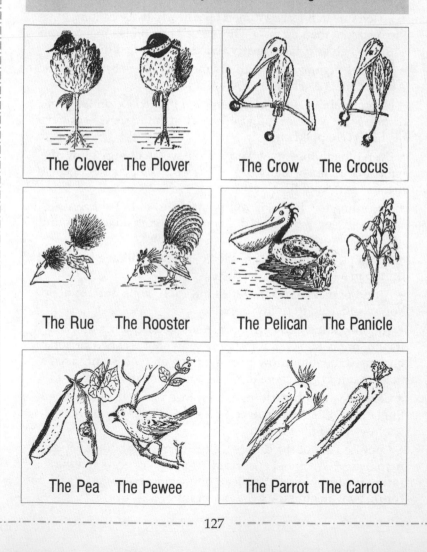

The Clover   The Plover

The Crow   The Crocus

The Rue   The Rooster

The Pelican   The Panicle

The Pea   The Pewee

The Parrot   The Carrot

Potty Pourri

RANDOM KINDS OF FACTNESS

• Listen up, architects: Women take nearly twice as long to use the restroom than men—a whopping 34 seconds longer. Women should, therefore, have nearly twice as many facilities.

• The U.S. organization with the most members is the American Automobile Association, or AAA.

• Hammurabi's Code of Law, enacted in 1780 B.C. in Babylon, dictated that a doctor found guilty of malpractice was to have his hands chopped off.

• Even though they may happen to have an orangy glow, the name orangutan actually comes from the Malay language and means "person of the forest."

• According to Gillette, if you're male and didn't shave your face for sixteen years, you'd theoretically gain an extra pound in hair—a beard that runs about 30 feet long.

• In Egypt, where cats were sacred, citizens followed a rule of thumb in a house fire: Save the cat first.

• Afraid of picking up the latest infection while out in public? You're suffering from mysophobia.

• You may know red herrings are smoked herrings, and that they're pretty stinky. But did you know that escaped prisoners once used them to throw tracking dogs off their scent? That's how "red herring" came to mean "diversionary tactic."

• Christmas, plum pudding, and mince pie were made illegal in England and its American colonies in 1647. Blame Oliver Cromwell and the Puritans.

• Confused about the difference between molybdomancy and myomancy? We're not surprised. Molybdomancers tell the future by dropping melted lead into water; myomancers tell the future by watching the behavior of mice.

Warts and All

Sure, we have more effective ways to get rid of warts today, but they involve knives and chemicals. Here are some creative cures for warts from days gone by.

• Folk remedies from the Appalachian Mountains were plenty. One involved spit, heavy with tobacco juice, and an incantation. The other used fatty meat rubbed on the wart, then bound in white cloth and buried under running water.

• In Mongolia they used red thread. After tying the wart with the thread, the string was then hung over a door hinge. The wart was expected to be cured within days.

• Russians believed that smearing bear or beaver fat directly onto a wart would heal it quickly. This is still touted today among some country folk as a legitimate cure.

• In an old Native American cure, a pepper pod was tied around the wart daily until the wart disappeared.

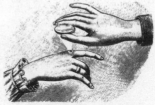

• In nineteenth century America, it wasn't uncommon to burn off a wart using the sun and a magnifying glass. A less painful way was to find some- one who would be willing to "buy"

The magnifying glass treatment

the wart. Still another was to secretly rub the wart against somebody who had fathered a child out of wedlock.

• In Merry Ol' England, *De Morbis Cutaneis* by Daniel Turner prescribed extracts from various medicinal herbs, but if that didn't work, patients were treated to a dose of corrosive brim- stone, or went under the knife.

• Another folk cure of the same place and time counseled folks to rub an apple on the wart and feed it to a pig.

• A traditional folk cure in Western Europe involved sprinkling a snail with salt, then rubbing the juices on the wart.

- Explorer and writer Francis Bacon rubbed pork fat on his warts, then hung the fat in the sun to rot. He swore by this method, which was especially apt, considering his name.
- In ancient Rome, at least one doctor was known for his unique method of curing warts. He bit off the skin that stuck out, then sucked on the place where the wart had once been.
- The Irish had a unique ceremony for wart removals: While rubbing the wart with a dirty washcloth, you must say, "Away, away, away," then bury the washcloth.
- A variation on this was to "conjure" the wart into a snail, then skewer the creature with a thorn and leave it there to die. As the snail dries up, so should the wart.
- Swiss misses once believed that if they rubbed their warts on stones and left them at an intersection, the next person to come along would contract the wart.
- "Take an sticke of greene oke woode laie that in the fier to burne and keepe the water therof which wil ishew out at the ends and therwith anoint the wartes. Use and follow that well twisse or thrisse a daie rubbing the warts well therwith and that will take them cleane awaie for ever as cleare as if youe never haid had any." —17th century wart-removing recipe from the National Archives of Scotland

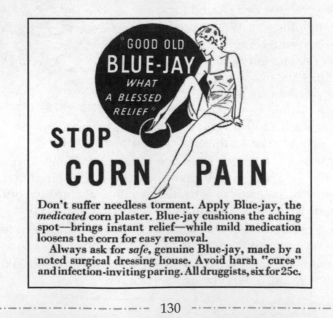

He Said/She Said

All's fair use in love and war.

"As long as a woman can look ten years younger than her own daughter, she is perfectly satisfied." —Oscar Wilde.

"Making coffee has become the great compromise of the decade. It's the only thing 'real' men do that doesn't seem to threaten their masculinity. To women, it's on the same domestic entry level as putting the spring back into the toilet-tissue holder or taking a chicken out of the freezer to thaw." —Erma Bombeck

"A woman's place is in the car." —Vinnie Barbarino, *Welcome Back, Kotter*

"Men read maps better than women because only men can understand the concept of an inch equaling a hundred miles." —Roseanne Barr

"Women: Can't live with 'em, can't stuff 'em in a sack." —Larry, *Newhart*

"The male is a domestic animal which, if treated with firmness and kindness, can be trained to do most things." —Jilly Cooper

"Direct thought is not an attribute of femininity. In this, women are now centuries behind man." —Thomas Edison

"Men are nothing but lazy lumps of drunken flesh. They crowd you in bed, get you all worked up, and then before you can say, 'Is that all there is?' that's all there is."
—Latka's mother, *Taxi*

"Women's intuition is the result of millions of years of not thinking."
—Rupert Hughes

"Men are such idiots and I married their king." —Peg Bundy, *Married ... with Children*

"When a woman becomes a scholar there is usually something wrong with her sexual organs."
—Friedrich Nietzsche

"What are the three words guaranteed to humiliate men everywhere? 'Hold my purse.'"
—Francois Morency

"Nature intended women to be our slaves. They are our property."
—Napoleon Bonaparte

"Whatever women do they must do twice as well as men to be thought half as good. Luckily, this is not difficult."
—Charlotte Whitton

"Men are superior to women. For one thing, men can urinate from a speeding car."
—Will Durst

"The only time a woman really succeeds in changing a man is when he's a baby."
—Natalie Wood

"Go see a girl? I'd rather smell a skunk!" —Beaver Cleaver, *Leave It to Beaver*

Clerk: *"You know what the fastest way to a man's heart is?"* **Roseanne:** *"Yeah, through his chest!"* —Roseanne Conner, *Roseanne*

"If women didn't exist, all the money in the world would have no meaning."
—Aristotle Onassis

"I married beneath me. All women do." —Nancy Astor

"I'll never understand women if I live to be thirty!"
—Richard Harrison, *The Patty Duke Show*

"Don't accept rides from strange men, and remember that all men are strange." —Robin Morgan

"A dame is like a bottle of milk: If she hangs around long enough, she turns sour."
—Bluto, *Popeye Cartoon Show*

"Men are simple things. They can survive a whole weekend with only three things: beer, boxer shorts and batteries for the remote control."
—Diana Jordan

"Women are like elephants. Everyone likes to look at them but no-one likes to have to keep one." —W. C. Fields

Strange Bible Tales

MIGHTY ODD STORIES FROM THE GOOD BOOK

There are a lot of Bible verses you won't necessarily hear
your preacher using as a text. In fact, most believers
haven't even run across them.

GOD ADMITS MAKING A MISTAKE. THEN HE CONTEMPLATES WIPING ALL LIFE OFF THE EARTH (GENESIS 6:5–7)

And God saw that the wickedness of humanity was great in the
world, and that every imagination of his thoughts and heart
were continuously evil.

And the Lord regretted that he had made people, and it
grieved him in his heart. And the Lord said, "I will destroy
man, whom I have created, from the face of the earth; man, and
beast, and every creeping thing, and the fowls of the air; for I
am sorry that I made them."

GOD SAYS YOU DIE IF YOU SMART OFF TO YOUR MOM (EXODUS 21:15)

"And he that curses his father, or his mother, shall surely be put
to death."

GOD SANCTIONS OWNING SLAVES, DIVIDING THEIR FAMILIES, AND BEATING THEM (WITHIN REASON) (EXODUS 21:2–6, 20–21)

"If you buy an Hebrew servant, six years he shall serve: and in
the seventh he shall go out free for nothing. If he came in by
himself, he shall go out by himself: if he were married, then his
wife shall go out with him. If his master has given him a wife,
and she have born him sons or daughter, the wife and her children shall be her master's, and he shall go out by himself.

"And if the servant shall plainly say, I love my master, my
wife, and my children; I will not go out free: Then his master
shall bring him unto the judges; he shall also bring him to the

door, or unto the door post; and his master shall bore his ear through with an awl; and he shall serve him for ever.

"However, if a man sells his daughter as a female slave, she is not to go free as the male slaves do.

"If a man smite his servant, or his maid, with a rod, and he die under his hand; he shall be surely punished. However, if the slave survives a day or two, the master shall not be punished, for he is his property."

EARTH GIRLS ARE EASY FOR THE SONS OF GOD (GENESIS 6:2–4)

Now it came about, when men began to multiply on the face of the land, and daughters were born to them, that the sons of God saw the daughters of men that they were fair; and they took them wives of all which they chose. And the Lord said, "My spirit shall not always strive with man, for that he also is flesh: yet his days shall be an hundred and twenty years."

There were giants in the earth in those days; and after the sons of God came in to the daughters of men, they bore children with them also, which became mighty men of renown.

GOD GOES TO AN INN TO KILL MOSES FOR NOT CIRCUMSIZING HIS SON, BUT HIS WIFE SAVES HIM WITH A QUICK CUT (EXODUS 4:23–26)

And it came to pass by the way in the inn, that the Lord met him, and sought to kill him. Then Zipporah took a sharp stone, and cut off the foreskin of her son, and cast it at his feet, and said, "Surely a bloody husband you are to me." So he let him go: then she said, "A bloody husband thou art, because of the circumcision."

GOD KILLS ONE OF JUDAH'S SONS FOR WICKEDNESS, THEN ANOTHER FOR PRACTICING COITUS INTERRUPTUS WITH HIS BROTHER'S WIDOW. MEANWHILE, JUDAH UNKNOWINGLY IMPREGNATES THE SAME WOMAN (HIS DAUGHTER-IN-LAW), & DECIDES TO BURN HER ALIVE... (GENESIS 36:2–27)

Judah saw there a daughter of a certain Canaanite whose name was Shua. And he took her, and went in unto her. And she conceived, and bare a son; and he called his name Er. And she conceived again, and bare a son; and she called his name Onan. And she yet again bare a son, and called his name Shelah: and he was at Chezib, when she bare him.

And Judah took a wife for Er his firstborn, and her name was Tamar. And Er, Judah's firstborn, was wicked in the sight of Jehovah. So God killed him.

And Judah said unto Onan, "Go in unto thy brother's wife, and perform the duty of a husband's brother unto her, and raise up seed to your brother."

But Onan knew that the seed would not be his; and it came to pass, when he went in unto his brother's wife, that he spilled his seed on the ground, lest he should give seed to his brother. And the thing which he did was evil in the sight of Jehovah. God killed him also.

Then Judah said to Tamar his daughter-in-law, "Remain a widow in thy father's house, till Shelah my son be grown up, lest he also die, like his brethren." And Tamar went and dwelt in her father's house.

And in process of time Shua's daughter, the wife of Judah, died; and Judah was comforted, and went up unto his sheep-shearers to Timnah, he and his friend Hirah the Adullamite.

And it was told Tamar, saying, "Behold, thy father-in-law goes up to Timnah to shear his sheep." And she put off from her the garments of her widowhood, and covered herself with her veil, and wrapped herself, and sat in the gate of Enaim, which is by the way to Timnah; for she saw that Shelah had grown up, but she was not given unto him to wife.

When Judah saw her, he thought her to be a harlot; for she had covered her face. And he turned unto her by the way, and said, "Come, I pray, let me come into you," for he knew not that she was his daughter-in-law. And she said, "What will you give me, that you may come in unto me?"

And he said, "I will send you a kid from my goat flock." And she said, "Will you give me a pledge, until you send it?" And he said, "What pledge shall I give you?" And she said, "Your seal, your cord, and your staff." And he gave them to her, and came in to her, and she conceived by him.

And she arose, and went away, and put off her veil from her, and put on the garments of her widowhood. And Judah sent the his friend Adullamite to deliver the kid of the goats and retrieve the pledge: but he found her not. Then he asked the men of her place, saying, "Where is the temple prostitute, that was at Enaim by the wayside?" And they said, "There has been no prostitute here." And he returned to Judah, and said, "I have not found her; and also the men of the place said, 'There has been no prostitute here.'" And Judah said, "Let her keep them before we become a laughingstock: I sent this kid, but you did not find her."

About three months later, Judah was told, "Tamar your daughter-in-law hath played the harlot; and moreover, she is with child by whoredom." And Judah said, "Bring her forth, and let her be burnt!" When she was brought forth, she sent to her father-in-law, saying, "By the man, whose these are, am I with child," and she said, "Look and see, whose are these, the seal, the cords, and the staff?"

And Judah acknowledged them, and said, "She is more righteous than I; considering that I gave her not to Shelah my son." And he did not have sex with her ever again.

GOD KILLS THE FIRSTBORN CHILDREN OF EGYPTIANS ... AND FOR GOOD MEASURE, THE FIRSTBORN CATTLE, TOO (EXODUS 12:29)
And it came to pass, that at midnight the Lord smote all the firstborn in the land of Egypt, from the firstborn of Pharaoh that sat on his throne unto the firstborn of the captive that was in the dungeon; and all the firstborn of cattle.

GOD COMMANDS GENOCIDE AND LIVESTOCK KILLING; THE ISRAELIS KILL THE PEOPLE, BUT KEEP THE LIVESTOCK (I SAMUEL 15:2–9)
Thus said the Lord of hosts, "I remember that which Amalek did to Israel, how he laid wait for him in the way, when he came up from Egypt. Now go and smite Amalek, and utterly destroy all that they have, and spare them not; but slay both man and woman, infant and suckling, ox and sheep, camel and ass."

And Saul gathered the people together, and numbered them in Telaim, 200,000 footmen, and 10,000 men of Judah.... And Saul took Agag the king of the Amalekites alive, and utterly destroyed all the people with the edge of the sword. But Saul and the people spared Agag, and the best of the sheep, and of the oxen, and of the fatlings, and the lambs, and all that was good, and would not utterly destroy them: but every thing that was vile and refuse, that they destroyed utterly.

Gone Today...
Hair Tomorrow

You say Rogaine hasn't done the trick? Consider some of these old folk remedies for baldness.

• Medieval doctors from Western Europe would've prescribed an ointment made of oil and the ashes of burned bees.

• Another medieval cure consisted of rubbing goose pellets directly onto the scalp.

• Globe-topped citizens in the West Indies still rub the oils of hot chili peppers onto their scalps until they feel the tingle. (The main chemical in chilis is capsicum—the same tingling ingredient in the dandruff shampoo Denorex. It doesn't cure baldness and it doesn't get rid of dandruff, but it sure feels like it's doing *something* up there.)

• Native Americans also used chili pepper oil, but they mixed it with yucca root. This mixture (or variations) were sold to balding men well into the twentieth century. The silent movie director D. W. Griffith had an early career as a traveling salesman, hawking this very remedy under the name "Yuccatone."

• Doctors in ancient Egypt mixed up a quick solution of hedgehog hairs, human fingernails in hippo, lion, or crocodile fat to bring back hair.

• In America in the 1800s, cantharidine and rosemary were used in hair tonics to cure baldness. Cantharidine is a burning chemical derived from crushed beetles, also known as Spanish Fly.

• As tea is the cure to all ills in England, it's not surprising that balding Englishmen in the 1600s used a combination of lemon with tea imported from India.

• It pays to be a famous doctor. When ancient Greek Hypocrites was going bald, he used flower oil, dove poop, and opium to stop the hair loss. It didn't work, but hey, he was happy, although stinky.

• If you can't beat 'em....When the usual ancient Roman cure of boiled snake tonic didn't work, they just painted curls right onto their heads.

• When treating hair loss in thirteenth-century Hungary, nothing short of a rosemary and wine ointment would do.

• From an early eighteenth-century course on Herbalism, held at the Royal College of Physicians and Surgeons of Glasgow, Scotland: "Some choice medices fo the fulling of the heir from the head: 1. Beat linseeds very well: and mix them with sillet oyl and when you have well mixed them anoint the head therwith and in three or four times rinsing it: it will help you. 2. For the falling of the haire by reson of a scald head warm a litle oil of tartar that which is made by deliguium and rub your head with it and in a litle the heare will come again. 3. For beldiness in the head Anoint with the oil of Lizeards and the beldness will grow once again."

• As recently as the early 1900s, such methods as electric hair brushes were used to cure baldness. It was believed to shock hair follicles into producing again. At the same time, scalp vacuuming came into vogue. Charlatans hawking this service claimed the vacuum would unclog blocked pores.

> *"The tenderest spot in a man's makeup is sometimes the bald spot on top of his head."* —Helen Rowland

Razor's Edge

A MAN WHO WOULD BE KING GIVES A CLOSE SHAVE

You can measure success by how close you come to your aspirations. King C. Gillette became an inventor of a new way to remove hair. But what he *really* wanted was to be president of the world.

King Camp Gillette was an eccentric who wanted to be leader of the world, but at least he came by his eccentricity honestly. First of all, there was his name, given in honor of his father's friend, Judge King (that was his given name—just as King Gillette wasn't really a king, Judge wasn't really a judge).

Then there was his mom, Fanny Lemira Camp, who was author of *The White House Cookbook*, a classic cookbook that made its debut in 1887; for most of King's childhood, his mom served up experimental recipes like Georgia Possum Pie or Rattlesnake Filet and took post-dinner polls on whether to include them in her cookbook.

Gillette's father, George, was a postmaster and part-time inventor whose hardware supply business had been wiped out by the Chicago Fire in 1871. In 1872, seventeen-ear-old King followed his father's footsteps and joined a hardware supply business as a traveling sales rep. While on the road, King filled his spare time by inventing things. In 1879, he patented a combination bushing and valve for faucets. Ten years later he patented two new types  of electrical conduits. None of his inventions made him any significant money, but he continued his tinkering.

One of his bosses understood his drive to invent. He was William Painter, president of the Baltimore Seal Company, himself a successful inventor. One of Painter's money-making inventions was a soft rubber valve used in emptying cesspools and privy pits. But the one that made him rich beyond dreams was the Crown Cork, the cork-lined metal bottle cap still in use today.

Painter adopted Gillette as a protégé and personal friend. In 1885, he gave Gillette a piece of advice that eventually changed his life: "Why don't you try to come up with something like the Crown Cork, which, when used, is thrown away? The customer keeps coming back for more; with each additional customer you get, you are building a foundation of profit."

"That sounds simple enough," replied King, "but how many things are there like corks, pins, and needles?"

Painter paused, thoughtfully. "You don't know. It isn't probable that you will ever find anything that is like the Crown Cork, but it won't do any harm to think about it." King did, to a point of obsession. He kept his mind constantly busy, watching life around him and waiting for inspiration to hit. He went through the dictionary, compiling page after page of things people needed, but for the longest time, he couldn't think of anything that people would want to use once and then throw away.

That's when a different kind of revelation hit. It had nothing to do with inventing things. It was bigger than that, *much* bigger. Gillette's revelation had to do with reinventing humanity's place in the entire social and economic system.

It came to him in a hotel room in Scranton, Pennsylvania. A heavy storm was raging and the rain fell in torrents. Normally dependable to a fault, Gillette decided to cancel his appointments for the day. He sat in his room, looking out at the rain-snarled traffic below his window. In the wind and rain, a disorganized mess of horses, buggies, and pedestrians had achieved a pre-auto state of gridlock.

First, Gillette tried to figure out ways that the snarl could have been avoided; then his mind was blown far adrift. Looking down on the disabled grocery wagon that had caused the snarl, he began imagining what was inside and where it came from, tracing coffee back through grinding and roasting to plantations in Brazil, sugar back to the cane fields of Cuba, and spices back to Asia.

Until that point, he wrote later, he had always thought of the world's industries as separate, independent entities. But suddenly "came the thought that is destined to change man's conception of industry. THE THOUGHT—Industry as a whole is one vast operative mechanism. Included in it are the governments of every country, and

our combined system of social, political and industrial economy." He began seeing the whole world as one giant machine. But that machine was running inefficiently and needed someone who could put it back in order through "the displacement of governments and the amalgamation of all the people in the world into one corporate body, with one corporate brain."

Gillette decided that he was that someone. He decided to write a book: a practical, step-by-step guide to centralize the entire world into one gigantic corporation. He put away the idea of inventing gadgets and began reinventing the world.

In the summer of 1894, he finished his book, *The Human Drift*, and got it published. He sat back and waited for the world to see the rightness of his cause and began readying himself to take over as head of the worldwide Twentieth Century Company. His book began getting glowing reviews in utopian and socialist publications. Letters of support started filling his mailbox, some of them containing money to buy shares in Twentieth Century.

But, as he waited to become the world's chairman of the board, the next revelation struck, the one that would sidetrack him from his world-saving goals.

It happened while doing his morning ablutions in a hotel room. "On one particular morning when I started to shave, I found my razor dull, and it was not only dull, but was beyond the point of successful stropping and it needed honing, for which it must be taken to a barber or a cutler," he wrote years later. "As I stood there with the razor in my hand, my eyes resting on it lightly as a bird settling down on its nest...the thought occurred to me that no radical improvements had been made in razors, especially in razor blades, for several centuries, and it flashed through my mind that if by any possibility razor blades could be constructed and made cheap enough to do away with honing and stropping and permit the user to replace dull blades by new ones, such improvements would be highly important in that art.... The Gillette razor was born."

Well, not quite. It took another eight years for Gillette to work out the practical details, assisted by an engineer with the name William E. Nickerson (can you imagine the marketing difficulties if the razor had been named after him?). Expert cutlers and metallurgists said that it couldn't be done, but Gillette continued trying new metals and various designs. He finally worked out all the bugs and made the razor available to the public in 1903.

His company sold only 51 razors and 168 blades that year. Gillette continued to earn his living as a traveling salesman for Crown Cork and Seal. In September that year, he was assigned to a selling route in England, giving him a raise he couldn't afford to turn down. He went across the sea, reluctantly leaving the Gillette Razor Company in the hands of its board of directors.

While he was gone, the company seemed about to go under and the board considered selling its assets and going out of business. But suddenly sales figures began to climb, helped along by good word-of-mouth and an extremely modest level of advertising. The company sold 91,000 razors and 123,000 blades in 1904. In November of that year, Gillette resigned his sales position and returned home.

But he was still interested in utopian politics. He wrote more books. He put his name and picture on each package of blades to increase his fame, still hoping to be made leader of the world by public acclaim. Later, when it became clear that the world was not buying  his leadership role, he offered the former president, Teddy Roosevelt, $1 million to serve as the head of the "World Corporation." But Teddy declined, and when Gillette died in 1931, the world revolution he dreamed about still had not come about. To his profound disappointment, Gillette didn't become renowned for having *saved* humanity; instead, he became famous for having *shaved* it.

Escape Artist

How to Avoid a Tiger Attack

Tigers attack humans often. Not because they like the way we taste (we're pretty bony and bland) but because they're ultimately lazy animals that will take what they can get.

Although it probably won't happen often at your local zoo, tigers munch down on dozens of humans a year. Here are a few ways to avoid being a tiger's next lunch:

1. When you're out in the wild, be aware of your surroundings. Is there dense jungle where something could hide without being noticed? Are you near a river that's a known watering hole for wild animals? If so, stay clear of these places.

2. But say your route must take you through the jungle. Then what? Use your nose. Tigers are solitary creatures like our house cats, and spray their scent to mark their territory. Their urine smells very similar to buttered popcorn. So if you start smelling something in the jungle that smells like a movie snack bar, watch out. You could be in a tiger's territory.

3. People swear this works: wear a mask on the back of your head. Tigers only pounce from behind. If you're not offering them a behind, they've been known to get confused and give up. Many natives in India have tried this method and found the tigers eventually slink off into the jungle, thoroughly demoralized.

4. But say your stalking tiger is smart and your mask fails you. Then what? Well, you can't outrun a tiger, so the only chance you've got is to face the tiger—again, taking away the option of attacking from behind—and stand your ground. Showing fear will be your downfall, so stand your ground. Good luck!

Lemming Aid

TRACKING THE MYTH OF LEMMING SUICIDE

The metaphor of lemmings following the crowd to their death is such an irresistible story. Too bad it's not true.

HOW DID THE MYTH BEGIN that lemmings commit suicide *en masse*? They don't, you know. Not even the really, really depressed ones. Yet, people still want to believe the story and use it as a metaphor for everything from the behavior of stock market investors to religious cult members to the peer group behavior of teens.

Not that many would care if lemmings really did have a tendency for mass suicide. They're nasty little things that look like voles. They reproduce like rabbits, popping out as many as thirteen babies every three weeks.

While there are other breeds, including an American variety, the most famous is the Norway lemming that lives in the tundra and grasslands of Scandinavia. These are the ones that are allegedly suicidal. In reality, though, that's wishful thinking, because lemmings are actually *homicidal*. As we said, they're nasty little things.

WHY LEMMINGS ARE SO DARNED NASTY

In the warm spring when grass is plentiful, the lemming population rises at an alarmingly unsustainable rate. By summer, desperation kicks in, and things turn ugly. Adults fight to the death for breeding territory; lemming moms raid the nests of their neighbors and kill their young, no doubt laughing maniacally while they do so.

Since all this carnage isn't enough to solve the population problem, the animals disperse from their nesting grounds in search of food and living space. They don't formally migrate in a huge mass; it just looks that way. "A booming population of near-sighted, physically clumsy rodents stumbling down Norway's numerous funnel-shaped gullies is what produced the massive migration look," reported an article in *Canadian Geographic*. True, a number of lemmings may accidentally fall over the edge of a narrow mountain path or get washed away while fording fjords and streams, but they don't intentionally kill themselves. Actually, most of the lemmings that die along the way are eaten by predators taking advantage of the free protein that's ambling by.

THE DISNEY CONNECTION

Which brings up another layer of lemming-suicide myth: that a Disney film crew simply made up the suicide myth and then shot phony footage to document it.

Granted, the Disney people have a lot to answer for in spreading the story. Disney cameramen filming lemmings for *White Wilderness* (1958) were instructed by the producers to "throw them over the cliff by the bucketful if

necessary" to create the spectacle of lemmings plunging into the ocean to drown.

While that is despicable on humanitarian grounds, the Disney producers didn't *create* the myth, but were in fact victims of it as well. In their cruel and dubious shenanigans, they were merely trying to capture on film an ancient story that they themselves believed to be true.

RAINING CATS & LEMMINGS

In reality, the myth goes back long before Disney. Lemming suicide stories emerged centuries earlier in Scandinavia, where people had witnessed masses of the clumsy animals falling and drowning. Over time, these myths became even more bizarre. In 1555, Swedish archbishop Olaus Magnus, in *The History of Northern Peoples,* speculated that that the only explanation for the sudden explosions of lemming populations was that they rained from the sky. This echoes an Inuit myth about the collared lemming, which they call Kilangmiutak ("that which falls from the sky").

Too bad Disney didn't show that!

Edward Lear

Landscape artist Edward Lear (1812–1888) wrote and illustrated limericks. His Book of Nonsense *is considered a masterpiece of children's literature. Just for fun, here are some excerpts.*

There was an Old Man with a beard,
Who said, "It is just as I feared!
Two Owls and a Hen,
Four Larks and a Wren,
Have all built their nests in my beard!"

There was an Old Man with a nose,
Who said, "If you choose to suppose,
That my nose is too long,
You are certainly wrong!"
That remarkable Man with a nose.

There was a Young Lady whose bonnet,
Came untied when the birds sat upon it;
But she said: "I don't care!
All the birds in the air
Are welcome to sit on my bonnet!"

There was an Old Man in a boat,
Who said, "I'm afloat, I'm afloat!"
When they said, "No! you ain't!"
He was ready to faint,
That unhappy Old Man in a boat.

There was a Young Lady of Portugal,
Whose ideas were excessively nautical:
She climbed up a tree,
To examine the sea,
But declared she would never leave Portugal.

There was a Young Lady whose eyes,
Were unique as to colour and size;
When she opened them wide,
People all turned aside,
And started away in surprise.

The was a Young Lady of Bute,
Who played on a silver-gilt flute;
She played several jigs,
To her uncle's white pigs,
That amusing Young Lady of Bute.

There was a Young Lady whose nose,
Was so long that it reached to her toes;
So she hired an Old Lady,
Whose conduct was steady,
To carry that wonderful nose.

There was an Old Lady whose folly,
Induced her to sit on a holly;
Whereon by a thorn,
Her dress being torn,
She quickly became melancholy.

There was an Old Man of Cape Horn,
Who wished he had never been born;
So he sat on a chair,
Till he died of despair,
That dolorous Man of Cape Horn.

There was an Old Man of the Nile,
Who sharpened his nails with a file,
Till he cut out his thumbs,
And said calmly, "This comes
Of sharpening one's nails with a file!"

Believe It's Not Butter

THINGS YOU DIDN'T KNOW ABOUT MARGARINE

Have you ever wondered what that stuff is as you spread it on your bread? We give you the sometimes unsavory story behind margarine.

WHAT'S IN A NAME?

"Margarine" comes from margaric acid—an acid rendered from fat. A man named Michael Chevreul managed to isolate it almost fifty years before anyone found a use for it. Since the acid forms in shiny droplets, Chevreul named it "margaric" from the Greek word *margarites*, meaning "pearl."

THE CREATOR

Margarine itself was originally created by a man named Hippolyte Mege-Mouries in 1870. Napoleon's wars were costing the French a lot of money, and butter was in short supply. The emperor called for someone to find a substitute that could meet the demands of the people. Mege-Mouries did a little research and realized that even starving cows could produce milk that had milk fat in it. He deduced that this fat must be coming not from food intake, but from the fat of the cow itself. To test his theory,

Mege-Mouries

he squeezed out the fatty acids from beef fat, mixed it with milk and created oleomargarine (*oleo* being French for "beef fat"). It was a big success, and Mege-Mouries won a prize from Napoleon.

MARGARINE COMES TO NORTH AMERICA

When the war ended in 1873 Mege-Mouries found himself with a margarine factory and zero demand for his product. He applied for a patent in the United States and moved across the Atlantic to set up shop. Things didn't pan out as he'd hoped for his company there, either, and he died in relative poverty and obscurity.

However, in 1874, the U.S. Dairy Company had bought the rights from Mege-Mouries for his invention. It built factories all over the country and began using left-over beef by-products to manufacture their "artificial butter." By 1882, the company was manufac-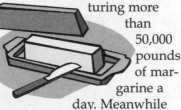turing more than 50,000 pounds of margarine a day. Meanwhile in Europe, the Lever Brothers and the Dutch Margarine Union also began marketing Mege-Mouries's spread.

DAIRY TRIES A SQUEEZE PLAY

With cheap margarine sweeping the Western world, dairy farmers were naturally getting worried. By 1877 they had begun using their clout to pass anti-margarine laws. In several states, for example, margarine manufacturers became subject to a $100 fine and 30 days in jail if their labels didn't clearly state that the product was margarine and not butter.

Fair enough. Unfortunately, the law didn't have the desired effect of reducing demand for margarine, so dairy interests convinced Congress to pass the Margarine Act of 1886, which mandated hefty fees for anyone making, distributing, or selling margarine. On top of that, the law levied a special tax of 2¢ for every pound of margarine consumers bought. However, margarine was still cheaper than butter, and sales didn't slow. Finally in 1902, the butter lobby got another federal tax levied: a 10¢ tax on yellow-colored margarine. Since margarine had been selling for 20¢ a pound, the tax increased the price fifty percent and made it more expensive than butter.

COLOR ME LEGAL

Dairy farmers lobbied state governments to pass more restrictive margarine laws. When consumers continued to buy the white product, states passed laws requiring margarine manufacturers to color their product an unappetizing pink. This time the dairy interests went to far: the Supreme Court ruled that the "pink margarine" law was unconstitutional.

Margarine manufacturers finally started fighting back against the restrictive laws. For example, manufacturers discovered that there was nothing in the law that prevented them from selling margarine inside a cellophane bag with a pellet of yellow food dye. Consumers could get yellow margarine by simply kneading the bag for a few minutes. Manufacturers also started making margarine from vegetable oil instead of animal fats. For years, the dairy industry had had a field day with lurid tales of diseased animals being made into margarine—vegetable oils not only preempted that campaign, but also produced a margarine with a naturally yellow hue.

A WINNING SPREAD

Dairy farmers kept fighting (and usually winning) legal battles on state and federal levels. However, the Great Depression and two World Wars solidified margarine's position in the marketplace, when consumers turned to margarine because butter was too expensive or rationed. Margarine producers teamed with the makers of vegetable oils and got the national tax on yellow margarine rescinded in 1950. Within five years

every state except Minnesota and Wisconsin had repealed the laws against coloring margarine yellow (Minnesota repealed the law in 1963; Wisconsin, "The Dairy State" held out until 1967.)

Pretty much the same: Margarine is 80% fat. Butter is 85%.

QUICK FACTS

• In the year 1930, consumers in the United States ingested about 2.6 pounds of margarine per capita, and 17.6 pounds of butter. Now butter's down to 4.2 pounds per capita while margarine's up to 8.3 pounds.

• To be called "margarine" in the United States, a spread must contain at least 15,000 IUs of vitamin A. Oil must make up eighty percent of the spread.

• If it's called a "spread" instead of "margarine," it just means that it doesn't meet the above legal standard.

The Devil's Dictionary: E

More of *The Devil's Dictionary* by Ambrose Bierce (1842–1914?)

ECCENTRICITY, *n.* A method of distinction so cheap that fools employ it to accentuate their incapacity.

ECONOMY, *n.* Purchasing the barrel of whiskey that you do not need for the price of the cow that you cannot afford.

EDIBLE, *adj.* Good to eat, and wholesome to digest, as a worm to a toad, a toad to a snake, a snake to a pig, a pig to a man, and a man to a worm.

EDUCATION, *n.* That which discloses to the wise and disguises from the foolish their lack of understanding.

EFFECT, *n.* The second of two phenomena which always occur together in the same order. The first, called a Cause, is said to generate the other—which is no more sensible than it would be for one who has never seen a dog except in the pursuit of a rabbit to declare the rabbit the cause of a dog.

EGOTIST, *n.* A person of low taste, more interested in himself than in me.

ELOQUENCE, *n.* The art of orally persuading fools that white is the color that it appears to be. It includes the gift of making any color appear white.

EMBALM, *v.i.* To cheat vegetation by locking up gases upon which it feeds. Many a dead man who ought now to be ornamenting his neighbor's lawn as a tree, or enriching his table as a bunch of radishes, is doomed to a long inutility.

ENTERTAINMENT, *n.* Any kind of amusement whose inroads stop short of death by injection.

ENTHUSIASM, *n.* A distemper of youth, curable by small doses of repentance in connection with outward applications of experience.

EPAULET, *n.* An ornamented badge, serving to distinguish a military officer from the enemy—that is to say, from the officer of lower rank to whom his death would give promotion.

EPITAPH, *n.* An inscription on a tomb, showing that virtues acquired by death have a retroactive effect.

ERUDITION, *n.* Dust shaken out of a book into an empty skull.

EXHORT, *v.t.* In religious affairs, to put the conscience of another upon the spit and roast it to a nut-brown discomfort.

EXILE, *n.* One who serves his country by residing abroad, yet is not an ambassador.

One Hump or 2?
THINGS YOU MIGHT NOT KNOW ABOUT CAMELS

They may be the Ships of the Desert, but most people don't know much about camels beyond their humps, bad tempers, and ungainly walk. Here's a quick primer.

WHAT'S IN THOSE HUMPS

Despite legend, camels don't really store water in their humps. The humps are big chunks of fat, which makes it possible for camels to go weeks without food in the desert. Why isn't their fat distributed over their bodies, like other animals? Well, ask any polar bear and you'll learn that fat is not just stored energy, it also makes a really good insulating jacket. It's why polar animals tend to look more like sumo wrestlers than ballerinas and why even penguins have a thick layer of fat on the bottoms of their feet. The last thing you'd want in the desert would be a warm layer of fat, so camels have evolved to a point where they've localized their fat in one (if Arabian) or two (if Asian) high-cholesterol lumps on the top of their bodies.

As a camel uses the stored fat in its hump, the hump gets floppy and bounces around from side to side.

HOW THEY GO WITHOUT WATER

There are other unusual heat-coping features that make camels the preferred ship of the desert. For starters, their kidneys are designed to absorb a high level of moisture from their urine. Also, their body temperature rises with the heat from 95° F. at night to more than 104° during the day—not an unusual thing with fish and amphibians, but almost never seen in mammals. It's only at the higher temperature that camels begin to sweat, and they're unusual in that they lose moisture evenly from all tissues of the body instead of just from the blood like most mammals. This allows a camel to lose 40 percent of its body weight in water loss before its life is endangered. Camels make up this water loss with binge drinking, staggering into an oasis and sucking down as much as 50 gallons at a time.

OPERATING ON A CAMEL

Camels can't lie flat on their backs, so how do veterinarian surgeons operate on them? In the Dubai Camel Hospital, it's done on a slab with a hole in the center. The operating slab tilts so that it fits down over the hump of an upright camel. After the camel is anesthetized, the table tilts back, allowing what camels can't normally do in nature: lie with all four legs in the air.

MANGY CAMELS

In the spring and summer, camels shed their winter coats in huge ugly patches—about 5 pounds total. It looks alarming, as though the large beast were falling apart. Believe it or not, though, this matted wool is valued as clothing fiber around the world. What looks grotesque when falling off the camel looks good when woven into a coat or a kicky little beret.

CAMEL HAIR BRUSHES

Are the bristles of a "camel hair brush" really made from camel hair? Usually not. The cheap ones come from a pony's tail or mane. Better ones come from an ox, ferret, goat, or squirrel.

THE EYE OF A CAMEL

Camels have a double set of eyelashes to keep the sand out of their eyes, and an inner eyelid that blinks to wash away any stray grains. Its eyebrow protrudes over the eyeball, shading it from the glaring sun. All of these things combined give the camel's eye a deceptively gentle look. Don't go up and try to squeeze its cute little cheeks, though. (Keep reading.)

SPITTING IMAGE

Camels are very territorial, and if they feel threatened, they spit. If you do get caught in the crossfire, it can get pretty vile, since the camel launches stomach bile mixed with saliva. Contrary to popular myth, camel spit is harmless—it won't burn or blind you. If one does spit, it's the camel's way of saying, "Get out of my way, or I'll really

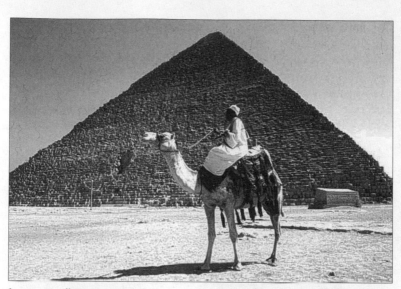

hurt you." Best to heed the spit and split.

AMERICAN ROOTS?

Camels in America? Many natural history experts believe that camels originated in North America 40 million years ago and migrated through Alaska and into Asia prior to the Ice Age.

PACKING A HUMP

Camels were used as pack animals in the western parts of the U.S. deserts. In 1855, then-Secretary of War Jefferson Davis gave the Army $30,000 for the purchase of seventy-seven camels. They arrived in Texas from the Middle East, along with a native fellow named Hadji Ali to help lead the camel cara-

vans. When Davis requested more funds from Congress in 1858 for 1,000 more camels, it looked like the camel might become a fixture of the American West. However, because of brewing Civil War tensions, the funds were never appropriated, and the Army camel experiment died a quiet death.

ROCKY RIDE

Camels move their legs on each side of their body together. Unlike most animals, their two right legs step forward, and then their two left legs. The rocking motion can be very hard for new riders. Many travelers have tales of "seasickness" upon their first few rides behind the hump of the desert ship.

THIS JARGON'S A BEDOUIN

The Bedouin name for the camel is *ata Allah*, or "God's gift." The Bedouins have over 160 specific words in their language to describe camels and their traits.

CAMEL RACES

Camels have been clocked upward of 40 miles an hour. This pace slows considerably as a race progresses, however. The average speed of a racing camel is about 25 miles per hour. In 1892, a horse and a camel competed in a famous one-day, 109.4-mile race in Australia. The horse won by a hair, then promptly collapsed and died. The camel, though second, crossed the finish line relatively unfazed by the experience.

NAR WAY!

Can one-hump and two-hump camels mate? Yes. You get what's called a "Nar" with one elongated hump.

1776 TERRORISM: TAR AND FEATHERS

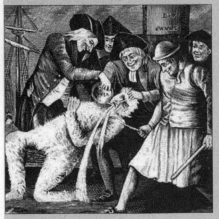

Before the American Revolution, attacking Crown-appointed officeholders became a tactic used again and again to terrorize them into resigning their posts. Tarring and feathering added both insult and injury to the mix. The practice was not invented by the Americans—British mobs had used it against tax collectors and other pests back in the days of Richard the Lionhearted.

The idea was simple: to cover the victim with tar and then pour feathers on him to make him look like a large chicken. It sounds humiliating, and it was. It also could cause great injury, because the pine tar had to be burning hot to get the right consistency. Afterward, it was difficult and painful to get off.

Mob violence got rougher with time. After tarring and feathering a Loyalist minister, the mob hanged him and burned his body. A Loyalist physician was blistered by the tar, and hog dung was forced into his mouth. The Revolutionary leaders finally decided things had gotten out of hand and began reining in the practice.

Smoke Screen

QUOTES FROM THE TOBACCO INDUSTRY

What if you were selling an addictive product that you knew was killing your customers? How would you justify that to yourself and explain it to the rest of the world? Not like this, we hope.

- "Cigarettes are not addictive." — Brennan Dawson, Tobacco Institute, 1994
- "I think we overuse the word 'addictive.' I think smoking can be a habit." — Brennan Dawson, Tobacco Institute, 1991
- "If I saw or thought that there were any evidence whatsoever that conclusively proved that, in some way, tobacco was harmful to people, and I believed it in my heart and my soul, then I would get out of the business and I wouldn't be involved in it. Honestly, I have not seen one piece of medical evidence that has been presented by anybody, anywhere that absolutely, totally said that smoking caused the disease or created it. I believe this. I'm sitting here talking to you with an extremely clear conscience." — Gerald H. Long, president of R. J. Reynolds Tobacco Company, May 19, 1986, as quoted in *The Washington Times*
- "Gosh, we're awed at how a story can be told and retold by the anti-cigarette people, and how little attention is given in the press to claims *for* cigarettes." — James C. Bowling, assistant to the president of Philip Morris
- "It's part of the whole anti-business movement, the Green Movement. If you think it's bad here, it's even worse in Europe. People have more time to think these days, and so they're more and more critical of everything. Look how critical they are of

governments. And there's this health-consciousness movement running through the world." —John Dollisson, vice president of corporate affairs of Phillip Morris, explaining the anti-smoking movement

• "I think that if it were ever conclusively shown that there was some connection between smoking and, say, lung cancer, most ad agencies would not be advertising cigarettes. But it's easy to get stampeded, and the tobacco industry is being very much maligned.... The fact is that I have never met a finer group in my life than the people in the tobacco industry ... and tobacco has given pleasure to an awful lot of people. You should never act on hunches, suspicions, and stir-ups." —Henry Pattison, account executive for Philip Morris at the Benton and Bowles Agency, 1969

•"Just what the doctor ordered." —Ad, L & M cigarettes, 1956

• "If it was legal to sell to 'em, we'd be glad to. But it's not." —Walker Merryman, Tobacco Institute, August 5, 1992, discussing tobacco use by minors

"It's always been our policy that young people shouldn't smoke." —Brennan Dawson, Tobacco Institute, 1991

• "Realistically, if our company is to survive and prosper, over the long term, we must get our share of the youth market. In my opinion, this will require new brands tailored to the youth market." —In-house memo by Claude Teague of R. J. Reynolds, February 2, 1973

• "There is no science behind the accusation that advertising causes smoking initiation." —Thomas Lauria, Tobacco Institute, 1991

• "This attempt to ban smoking is an example of social engineering on a vast scale. Such massive intervention in the private lives and choices of one quarter of our adult population recalls the extremism of Prohibition, the last national crusade against a supposed social evil." —Charles Whitley, Tobacco Institute, 1990

• LAST WORD ON THE SUBJECT: "Tobacco is lothesome to the eye, hatefull to the Nose, harmfull to the braine, dangerous to the Lungs; and in the stinking fume thereof nearest resembling the horrific Stigian smoke of the pit that is bottomless." —King James I, banning tobacco in 1604

Penguin Love

THEIR SECRETS LAID OUT IN BLACK & WHITE

Penguins mate for life, and the fathers take an active role in their chicks' upbringing. Are these little waddlers a role model for us all, or what?

FIRST OF ALL, penguins are not particularly lusty birds. True, they mate for life, but they typically have sex only once a year.

They are, however, good parents. Yes, even the mothers, despite the rumors you might've heard. It's true that penguin moms don't look good in a straight retelling of the facts: they lay eggs, immediately go AWOL, and don't come back until after the eggs are hatched. But to come to the moms' defense, there are extenuating circumstances. Let's start at the beginning.

NORTH, SOUTH, EAST ... THEN NEST

Penguins don't normally spend much time on land because all of their food is in the water. However, nesting changes the rules. The penguins take to the same land where they were born, colonies of thousands of the birds walking single file in the same, often absurdly circuitous path that their forepenguins walked for untold generations. (How do we know this? Because scientists have found penguin paths worn into soil, ice, and rocks from the feet of millions of birds waddling through over time.)

Nest styles differ. Penguins in warmer regions may dig shallow burrows for nests; because of the hardness of the earth, many Antarctic penguins build nests of pebbles. Emperor and king penguins, though, don't build nests at all. Instead, they balance the eggs on the tops of their feet and keep them warm by covering them with their ample bellies.

With few exceptions, typically the penguin love schedule goes like this: In the same way that human lovers tune into each other over the hubbub of a crowded room, the two penguin guin mates find each other in the nesting areas by the sound of  the other's voice. They mate, and the male stakes out a nesting area. He spends weeks defending it from interlopers, neither parent leaving the nesting area to find food. Finally, Mom lays the eggs.

She, more depleted than the father after manufacturing the eggs, immediately makes a rush to the sea to binge eat, replenish her famished self, and stave off post-ovum depression. The father stays around to keep the eggs warm.

DAD LOVES HIS EGGS

Of course, keeping eggs warm in Antarctica is harder than it sounds. The eggs have to be constantly heated at body temperature for 30 to 65 days, which requires extraordinary paternal efforts. For example, the male emperor penguin spends weeks standing stationary 24 hours a day with an egg cradled on his feet in the dead of winter. To keep warm in weather that stays close to –40° is nearly impossible for a single dad, but they've found a solution. Thousands of emperor penguin dads huddle together in a tight group, the penguins on the outside of the crowd rotating in toward the center to share the warmth and keep from freezing. Other types of penguin dads spend a lonely vigil sitting on a pebbly nest.

Shortly before the eggs are supposed to hatch, the prodigal mother penguin returns. She typically takes over the egg tending, and her exhausted, hungry mate takes off. He heads to the sea and replenishes his blubber in a remarkably short time, returning shortly after the eggs hatch with food for the baby. After that, the parents continue to alternate between taking care of the young and eating until the chicks are old enough to fend for themselves.

To the Pillory!

CRUEL BUT USUAL PUNISHMENT IN AMERICA

Changing the hearts, minds, and behaviors of lawbreakers has long been the goal of criminologists. Unfortunately, their attempts have often been ineffective and sometimes just plain criminal.

ANYBODY WITH ANY HONESTY would admit we don't do a great job dealing with criminals. America has a larger percentage of its citizens locked up in prisons than any other country in the world, including Russia, China, and Iraq. It is one of the few advanced countries that still has the death penalty. And yet, despite being increasingly "tough on crime," America continues time after time to lead the lists of serious violence and crime in industrialized countries.

The Pillory.

But as ineffectually inhumane as the present system is, it could always be worse. In fact, it *was* worse, back in a time that we romanticize now — the time when Pilgrims and Puritans ruled the new settlements in America. Justice in the New World was based on England's justice, which was not just at all. Different punishments were given to gentlemen, common people, and slaves. Brutality and death were common for even minor crimes, such as belonging to the wrong religious denomination, writing a book without authorization, or criticizing the authorities. Pain and public scorn were powerful weapons, and the civil/religious authorities used them creatively and often.

STOCKS & BONDAGE

Public humiliation was the point of the stocks. They descended from England's *bilboes*, which were heavy metal bars with foot shackles, designed to keep a prisoner from moving from the spot.

The Stocks.

Bilboes were impractical in the New World because of a shortage of skilled metal workers, but America had plenty of trees, so a wooden version became common. (In fact, judges sometimes demanded that the prisoner provide wood and make stocks to bind himself.) Being stuck sitting with feet imprisoned between wooden slats on a Sunday between the morning and evening services was considered a suitable punishment for such things as drunkenness, mild profanity, breaching the Sabbath, and the like. Besides the discomfort and boredom, prisoners in stocks had to put up with the censure, jibes, and jests of other townspeople.

THE PILLORY

Also known as the "stretch-neck," the pillory was for more serious crimes. It was more painful than the stocks and made the prisoner subject to much worse than jibes and jests. Standing uncomfortably with hands and head immobilized allowed every ruffian in town the sport of pelting the prisoner with rotten eggs, garbage, offal, and dung. Sometimes, to drive the point further, city officials nailed the prisoner's ears to the wood on either side of the head hole. The pillory—sometimes in conjunction with branding, mutilation, fines, and other penalties—was a one-size-fits-all punishment for treason, sedition, arson, blasphemy, witchcraft, perjury, wife-beating, cheating, forging, gaming, quarreling, lying, slander, drunkenness, begging, speculating in commodities futures, impudence, and general mischief.

THE DUCKING STOOL

The ducking stool was a milder punishment, used mostly for scolding and nagging women, but sometimes also for men a little too loose in their tongues: rumor mongers, whiners, and slanderers. The punishment was to repeatedly duck offenders under water until they emerged choking and thoroughly dispirited. A poem written in 1780 explained:

> There stands, my friend, in yonder pool
> An engine called the ducking stool....
> If noisy dames should once begin
> To drive your house with noisy din,
> Away you cry, you'll grace the stool;
> We'll teach how your tongue to rule....
> No brawling wives, no furious wenches
> No fire so hot but water quenches.

BRANKS, GAGS, & SPLIT STICKS

If the ducking stool didn't work on chronically harping women, there were more direct behavior modification techniques. Branks were a type of iron headgear with a sharp protrusion into the mouth that would injure the tongue if the wearer spoke.

A similar punishment was the "cleft stick" — cutting a split into a wooden stick and forcing it onto the tongue of a person deemed guilty of nagging, scolding, complaining, or criticizing the authorities.

SCARLET LETTER

Anybody who read *The Scarlet Letter* in school knows about this one: a person forced to wear a letter to advertise to the world his or her dire depravity. Hester Prynne had to wear an *A* for adultery. Other letters included *B* for blasphemy, *V* for viciousness, and *D* for drunkenness. To prevent poor people from receiving charity from more than one church parish, they had to wear letters to indicate where they lived.

WHIPPING

Like most of the early colonial punishments, whippings were likely to be given on

The Ducking-Stool

Sabbath days in conjunction with church services, in order teach a moral lesson. A good whipping, each lash causing deep injury and permanent scars, was meant to correct serious offenses. Whippings were meted out for stealing a loaf of bread, shooting fowl on the Sabbath, sleeping in church, falling in love with an unsuitable suitor, and complaining about the government. To avoid killing the prisoner, judges generally limited the whippings to a maximum of 39 lashes at a time; for modesty's sake, women were sometimes whipped behind walls instead of in public.

THE WOOD HORSE

Riding the wooden horse was a military punishment in both the British and American armies:

Rule-breaking soldiers were forced to straddle a sharpened wooden rail, sometimes with cannonballs tied to their feet, sometimes for hours or days at a time.

BRANDING & MAIMING

Being subjected to permanent injury (including death) was the punishment for more serious crimes. For example, here's an account of the punishment given a man who was convicted of the "crime" of being a Quaker in New Haven, Connecticut:

The Drum was Beat, the People gather'd, Norton was fetch'd and stripp'd to the Waste, and set with his Back to the Magistrates, and given in their View Thirty-six cruel Stripes with a knotted cord, and his hand made fast in the Stocks where they had set his Body before, and burn'd very deep with a Red-hot Iron with H for Heresie.

In Massachusetts, Quakers were banished from all settlements. If they returned, read a 1657 law, "a Quaker if male for the first offense shall have one of his eares cutt off; for the second offense have his other eare cutt off; a woman shall be severely whipt; for the third offense, he or she shall have their tongues bored through with a hot iron."

In early Virginia, a first-time hog thief might be heavily fined and have his ears cropped; if he repeated the crime, he might pay the same fine and have H branded on his forehead; the third time, he would be put to death.

Maryland law required that all towns have a set of branding irons for burning the cheeks of criminals: SL for "seditious libel" (criticizing the authorities); M for manslaughter; T for thief; R for rogue or vagabond; F for forgers, and so on.

Someone convicted of a misdemeanor might have his nose or ears slit or cut as a lesson to the miscreant and a warning to others.

A Toast to Toasters

BRED FOR BREAD ... AND SO MUCH MORE

Stoves are unwieldy; microwaves have no soul. But a toaster is like a small, tabletop hearth; the smells and foods that emerge from it seem to whisper, "Home!"

ONSIDER THE TOASTER: Its function is modest—to singe both sides of a slice of bread to just the right temperature—yet that function is considered so crucial that 88 percent of all American households have at least one toaster.

Despite the ascendency of fad kitchen gadgets and microwave ovens, the toaster continues to hang on to its counter space in a way that lesser appliances have not. Of course, it's not just all about the bread. Thanks to the ingenuity of the food industry, a toaster can prepare main courses from waffles to pizza, exotic faux-international foods like bagels and English muffins, and even desserts, thanks to that class of foods known as "toaster pastries."

THE RISE OF BREAD

To understand the toaster, you have to begin with bread. And not just any bread, but fluffy bread. Even before the beginning of agriculture, people baked a flat, hard bread made from the seeds of grasses. As the varieties of these grains were recognized and purposely planted, breadmaking continued, but it was still flat, unleavened bread totally unsuited for toasting (and barely suitable for eating).

About 6,000 years ago, Egyptian bakers changed all that when they invented fluffy bread.

It was most likely an accident: If you've ever made bread from scratch, you can imagine the difficulty of kneading huge quantities of dough day in and day out. We can surmise that one of the bakers had a brilliant thought to save the constant strain on his arms, shoulders, and back: "If winemakers find it easier to crush grapes with their feet, why don't we try the same thing to knead our bread?"

Ancient Egyptian breadmakers kneading bread dough with their feet

PEDICUREAN DELIGHT

It wasn't a time of great cleanliness in food preparation. While it's true that their feet weren't particularly clean, their hands may have been just as bad or worse. One key difference between the two, though, was the yeast between the bakers' toes. We've all got it—it's the stuff that makes your feet smell cheesy. Wine and beer need yeast to ferment. Bread needs yeast to rise. And sure enough, the first batches of foot-kneaded bread came out of the oven radically different from what had ever come out before: they were light, fluffy, and chewy. (One "foot" note to think about next time you're having grilled cheese sandwiches: The yeast used in cheesemaking has a similar toejam pedigree.)

The bakers didn't have a clue why their foot-kneaded bread came out fluffy, but they did know that it was easier to make and that their customers seemed to like it. So they kept kneading bread that way, and the practice spread.

Despite its downtrodden origins, this softer bread became so valued that Egyptian workers accepted it as payment at the end of the workday, making them the first "breadwinners" in history.

ROMAN MEAL

It took the ancient Romans to take bread to its next logical step: toast! Toasting was first used as a way of preserving bread longer for the Roman Army, but it became popular as a tasty side dish among

Romans. who gave it its modern name (*tostum* means "scorch") and spread toast from Africa to Britain.

In the first millennia of toast, "toasters" were primitive things—often simply a stick to hold bread to within browning distance of a fire's flames. However, human ingenuity resulted in other solutions as well. For example, toasters in the 1800s consisted of bread-holding wire racks that stood next to the fireplace. Like all pre-electric toasters, they required constant monitoring to avoid burning the bread.

The first successful electric toaster didn't appear until 1909. Made by the General Electric Company, it plugged into a lightbulb socket (wall outlets weren't a common thing yet), toasted one side of

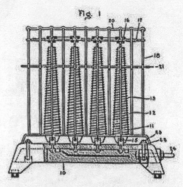

Patent drawing for General Electric's 1909 toaster. Note that it's just four electric coils with a wire bread stand.

bread at a time, and wasn't automatic—when the toast looked good to you, you unscrewed the plug.

Ten years later, Charles Strite finally got it right. He invented the modern, timer-activated, pop-up toaster. The innovation of pre-sliced bread from Wonder in 1930 advanced toasting technology even further.

MORE TOAST FACTS

• The optimal temperature for making toast is about 310°.

• Chemical changes occur when you make toast—the bread's starches and sugars caramelize into intense new flavors. It's even got a name: "the Malllard Reaction" in honor of L. C. Maillard, the chemist who identified it in 1912.

• Maybe you've heard "milktoast" used as an insult, but do you know what it is? It's a British concoction: toast in a bowl covered with milk and flavored with butter, salt, and pepper.

• Our favorite toaster? A yellow one from the early 1970s with Charlie Brown's dog on it and the inscription: "Happiness is a Snoopy Toaster." Awww!

Life Lessons
HOW TO MILK A COW

Say you're out in the middle of dairy country with nothing on you but the shirt on your back. What are you going to do—eat tumbleweed? Well, we're here to help with a quick primer on how to milk a cow. It could save your life.

IF YOU CAN IGNORE the potentially lethal kicking legs and the shifting half ton of weight, it's really not so hard to milk a cow. Here we go step by step:

1. The pail of milk should be protected. It'll help if you can find a neck and leg harness for Bossie in order to keep her still. If you have no idea what these things are, you're on your own.

2. Hay is a good distracter. It'll keep the cow's interest off kicking you as you begin.

3. If you've got it, use anti-bacterial soap to wash your hands and the teats. Cows aren't the cleanest things, and you likely don't want invisible germs swimming around in your milk.

4. In order for the milk to "let down" (begin to flow), the cow's teats need to be stimulated. This isn't foreplay; you use your thumb and forefinger on each of the cow's teats to squeeze out a little milk before the official milking begins.

5. Now the fun begins. Take your forefinger and wrap it around an individual teat while pressing your thumb from the opposite side. Roll your forefinger in a downward motion, apply pressure as evenly as possible. If you're having trouble with this, visualize your fingers as a calf's mouth sucking like a baby.

6. This will take a while, so sit back and enjoy the process and the exercise. It'll take about 350 squirts to fill your typical five gallon bucket. A cow produces enough milk to fill one of these a day. That's a heap of milk for one body, so start dreaming up creamy recipes.

Snow Business
HOW TO BUILD AN IGLOO

For most kids, building an igloo on snow days was a continuously unrealized goal. But it's not that hard ... if you learn from an expert.

THE PROBLEM BUILDING AN IGLOO is getting that round shape without having the roof cave in. At least, that's what doomed our childhood attempts so thoroughly we never even considered building one as we got older. So we were glad to run across an account of igloo building by native Canadians in a book called *The Igloo* by David and Charlotte Yue (Houghton-Mifflin, 1988). We learned enough from their observations to be able to put together our own igloo.

SOME THINGS WE LEARNED ALONG THE WAY
• *Iglu* is a native word meaning any kind of house.

• Not all native groups in the Arctic used snow igloos; some never used them, while others used them only as temporary shelter while traveling.

• A good builder can build a basic igloo in a little over an hour.

• The dome structure is energy efficient, offering the minimum amount of surface area, and snow is a great insulator. As a result, a good igloo can be 65° warmer inside than it is outside.

• Domes built by a competent builder were strong enough that native kids used to slide down them for fun.

WHAT YOU'LL NEED

- A 3-foot-deep drift of packed snow as big as your intended igloo. (If necessary, make one: pile some snow, pack it down, and let it sit.)

- A large kitchen knife. A curved blade made of caribou antler is traditional, but few homes stock them any more. If kids are involved in your project, keep them away from the knife.

HOW YOU DO IT

1. Draw a circle in the snow as a guideline. For sleeping 4 or 5 people, make it about 9–12 feet in diameter (but smaller igloos are possible).

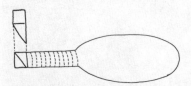

2. Draw the entrance passageway—two 6 foot parallel lines about 30–40 inches apart.

3. Cut 1–2 feet deep into the end of your two parallel lines. Remove and discard a wedge-shaped block from the end to give your igloo a ramped entrance and allow you room when cutting blocks.

4. Start cutting some building blocks from between your two cuts. Make them "curving rectangles" for the circle shape of the igloo, 1–2 feet deep, 4–6 inches thick, and as wide as your passageway. Cut and dig up to and then through the circle you've drawn.

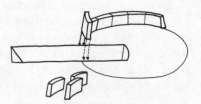

5. When you've accumulated a dozen blocks and cut out some working room inside the circle, jam one of the blocks back into the trough exactly where the opening of the igloo will go.

6. Next arrange your blocks in a layer around your circle, shaving a wedge off the bottom and sides of each so it leans inward. Each will support the others so that your walls should stay in place without additional props.

7. Before you add the next

layer of blocks, take your knife and cut two standing blocks in a diagonal from the far lower corner of one to the far upper corner of the other (see below). This allows you to place the rest of the blocks in an upward spiral.

8. From here on, you'll work

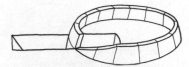

from the inside of the igloo, cutting blocks out from the "floor," shaping them, and positioning them on the spiral. After you place a block, run your knife along where it touches the other blocks. This softens the snow and smooths out irregularities, allowing for an airtight fit.

9. As you get closer to the top, you need to make your blocks more and more trapezoidal, so each layer will lean a little more toward the center.

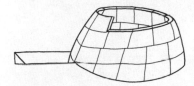

10. When your hole at top is too small for a full block, cut a custom-shaped block slightly bigger than the hole. From the inside, tilt it so you can slide it out through the opening. Standing inside the igloo, lower it into the hole while shaving it with your knife until it settles snugly in place.

11. You're now inside a fully enclosed dome. There shouldn't be any holes in the walls— if you see any, patch them with soft snow.

12. For ventilation and light, cut a small hole (up to 6 inches in diameter) into the top. If windy, put it slightly off-center, away from the wind.

13. Find the temporary block you put in the passageway, and cut a hole big enough to crawl through.

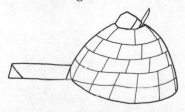

14. Inside the dome, cut blocks to enclose the passageway, creating ledges for sitting, lying, and working on. Shape the blocks so they'll curve inward, and arch them over your passageway. Save a big block for a door.

15. A candle or small lamp inside will give you light, and it will also melt a thin layer of snow, sealing the igloo walls and making it warmer.

16. **_IMPORTANT SAFETY WARNING: Never use a fire or heater inside your igloo— even with a vent hole— because you will suffocate. If using a lamp or candle, make sure that you have the doorway open and an adequate vent hole on top._**

17. If the igloo gets too stuffy from having people inside, enlarge the vent hole up to 8 inches. If it gets too cold, stuff a rag or mitten loosely into it. Don't seal it completely, though, because you want some ventilation.

18. When your igloo melts away, don't feel bad. Even in the Arctic, people use an igloo for a only month or so before abandoning it and starting over again with new snow (sure beats house-cleaning).

Great Danes

Here's a question people ask: Why didn't any of the countries conquered by Hitler refuse to go along with the Holocaust? The answer is, one did, and in a big way: Denmark.

Outgunned and vulnerable on the northern border of Germany, Denmark surrendered to the Nazis in 1940. However, unlike many other conquered countries, the Danes had no tradition of antisemitism for the Nazis to tap into. In fact, the government so strongly objected to singling out the Jews that the Nazis didn't make them wear Stars of David as in other occupied countries. (The story that they did and the King of Denmark wore one too is heartwarming, but a myth.)

When, in 1943, the Nazis did try to round up Denmark's Jews, they met with little success. Thousands of Danes banded together into a widespread conspiracy called the Freedom Council. Within days they began smuggling Jews to Sweden using fleets of cars, taxis, trucks, and fishing boats. Of the 7,500 Danish Jews, 7,000 were smuggled to safety. Meanwhile, the Danish government objected loudly about the 500 Jewish Danes who were sent to concentration camps, and probably saved lives: Of the 500, only 51 died.

Tom's Whitewash
A Classic Tale for Kids of All Ages

Mark Twain was a great observer of the best and worst of humanity.
He lays out a sly lesson in psychology in this funny story
from *The Adventures of Tom Sawyer*.

SATURDAY MORNING WAS COME, and all the summer world
was bright and fresh, and brimming with life. There was a
song in every heart; and if the heart was young the music
issued at the lips. There was cheer in every face and a spring in
every step. The locust-trees were in bloom and the fragrance of
the blossoms filled the air. Cardiff Hill, beyond the village and
above it, was green with vegetation and lay just far enough
away to seem a Delectable Land, dreamy, reposeful, and inviting.

Tom appeared on the sidewalk with a bucket of whitewash
and a long-handled brush. He surveyed the fence, and all glad-
ness left him and a deep melancholy settled down upon his
spirit. Thirty yards of board fence nine feet high. Life to him
seemed hollow, and existence but a burden. Sighing, he dipped
his brush and passed it along the topmost plank; repeated the
operation; did it again; compared the insignificant whitewashed
streak with the far-reaching continent of unwhitewashed fence,
and sat down on a tree-box discouraged.

He began to think of the fun he had planned for this day, and
his sorrows multiplied. Soon the free boys would come tripping
along on all sorts of delicious expeditions, and they would
make a world of fun of him for having to work—the very
thought of it burnt him like fire. He got out his worldly wealth
and examined it—bits of toys, marbles, and trash; enough to
buy an exchange of work, maybe, but not half enough to buy so

much as half an hour of pure freedom. So he returned his strait-
ened means to his pocket, and gave up the idea of trying to buy
the boys. At this dark and hopeless moment an inspiration
burst upon him! Nothing less than a great, magnificent inspiration.

He took up his brush and went tranquilly to work. Ben
Rogers hove in sight presently—the very boy, of all boys, whose
ridicule he had been dreading. Ben's gait was the hop-skip-and-
jump—proof enough that his heart was light and his anticipa-
tions high. He was eating an apple, and giving a long, melodi-
ous whoop, at intervals, followed by a deep-toned ding-dong-
dong, ding-dong-dong, for he was personating a steamboat. As
he drew near, he slackened speed, took the middle of the street,
leaned far over to star-board and rounded to ponderously and
with laborious pomp and circumstance—for he was personating the *Big Missouri*, and considered himself to be drawing nine
feet of water. He was boat and captain and engine-bells combined, so he had to imagine himself standing on his own hurri-
cane-deck giving the orders and executing them:

"Stop the stabboard! Ting-a-ling-ling! Stop the labboard!
Come ahead on the stabboard! Stop her! Let your outside turn
over slow! Ting-a-ling-ling! Chow-ow-ow! Get out that headline! Lively now! Come—out with your spring-line—what're
you about there! Take a turn round that stump with the bight of
it! Stand by that stage, now—let her go! Done with the engines,
sir! Ting-a-ling-ling! Sh't! s'h't! sh't!" (trying the gauge-cocks).

Tom went on whitewashing—paid no attention to the steamboat. Ben stared a moment and then said: "Hi- yi ! You're up a
stump, ain't you!"

No answer. Tom surveyed his last touch with the eye of an
artist, then he gave his brush another gentle sweep and surveyed the result, as before. Ben ranged up alongside of him.
Tom's mouth watered for the apple, but he stuck to his work.
Ben said: "Hello, old chap, you got to work, hey?"

Tom wheeled suddenly and said: "Why, it's you, Ben! I warn't
noticing."

"Say—I'm going in a-swimming, I am. Don't you wish you
could? But of course you'd druther work—wouldn't you?
Course you would!"

Tom contemplated the boy a bit, and said: "What do you call work?"

"Why, ain't that work?"

Tom resumed his whitewashing, and answered carelessly: "Well, maybe it is, and maybe it ain't. All I know, is, it suits Tom Sawyer."

"Oh come, now, you don't mean to let on that you like it?"

The brush continued to move. "Like it? Well, I don't see why I oughtn't to like it. Does a boy get a chance to whitewash a fence every day?"

That put the thing in a new light. Ben stopped nibbling his apple. Tom swept his brush daintily back and forth—stepped back to note the effect—added a touch here and there—criticized the effect again—Ben watching every move and getting more and more interested, more and more absorbed. Presently he said: "Say, Tom, let me whitewash a little."

'AIN'T THAT WORK?

Tom considered, was about to consent; but he altered his mind: "No—no—I reckon it wouldn't hardly do, Ben. You see, Aunt Polly's awful particular about this fence—right here on the street, you know—but if it was the back fence I wouldn't mind and she wouldn't. Yes, she's awful particular about this fence; it's got to be done very careful; I reckon there ain't one boy in a thousand, maybe two thousand, that can do it the way it's got to be done."

"No—is that so? Oh come, now—lemme just try. Only just a little—I'd let you, if you was me, Tom."

"Ben, I'd like to, honest injun; but Aunt Polly—well, Jim wanted to do it, but she wouldn't let him; Sid wanted to do it, and she wouldn't let Sid. Now don't you see I'm fixed? If you was to tackle this fence and anything was to happen to it—"

"Oh, shucks, I'll be just as careful. Now lemme try. Say—I'll give you the core of my apple."

"Well, here—No, Ben, now don't. I'm afeard—"

"I'll give you all of it!"

Tom gave up the brush with reluctance in his face, but alacrity in his heart. And while the late steamer Big Missouri worked and sweated in the sun, the retired artist sat on a barrel in the shade close by, dangled his legs, munched his apple, and planned the slaughter of more innocents. There was no lack of material; boys happened along every little while; they came to jeer, but remained to whitewash. By the time Ben was fagged out, Tom had traded the next chance to Billy Fisher for a kite, in good repair; and when he played out, Johnny Miller bought in for a dead rat and a string to swing it with—and so on, and so on, hour after hour. And when the middle of the afternoon came, from being a poor poverty-stricken boy in the morning, Tom was literally rolling in wealth. He had besides the things before mentioned, twelve marbles, part of a jews-harp, a piece of blue bottle-glass to look through, a spool cannon, a key that wouldn't unlock anything, a fragment of chalk, a glass stopper of a decanter, a tin soldier, a couple of tadpoles, six fire-crackers,

a kitten with only one eye, a brass door-knob, a dog-collar—but no dog—the handle of a knife, four pieces of orange-peel, and a dilapidated old window sash.

He had had a nice, good, idle time all the while—plenty of company—and the fence had three coats of whitewash on it! If he hadn't run out of whitewash he would have bankrupted every boy in the village.

Tom said to himself that it was not such a hollow world, after all. He had discovered a great law of human action, without knowing it—namely, that in order to make a man or a boy covet a thing, it is only necessary to make the thing difficult to attain. If he had been a great and wise philosopher, like the writer of this book, he would now have comprehended that Work consists of whatever a body is obliged to do, and that Play consists of whatever a body is not obliged to do. And this would help him to understand why constructing artificial flowers or performing on a tread-mill is work, while rolling ten-pins or climbing Mont Blanc is only amusement. There are wealthy gentlemen in England who drive four-horse passenger-coaches twenty or thirty miles on a daily line, in the summer, because the privilege costs them considerable money; but if they were offered wages for the service, that would turn it into work and then they would resign.

The boy mused awhile over the substantial change which had taken place in his worldly circumstances, and then wended toward headquarters to report.

THINGS JUST SOUND SMARTER IN LATIN

"Accipere quam facere praestat injuriam." (It is better to suffer an injustice than to do an injustice.) –Marcus Tullius Cicero (106–43 B.C.)

"Nec quicquam insipiente fortunato intolerabilius fieri potest." (Nothing's more insufferable than a successful fool.) –Ibid

"Amor est melle et felle est fecundissimus." (Love is rich with both honey and venom.) –Titus Maccius Plautus (250–184 B.C.)

"Bene qui latuit, bene vixit." (One who lives well, lives unnoticed.) –Publius Ovidius Naso (43 B.C.–17 A.D.)

"Crescit amor nummi, quantum ipsa pecunia crevit." (The love of wealth grows as wealth grows.) –Decimus Junius Juvenalis (A.D. 60–135)

"Facilius est multa facere quam diu." (It is easier to do many things than to do one for a long time.) –Marcus Fabius Quintilianus (A.D. 35–100)

"Hoc tempore obsequium amicos, veritas odium parit." (Nowadays friends are won through flattery, truth gives birth to hate.) –Ibid

Expert Advice

THINGS TO NEVER, EVER DO

"Never wear anything that panics the cat." — P. J. O'Rourke

"Never jog while wearing wingtips …unless you are attending the Nerd Convention in Atlantic City." — Mark Russell

"Never eat in a restaurant that's over a hundred feet off the ground and won't stand still." — Calvin Trillin

"Never eat Chinese food in Oklahoma." — David Bryan

"Never slap a man who chews tobacco." — Willard Scott

"Never commit yourself to a cheese without having first examined it." — T.S. Eliot

"Never eat anything with suction cups." — Alf

"Never touch your eye but with your elbow." — English proverb

"Never run after your own hat — others will be delighted to do it; why spoil their fun?" — Mark Twain

"Never put a razor inside your nose, even as a joke." — Jake Johansen

"Never drop your gun to hug a bear." — H. E. Palmer

"Never face facts; if you do you'll never get up in the morning." — Marlo Thomas

"Never kill a boy on the first date." — Buffy, the vampire slayer

"Never trust a computer you can't throw out a window." — Steve Wozniak

Slogos 2!

Test your knowledge of slogans and logos in this big "O" Slogo quiz. We're going to give you pictures of distinctive "O's" from the packaging of well-known products. match the "O" with the right slogan. Rated: Medium difficulty.

1

A. "And I helped"
B. "Shot from guns"
C. "They plump when you cook 'em"
D. "Uh-Oh!"
E. "dot–dot–dot, dash–dash–dash, dot–dot–dot!"

2

A. "Uh-Oh!"
B. "Do the Twist"
C. "Strong enough for a man"
D. "... not in your hand"
E. "Built Ram Tough"

3

A. "Do the Twist"
B. "And I helped"
C. "Watch it Wiggle"
D. "Shot from guns"
E. "dot–dot–dot, dash–dash–dash, dot–dot–dot!"

4

A. "Honey of an O"
B. "It's a meal in itself"
C. "They plump when you cook 'em"
D. "Strong enough for a man"
E. "... not in your hand"

5

O.

A. "It's a meal in itself"
B. "dot–dot–dot, dash–dash–dash, dot–dot–dot!"
C. "Do the Twist"
D. "Built Ram Tough"
E. "They plump when you cook 'em"

6

A. "Strong enough for a man"
B. "Shot from guns"
C. "… and she knows how to use them"
D. "I love what you do for me!"
E. "It's a meal in itself"

Answers: 1. D: You remember the old SpaghettiOs jingle: "Uh-oh, SpaghettiOs!" and "The neat new spaghetti you can eat with a spoon!" **2. B:** In 1990, Nabisco signed creator of "The Twist," Chubby Checker, to a series of commercials in which he urged tv viewers to "do the twist"; **3. C:** "Watch it wiggle; see it jiggle." It's Jell-O! **4. A:** "It's a honey of an "O," Honey Nut Cheerios." **5. B:** S.O.S scouring pads. Some people mistakenly think that the last period after the second "S" in the logo is missing by accident. Not so. The Morse code distress symbol—S.O.S.—can't be trademarked. By removing the last dot, the company was able to register the name. **6. E:** Oh Henry candy bar ads once claimed "It's a meal in itself." If you're counting calories and fat, that'd be about right.

Fat Free Diet

From The Odd Index *by Stephen Spignesi, here are the foods that are most laden with cholesterol:*

1. 3 oz. of cooked pork brains (2,169 mg)
2. 3 oz. cooked beef brains (1,746 mg.)
3. 6 oz. cooked beef sweetbreads (thymus) (1,560 mg.)
4. 1 cup egg salad (1,124 mg.)
5. 7 oz. braised lamb sweetbreads (932 mg.)
6. 1 cup stewed chicken liver (884 mg.)
7. 1 cup stewed turkey liver (876 mg.)
8. 6 oz. braised pork spleen (856 mg.)
9. 1 cup scrambled eggs (854 mg.)
10. 1 whole chicken, batter dipped and fried (810 mg.)

Corporate Tags
HOW MUCH FOR A SUCCESSFUL LOGO?

"Repetition means remembrance," says logo designer Saul Bass. A successful corporate logo can be worth billions of dollars in Pavlovian response from consumers. So how much did companies pay the designers? You may be surprised....

Company: Federal Express
Cost of logo: Almost $5,000,000
In 1992, Federal Express hired Landor & Associates, a "corporate identity" company, to update its image. After two years of tests, Landor designed a purple and orange logo featuring the company's nickname and a subliminal arrow between the E and X. The cost? "Less than $5 million," said a company official, adding that it's worth the money because the mark on all those double-parked trucks is the equivalent of $160 million in outdoor advertising.

Company: Nike
Cost of logo: $35
When Nike was trying to get a foothold in 1971, the founders decid-ed that their shoes needed a distinctive marking like the Adidas stripes, so they hired Carolyn Davis, an art student from Portland State. The founders were at first unenthusiastic about her design but didn't have time to revise it. Since then, the "swoosh" has graced a zillion pieces of sporting equipment. For her work, Davis got $35, which doesn't sound like much, but it's a fortune compared to the 20–30¢ an hour that Nike pays its workers in Third World countries.

Company: Coca-Cola
Cost of logo: $0
The lifespan of a logo is typically fifteen to twenty years, but good ones can last much longer. In 1887, Coke's advertising director, Frank Robinson, had an annual budget of only $150. Robinson, who had named the drink a

few years earlier, saved money by drawing the logo himself. His reward? Robinson believed that he was an owner in the fledgling company, but his "partners" sold the company to tycoon Asa Candler and ran. Robinson, now broke, continued on as advertising director, making Coke the most successful soft drink ever. However, when Candler's nephew decided he wanted the ad director job in 1906, Robinson was moved into a meaningless position until he retired in 1913.

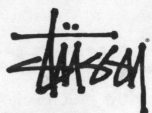

Company: Stussy
Cost of logo: $0
Californian beach boy Shawn Stussy first designed surfboards, but later branched out more successfully into clothes.The graffiti-like logo has umlauts to give it that heavy-metal band look and to increase the chance that people pronounce the name right. "It's his real signature," insists a Stussy spokesman. "He even signs his checks with it."

Company: MTV
Cost of logo: $1,000
A rock music channel was an unlikely joint venture of American Express and Warner Communications. They wanted to call it "TV-1," but the name was already taken. Second choice was TV-M (Television Music), until programming director Steve Casey suddenly blurted out, "Don't you think that MTV sounds better than TV-M?" They sent the name out to several designers, but especially liked one from a small shop called Manhattan Design. For their efforts, the designers walked away with a measly grand.

Company: Lucent
Cost of logo: Secret, but more than FedEx
AT&T hired Landor & Associates to provide a new identity for its new spinoff. Landor winnowed fifty names from a list of 700 possibilities and screened them for obnoxious connotations in nine countries and thirteen languages. They used a similar process with logo designs. Several

million dollars later, Landor came up with a name that means "clear" or "glowing" in English, and a logo that's been compared to a coffee stain. Lucent Technologies launched itself with a $50 million ad campaign.

Company: Playboy
Cost of logo: $0
When Hugh Hefner launched *Playboy* in the early 1960s, he chose the rabbit as his mascot because of its reputation as an unusually sexual creature. As part of his regular duties, art director Arthur Paul sketched out a simple black and white design that would look good as a tiny dingbat at the bottom of stories, but the image's size grew as its popularity grew, making its way to every cover for four

decades. Playboy licensed it to manufacturers, and it has appeared on everything from pinball machines to air fresheners.

Company: Ben & Jerry's
Cost of logo: $6 an hour
When Ben Cohen and Jerry Greenfield began packaging their ice cream, they needed a logo and package design but didn't have much money. Vermont designer Lyn Severance came up with a homemade look that fit their philosophy as well as their budget, using hand lettering and hand-drawn lines. This was fine with Jerry and Ben because it was cheaper to put her on staff at $6 an hour than buy typesetting and border tape.

Hot & Culinary

• "The hymn 'Onward Christian Soldiers,' sung to the right tune and in a not-too-brisk tempo, makes a very good egg timer. If you put the egg into boiling water and sing all five verses and chorus, the egg will be just right when you come to Amen." —Letter to the *London Daily Telegraph*

• "If you intend to tap a sugar maple tree for syrup, keep in mind that it should be at least 40 years old, 60 feet tall, and a foot wide. Each tree will yield about 10 gallons of sap; when boiled down, these 10 gallons will become one quart of syrup." —*American Farm Companion*

Pot Shots

Some of our favorite bathroom shots. Send us yours! (See page 478.)

a. Straddle toilet in Kenya (note feet)
b. Nevada ghost town outhouses
c. Outhouse at Anchor Bay, Malta
d. Sign at Glacier National Park
e. Extra-tall in Brazil
f. Rustic outhouse in Baja, Mexico

Vrooom!

HOW THE HARLEY BECAME AMERICA'S BIKE

Whether a Hells Angel or a mild-mannered desk jockey, for many
motorcyclists only a noisy, rough-riding Harley can fuel
their outlaw dreams.

MOST MOTORCYCLISTS LIVE A CERTAIN CONTRADICTION: They
swear they're just law-abiding folk who like to ride ...
but at the same time cherish the biker image that
transforms mild-mannered CPAs and computer nerds into
weekend outlaws. And outlaws drive Harleys; that's the way it
is. Even Sonny Barger, longtime head of the Hells Angels, told a
reporter that he likes Japanese bikes better, but drives a Harley
because of pressure from the other members of the club.

But it wasn't always so. Motorcycles were once just a cheap
way of getting around town, and Harley-Davidson was once
just a small start-up in a Milwaukee shack.

WHEEL-LIFE ADVENTURES

Putting a motor on a bicycle seemed like a logical idea from the
early days of steam engines. The problem was getting the
engine small enough to fit on a
bike and powerful enough to
move it. When that first happened
still isn't clear, but the earliest
known attempt is pictured in an
1818 drawing of a steam-powered
"Velocipedraisiavaporianna"
being tested in Paris's
Luxembourg Gardens. In 1869,
both a French team and American

French steam velocipede, 1869

Sylvester Roper successfully built "steam velocipedes" that could go faster than a horse.

However, there were some problems with the steam-powered bikes. They didn't have much power, for one. For another, they had a tendency to explode now and then. And even at their best, you had to continuously add water and coal into the hissing, smoking engine between your legs. Inventors looked for other approaches. For example, the "Cynosphere," invented by M. Huret of Paris in 1875, was powered by two dogs running on the wheels.

Dogs on hogs: The Cynosphere

Finally, in 1876, the internal combustion gasoline engine came into being, thanks to N. A. Otto of Germany. Nine years later, his former assistant, Gottlieb Daimler, fathered the first modern motorcycle. Not that it was perfect—the spark plug had not yet been invented, and so

to ignite the gas and air mixture, Daimler provided a Bunsen burner to heat up a metal tube that extended into the engine's cylinder. The problem, of course, was that the flame occasionally blew out in the wind. Worse, it would occasionally catch the rider's pants on fire or, in the event of dumping the bike, ignite spilled gasoline. Then came 1895, a year that brought the twin miracles of electrical ignition and inflatable tires.

Motorcycles began evolving away from being merely bicycles with motors strapped to them. In 1901, a French company designed a motorcycle in which the engine was not just a clip-on, but an integral part of the design. The designers were so confident that their motor would dependably propel the cycle that they even left off the bicycle pedals. This design was the true forerunner of the modern motorcycle, the one the world copied ... including some young guys in a shack in Milwaukee.

HARLEY-DAVIDSON-DAVIDSON ...
In 1901, Arthur Davidson, a twenty-year-old pattern maker, teamed up with a

twenty-one-year-old drafts-
man named Bill Harley.
Inspired by the European
motorcycles, they decided to
tinker after work hours on
their own design.

The two partners recruited
a second Davidson brother
(Walter, a railroad machinist)
and then a third (William, a
toolmaker). Rounding out the
team with ideas and advice
was a friend named Ole
Evinrude (who later went off
and started his own company
that made Evinrude outboard
boat motors).

SCARING THE HORSES

Needing a place to work, the
Davidson boys convinced
their father, a cabinet maker,
to build a shed in their backyard. They put together a
two-horsepower engine from
scrounged scraps (including a
tomato-can carburetor) and
attached it to a bicycle. Eventually they worked out the
bugs and began tooling
around town at 25 mph on
motorized bicycles, amazing
the citizens and scaring the
horses. Pretty soon, people
started asking if the bikes
were for sale. The company
sold three motorcycles in its
first year.

The after-hours business

grew slowly. From three
motorcycles in 1903, the company increase its output 66
percent the following year,
assembling five motorcycles,
and then again 60 percent the
following year, making eight.

This dizzying growth curve
convinced the partners to
build a new, 28-by-80-foot
headquarters next to a rail
spur. Unfortunately, they discovered afterward that they'd

World headquarters, 1903

built it dangerously close to
the track. Rather than dis-
mantle it, they got together a
dozen of their huskiest
friends and had them lift the
building a legal distance
away. (The company head-
quarters still stands on this
site, a safe distance from the
tracks.)

Meanwhile, the partners
decided they needed some
capital so they could quit
their day jobs. They turned to
another Davidson, who the
boys called their "honey
uncle" because he was a bee-

keeper, and borrowed enough to get serious about manufacturing their bikes.

Ironically, Harley's first model was designed to be unobtrusive and quiet. The partners had decided that people hated the noise and flash of the new contraptions, so William designed a grey motorcycle and an effective muffler. The result was dubbed "The Silent Grey Fellow." While the company sold all they could make, the silence was short-lived. It turned out that motorcyclists *liked* making a disturbance.

In 1907, when annual production was up to 150 units, William Harley accidentally created Harley's distinctively

The Silent Grey Fellow

rough staccato "potato-potato" engine sound. It was the result of taking a fairly inept design shortcut while trying to increase engine power. Rather than designing a two-cylinder engine from scratch, he merely welded a second cylinder to his one-cylinder design, using a forked connecting rod to join both pistons to a single crankshaft "throw." The result was an engine that ran rough and produced an excessive amount of vibration ... which, for better or worse, has become the famous sound and feel of a Harley.

Despite the odd engine design, Harleys became the heavyweight bike of choice for American motorcyclists, accounting for more than half of U.S. sales.

In the century since its founding, the company walks a tightrope between keeping its traditional outlaw biker market happy and also selling hogs to the rebel dentists, lawyers, and CPAs who make up a large part of their customer base now. Whether they can keep pleasing everybody without ending up pleasing nobody remains to be seen. Still, the Harley mystique continues, even as their owners cheerfully complain about them. For example: "Harleys leak oil, they vibrate bad, and you can't turn the things," groused one biker to *Forbes*. So why does he keep buying them? "You get laid."

Change Your Looks
A Spy Manual from 1944 Tells How

This not-so-politically-correct manual from the Office of Strategic Services (forerunner to the CIA) suggests that all you really need to disguise yourself are newspapers, spirit gum, make-up, rubber tubing, and a couple of pencil erasers. Here's how to use them.

O NE MAIN POINT should be stressed again and again: **Disguise must be to a great extent an *internal* matter. The less there is of it on the outside, the better.** First: You must study yourself and check up on your habits. Each individual has peculiar mannerisms. They must be analyzed and eliminated. Second: You must know your cover story thoroughly. Keep in mind that if you tell a lie often enough you believe it yourself.

The type of clothes you will be wearing will determine, to some degree, the amount of change you can make. It will be much easier to switch from a bank clerk to a tramp, for example, than vice versa. Consider also the district you have to pass through in making your escape. If it is the wharves, you will be less noticeable as a seaman or a stevedore. If it is the financial district, become the most typical of clerks. Be one of the crowd.

SHAPE OF BODY

To make yourself taller, $2-2^1/_2$ inches can be quickly added to your height by folding a newspaper to form a ramp in the heels of your shoes. Such ramps offer an added advantage in that they also change your walk and posture. Restyle the crown of your hat, using its complete height. Hoist your trousers way up and tighten the belt. This will make your legs look longer. Pull your collar down, showing as much neck as you can.

To appear shorter, the reverse of everything above should be done. Also, slump down and bend your knees a bit.

FACE, HAIR, AND HANDS

Pick out your most prominent features. These are the ones to disguise. Wads of cotton or paper between the teeth and cheeks will change a thin face to a fuller one. Under the upper or lower lip, or both, will radically change the profile.

A nose can be narrowed by shadowing it on both sides and highlighting the top down its length. A narrow nose is widened or twisted by the use of nose plugs. These can be made of rubber tubing, approximately one-half inch in outside diameter and cut into half-inch lengths. Place them in the nostrils just up out of sight, being careful not to let them slip into the nasal cavity. The firm upper part of a baby's rubber nipple can be used.

If you are wearing a mustache, remove it or cut it down to a stubble so that it loses its previous character. If you don't have one, it is possible to make one on the spot in a few minutes, using your own body hair, provided you have taken the trouble to carry with you a small vial of liquid adhesive or spirit gum. If you have glasses put them on or remove them.

A good swarthy or dirty skin color can be had by wetting your hands and rubbing them on an old piece of rusty iron. Its advantages are readily apparent when one realizes that when white officers and men go in with native troops, it is usually the white faces that the Japs shoot at first. Don't forget the hands. They too much match.

Soot from inside a water heater or stove pipe can darken the eyebrows and hair. Try using a little of the black mixed with the rust to accentuate "bags" under the eyes, hollows in cheeks, or even a broken nose effect.

For graying hair, mustache, or eyebrows, try grey ashes powdered by rubbing them in the palm of the hand; try talcum powder, flour, or shoe-white. The effect of a stubble beard is best put on by using a dark thick grease and a rough sponge.

POSTURE AND GAIT

If you have round shoulders, a "figure eight" cord around both arms and crossed in the back, will serve as a reminder to throw out your chest and stand up straight. Tying your suspenders together high up in the back will do the same thing to a lesser extent.

If you want round shoulders, cross the figure eight cord in front. Try the old trick of buttoning your pants to your vest to acquire a stoop. Another way is a strip of adhesive plaster stuck from just above the navel up to the hair on the chest, applied while slouched over. Then try to straighten up!

Even without making a clothes change, a student can assume a completely different cover merely by changing his gait and switching to the exact opposite of the tempo used in the first cover. Start now to observe how men of different classes of society and age sit, stand and walk. One section of the crowd will move with a purpose, preoccupied with their own important little lives. Another group will slouch or waddle along, like dully curious animals. Any little object catches their interest for a fleeting moment. They have no goals in life and every movement and line of their bodies show it.

Building up the inside of one shoe-heel will give a "short-leg" limp. With the same device it is easy to assume the walk of someone who has been paralyzed on one side. Build up your left heel about $1^1/_2$ inches, crook your right arm into a useless set, drop the right shoulder, and swing the right half-dead leg forward. Be sure your face has that drooped, dull, set expression of one who has had a stroke. The eyes are usually all that move, with a bewildered, anxious expression as though the person does not quite know what has happened to him. This cover, if not overplayed, has a good psychological angle because one's natural impulse is to look away from such cripples.

A small stone in one sock heel will produce a convincing limp. Slightly larger ones in the arch of each foot will produce a "fiat foot" walk. Detachable rubber pencil erasers are best for this because they do not bruise the foot so much over a period of time. Putting them inside the sock helps keep them in place. For an "old age" gait, try a tight bandage around the calf of your leg with something under it to hurt the muscle as the weight is put on that foot.

Try the "lost arm," which is best done when wearing a double-breasted coat. Take the left arm from the coat sleeve. Tuck the empty sleeve in the coat pocket. Hold the elbow close to the waist at the side front and put your forearm around your waist with the left hand resting on the right hip.

WOMEN STUDENTS

While many of the suggestions outlined in this volume are applicable to both men and women students, the following section is written solely for the women.

A change of hair style is one of the most simple and effective aids in changing a woman's appearance. The style chosen should be one that a woman can arrange herself without recourse to a beauty parlor. An important point to remember is that the most unbecoming hair style will probably change the wearer's appearance more than any other.

It should be borne in mind that in many parts of the world women do not get or use much make-up. If lipstick is used, however, making a different lip line will alter the appearance greatly, as will changing the shape of the eyebrows.

If a woman does not want to be noticed, she should strive to look mousy or old or dumpy. If the work calls for glamour, an expert on make-up should be consulted. A woman who normally chooses bright and colorful clothes should change to something darker, say a grey dress or suit. The point is to achieve a complete contrast from the clothes usually worn.

Before   After

A woman of 30–40 years of age can easily add 10–15 years to her apparent age. She should clean off all make-up, wrinkle up her face, and with a very sharp brown eyebrow pencil lightly line all of the creases. Rub these down to the point where they are only soft shadows. A very thin application of the brown pencil mixed with Max Factor's No. 6 blue-grey liner, close to the bridge of the nose and accentuating circles under the eyes, will add to the effect. Next, a light-colored make-up should be used on all the high spots—the cheek bones, nose, chin and the tops of all wrinkles, care being taken to blend all edges out. If any lipstick is used at all, it should be thin and light-colored and blotted off. Next, the lips should be puckered and powder added on top of the lipstick. If the student wears dental plates or removable bridges, she should take them out. The neck and hands must not be overlooked; all must tie in together. A little hair white should be combed in at the temples or streaked through the whole head and the hair done up in an older style.

PERMANENT DISGUISE
Permanent disguise requires the services of a plastic surgeon. Its use has been successfully employed on a particularly noticeable feature, such as a prominent nose, ears that stick far out, or an easily remembered scar, that might be recognized on returning to the field.

Surgery has been used to alter the racial characteristics of Jewish students. Broken, bulbous and sharp Roman noses have also been successfully changed to shapes less eye-catching.

Prominent ears are dealt with by pinning them back. This leaves a small inconspicuous scar where the skin joins the ear to the head.

Scars should always be eliminated if possible. They can be removed surgically by a specialist without requiring hospitalization. An operation lasting two to three hours and removal of stitches after seven to ten days are all that are necessary.

Tattoo marks are extremely difficult to remove. The process is long and painful and is not recommended. A more satisfactory treatment is re-tattooing with a larger, more elaborate design. Skillful blending can achieve very satisfactory results. It has the advantage of speed and there is much less discomfort to the subject.

Listen Up

MORE LIFE ADVICE FROM THE RICH & FAMOUS

"You can't be happy with a woman who pronounces both Ds in Wednesday." — Peter DeVries

"Money is better than poverty, if only for financial reasons." — Woody Allen

"All Southern literature can be summed up in these words: 'On the night the hogs ate Willie, Mama died when she heard what Daddy did to sister.'" — Pat Conroy's mother (according to Pat)

"Don't tap your foot, it makes your arms get tired." — Thelonious Monk

"When in doubt, sing loud." — Robert Merrill

"Eat cereal for breakfast and write good prose." — Raymond Carver

"When you are smashing monuments, save the pedestals. They always come in handy." — Stanislaw Lec

"Cynicism is more than a pose; it's also a handy time saver. By deflating your companion's enthusiasm, you can cut conversations in half." — Lisa Birnbach

"Live each moment as if your hair is on fire." — Suzannah B. Troy

"I've always wanted to be somebody. But now I see I should have been more specific." — Jane Wagner

"I don't know the key to success, but the key to failure is to try to please everyone." — Bill Cosby

"The thermometer of success is the level of jealousy from the malcontents." — Salvador Dali

Elephant Jokes

WHY DO ELEPHANTS HAVE FLAT FEET?

Elephant jokes were a fad in the mid-1960s. Their surreal humor—half non-sequitur, half Zen koan—matched the tone of the times perfectly.

How do elephants communicate? *They talk on the elephone.*

How can you tell if an elephant's been in your refrigerator? *His footprints are in the Jell-O.*

How can you tell if two elephants have been in your refrigerator? *There are two sets of footprints in the Jell-O.*

How can you tell if three elephants are in your refrigerator? *The door won't close.*

How many hippos will fit in the refrigerator? *None. There are too many elephants in there.*

How do you make an elephant float? *Two scoops of ice-cream, a bottle of cola, and one elephant.*

Why do elephants paint their toenails red? *So they can hide in the strawberry patch.*

But there aren't any elephants in the strawberry patch! *See? It's working.*

How do you get an elephant to the top of an oak tree? *Plant an acorn under him and wait fifty years.*

How do you get an elephant down from an oak tree? *Tell him to sit on a leaf and wait until fall.*

What's the difference between an elephant and an egg? *You don't know? I guess I'm not sending YOU to the store!*

What do you do with a blue elephant? *Cheer him up.*

How do you keep an elephant from charging? *Take away his credit cards.*

Why were the elephants kicked off the beach? *They were walking around with their trunks down.*

Why do ducks have flat feet? *From stomping out forest fires.*

Why do elephants have flat feet? *From stomping out burning ducks.*

How do you get down from an elephant? *You don't — you get down from a duck.*

I Curse Thee!

"Ye little gayle hather mammothrept!" Jeffrey Racirk, author of the *Long Lost Insults Knowledge Cards*, has compiled an extensive list of long-forgotten English slurs. Test-marketed on our siblings and friends, here are some of our favorites.

GUDDLER: "A greedy drinker, one who is fond of liquor: [from] guddle, to drink much and greedily." — James Jennings's *Dialect of Somersetshire*, 1869

MUNZ-WATCHER: "One of those sneaks that makes a practice of watching the movements, etc., of sweethearts on their nightly walks, and if any impropriety is witnessed, demanding hush-money to keep the matter secret." — Joseph Wright's *English Dialect Dictionary*, 1896–1905

RUM-DAGGER: "A cheat who tells wonderful stories of his sufferings at sea to obtain money." — Admiral William Smyth's *Sailor's Word-book*, 1867

SHEEP-BITER: "A poor, sorry, sneaking, ill-lookt fellow." — B.E.'s *Dictionary of the Canting Crew*, 1698–1699

SLACKUMTRANCE: "A slovenly or dirty woman." — W. H. Long's *Dictionary of the Isle of Wight Dialect*, 1886

THEOLOGASTER: "A quack in theology; a shallow or pretended theologian." — William Whitney's *Century Dictionary*, 1889

ZOUNDERKITE: "Usually applied to one whose stupid conduct results in awkward mistakes." — C. Clough Robinson's *Dialect of Mid-Yorkshire*, 1876

Fabled Humans

AESOP TALES WITH PEOPLE IN THEM

Most Aesop fables use animals to tell a story and deliver a lesson, but they occasionally include humans, sometimes at their worst and sometimes at their best.

THE WOODMAN AND THE SERPENT

One wintry day a Woodman was tramping home from his work when he saw something black lying on the snow. When he came closer he saw it was a Serpent to all appearance dead. But he took it up and put it in his bosom to warm while he hurried home. As soon as he got indoors he put the Serpent down on the hearth before the fire. The children watched it and saw it slowly come to life again. Then one of them stooped down to stroke it, but the Serpent raised its head and put out its fangs and was about to sting the child to death. So the Woodman seized his axe, and with one stroke cut the Serpent in two. "Ah," said he,

"No gratitude from the wicked."

THE WOLF AND THE KID

A Child was perched up on the top of a house, and looking down saw a Wolf passing under him. Immediately he began to revile and attack his enemy. "Murderer and thief," he cried, "what do you here near honest folks' houses? How dare you make an appearance where your vile deeds are known?"

"Curse away, my young friend," said the Wolf.

"It is easy to be brave from a safe distance."

THE MAN AND THE WOOD

A Man came into a Wood one day with an axe in his hand, and begged all the Trees to give him a small branch which he wanted for a particular purpose. The Trees were good-natured and gave him one of their branches. What did the Man do but fix it into the axe head, and soon set to work cutting down tree after tree. Then the Trees saw how foolish they had been.

Don't give an enemy the means to destroy you.

"But a Wolf actually did come..."

THE SHEPHERD BOY

There was once a young Shepherd Boy who tended his sheep at the foot of a mountain near a dark forest. It was rather lonely for him all day, so he thought upon a plan by which he could get a little company and some excitement. He rushed down toward the village calling out "Wolf, Wolf," and the villagers came out to meet him, and some of them stopped with him for a considerable time. This pleased the boy so much that a few days afterward he tried the same trick, and again the villagers came to his help. But shortly after this a Wolf actually did come out from the forest, and began to worry the sheep, and the boy of course cried out, "Wolf, Wolf," still louder than before. But this time the villagers, who had been fooled twice before, thought the boy was again deceiving them, and nobody stirred to come to his help. So the Wolf made a good meal off the boy's flock, and when the boy complained, the wise man of the village said:

"A liar will not be believed, even when he speaks the truth."

THE THIEF AND HIS MOTHER

A young Man had been caught in a daring act of theft and had been condemned to be executed for it. He expressed his desire to see his Mother, and to speak with her before he was led to execution, and of course this was granted. When his Mother came to him he said: "I want to whisper to you," and when she brought her ear near him, he nearly bit it off. All the bystanders were horrified, and asked him what he could mean by such brutal and inhuman conduct. "It is to punish her," he said. "When I was young I began with stealing little things, and brought them home to Mother. Instead of rebuking and punishing me, she laughed and said: 'It will not be noticed.' It is because of her that I am here today."

"He is right, woman," said the Priest; "the gods hath said:

"Train up a child in the way he should go; and when he is old he will not depart therefrom."

THE MAN AND HIS TWO WIVES

In the old days, when men were allowed to have many wives, a middle-aged Man had one wife who was old and one who was young; each loved him very much, and desired to see him like herself. Now the Man's hair was turning grey, which the young Wife did not like, as it made him look too old for her husband. So every night she used to comb his hair and pick out the white ones. But the elder Wife saw her husband growing grey with great pleasure, for she did not like to be mistaken for his mother. So every morning she used to arrange his hair and pick out as many of the black ones as she could. The consequence was the Man soon found himself entirely bald.

Yield to all and you will soon have nothing to yield.

TWO FELLOWS AND A BEAR

Two Fellows were traveling together through a wood, when a Bear rushed out upon them. One of the travelers happened to be in front, and he seized hold of the branch of a tree, and hid himself among the leaves. The other, seeing no help for it, threw himself flat down upon the ground, with his face in the dust. The Bear, coming up to him, put his muzzle close to his ear, and sniffed and sniffed. But at last with a growl he shook his head and slouched off, for bears will not touch dead meat. Then the fellow in the tree came down to his comrade, and, laughing, said "What was it that Master Bruin whispered to you?"

"He told me," said the other,

"Never trust a friend who deserts you at a pinch."

THE MILKMAID AND HER PAIL

Patty the Milkmaid was going to market carrying her milk in a Pail on her head. As she went along she began calculating what she would do with the money she would get for the milk. "I'll buy some fowls from Farmer Brown," said she, "and they will lay eggs each morning, which I will sell to the parson's wife. With the money that I get from the sale of these eggs I'll buy myself a new dimity frock and a chip hat; and when I go to market, won't all the young men come up and speak to me! Polly Shaw will be that jealous; but I don't care. I shall just look at her and toss my head like this." As she spoke she tossed her head back, the Pail fell off it, and all the milk was spilt. So she had to go home and tell her mother what had occurred.

"Ah, my child," said the mother,

"Do not count your chickens before they are hatched."

THE MAN BITTEN BY A DOG

A man who had been bitten by a Dog went about in quest of someone who might heal him. A friend, meeting him and learning what he wanted, said, "If you would be cured, take a piece of bread, and dip it in the blood from your wound, and go and give it to the Dog that bit you." The Man who had been bitten laughed at this advice and said, "Why? If I should do so, it would be as if I should beg every Dog in the town to bite me."

Benefits bestowed upon the evil-disposed increase their means of injuring you.

OLD WOMAN AND THE WINE JAR

You must know that sometimes old women like a glass of wine. One of this sort once found a Wine Jar lying in the road, and eagerly went up to it hoping to find it full. But when she took it up she found that all the wine had been drunk out of it. Still she took a long sniff at the mouth of the Jar. "Ah," she cried,

"What memories cling 'round the instruments of our pleasure."

"Go, give it to the Dog that bit you."

Stately Knowledge

12 REASONS WHY YA GOTTA LOVE RHODE ISLAND

We've searched the vaults and come up with some pretty impressive
facts and stories about Rhode Island. Here are a
dozen of our favorites.

1 It's the smallest state in the country. It has the shortest slogan of all the states: "Hope." But it has the longest official
name: "State of Rhode Island and Provid-
ence Plantations."

2 Rhode Island would fit inside the
state of Alaska 483 times.

3 Despite the name, Rhode Island is
not an island like Hawaii. It does,
however, have thirty-six islands along its
coast. In 1524, explorer Giovanni da
Verrazzano decided that one of them
looked like the island of Rhodes in
Greece, and so he called it Rhode Island.
The name got stuck on the whole region.

4 Rhode Island was founded on the idea of tolerance for *all*
religions and fair treatment of the Indians by Roger
Williams. Those were both shockingly controversial ideas at the
time, so most other American settlements shunned contact with
Rhode Island. Rhode Island can claim both the first Baptist
church, founded by Williams himself in 1639, and the oldest
synagogue in America, the Touro Synagogue in Newport, established in 1763.

5 You'll have a problem, though, if you want to see Roger William's gravesite. His earthly remains were eaten by an apple tree. Centuries after his death, the Rhode Island Historical Society wanted to bury him in a better resting place, but when they dug up his grave they discovered that Williams was completely gone, bones and all. An apple tree's roots had entered his coffin near his head and—apparently liking what it found—grew down his spine, even branching into his legs and arms.

6 Famous Rhode Islanders include songwriter George M. Cohan, (he wrote "You're a Grand Old Flag" and "I'm a Yankee Doodle Dandy"), painter Gilbert Stuart (his portraits of Washington are on the dollar bill and quarter), actors Van Johnson, Harry Anderson, James Wood, Anthony Quinn, and political commentator John McLaughlin.

7 More silverware is produced in Providence, Rhode Island, than anywhere else on Earth.

8 Rhode Island's state bird is a common chicken— the Rhode Island Red, bred in the village of Adamsville in Little Compton. You can see a granite monument with an image of the chicken on it. How can you tell if your morning eggs are from a Rhode Island Red? The shells are brown instead of white.

9 Newport, Rhode Island firsts: First game of polo played in America (1876). First jail sentence for speeding in an automobile (August, 1904). First circus in the United States (1774). The country's oldest tavern (the White Horse, 1673). And the first street illuminated by gas lights (Pelham Street, 1806).

10 Rhode Island's Official State Drink is "Coffee Milk"—half coffee, half milk, heavily sugared.

11 You may have been to Disney World, but how about Dairy World? It's really just the Nature's Best Dairy plant—featuring factory tours and dairy museum— in Cranston, Rhode Island.

12 The world's largest toy company, Hasbro, is headquartered in Pawtucket, Rhode Island. One of their bigger selling toys, Mr. Potato Head, was named the state's Official Travel Ambassador by the governor.

Dotty Detours

W. C. Privy's "Don't Miss" Attractions

Next time you head out to visit the Grand Canyon, Niagara Falls, or Disney World, don't forget to add these places to your Must-See list.

BEAN FEST & CHAMPIONSHIP OUTHOUSE RACE
Mountain View, Alaska
Cost: Free admission, cornbread, and beans

This event takes place on the last Saturday in October. Lots of beans and fast-rolling outhouses; the winner gets a gold-painted toilet seat.

THE HAIR MUSEUM
In the office of Lelia Cohoon, College of Cosmetology, Independence, Missouri
Cost: $3, but you get a discount on a hair cut

Lelia opened The Hair Museum to honor the old artistic tradition of hair art, which reached its height of popularity at the turn of the twentieth century. At this museum you'll find wreaths, butterflies, bracelet, and flower arrangements, among other things.

THE TOILET SEAT ART MUSEUM
239 Abiso, Alamo Heights, Texas
Cost: Free

"Doc" Barney Smith—a lifelong plumber and artist—has painted well over 650 toilet seats, and displayed them in his garage for folks to come and take a gander at. None are for sale. Open most afternoons, but call first: 210-824-7791.

TOILET ROCK

City of Rocks, New Mexico
Cost: No fee for daytime use, small camping fee

The name says it all: It's a rock shaped like a giant toilet.

LINGERIE MUSEUM AND CELEBRITY LINGERIE HALL OF FAME

Behind Frederick's of Hollywood store, Hollywood, California
Cost: Free

Here you'll see negligees once owned by Mae West and Loni Anderson, Madonna's bustier, and bras worn by Cher, Phyllis Diller, and Natalie Wood. Also a pair of Robert Redford's striped boxers, and other celebrity scanties.

THE DONNER PARTY MUSEUM

Donner Memorial State Park, Truckee, California
Cost: $1

Today it's called the Emigrant Trail Museum and Statue, dedicated to the pioneering spirit. However, that's been a recent change. The museum still heavily features the Donner Party's badly planned journey that ended up in misery, wintry deaths, and cannibalism.

THE MUSEUM OF QUESTIONABLE MEDICAL DEVICES

Science Museum of Minnesota, St. Paul, Minnesota

Cost: $7 adults, $5 kids and seniors

Here's a blurb from the museum's Web site: "The world's largest display of what the human mind has devised to cure itself without the benefit of either scientific method or common sense."

THE SPAM MUSEUM

1937 Spam Blvd., Austin, Minnesota
Cost: Free

Austin is the hometown of George A. Hormel's first meat-processing plant (opened in 1891). You enter the museum through a huge Spam can, and are greeted with case after case of packaging, old advertisements, and artifacts.

THE TESTICLE FESTIVAL

Just outside Clinton, Montana
Cost: $10 for five-day pass

In mid-September the Rock Creek Lodge hosts a Testicle Festival, honoring the eating of bull testicles ("Rocky Mountain Oysters").This one may not be fit for the kids, since public nudity, drinking, and general acting out seems to be a large part of the celebration. "In addition to 'nuts,'" says the Web site, "the festival provides chicken, music, group games and a little bit of 'crazy.'"

Tales of Gods

AESOP'S FABLES ABOUT DEITIES

Considering how much the ancient Greeks valued their gods, it's surprising there aren't more in Aesop's fables. We searched heaven and earth for these.

AVARICE AND ENVY

Two neighbors came before Jupiter and prayed him to grant their hearts' desire. Now the one was full of avarice, and the other eaten up with envy. So to punish them both, Jupiter granted that each might have whatever he wished for himself, but only on condition that his neighbor had twice as much. The Avaricious man prayed to have a room full of gold. No sooner said than done; but all his joy was turned to grief when he found that his neighbor had two rooms full of the precious metal. Then came the turn of the Envious man, who could not bear to think that his neighbor had any joy at all. So he prayed that he might have one of his own eyes put out, by which means his companion would become totally blind.

Vices are their own punishment.

HERCULES AND THE WAGONER

A Wagoner was once driving a heavy load along a very muddy way. At last he came to a part of the road where the wheels sank halfway into the mire, and the more the horses pulled, the deeper sank the wheels. So the Wagoner threw down his whip, and knelt down and prayed to Hercules the Strong. "O Hercules, help me in this my hour of distress," quoth he. But Hercules appeared to him, and said:"Tut, man, don't sprawl there. Get up and put your shoulder to the wheel:

"The gods help them that help themselves."

MERCURY AND THE WOODMAN

A Woodman was felling a tree on the bank of a river, when his axe, glancing off the trunk, flew out of his hands and fell into the water. As he stood by the water's edge lamenting his loss, Mercury appeared and asked him the reason for his grief. On learning what had happened, out of pity for his distress, Mercury dived into the river and, bringing up a golden axe, asked him if that was the one he had lost. The Woodman replied that it was not, and Mercury then dived a second time, and, bringing up a silver axe, asked if that was his. "No, that is not mine either," said the Woodman. Once more Mercury dived into the river, and brought up the missing axe. The Woodman was overjoyed at recovering his property, and thanked his benefactor warmly; and the latter was so pleased with his honesty that he made him a present of the other two axes. When the Woodman told the story to his companions, one of these was filled with envy of his good fortune and determined to try his luck for himself. So he went and began to fell a tree at the edge of the river, and presently contrived to let his axe drop into the water. Mercury appeared as before, and, on learning that his axe had fallen in, he dived and brought up a golden axe, as he had done on the previous occasion. Without waiting to be asked whether it was his or not, the fellow cried, "That's mine, that's mine," and stretched out his hand eagerly for the prize: but Mercury was so disgusted at his dishonesty that he not only declined to give him the golden axe, but also refused to recover for him the one he had let fall into the stream.

Honesty is the best policy.

THE OLD MAN AND DEATH

An old laborer, bent double with age and toil, was gathering sticks in a forest. At last he grew so tired and hopeless that he threw down the bundle of sticks, and cried out: "I cannot bear this life any longer. Ah, I wish Death would only come and take me!"

As he spoke, Death, a grisly skeleton, appeared and said to him: "What wouldst thou, Mortal? I heard thee call me."

"Please, sir," replied the woodcutter, "would you kindly help me to lift this bundle of sticks onto my shoulder?"

We would often be sorry if our wishes were gratified.

THE MAN AND THE SATYR

A man and a Satyr once drank together in token of a bond of alliance being formed between them. One very cold wintry day, as they talked, the Man put his fingers to his mouth and blew on them. When the Satyr asked the reason for this, he told him that he did it to warm his hands because they were so cold. Later on in the day they sat down to eat, and the food prepared was quite scalding. The Man raised one of the dishes a little towards his mouth and blew in it. When the Satyr again inquired the reason, he said that he did it to cool the meat, which was too hot. "I can no longer consider you as a friend," said the Satyr:

"A friend should not with the same breath blow hot and cold."

THE MAN AND THE WOODEN GOD

Long ago men used to worship sticks, stones and idols, and prayed to them for luck. It happened that a Man had often prayed to a wooden idol he had received from his father, but his luck never changed. He prayed and prayed, but still he remained unlucky. One day in a great rage he went to the Wooden God, and with a blow swept it down from its pedestal. The idol broke in two, and what did he see? An immense number of coins that had been inside all the time.

Having no god is better than one that does no good.

Juno refused the peacock's request.

THE PEACOCK AND JUNO

A Peacock once placed a petition before Juno desiring to have the voice of a nightingale in addition to his other attractions; however, Juno refused his request. When he persisted, and pointed out that he was her favorite bird, she said:

"Be content with your lot; one cannot be first in everything."

Potty Pourri

RANDOM KINDS OF FACTNESS

- July, for some reason, is the most dangerous month for fatal auto accidents. February's next.

- Most barns in the 1800s really were painted red. Why was that? Red paint hid dirt well and was easy to make without having to resort to expensive store-bought paint. Here's the recipe: Mix skim milk with some linseed oil and lime. Add rust.

- The Hebrew word *musar* means both "education" and "corporal punishment."

- Put a Twinkie snack cake in a microwave oven, and in about 45 seconds, the Twinkie will explode.

- Your average cat usually has twelve whiskers on each side of its face.

- In Tudor-era England, doctors were expected to move in with the patient until they were nursed back to health.

- The term "freelancing" dates from the twelfth century when knights who lost employment with royal houses offered themselves as mercenaries.

- Because of "Blue Laws" forbidding such things on the sabbath, pro baseball didn't start playing Sunday games until 1933. Not that the laws changed—the baseball leagues just decided to ignore them.

- Ant queens never leave the ground except to mate. They do so after shooting straight up in the air. When they come back down, their minions pull off their wings and they never fly again.

- Roll out those lazy, hazy, crazy days of summer: A disproportionate number of people are admitted into mental institutions during the summer months.

- Watch out for cherry trees. Even though the fruit is divine, eating the leaves and limbs can be fatal.

Empty Soles

HOW NIKE TURNED TENNIES INTO A STATUS ITEM

In the old days sports shoes were called tennies and cost a few bucks. Both of these things changed with the Nike Air sports shoe lines. Here's the story.

DID YOU KNOW that the first air sole was patented in 1882? Since then, more than seventy different air-filled shoes have been registered with the U.S. Patent Office. Almost all of them, however, failed because of technical or commercial problems. It was Nike that made the air sole practical ... and sold it first for sports, and then status.

BIRTH OF THE NOTION

In 1969, Frank Rudy left a director-of-new-products job in the aerospace industry and started thinking about ski equipment. He decided to design an improved ski boot, since most of the current models were unnecessarily uncomfortable. He was joined in his quest by another aerospace industry guy named Bob Bogert, who had been a designer.

In a few years, they had come up with a practical air-filled boot liner. They took it to Howard Head, owner of Head Skis, who licensed the design. He began manufacturing boots with air soles inside. Unfortunately, not long afterward, he sold Head Skis to the AMF company. AMF decided to discontinue the line.

Meanwhile, the recreational running trend began taking hold. Rudy and Bogert decided to design a running shoe model of their air sole, figuring that the air would absorb some of the pavement shock that long-distance runners suffer from. After many attempts, they successfully designed a thin polyurethane air bag for the inside of running shoes and convinced the Bata shoe company to try them out.

A HURDLE OR TWO

The first prototypes worked great. The company ordered fifty more. Unfortunately, the oil embargo of 1974 was in full swing, and their supplier, without telling them, changed the formula for its polyurethane to use less oil. The new formula wasn't as strong as the old one. When the soles warmed up, the air inside expanded ... and the sole exploded with a bang. Bata suddenly lost interest.

Nearly broke and desperate, Rudy flew to France to meet with executives at Adidas. But talks broke down over terms and whether it was technically possible to mass produce shoes with air inside. Then a fortuitous thing happened: While hanging around the offices, Rudy overheard an Adidas employee mention a new little company named Nike that was selling a lot of running shoes

Nike, Greek goddess of Victory

in the United States. Rudy made some calls, found out that there was a running shoe trade show going on that weekend in Anaheim, and caught the next flight back to Southern California.

He stopped by the booth in Anaheim just as it was closing and found out the name of the company's president, Phil Knight. Rudy found a pay phone and called Knight at headquarters in Oregon. Knight listened to Rudy's story and invited him up to Nike headquarters.

KNIGHT IN SHINING SNEAKERS

Knight had started Nike a few years before as Blue Ribbon Sports, distributing Tigers, an inexpensive Japanese running shoe. With time, Knight decided to manufacture his own shoes. An associate suggested the name Nike, after the winged Greek goddess of victory. Knight didn't like it much, but it was better than other names they'd come up with (among them Falcon, Bengal, and Dimension 6). Besides, it fit on the shoes and complemented the winged logo design.

After years of struggling, Nike was finally making strides in the recreational shoe business. Knight, an amateur runner, had seen the jogging boom coming and recognized the need for specialized shoes. He took Rudy's air-filled shoes for a run. They slowly deflated as he ran, but he saw the potential. "It was a great ride while it lasted," he told Rudy, and put him on six-month retainer to see if he could make something out of his idea.

Not long after, Nike decided that air soles were impractical. Sure, the air cushioned the road, but the friction from running heated the air to a level of discomfort and caused blisters. They tried putting an inflated midsole between a traditional sole and the runner's foot, which worked better.

They rushed the design into production. When the new shoe, called the Tailwind, hit the market, problems immediately started showing up. First of all, its price was $50, higher than any mass-produced running shoe up to that time. Then a last-minute fabric switch resulted in a shoe that fell apart quickly, infuriating customers. Just about half of the shoes were returned as defective.

But serious runners quickly saw some potential. An in-house study found that the air midsoles reduced impact by about 10 percent and decreased energy use by 2.8 percent. Some runners patched their shoes with duct tape and kept on running. The company eventually got the bugs out and prepared to promote them.

THE BOTTOM LINE

Up until this point, Nike had been signing up pros for between $8,000 and $100,000, each to wear and endorse their shoes. They "owned" about half of the players in the NBA (and all-in-all, about 2,000 expensive athletes from various sports) at a cost of millions of dollars a year.

For the new shoe models, they decided to find one promising rookie who had the potential to become a superstar and put all their eggs in his basket early, before he had a chance to get pricey. Charles Barkley was one candidate. Patrick Ewing was another. But the compa-

Air Jordans' logo

ny finally settled on 20-year-old college junior named Michael Jordan. They decided that they would design a brand new shoe for him, push it hard, and tie the product to the man and vice versa, so that when consumers saw the player, they thought "shoes!"

Nike offered Jordan $2.5 million for a five-year contract, plus royalties on every Air Jordan shoe sold (they thought about calling them Jordan Airs, but decided it would cause too much confusion with the Mid-East airline and Elvis Presley's longtime backup group).

Nike came up with a proposed shoe, a logo, and an advertising campaign. There was only one stumbling block: Jordan didn't particularly like Nike shoes. He tried to work out a deal with Adidas, but they weren't willing to give even a fraction of what Nike offered him.

So in August 1984, Jordan signed with Nike. Nike came up with the distinctive black and red design for him. It was so distinctive, in fact, that NBA Commissioner David Stern threatened to fine him $1,000 if he wore the shoes during a game because they violated the NBA "uniformity of uniform" clause. He wore them anyway, creating an uproar in the stands and in the press ("Michael Jordan is not the most incredible, the most colorful, the most amazing, the most flashy, or the most mind-boggling thing in the NBA," wrote *Chicago Journal* sportswriter Steve Aschberner the next day. "His shoes are.")

IN THE END

Nike gladly paid Jordan's fine. It was the beginning of a brilliant PR and advertising campaign—a win-win situation for both parties. The Air Jordans endorsement went on to become the most successful in athletic history Over $100 million in shoes sold in the first year alone. The dark side: It became dangerous to wear the shoes in some cities as kids began killing other kids for their $110 sneakers. Meanwhile, despite the inflated price for the inflating shoes, Nike's workers in foreign plants were still being paid pennies an hour in sweatshops....

Despite the name, Nike Air soles don't have air in them. Instead, they contain a gas that has larger molecules than air so it don't leak through the airbag material as easily as air molecules would.

Stately Knowledge

12 REASONS WHY YA GOTTA LOVE MARYLAND

We've searched the vaults and come up with some pretty impressive facts about Maryland. Here are a dozen of our favorites.

1 You may know that the state slogan is "Maryland is for Crabs!" But the state motto is downright dated for these nonsexist times: *Fatti masdhii, parole femine,* which means "Manly deeds, womanly words."

2 Sea Monkeys—the "pet" that is simply reconstituted brine shrimp—come from Bryans Road, Maryland, near the salty Atlantic Coast.

3 Back in 1988, Bob Rivers, a DJ at Baltimore, Maryland's WIYY radio station, vowed to stay on the air until the baseball team, the Baltimore Orioles, won a game. He didn't know what he'd gotten himself into. After ten losing games, and Rivers making the pledge, the Orioles continued to lose, keeping the DJ on the air 24 hours a day. Rivers took quick naps during songs, news, and commercial breaks. Finally, after eleven more losses in almost that many days, the Orioles beat the Chicago White Sox 9–0. Rivers played "I'm Free" by the Who and then went home to a well-deserved rest.

4 Maryland has more doctors per thousand people than any other state.

5 The first airmail flight in the United States landed in a cow pasture in Maryland. It wasn't supposed to. When the mail plane was launched with great ceremony in 1918, its scheduled route was supposed

to be from Washington, D.C. to New York. Unfortunately, the pilot discovered shortly after takeoff that somebody had forgotten to fill the plane's fuel tank.

6 There's something wrong about the sculpture of champion baseballer Babe Ruth at Baltimore's Oriole Park. Ruth grew up in Baltimore, so the 9-foot statue was supposed to be perfect, and it was, except for one thing: The Babe is shown leaning on a bat and clutching a right-handed fielder's glove. The real-life Babe Ruth was a lefty.

7 Boring, Maryland. It's not necessarily a description, it's the name of a town.

8 Maryland has no natural lakes. All of its lakes were made by humans digging and damming.

9 Famous Maryland residents include assassin John Wilkes Booth, anti-slavery activists Harriet Tubman and Frederick Douglass, polar explorer Matthew Henson, singer Billie Holiday, lawyer and writer of the National Anthem Francis Scott Key, chicken man Frank Perdue, Supreme Court Justice Thurgood Marshall, athletes Babe Ruth and Cal Ripken, Jr., authors H. L. Mencken,

Upton Sinclair, Tom Clancy, and Leon Uris, weird musician Frank Zappa, and the first American-born saint of the Roman Catholic church, Elizabeth Seton.

10 Here's a fact for a rainy day: The world's first umbrella factory was opened in Baltimore in 1828, boasting the catchy slogan, "Born in Baltimore—Raised Everywhere." Get it?

11 Camp David, near Thurmont, Maryland. It was called Shangri-La until Dwight D. Eisenhower decided to rename it Camp David in honor of his grandson and his father—both named David.

12 Maryland was a leader in naming an official state sport—jousting. Several tournaments are held during the year, but, alas, it's the wimpy kind where they spear rings, not each other.

The Five Senses

A FEW SENSORY NOTES

Bathroom Companion correspondent Kathie Meyer has found some intriguing tidbits and odd stories on the things we use to navigate the world—the five senses.

NOSING AROUND AT THE OLFACTORY

• At the upper end of each nostril are the olfactory regions, a yellow, moist, fatty substance. Heredity determines the shade of yellow of this body part, and the richer the color of yellow, the more acute one's sense of smell. People with darker skin have more sensitive noses than those with lighter skin. Albinos have an especially poor sense of smell.

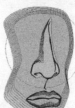

• There are odor technicians in the perfume trade who reportedly have the olfactory skills to distinguish 20,000 odors at twenty levels of intensity.

• Harry "the Nose" Jongen is a "remains identification expert" in the Netherlands. He's won worldwide attention for his ability to smell out the dead, even buried underground, and his skills are usually used for police work. However, not always. A Jewish man asked Harry if he would help him find an available plot in an old Jewish graveyard where he wanted to be buried. The problem was that the graveyard had been left untouched for more than 300 years, and the Jewish faith precludes graves from being disturbed. "We knew Harry only needs a stick to poke in the earth and, by the look and the odor of the ground, he can find out if someone has been buried there before," said a spokesman of the Jewish community. Sure enough, Harry found an empty grave site for the guy.

OPTICAL ALLUSIONS

• A newborn baby's eye is remarkably close to its full adult size. At birth the length of the eye is around 17 mm, growing to full adult size of 23 mm. This explains why so many babies are admired for having such "big, beautiful eyes." Your ears and nose, on the other hand, continue to grow throughout your entire life.

• A bird's eye takes up about fifty percent of its head; a human's eyes take up about five percent of the head.

• Humans can't perceive color in bright moonlight. "Get up on a dark moonlit night and look around," suggests David Hubel of Harvard Medical School, Nobel prize-winner for his vision research. "Although you can see shapes fairly well, colors are completely absent. It is remarkable how few people realize that they do without color vision in dim light."

• Anton's Syndrome is characterized by a person's complete blindness coupled with a firm belief that they can still see. Medically, it is a cortical blindness associated with dementia and delirium, and otherwise downright weird.

• George Edgar Lizarralde, a legally blind man, failed to gain a California driver's license the first three times he took the test. On the fourth try, even though he failed the vision test, the DMV granted him the much coveted license. Five years later, Lizarralde plowed into a woman in a crosswalk, and a court ruled it was the DMV's negligence.

• The average human eye can distinguish about 500 different shades of gray.

• There are 1,200,000 fibers in a human optic nerve.

• The average person's field of vision encompasses a 200-degree wide angle.

YOU GOT SOME NERVE, PAL!

• Electrical impulses travel from the skin to the spinal cord at a rate of up to 425 feet per second.

• The star-nosed mole is said to have the most delicate sense of touch in the animal kingdom. This nosey beast boasts twenty-two pink tentacles on its snout.

• Heel, boy! Although the benefits of stroking your pet are widely documented in touch research, *The New England Journal of Medicine* revealed one unexpected detriment. A woman's mysterious, chronic heel pain was found to be due to an accumulation of dog hairs embedded in her skin over the Achilles tendon. The woman had a long history of using her bare heel to pet her Scottish terrier. We wonder who had the worse end of that deal....

• Babies who are frequently touched gain weight fifty percent faster than unmassaged babies and cry less often.

•Here's something to rub you the wrong way: Massage therapy is covered by only eleven percent of all HMOs.

EARS LOOKIN' AT YOU, KID

• A New York judge dismissed a lawsuit by Clifford Goldberg against the heavy metal group, Motley Crüe. Goldberg said the music gave 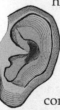 him a "searing pain" through his ears. The judge ruled that Goldberg had no case—everyone at a Motley Crüe concert knows it's going to be loud.

• Continual exposure to noises above 85 decibels is potentially damaging to your hearing.

Sixty decibels is normal conversation. Exposing yourself to 90 decibels (a lawnmower) for more than eight hours, 100 decibels (a chainsaw or snowmobile) for more than two hours, 115 decibels (a rock concert or auto horn) for more than 15 minutes per day, or 140 decibels (a gun blast or jet engine) will most assuredly cause damage.

• In 1995, Carty Finkbeiner, mayor of Toledo, Ohio, came up with a politically tone deaf solution for the homeowners in the neighborhood nearest the airport: If they didn't like the noise, they could just sell their homes to the deaf. Several days later, the mayor issued an apology for this idea, which, as you might suspect, never really got a fair hearing.

• During World War I, before radar, birds were used in aerial warfare. Because of their acute hearing, the Army kept parrots on the Eiffel Tower to squawk out a warning of approaching enemy aeroplanes long before they could be seen or heard by humans.

• The first electrical hearing aid was invented in 1901 by Miller R. Hutchinson. It was a rather large appliance, too large to carry comfortably—in fact, it worked best to build it into a chair.

• American deaf people have better driving records than their hearing counterparts.

THE BETTER TO TASTE YOU WITH, MY DEAR

• Taste buds can perceive four things: salt, bitter, sour, and sweet. Some experts believe there's a fifth taste category, known as *umami*, found in soy products.

• Humans have approximately 9–10,000 taste buds. Cats have only 473.

• Eat your favorite foods when you're young, because by the age of seventy half of your taste buds will be gone.

• There are people known as "supertasters" who may have more than 1,000 taste buds  per square centimeter on their tongues, as opposed to the average person who has fewer than forty. Women are more likely to be "supertasters" than men, and hormones such as estrogen are thought to play an additional role in taste perception. For instance, during the first trimester of pregnancy, many women are more sensitive to bitter flavors. This may explain the whole pickle-and-ice-cream thing.

• The official taste tester for Dreyers and Edy's Ice Cream, John Harrison, had his taste buds insured for a cool $1 million.

• If you're a supertaster and don't care for ice cream, there still may be a place for you as a professional tea taster, wine taster, beer taster ... in fact, you can probably name your food group, because the food and drink industry employs professional tasters in a variety of categories.

• New York gourmet chef Howard Schaeffer believed a traffic accident caused him to lose his senses of smell and taste. He sued for $1.1 million. When asked later why he still ate well enough to weigh over 200 pounds, he said he found other ways to enjoy his food, explaining, "It's amazing how quickly you can get into texture." He was awarded the money.

Dear Sir or Madame

"I regret the American public is not interested in anything on China." —an editor's 1931 rejection of Pearl S. Buck's now-classic *The Good Earth.*

The Eyes Have It

THINGS ARE A LITTLE DOTTY

Are the dots really flashing, or are your eyes playing tricks?

Stare at the black dot. What happens to the haze around it?

Every Picture Tells a Story

Washington Crossing the Delaware **by Emanuel Gottlieb Leutze**

• It is perhaps the most lasting image of the Revolutionary War, although it was painted eighty-five years later in Germany using the Rhine to stand in for the Delaware. Ironically, it commemorates a minor victory in the war, in which Americans made a sneak Christmas morning attack and captured 900 German troops, hired by the British.

• The painting is huge, about 21 feet long.

• The black man half-standing behind the flag bearer represents Prince Whipple, a slave emancipated during the war who served as bodyguard for his former master, Gen. William Whipple, a signer of of the Declaration of Independence and an aide to Washington.

• Nitpickers like to point out some problems with the painting:

1. Standing up in a boat in icy water is a really stupid idea.

2. The boat is too small for that many people (Washington's troops really used 30-footers).

3. The ice is all wrong.

4. The flag pictured wouldn't exist for another six months.

5. The sky shows a clear dawn, but the Americans crossed at 3 AM in a driving storm.

Shell Games

Aesop's Tales about Things with Shells

You know the Tortoise and the Hare, but perhaps these more obscure fables will also delight you. Shell-related, they're everything they're cracked up to be.

THE HARE AND THE TORTOISE

The Hare was once boasting of his speed before the other animals. "I have never yet been beaten," said he, "when I put forth my full speed. I challenge any one here to race with me."

The Tortoise said quietly, "I accept your challenge."

"That is a good joke," said the Hare; "I could dance round you all the way."

"Keep your boasting till you've beaten," answered the Tortoise. "Shall we race?"

So a course was fixed and a start was made. The Hare darted almost out of sight at once, but soon stopped and, to show his contempt for the Tortoise, lay down to have a nap. The Tortoise plodded on and plodded on, and when the Hare awoke from his nap, he saw the Tortoise just near the winning-post and could not run up in time to save the race. Said the Tortoise:

"Plodding forward steadily wins the race."

THE GOOSE WITH THE GOLDEN EGG

One day a countryman going to the nest of his Goose found there an egg all yellow and glittering. When he took it up it was as heavy as lead and he was going to throw it away, because he thought a trick had been played upon him. But he took it home on second thoughts, and soon found to his delight that it was an egg of pure gold. Every morning the same thing occurred, and he soon became rich by selling his eggs. As he grew rich he grew greedy; and thinking to get at once all the gold the Goose could give, he killed it and opened it only to find nothing.

Greed oft o'er reaches itself.

Seizing the Tortoise by the shell with her talons, she soared aloft

THE TORTOISE AND THE BIRDS

A Tortoise desired to change its place of residence, so he asked an Eagle to carry him to his new home, promising her a rich reward for her trouble. The Eagle agreed and seizing the Tortoise by the shell with her talons soared aloft. On their way they met a Crow, who said to the Eagle: "Tortoise is very good eating." "The shell is too hard," said the Eagle in reply. "The rocks will soon crack the shell," was the Crow's answer; and the Eagle, taking the hint, let fall the Tortoise on a sharp rock, and the two birds made a hearty meal of the Tortoise.

Never soar aloft on an enemy's pinions.

THE TWO CRABS

One fine day two Crabs came out from their home to take a stroll on the sand. "Child," said the mother, "you are walking very ungracefully. You should accustom yourself to walking straight forward without twisting from side to side."

"Pray, mother," said the young one, "do but set the example yourself, and I will follow you."

Example is the best precept.

THE BOY AND THE FILBERTS

A boy put his hand into a pitcher full of filberts. He grasped as many as he could possibly hold, but when he tried to pull out his hand, he was prevented from doing so by the neck of the pitcher. Unwilling to lose his filberts, and yet unable to withdraw his hand, he burst into tears and bitterly lamented his disappointment. A bystander said to him, "Be satisfied with half the quantity, and you will readily draw out your hand."

Do not attempt too much at once.

Stately Knowledge

12 REASONS WHY YA GOTTA LOVE TEXAS

We've searched the vaults and come up with some pretty impressive facts and stories about Texas. Here are a dozen of our favorites.

1 Dr Pepper was invented in Waco, Texas, but not by a guy named Dr Pepper. The guy who invented the drink, Wade Morrison, named it after his former boss, a Virginia druggist named Dr. Kenneth Pepper.

2 You can visit a lot of the solar system without leaving Texas, because it has towns named Earth, Mercury and Pluto.

3 In 1987, Gene Gordon of Fort Worth, Texas, was in his backyard when he heard a loud bang in his house. He ran inside and found a large hole in his roof and smelly, bright blue ice melting in his attic. What do you suppose happened? He finally figured it out: A plane had a leaky toilet tank. The contents of the tank, including the bright blue liquid that flushes the toilet bowl, had dripped out and frozen on the bottom of the airplane. After a while, the blue ice let go ... right above Gordon's house. Yech!

4 Our favorite Texan? "Country" Bill White, who lived 341 days in a coffin more than six feet underground. His only connection to the outside world was a four-inch wide tube used for feeding and oxygen. Why'd he do it? Just to prove it could be done.

5 Texan Gail Borden invented condensed milk. He also coined the slogan, "Remember the Alamo!"

Texas!

6 The King Ranch in southern Texas can lay claim to developing the very first new breed of beef cattle in the Western hemisphere—the Santa Gertrudis Cattle.

7 The first laundromat opened in Fort Worth, Texas, in 1934.

8 The largest tumor removed from a person's body came from a woman in Galveston, Texas, in 1905. It weighed 328 pounds.

9 The gas found in blimps and balloons is a natural substance that helium drillers drill for. Most of the world's helium comes from the ground under Texas. The largest helium well is in Amarillo, Texas.

10 There are not one but two statues of Popeye in Crystal City, Texas. They're there to celebrate Crystal City's main crop. Guess what that leafy vegetable might be?

Fire ants swarming toward the Festival

11 Under the 1845 annexation treaty that brought Texas into the Union, the state has what's called the "Right to Divide." That means at any time the state can legally divide into as many as five separate states.

12 Our favorite city in the lone star state is Marshall, located near the eastern border near Louisiana. It has a rich history and culture that embodies the Texan spirit. For starters, during the Civil War, Missouri governor Thomas Reynolds, running from Union forces, holed up in Marshall and made the Texas city the capital of Missouri. As far as we know, Marshall is the only city to be used as another state's capital. More recently, Marshall has played host to the annual Fire Ant Festival. In case you've never experienced a fire ant up close and personal, the little buggers are sort of like killer bees without wings; they're mean. The people of Marshall decided that since they can't seem to get rid of them, they might as well have some fun with them. They have fire ant calling contests, fire ant roundup competitions, and even a fire ant cook-off, featuring recipes made with fire ants.

Cosmic Pekoe
TEA READING TO THE GREAT BEYOND

Today it's virtually unheard of, but it used to be common. In tearooms and coffee houses across the land, a dark, mysterious stranger would approach when you'd reached the end of your cup and offer to read your future for a few coins. After a mysterious ritual of stirring and dumping the cup's dregs, the reader would point out pictures in the leaves and tell you what they meant.

THE HISTORY OF TEALEAF READING

Telling the future with tea leaves (called tasseography, by the way) goes so far back that there's no way to trace its history. Suffice it to say that reading coffee grounds and tea leaves has been around for thousands of years in a number of cultures. (A similar technique appears in Genesis 44:5, in which Joseph reads wine dregs from a special silver cup to foretell the future.)

Sadly, reading tea leaves and coffee grounds has nearly died out in our time. The reasons are simple and concrete: tea bags and coffee filters. But we can work around that. In the really old days, people drank hot beverages through clenched teeth to strain out loose leaves and coffee grounds. Get used to the idea, because it's something you'll need to do when telling fortunes.

HOW DOES IT WORK?

Interpretation is a lot like inkblots in a psychiatrist's office. This is especially true when you start realizing that it's awfully hard to differentiate between, for example, a tea-leaf dog ("faithful friends") and a wolf ("jealous friends"), or between a toad ("unknown enemy") and a frog ("arrogant French person"). So, in this way, tea-leaf reading can be a reflection of your subconscious mind.

Throw in a reader who is also a good and intuitive judge of people, which many tea-leaf readers have proven to be, and you can see how effective fortunetelling with tea can be.

The best thing about tea and coffee reading, though, is that it can be done anytime you stop and have a cup of something, so it allows a relaxing moment by yourself or a social, self-revealing one when you're with friends.

READING THE LEAVES
• Use a cup with a wide opening, the kind that comes with a saucer, not a mug. The inside of the cup should be light-colored and patternless so that you can see the leaves clearly.

• Use loose tea if you can find it in the store, preferably with big leaves. Otherwise, simply cut open a tea bag or two and dump the contents into a cup. If you're making coffee, dump the loose ground coffee (instant coffee won't work) right into the cup, add hot water, and wait for a few minutes before adding cream or sugar.

• The room should be peaceful, if possible, and the light dim with one spot of light—either artificial or a ray of moonlight—illuminating the cup. Clear your mind and relax, concentrating on your future and asking whatever power is involved for an accurate reading.

1. Don't drink to the last drop. Instead, save the leaves or grounds with a little liquid in the bottom (not too much, one or two teaspoonsful).

2. Take the cup in your left hand and spin it three times clockwise. (At least, that's what most tea leaf readers say, although we found one source that said you should do it *counter*clockwise. So, either this one is wrong, or it doesn't really matter which way you turn it ... or, perhaps

this advice is for leaf readers in the Southern Hemisphere.)

3. Immediately after swirling it, turn the cup over on a saucer or plate. After all the liquid drains out, set it back up upright, with the handle pointing toward you.

INTERPRETING

• The handle is like a YOU ARE HERE arrow on a map— it represents you and your sphere of influence and home, and a symbol found near the handle indicates something that will literally strike close to home. Leaf configurations stuck near the rim represent your present; the walls, your immediate future; and the bottom, the distant future.

• Look carefully into the cup, tipping it and noting all walls and the bottom, noting the leafs or grounds stuck to them from all angles. At first they may look like random clumps and glops, but see if their shapes remind you of anything. This will take some imagination, like when you were a kid and looked for pictures in the clouds. Also notice their size and relative positioning, because two images next to each other can influence each other.

• The bigger and clearer an image is, the more significant it is. A small or blurry image has substantially less significance. If all the images are blurry, it indicates that you'll be troubled by delay and disturbance before the events come to pass. If the cup itself is blurry, too, it signifies that you'll soon be receiving bad news from your optometrist.

• You may see just a few symbols, or dozens, in one cup. The idea is to note all of them in a big picture and see how they interact with each other instead of trying to isolate each one as a separate thing. As in life, each component influences and is influenced by each of the other components.

• Your message doesn't lie in any one symbol, but within the unique relationship of all the elements. Bad omens may be weakened or canceled out by nearby good omens and vice versa. For example, something that looks like a snake ("bad luck") that appears near something looks like the letter M may indicate that you should be on guard against an enemy whose name begins with M. A number 6 next to a travel symbol may mean you'll be gone for that many days, weeks ... or even years (no matter what the Skipper and Gilligan promised about it being "a three-hour tour").

• Start with the images near the rim ("the present"), then work your way inward into the future.

Below are some of the images you might see.

SYMBOL KEY

Acorn: Good health, good luck (especially if you're reading for a squirrel)

Ants: Bad news, hard work (perhaps a disastrous picnic)

Apple: Long life, gain in business (may be incompatibility with other PCs)

Arch: Trip abroad (or maybe to McDonalds); if blurred, a bad trip

Bat: Fruitless endeavor (unless it's a fruit bat, perhaps)

Boat: Friendly visitor (howdy, sailor!)

Cat: Treachery, insincere friends

Comet: Unexpected visitor (or maybe clean sinks)

Cross: Trouble (if your father was a god and your mother a virgin, *big* trouble)

Crown: Success

Desk: Prosperity (or at least a cubicle of your own)

Dog: Faithful friends (some of whom perhaps will gladly hump your leg)

Dragon: Sudden change

Egg: Some say good fortune; others, that you'll lose your savings

Fan: Good luck with the opposite sex

Frog: Beware of excessive pride, arrogance (or French people ... but I repeat myself)

Goat: You're surrounded by enemies

Grasshopper: A friend will leave, maybe not return (or perhaps you'll be cast in the remake of *Kung-Fu*)

Hen: New addition to family

Hourglass: Danger nearby

Monkey: Success

Mountain: Friends in high places

Mouse: Thief nearby

Owl: Failure, sickness, poverty, maybe death (but have a nice day anyway)

Square: Peace, or no marriage (actually, the two may go together)

Violin: Excessive vanity

Wolf: Jealous friends

Worms: Secret enemies

ONE LAST ODD FACT

In China, a country full of both divination and tea, reading tea leaves is all but unknown.

Foodonyms

A Bunch of Fruits and Nuts

Did you know that there's a reason we call it a Bartlett pear or a macadamia nut? The origins of some of these names may surprise you as much as they did us.

Granny Smith apple: In the 1860s, Australian grandmother Maria Ann Smith created this tart apple by mixing a late-ripening crabapple with her regular orchard apples.

McIntosh apple: John McIntosh immigrated to Canada in the 1700s. He found a grove of wild apple trees growing near his farm. Word soon spread of their flavor and the McIntosh Red apple was born. The trees were probably cultivated by an earlier Indian settlement.

filbert: The filbert, also known as the hazelnut, got its name from St. Philbert. In Greece, Italy, and Turkey, where the plant is native, the bush blooms around the Catholic saint's feast day.

loganberry: This berry from the raspberry family was cultivated in the home garden of California lawyer James Logan in 1881.

boysenberry: Using the loganberry, raspberry, and blackberry, botanist Rudolph Boysen developed this hybrid in the 1920s and '30s.

macadamia: This nut, native to Australia, was discovered by European settlers in the 1800s. It was named in 1859 by Australian botanist Ferdinand Von Mueller in honor of his friend, Scottish scientist Dr. John Macadam. Macadam died at 38 without ever tasting the nut that bore his name.

Bartlett pear: In the 1600s, an English schoolteacher named John Stair created a pear variety. A horticulturist named Williams did some further breeding and named the result after himself. Massachusetts nursery owner Enoch Bartlett became known for selling this variety. Locals called the pear "Bartlett," and this time the name stuck.

Potty Pourri
RANDOM KINDS OF FACTNESS

• Dr. Pearl Zane Grey was only a moderately successful dentist. He did much better as "Zane Grey," writing Western novels between patients.

• Mexican jumping beans jump because there's a caterpillar inside. The "bean" is from a shrub that grows south of the border, and the caterpillar eats out the inside, jerking now and again to scare away birds and other seed-eaters. Eventually the caterpillar grows up and emerges from the seed as a butterfly.

• When he was a desperately poor child, Charles Dickens was forced to work at a shoe polish factory in London.

• How many ridges are there around the edge of a United States dime? 118. Don't believe us? Count 'em yourself.

• The oldest letter in our alphabet is *o*, first used by the Egyptians in about 3000 B.C.

• The newest letters are *j* and *v*. *J* was derived from *i* in about 1600. *V* had double-duty as vowel and consonant until someone got the bright idea to round the bottom and create a separate letter, *u*. This happened during the Renaissance.

• A 216-minute movie with a cast of thousands, yet not a single woman in a speaking role: That's one way of describing *Lawrence of Arabia*.

• In a poll, American speech teachers came up with the ugliest sounding words in the English language. The list included "plump," "gripe," "sap," "jazz," "crunch," "treachery," "cacophony," "phlegmatic," "plutocrat," and "flatulence."

• If you're dealing in Polish currency, just remember that it takes 100 groszy to make one zloty.

• Each of your eyeballs weighs about an ounce.

• In ancient China, the color of your fingernail polish was an indicator of your rank and position.

The Stalled Ox

A Short Story by Saki (Hector Monro)

Before he was killed in World War I, Hector Monro wrote short
stories with a twist under the pen name "Saki." In this one,
a bull in a garden inspires a major career change....

THEOPHIL ESHLEY WAS AN ARTIST by profession, a painter of
cattle by force of environment. Not that he lived on a
ranch or a dairy farm, in an atmosphere pervaded with
horn and hoof, milking-stool, and branding-iron. His home was
in a villa-dotted district that only just escaped being suburban.
On one side of his garden there abutted a small, picturesque
meadow, in which an enterprising neighbor pastured some
small picturesque cows of the Channel Island persuasion.

In summertime the cows stood in meadow-grass under walnut trees with sunlight falling in dappled patches on their
mouse-sleek coats. Eshley had executed a dainty picture of two
reposeful milk-cows in filtered sunbeam, and the Royal Academy had duly exposed the same in its Summer Exhibition.

As he had begun, so, of necessity, he went on. His "Noontide
Peace," was followed by "A Mid-day Sanctuary," a study of a
walnut tree with two dun cows under it. In due succession
there came "Where the Gad-Flies Cease from Troubling," "The
Haven of the Herd," and "A-dream in Dairyland," all studies of
walnut trees and dun cows. His two attempts to break away
from his own tradition were signal failures: "Turtle Doves
Alarmed by Sparrow-hawk" and "Wolves on the Roman
Campagna" came back to his studio as abominable heresies,
until Eshley climbed back into grace and the public gaze with
"A Shaded Nook where Drowsy Milkers Dream."

On a fine late-autumn afternoon he was putting finishing
touches to a study of meadow weeds when his neighbor, Adela
Pingsford, assailed the door of his studio with loud knockings.

"I paint dairy cows, certainly," admitted Eshley, "but I cannot claim any experience in rounding-up stray oxen."

"There is an ox in my garden," she announced, in explanation of the tempestuous intrusion.

"An ox," said Eshley blankly; "what kind of ox?"

"I don't know what kind," snapped the lady. "A common or garden ox, to use the slang expression. It is the garden part of it that I object to. My garden has just been put straight for the winter, and the chrysanthemums are just coming into flower."

"How did it get into the garden?" asked Eshley.

"I imagine it came in by the gate," said the lady impatiently; "it couldn't have climbed the walls, and I don't suppose any-one dropped it from an aeroplane. The immediately important question is not how it got in, but how to get it out."

"Won't it go?" said Eshley.

"If it were anxious to go," said Adela Pingsford rather angri-ly, "I would not have come to chat with you about it. I'm practi-cally all alone; the housemaid is out and the cook is lying down with neuralgia. Anything that I may have learned at school or life about how to remove a large ox from a small garden seems to have escaped my memory. All I could think of was that you were a cattle painter, presumably familiar with the subject, and that you might be of some assistance. Possibly I was mistaken."

"I paint dairy cows, certainly," admitted Eshley, "but I cannot claim any experience in rounding-up stray oxen. I've seen it done in a cinema film, of course, but there were always horses and lots of other accessories; besides, one never knows how much of those pictures are faked."

Adela Pingsford said nothing, but led the way to her garden. It was a fair-sized garden, but looked small in comparison with the ox, a huge mottled brute, dull red with shaggy ears and large blood-shot eyes. It bore about as much resemblance to the dainty paddock heifers that Eshley painted as the chief of a Kurdish nomad clan would to a Japanese tea-shop girl. Eshley stood very near the gate while he studied the animal's appearance and demeanor. Adela Pingsford continued to say nothing.

"It's eating a chrysanthemum," said Eshley at last, when the silence had become unbearable.

"How observant you are," said Adela bitterly. "You seem to notice everything. As a matter of fact, it has got six chrysanthemums in its mouth at the present moment."

The necessity for doing something was becoming imperative. Eshley took a step or two in the direction of the animal, clapped his hands, and made noises of the "Hish" and "Shoo" variety. If the ox heard them it gave no outward indication of the fact.

"If any hens should ever stray into my garden," said Adela, "I should certainly send for you. Meanwhile, do you mind trying to drive that ox away? That is a *Mademoiselle Louise Bichot* that he's begun on now," she added in icy calm, as a glowing orange head was crushed into the huge munching mouth.

"Since you have been so frank about the mum's variety," said Eshley, "I don't mind telling you that this is an Ayrshire ox."

The icy calm broke down; Adela Pingsford used language that sent the artist nearer to the ox. He picked up a pea-stick and flung it with some determination against the animal's mottled flanks. The mashing of the flowers into a petal salad was suspended for a long moment, while the ox gazed with concentrated inquiry at the stick-thrower. Adela gazed with equal concentration and more obvious hostility at the same focus.

As the beast neither lowered its head nor stamped its feet, Eshley threw another pea-stick. The ox seemed to realize that it was to go; it gave a hurried final pluck, and strode swiftly up the garden. Eshley ran to head it towards the gate, but only succeeded in quickening its pace to a lumbering trot. With no real hesitation, it pushed its way through an open French window into the morning-room. Some chrysanthemums and autumn herbage stood about the room in vases, and the animal resumed its browsing; Eshley fancied that a hunted look had come into its eyes, a look that counseled respect. He discontinued his attempt to interfere with its choice of surroundings.

"Mr. Eshley," said Adela in a shaking voice, "I asked you to drive that beast out of my garden, but I did not ask you to drive it into my house. If I must have it anywhere on the premises I prefer the garden to the morning-room."

"Cattle drives are not in my line," said Eshley; "if I remember I told you so at the outset." "I quite agree," retorted the lady, "painting pretty pictures of pretty little cows is what you're suited for. Perhaps you'd like to do a nice sketch of that ox making itself at home in my morning-room?"

The worm had turned; Eshley began striding away.

"Where are you going?" screamed Adela.

"To fetch implements," was the answer.

"Implements? I won't have you use a lasso. The room will be wrecked if there's a struggle."

But the artist marched out of the garden. In minutes he returned with easel, sketching-stool, and painting materials.

"Do you mean to say that you're going to sit and paint that brute while it's destroying my morning-room?" gasped Adela.

"It was your suggestion," said Eshley, setting canvas in place.

"I forbid it; I absolutely forbid it!" stormed Adela.

"I don't see what say you have in the matter," said the artist. "You can hardly pretend that it's your ox, even by adoption."

"You seem to forget that it's in my morning-room, eating my flowers," came the raging retort.

"You seem to forget that the cook has neuralgia," said Eshley. "Your outcry will waken her. Consideration for others should be the guiding principle of people in our station of life."

"The man is mad!" exclaimed Adela. A moment later it was Adela herself who appeared to go mad. The ox had finished the vase-flowers and the cover of *Israel Kalisch,* and appeared to be thinking of leaving its restricted quarters. Eshley noticed its restlessness and promptly flung it some bunches of Virginia creeper as an inducement to continue the sitting.

"I forget how the proverb runs," he observed. "Something about 'better a dinner of herbs than a stalled ox where hate is.' We seem to have all the ingredients for the proverb at hand."

"I shall go to the Public Library and get them to telephone for the police," announced Adela, and, raging, she departed.

Some minutes later the ox, awakening probably to the suspicion that oil cake and chopped mangold was waiting for it in some appointed barn, stepped with much precaution out of the morning-room, stared with grave inquiry at the no longer obtrusive and pea-stick-throwing human, and then lumbered heavily out of the garden. Eshley packed up his tools and followed the animal's example.

The episode was the turning-point in Eshley's artistic career. His remarkable picture, "Ox in a Morning-Room, Late Autumn," was one of the sensations of the next Paris Salon, and when it was subsequently exhibited at Munich it was bought by the Bavarian Government, after spirited bidding among three meat-packing firms. From then on his success was assured, and the Royal Academy was thankful, two years later, to give a conspicuous position on its walls to his large canvas "Barbary Apes Wrecking a Boudoir."

Eshley presented Adela Pingsford with a new copy of *Israel Kalisch,* and a couple of finely flowering pots of *Madame Andre Blusset,* but nothing in the nature of a real reconciliation has taken place between them.

Would "Little Worms" by Any Other Name Taste as Good?

Sometimes food just sounds better in a foreign language. For example, would pasta taste nearly as good if we translated the word from the Italian ("dough paste")? And how would you feel about eating these pastas translated?

- •"large reeds" (cannelloni)
- •"butterflies" (farfalle)
- •"small ribbons" (fettucine)
- •"small muffs" (manicotti)
- •"small twists" (tortellini)

- •"little strings" (spaghetti)
- •"little worms" (vermicelli)
- •"little turnips" (ravioli)
- •"little tongues" (linguine)

Word Thieves 3

Some Terms We've Borrowed from the Africans

When African natives were kidnapped and enslaved they brought remnants of their cultures and languages with them. Some of their words ended up as part of American English.

banana: First a West African word, may have been borrowed by them from a word in the Arabic language, pronounced *banayna, and* meaning "fingers" or "toes."

banjo: Probably from the Kimbundu word, *mbanya,* which refers to a stringed instrument.

chigger: First used to indicate any biting insect, the word came from the Wolof language's *jiga* ("insect").

cooter: Most famous as a nickname for the box turtle in Alabama and Georgia. It most likely came from the West African word *kuta* or the Kongo tribe's *nkuda* meaning "turtle."

goober: This alternative name for a peanut comes from the Bantu *nguba.*

gumbo: *Kingombo* means "okra" in the Bantu language, and so the name got generalized to mean a thick stew made from okra pods.

juke: The word that goes into "juke joint" and "juke box" comes from the Wolof word *dzug,* which means leading a chaotic or wicked life.

Sambo: A common name among African American males in previous centuries, and now notorious because of a story called *Little Black Sambo.* Still, the name came from the Hausen people of Nigeria, and it means "second son."

tote: From the Western Congo word *tota* or *tuta* ("carry").

voodoo: From the Ewe tribe's *vodu* ("spirit").

yam: From the Vai *djambi* or the Sengal *nyami,* both of which mean "eat."

Lloyd's of London

HOW IT GOT OUT OF COFFEE & INTO HOT WATER

What would you think if Starbucks started selling insurance? Lloyd's of London started out as a dockside coffee shop where professional gamblers hung out. "Insurance" was just another bet you could make. Maybe it's not that different from today, actually....

LOYD'S OF LONDON is the most famous insurance syndicate in history. Its willingness to insure things like Betty Grable's legs and Bruce Springsteen's voice have made it a risk taker's heaven and a press agent's dream. It appears in the news whenever an unlucky disaster breaks. An unlucky streak in recent decades—including the collapse of the World Trade Center (the biggest single loss in the company's long history), the *Exxon Valdez* oil spill, the 1989 San Francisco earthquake, and Hurricane Hugo—has pushed some of its investors and underwriters to the edge of bankruptcy.

If Lloyd's doesn't survive as an insurance provider, though, maybe it can go back to the business where it began three centuries ago: a coffee house.

London was the major player in the maritime business in the seventeenth century, with merchant ships coming and going constantly from its bustling harbor. At the same time, coffee-drinking was becoming popular across Europe. Dutch colonists had recently established coffee plantations on the island of Java. In 1688, a man named Edward Lloyd opened a coffee house on Tower Street near the docks. Unlike taverns, where drunken revelry reigned, coffee houses were sober places where business people went to do serious wheeling and dealing.

Because of its location Lloyd's coffee house attracted a clientele of ship owners, captains, merchants, and insurance brokers. The concept of marine insurance had been introduced to England earlier in the century, allowing owners of ships and cargos to mitigate the financial hit they took if a ship went down.

But, although insurance in the modern sense existed, insurance companies did not (Lloyd's today is still a peculiar hybrid, as noted below). A merchant with ship or cargo hired a broker to go from one wealthy individual to another, selling a share of the risk in return for a share of the premium. It was essentially betting that a ship would make it safely: If nothing happened, the insurers got to keep the hefty premium; if disaster struck, they were personally liable for their share of the claim ... to the full extent of their personal fortunes, if necessary. Clearly, it was a field for gamblers with a lot of money they could afford to risk.

ONE LUMP OR TWO?

Because of the amount of ship talk he heard, Edward Lloyd gained a reputation for being  a trustworthy source of shipping news and gossip. His coffee house became recognized as the place to go to arrange for marine insurance. Lloyd himself was never directly involved in the insurance business, but he provided a congenial business atmosphere, semi-enclosed booths, and even writing materials for his patrons.

Lloyd's coffee house continued on after his death in 1713, and merchants continued to gather there. For decades, little separated those underwriters offering coverage in "respectable" marine underwriting from those betting on other things, like who would win a particular sports contest or war, or when the current king would die. Wanting to disassociate from their seamier brethren, a number of the respectable brokers broke away in 1769 to set up a coffee house in nearby Pope's Head Alley. They called it the "New Lloyd's Coffee House" and allowed business dealings in marine insurance only.

The building proved too small, and so a committee was formed to find new premises. Seventy-nine brokers, underwriters, and merchants each chipped in £100 to finance the move. When they moved, they left the coffee business behind. Nonetheless their new headquarters was still called "Lloyd's

Coffee House" for decades afterward.

THE "NAMES" ARE THE SAME

Over the following century, the Lloyd's society of underwriters evolved into its modern incarnation. They expanded to other kinds of insurance. In the 1990s, Lloyd's had 32,000 members (called "Names" because they put their "name," or full reputation and fortune, behind the risk), grouped into approximately 350 underwriting syndicates varying in size from a handful to a thousand. Each syndicate is managed by an agent and hires experts who determine the betting odds (and thereby the premium) for each insurance policy. As was the case three centuries ago, the Names are personally liable for claims, meaning that they can make money if things go well, but can lose their shirts if things go wrong. (There have been moves in recent years to limit this personal liability).

Over time, Lloyd's developed a reputation for fairness, holding to a rule that no policyholder with a legitimate claim went unpaid. For example, after the disastrous San Francisco earthquake of 1906 that destroyed most of the

city, every insurance company but one—Lloyd's—defaulted on their policies. In fact, when Lloyd's discovered that many of their policyholders had either fire insurance or earthquake insurance, but not both, Lloyd's leading underwriter cabled an unequivocal message to the company's San Francisco agent: "Pay all of our policyholders in full, irrespective of the terms of their policies."

Silly Policies from Lloyd's of London

Over the years, PR agents discovered that frivolous insurance policies with Lloyd's made for good publicity and that Lloyd's was a good sport about insuring just about anything. For example:

• Kid-show host Pinky Lee's lisp (a $50,000 policy)

• Jamie Lee Curtis's legs ($1,000,000 pair)

• Fred Astaire's legs ($150,000 each)

• Jimmy Durante's nose ($50,000)

• Bruce Springsteen's voice ($6,000,000)

• Dolly Parton's breasts ($600,000)

• A grain of rice with a tiny portrait of the Queen and the Duke of Edinburgh ($20,000)

• That Elvis wouldn't be found alive ($1,000,000)

• The beards of the "Whisker's Club" in Derbyshire against fire and "theft" (£20 each)

• A comedy troupe, against the risk of having members of the audience laugh themselves to death ($1,000,000)

• Skylab's disintegration and return to earth (£2,500,000 property damage, £500,000 for deaths)

• The world's largest cigar (£17,933.35)

• The body of underwear model Suzanne Mizzi (£10,000,000)

• That the Loch Ness monster wouldn't be captured (£1,000,000)

• Actress Kerry Wallace, who had to shave her head for a *Star Trek* movie, against the possibility that her hair wouldn't grow back right ($100,000)

• However, there are limits. Mr. Methane, a British entertainer who farts out melodies such as "Twinkle, Twinkle Little Star," sought to buy insurance against losing his talents. He was refused.

Crazy Like a Foxglove

Some touching, and some horrible, here's a sampling of the remedies used for insanity throughout the ages.

- To cure insanity, medieval kings and queens might've used a bag full of buttercups slung around the neck.

- The Welsh during this same time period preferred daisies — particularly daisy tea — as a remedy.

- The Irish buried their crazies up to their necks in dirt. After three days, they'd take them out, and if they weren't cured, they'd beat them until they couldn't move.

- In a special lake in Scotland, the insane were tied and dragged behind a boat. Once they reached an island, they were plunged into an icy well. This treatment apparently worked on more than one occasion.

- Ancient Mongolians boiled old animal bones that were found out on the steppes and collected the remaining juices. The prescription was to bathe in the juices for seven days to remove the affliction.

- Pearls were used for more than mere adornment by Europeans and Persians in the late Middle Ages. Wearing them was supposed to chase off insanity.

- Mayan priests were known to use the testicles of a black rooster to make an insanity-curing breakfast elixir.

- Early Arabians swore by *Vitex agnus castus* — Chasteberry — to cure crazy people. It was an herb also used to squelch sexual desire. It's still sold in Egypt for various purposes.

- Ancient Greeks used Hellebore, aka Christmas Rose, to cure insanity. Hellebore has strong purgative properties, is very poisonous, often causing violent reactions in those who come in contact with it. It's also a potent narcotic, which may explain its success with helping the mentally ill.

- The ancient Greeks as well as the Egyptians also used dance, song, and drama therapy in treating the mentally ill. In many temples, there were rooms set aside for the insane to sleep, believing that the holy place would ease their suffering.

- Later Greek medical cures included poisons and narcotics, donkey milk and bland foods.

- As religion invaded the medical profession of Western Europe, cures for insanity included beating, torturing, and starving. Trepanning—the practice of drilling a hole in the skull of the afflicted—soon became the preferred method of treatment, the belief being that the demons could escape the patient's body through the hole.

- But fennel, too, was believed to help the mentally ill.

- By the mid-1800s anesthesia was all the rage, so lobotomies were used to solve the problem—often altogether.

"The distance between insanity and genius is measured only by success."
—Bruce Feirstein

Family Feud

THE GRAPES OF WRATH

You would think that the gentility of wine would have a civilizing effect on the people who make it. The Ernest & Julio Gallo wine dynasty proved that idea wrong.

G IUSEPPE ("JOE") GALLO was a moody, violent man. He'd owned a saloon until Prohibition put him out of business. Since Prohibition still allowed individuals to bottle 200 gallons of "nonintoxicating cider and fruit juices exclusively for use in the home," Gallo shifted his business to growing wine grapes, which he sold all over the country to thirsty home winemakers. Most of his buyers, however, were bootleggers, making a lot more than the legal allotment.

Joe's oldest sons, Ernest and Julio, were drafted into working long, thankless hours on the family grape farm. Their younger brother, Joseph, Jr., wasn't old enough to help, and was able to enjoy the childhood that his older brothers had never had. Like his biblical namesake, Joseph was heartily resented by his brothers, and he paid for his favored position later.

Meanwhile, Joe, Sr.'s brother, Mike, was finishing up prison time he'd served for bribery and fraud. When he was released in 1918, he opened the San Pablo Bottling Shop in Oakland as a cover for an alcoholic distribution system. In addition to growing Mike's grapes, Joe was hired to supervise his production of brandy and wine. In 1922, Joe was arrested for running an illegal brandy still. Mike made a few calls to friends in  high places and the charges were mysteriously dropped.

By 1925, Joe had accumulated enough money to move to Modesto and build an $8,000 home on the edge of 70 acres of prime vineyards he paid for with cash. He began shipping grapes on a much larger scale. He also apparently continued winemaking: one night in total darkness, young son Joseph woke up to find his father digging a wide, deep hole with his tractor for a 32,000-gallon underground liquor-storing tank.

CHANGE OF FORTUNE

By winter of 1929, Big Joe was doing well enough to buy 160 more acres across the street from his house, this time paying $25,000 in cash. Julio and Ernest, full of late-teen contempt for their father, graduated from high school and went to work for him full-time, arguing with him over their $30 a month pay and for shares of the business. In 1933, anticipating the end of Prohibition, Ernest applied for a license to open a bonded wine storeroom in San Francisco, but his application was turned down because he didn't own a winery—it was all in his father's name.

That changed suddenly the next day. His parents were found shot to death on the family farm. After a hasty inquest, in which Ernest testified that maybe they'd had a financial reverse or something, their deaths were ruled a murder-suicide.

The three brothers were supposed to inherit equal thirds of the business, but Ernest immediately began maneuvering, according to author Ellen Hawkes in his book *Blood and Wine.* "While his two brothers mourned ... Ernest received permission from the probate court to continue his father's business." He applied for a winery permit twelve days after his parents' death in the name of himself and Julio, effectively cutting their younger brother out of his one-third inheritance. Little Joe essentially became their employee. He was soon chastised and fired for "an unwillingness to work hard" after he took a week's vacation.

NASTY, BRUTISH, AND SHORT

Neither brother knew much about making wine, so they learned what they could from a "how to make wine" pamphlet they found at the Modesto public library. Julio took over wine manufacturing and Ernest the marketing. "Ernest is the embodiment of the Hobbesian view of the world," one ex-employee was quoted as saying: "Nasty, brutish, and short." Ernest had a favorite saying: "Remember, people aren't led— they're driven."

The Gallo brothers built a successful company using hard-nosed competitive tactics. Its sales force was notorious for sabotaging the competition with tricks like counter-screwing their bottle caps tightly so that they couldn't be gotten off, or puncturing the caps with icepicks so the wine would go bad, or spraying light oil on the bottles so

dust would collect, making them look like they weren't selling. They deliberately littered ghetto neighborhoods with empty Thunderbird bottles to "advertise" the brand.

Building an empire on a foundation of cheap, flavored alcohol-fortified wines deliberately designed to appeal to heavy drinkers in low-income neighborhoods, the Gallo company eventually moved up the class chain to $60 Cabernets. Their winery factories in Modesto and Livingston are the size of oil refineries, pumping out 40 percent of all wine made in California, one-quarter of all wine sold in the United States— about 70 million cases a year.

NO GALLO CHEESE WITH WINE

Years later the two brothers successfully sued Joseph, Jr. for using his own last name on a line of cheese. Joe sued them unsuccessfully for a percentage of the Gallo winery. The judge, who had been a partner in the Fresno law firm that represented Ernest and Julio, ruled that Joseph hadn't actually proved that his brothers had overtly defrauded him out of his

Flornithology 2

HOW TO TELL THE BIRDS FROM THE FLOWERS

More entries from this helpful field guide by Robert Williams Wood (1868–1955) for those who may have trouble seeing the difference.

The Cowbird The Cowslip	A Sparrow Asparagus
The Tern The Turnip	The Old Gander The Oleander
Mountain Lory Morning Glory	The Quail The Kale

Strange Bible Tales
MORE ODD STUFF FROM THE GOOD BOOK

There are a lot of Bible verses you won't necessarily hear your preacher using as a text. Here are some of the strange things we found while thumbing through.

SEAFOOD'S OUT (LEVITICUS 11:10–11)
"And all that have not fins and scales in the seas, and in the rivers, of all that move in the waters, and of any living thing which is in the waters, they shall be an abomination unto you: They shall be even an abomination unto you; ye shall not eat of their flesh, but ye shall have their carcasses in abomination."

NO HAIRCUTS, SHAVES, OR TATTOOS (LEVITICUS 19:27–8)
"Ye shall not round the corners of your heads, neither shall you mar the corners of thy beard. Ye shall not make any cuttings in your flesh for the dead, nor print any marks upon you: I am the Lord."

BIBLICAL CURE FOR LEPROSY (LEVITICUS 14:1–7)
And the Lord spoke to Moses, saying, "This shall be the law of the leper in the day of his cleansing: He shall be brought unto the priest: And the priest shall go forth out of the camp; and the priest shall look, and, behold, if the plague of leprosy be healed in the leper; then shall the priest command to take for him that is to be cleansed two birds alive and clean, and cedar wood, and scarlet, and hyssop: And the priest shall command that one of the birds be killed in an earthen vessel over running water: As for the living bird, he shall take it, and the cedar wood, and the scarlet, and the hyssop, and shall dip them and the living bird in the blood of the bird that was killed over the running

water: And he shall sprinkle upon him that is to be cleansed from the leprosy seven times, and shall pronounce him clean, and shall let the living bird loose into the open field."

DAUGHTERS OF MINISTERS, BEWARE (LEVITICUS 21:9)

"And the daughter of any priest, if she profane herself by playing the whore, she profanes her father: she shall be burnt with fire."

NO PRIEST CAN HAVE GLASSES, A HANDICAP, A FLAT NOSE, OR CRUSHED TESTICLES (LEVITICUS 21:16–24)

And the Lord spoke unto Moses, saying, "Speak unto Aaron, saying, Whosoever he be of thy seed in their generations that has any defect, let him not approach the altar: a blind man, or a lame one, or he that has a flat nose, or any thing superfluous, or a man that is broken-footed, or broken-handed, or crook-backed, or a dwarf, or that has a defect in his eye, or be scurvy, or scabbed, or has his testicles crushed; no man of the seed of Aaron the priest who has a blemish shall come forward to offer the offerings of the Lord.

"He may eat the bread of his God, both of the most holy, and of the holy, only he shall not go in unto the veil, nor come near the altar, because he has a blemish, that he profane not my sanctuaries: for I the Lord do sanctify them."

GOD REALLY, REALLY DOESN'T LIKE WHINERS (NUMBERS 11:1–35)

And when the Israelis complained, it displeased the Lord: and the Lord heard it; and his anger was kindled; and he sent the fire of the Lord among them, and consumed the outskirts of the camp. And the people cried unto Moses; and when Moses prayed to the Lord, the fire died out.

And the children of Israel wept again, and said, "Who will give us meat to eat? We remember the fish, which we ate in Egypt freely; the cucumbers, melons, leeks, onions, and garlic. But now there is nothing at all except this manna."

The anger of the Lord was kindled greatly; Moses also was displeased. And Moses said to God,..."Whence should I have meat to give unto all this people? For they weep unto me, saying, 'Give us meat, that we may eat.'"

And the Lord said to Moses, "Say to the people,...'The Lord will give you meat, and you shall eat. You shall not eat one day, nor two days, nor five days, neither ten days, nor twenty days; but a whole month, until it comes out of your nostrils, and it be loathsome unto you, that because you have despised the Lord who is among you, and have wept in front of him, saying, 'Why did we ever leave Egypt?'"

And God brought forth a wind, and brought quails from the sea, and let them fall by the camp ... about two cubits high on the face of the earth. And the people stayed up all day and night, and they gathered the quails and they spread them out for themselves round about the camp.

And while the meat was yet between their teeth, before it was chewed, the wrath of the Lord was kindled against the people, and the Lord struck the people with a very great plague. So the name of that place became *Kilbroth-hattaavah* (Grave of the Greedy).

NO CROSS-DRESSING, SEED-MIXING, POLYESTER BLENDS, OR FRINGES (DEUTERONOMY 22:5–12)

"The woman shall not wear a man's clothes, neither shall a man put on a woman's garment: for all that do so are abomination unto the Lord thy God....

"You must not sow your vineyard with two kinds of seeds: or the fruit of your vineyard will be defiled.

"You shall not plow with an ox and an ass together.

"You shall not wear a garment of two fabrics, such as of wool and linen together.

"You shall not make fringes on your garment on the part that covers you."

IF RAPED, YOU MUST MARRY THE RAPIST (DEUTERONOMY 22:25–29)

"If a man finds a girl who is a virgin, who is not engaged, and forces her to have intercourse with him, and they are discovered, then the man shall give to the girl's father 50 shekels of silver, and she shall become his wife because he has violated her; he cannot divorce her all his days."

SORRY JOHN BOBBITT (DEUTERONOMY 23:1–2)

"No one who is emasculated, or has his male organ cut off, shall enter the assembly of God. No one of illegitimate birth shall enter the assembly; none of his descendants, even to the tenth generation, shall enter the assembly of the Lord."

JESUS DRIVES OUT DEMONS, KILLS A HERD OF PIGS, GETS RUN OUT OF TOWN (MATTHEW 8:28–32)

And when Jesus came into the country of the Gergesenes, he met two possessed with demons who were exceeding fierce, so that no man might pass by that way. They cried out, saying, "What have we to do with you, Jesus, you Son of God? Did you come here to torment us before the time?"

And there was a good way off from them an herd of many swine feeding. So the devils besought him, saying, "If thou cast us out, suffer us to go away into the herd of swine."

And he said to them, "Go." And when they left the men, they went into the herd of swine: and, behold, the whole herd of swine ran violently down a cliff into the sea, and perished in the waters. The sheepherders ran to the city and reported everything and the whole city came out to meet Jesus to send him away.

EYEWITNESS DESCRIBES GOD: "AMBER, FIERY FROM THE LOINS DOWN" (EZEKIAL 8:1–2)

And it came to pass in the sixth year, in the sixth month, in the fifth day of the month, as I sat in mine house, and the elders of Judah sat before me, that the hand of the Lord God fell there upon me. Then I beheld a likeness as the appearance of fire: from the appearance of his loins even downward, fire; and from his loins even upward, as the appearance of brightness, as the color of amber.

JESUS' BROTHERS AND SISTERS (MARK 6:3)

Is not this the carpenter, the son of Mary, the brother of James, and Joses, and of Juda, and Simon? And are not his sisters here with us?

GREAT EXPECTORATIONS (MARK 8:22–4)

They brought a blind man to him, and begged Jesus to touch him. And he took the blind man by the hand, and led him out of the town; and when he spat on his eyes and put his hands upon him, he asked him if he saw anything. And he looked up, and said, "I see men as trees, walking."

'Roos Clues

A POCKETFUL OF KANGAROO FACTS

Everyone loves kangaroos, right? It's no wonder. Here are just a few of the amazing reasons why kangaroos fascinate us so.

BEST HOPS FOR THE FUTURE

Kangaroos hop 33 feet per jump, for a maximum speed of about 40 miles per hour. Kangaroos couldn't run even if they wanted to, because their legs are completely unsuited for doing so. Centuries ago, when the lush Australian rain forests dried into deserts, kangaroos needed to be able to travel great distances to find the quantities of food they needed to stay alive. It turned out that hopping requires about 25 percent less energy than running. To add to its energy efficiency, its digestive organs bounce backward and forward with each hop, saving the energy that kangaroos normally have to expend breathing in and out.

BEANY BABIES

When a kangaroo baby's newly born, it's larger than a lima bean but smaller than a full-sized peanut. It's not at all cute, either, unless you're the kind of person who can love something that looks like a slimy pink intestinal worm. Marsupials give birth to tiny, hairless, helpless, blind, nearly larval young after a gestation that lasts only 30–40 days. Looking like undeveloped fetuses (which is essentially what they are), the young are instinctively capable of only two things: crawling up the fur of their mom to the safety of her *marsupium* (pouch) and finding a nipple there to suck upon.

The little joey stays attached to the mother's teat for six or seven months. After that time, the baby finally becomes a miniature version of its parents, leaving Mom's pouch for short hops before returning for protection and food.

TWO HEADS BETTER THAN ONE?
Like all marsupials, kangaroos have bifurcated (forked) penises, and their testicles lie in front of their penises instead of in back like other mammals. Female marsupials have two uteri and two vaginas that share a common fork-shaped opening. The birth canal forms from an opening in the connective tissue between the two vaginas.

WALLABIES AND WANNABES
People wonder if wallabies and wallaroos are the same as kangaroos, or are they just kangaroo wannabes? The truth is that they're all members of one big happy family (*Macropodidae* or "big foot"), which has fifty-five different species. Differences among them are not particularly apparent—what they're called is largely determined by their size and where they live:
- Kangaroos are generally bigger—up to 185 pounds for the red kangaroo—and they prefer congregating in large groups on open, dry, grassland plains.
- Wallaroos are not quite as tall, but they're stocky and

they live in small groups in hilly country.
- Wallabies are much smaller, some as small as rabbits, which works out pretty well since they hang out in places without much traveling space—in dense forests and thick vegetation along rivers and lakes. They also live in small groups.

Be warned, though, that even with these distinctions, there are exceptions. For example, the "tree kangaroo" lives in the forest and is smaller than most other kangaroos, which should arguably make it a "tree wallaby."

CLIMBING UP THE FAMILY TREE
All kangaroos once lived in trees, but as the Australian rain forests turned to desert, Kangaroos adapted into land-based animals. At some point in history, though, the tree kangaroo reversed course and climbed back into the trees, where it now spends most of its time, climbing instead of hoping.

RAT KANGAROOS
Rat kangaroos are not to be confused with kangaroo rats. The former live in the swamps and deserts of northeastern Australia; the latter, in the southwestern deserts of North America.

More Lear

More rhymes and drawings from Edward Lear's classic children's book, *The Book of Nonsense* (published 1846).

There was an Old Person of Rheims,
Who was troubled with horrible dreams;
So, to keep him awake,
They fed him with cake,
Which amused that Old Person of Rheims.

There was an Old Person of Troy,
Whose drink was warm brandy and soy;
Which he took with a spoon,
By the light of the moon,
In sight of the city of Troy.

There was an Old Person of Tring,
Who embellished his nose with a ring;
He gazed at the moon
Every evening in June,
That ecstatic Old Person in Tring.

There was an Old Man of Calcutta,
Who perpetually ate bread and butter,
Till a great bit of muffin,
On which he was stuffing,
Choked that horrid Old Man of Calcutta.

There was an Old Man of Coblenz,
The length of whose legs was immense;
He went with one prance
From Turkey to France,
That surprising Old Man of Coblenz.

There was an Old Man who said, "How
Shall I flee from that horrible cow?
I will sit on this stile,
And continue to smile,
Which may soften the heart of that cow."

There was a Young Lady of Hull,
Who was chased by a virulent bull;
But she seized on a spade,
And called out, "Who's afraid?"
Which distracted that virulent bull.

There was an Old Person of Dutton,
Whose head was as small as a button,
So, to make it look big,
He purchased a wig,
And rapidly rushed about Dutton.

There was an Old Man of the coast,
Who placidly sat on a post;
But when it was cold
He relinquished his hold
And called for some hot buttered toast.

There was an Old Man of Kamschatka,
Who possessed a remarkable fat cur;
His gait and his waddle
Were held as a model
To all the fat dogs in Kamschatka.

There was an Old Man who said, "Hush!
I perceive a young bird in this bush!"
When they said, "Is it small?"
He replied, "Not at all!
It is four times as big as the bush!"

Life Lessons

HOW TO USE A CRICKET AS A THERMOMETER

Have you ever been surprised by the weather outside? After all, how are you supposed to just know how cold it is without actually getting out of your bed or chair? Well, we've got a little trick that just may help.

True, you could go to the trouble of mounting a thermometer outside of your bedroom window.Or we suppose you might even step outside and try to estimate the temperature. But if you'd rather not go to such extreme efforts, you can depend on Nature's Thermometer, the cricket. Here's how:

1. Make sure you have a watch or clock handy that can calibrate seconds.

2. You'll need quiet for this one, so quiet your snoring partner, uproarious neighbors, and overactive children.

3. Sit perfectly still and listen to the outside ambiance through your windows and walls. Find one clear, crisp cricket chirp that's loud enough for you to keep track of its call.

4. Watch your watch and count the number of chirps you hear from your cricket within 14 seconds.

5. Add 40 to your chirp number, and you'll get the approximate number of degrees Fahrenheit outside. Dress accordingly.

H. L. Mencken vs. the World

H. L. Mencken (1880–1956) was a controversial curmudgeon who penned "Those who can't do, teach" and "No one ever went broke underestimating the taste of the American public."

- "Puritanism: The haunting fear that someone, somewhere may be happy."

- "Imagine the Creator as a low comedian, and at once the world becomes explicable."

- "The only really happy folk are married women and single men."

- "A cynic is a man who, when he smells flowers, looks around for a coffin."

- "We must respect the other fellow's religion, but only in the sense and to the extent that we respect his theory that his wife is beautiful and his children smart."

- "The kind of man who wants the government to adopt and enforce his ideas is always the kind of man whose ideas are idiotic."

- "For every problem, there is one solution which is simple, neat, and wrong."

- "Every failure teaches a man something; to wit, that he will probably fail again."

- "Women have simple tastes. They can get pleasure out of the conversation of children in arms and men in love."

- "On one issue at least, men and women agree: they both distrust women."

- "Conscience is the inner voice that warns us that somebody is looking."

- "God is the immemorial refuge of the incompetent, the helpless, the miserable. They find not only sanctuary in His arms, but also a kind of superiority, soothing to their macerated egos: He will set them above their betters."

- "Men become civilized, not in proportion to their willingness to believe, but in proportion to their readiness to doubt."

- "There are two kinds of books: those that no one reads and those that no one ought to read."

- "Democracy is the art and science of running the circus from the monkey cage."

- "Under democracy one party always devotes its chief energies to trying to prove that the other party is unfit to rule — and both commonly succeed, and are right."

- "The older I grow, the more I distrust the familiar doctrine that age brings wisdom."

- "Always remember this: If you don't attend the funerals of your friends, they will certainly not attend yours."

The Open Window

A SHORT STORY BY SAKI (HECTOR MONRO)

Before he was killed in World War I, Hector Monro wrote short stories with a twist under the pen name "Saki." In this one, a nervous man is confronted by the supernatural....

"**M**Y AUNT will be down presently, Mr. Nuttel," said a very self-possessed young lady of fifteen. "In the meantime you must try and put up with me."

Framton Nuttel endeavored to say the correct something which should duly flatter the niece of the moment without unduly discounting the aunt that was to come. Privately he doubted more than ever whether these formal visits on a succession of total strangers would do much toward helping the nerve cure which he was supposed to be undergoing.

"I know how it will be," his sister had said when he was preparing to migrate to this rural retreat; "you will bury yourself down there and not speak to a living soul, and your nerves will be worse than ever from moping. I shall just give you letters of introduction to all the people I know there. Some of them, as far as I can remember, were quite nice."

Framton wondered whether Mrs. Sappleton, the lady to whom he was presenting one of the letters of introduction, came into the nice division.

"Do you know many of the people round here?" asked the niece, when she judged that they had had sufficient silent communion.

"Hardly a soul," said Framton. "My sister was staying here, at the rectory, you know, some four years ago, and she gave me letters of introduction to some of the people here."

He made the last statement in a tone of distinct regret.

"Then you know practically nothing about my aunt?" pursued the self-possessed young lady.

"Only her name and address," admitted the caller. He was wondering whether Mrs. Sappleton was in the married or widowed state. An undefinable something about the room seemed to suggest masculine habitation.

"Her great tragedy happened just three years ago," said the child; "that would be since your sister's time."

"Her tragedy?" asked Framton; somehow in this restful country spot tragedies seemed out of place.

"You may wonder why we keep that window wide open on an October afternoon," said the niece, indicating a large French window that opened on to a lawn.

"It is quite warm for the time of the year," said Framton; "but has that window got anything to do with the tragedy?"

"Out through that window, three years ago to a day, her husband and her two young brothers went off for their day's shooting. They never came back. In crossing the moor to their favorite snipe-shooting ground they were all three engulfed in a treacherous piece of bog. It had been that dreadful wet summer, you know, and places that were safe in other years gave way suddenly without warning. Their bodies were never recovered. That was the dreadful part of it." Here the child's voice lost its self-possessed note and became falteringly human. "Poor aunt always thinks that they will come back some day, they and the little brown spaniel that was lost with them, and walk in at that window just as they used to do. That is why the window is kept open every evening till it is quite dusk. Poor dear aunt, she has often told me how they went out, her husband with his white waterproof coat over his arm, and Ronnie, her youngest brother, singing 'Bertie, why do you bound?' as he always did to tease her, because she said it got on her nerves. Do you know, sometimes on still, quiet evenings like this, I almost get a creepy feeling that they will all walk in through that window—"

She broke off with a little shudder. It was a relief to Framton when the aunt bustled into the room with a whirl of apologies for being late in making her appearance.

"I hope Vera has been amusing you?" she said.

"She has been very interesting," said Framton.

"I hope you don't mind the open window," said Mrs. Sappleton briskly; "my husband and brothers will be home directly from shooting, and they always come in this way. They've been out for snipe in the marshes today, so they'll make a fine mess over my poor carpets. So like you men-folk, isn't it?"

She rattled on cheerfully about the shooting and the scarcity of birds, and the prospects for duck in the winter. To Framton it was all purely horrible. He made a desperate but only partially successful effort to turn the talk on to a less ghastly topic; he was conscious that his hostess was giving him only a fragment of her attention, and her eyes were constantly straying past him to the open window and the lawn beyond. It was certainly an unfortunate coincidence that he should have paid his visit on this tragic anniversary.

"The doctors agree in ordering me complete rest, an absence of mental excitement, and avoidance of violent physical exercise," announced Framton, who labored under the tolerably wide-spread delusion that total strangers and chance acquaintances are hungry for the least detail of one's ailments and infirmities, their cause, and cure. "On the matter of diet they are not so much in agreement," he continued.

"No?" said Mrs. Sappleton, in a voice which only replaced a yawn at the last moment. Then she suddenly brightened into alert attention—but not to what Framton was saying.

"Here they are at last!" she cried. "Just in time for tea, and don't they look as if they were muddy up to the eyes!"

Framton shivered slightly and turned toward the niece with a look intended to convey sympathetic comprehension. The child was staring out through the open window with dazed horror in her eyes. In a chill shock of nameless fear Framton swung round in his seat and looked in the same direction.

In the deepening twilight three figures were walking across the lawn toward the window; they all carried guns under their arms, and one of them was additionally burdened with a white coat hung over his shoulders. A tired brown spaniel kept close at their heels. Noiselessly they neared the house, and then a hoarse young voice chanted out of the dusk: "I said, Bertie, why do you bound?"

Framton grabbed wildly at his stick and hat; the hall-door, the gravel-drive, and the front gate were dimly-noted stages in his headlong retreat. A cyclist coming along the road had to run into the hedge to avoid an imminent collision.

"Here we are, my dear," said the bearer of the white mackintosh, coming in through the window; "fairly muddy, but most of it's dry. Who was that who bolted out as we came up?"

"A most extraordinary man, a Mr. Nuttel," said Mrs. Sappleton; "could only talk about his illnesses, and dashed off without a word of good-bye or apology when you arrived. One would think he had seen a ghost."

"I expect it was the spaniel," said the niece calmly; "he told me he had a horror of dogs. He was once hunted into a cemetery somewhere on the banks of the Ganges by a pack of pariah dogs, and had to spend the night in a newly dug grave with the creatures snarling and grinning and foaming just above him. Enough to make anyone lose their nerve."

Romance at short notice was her speciality.

THE HISTORY OF THE HAWAIIAN SHIRT

THE HAWAIIAN SHIRT, that overly colorful garb favored by American tourists and extroverted college-age guys, is the result of missionaries sent to Hawaii in the 1800s. Scandalized by the overabundance of naked flesh, they introduced large, colorless, one-size-fits-all shirts and muumuus. The natives decided that if they had to wear clothes, they at least should be colorful, so they took the plain cotton garments and decorated them with bright Polynesian designs.

The 1920s brought a tourist boom to Hawaii. Tourists carried the gaudy, tropical shirts back to the mainland as souvenirs. Later, during World War II, soldiers and sailors on leave discovered that Hawaiian shirts made a cheap and colorful replacement for the drabness of their uniforms.

After two decades of depression and war, there was another big Hawaii tourist boom in the 1950s, followed by a faddish interest in the islands after they became an American state in 1959.

Cursed Opera

IS TOSCA AN OVERTURE TO DISASTER?

According to theater folklore, certain productions are staged only at
the risk of great peril.

THE HISTORICAL OPERA *TOSCA* is about intrigue and treachery
in the Vatican. According to backstage legend, it's also
cursed, and terrible things may happen to those who dare
perform it. Well, we're not so sure about that, but we're
impressed by the string of bad-luck stories, even though some
of them may only be legendary.

• In the first night of a 1995 production in Rome, tenor Mario
Cavaradossi was injured after debris fired from blanks punc-
tured his leg. The script called for Tosca (Raina Kabaivanska) to
rush to his fallen body; when she did so, his fallen body whispered to her, "Call an ambulance...." Kabaivanska promptly
passed out onstage at the sight of his blood, stopping the show.

• But the show must go on. After recuperating in the hospital,
Cavaradossi returned to the show hobbling and on crutches.
His first night back, he made it through most of the first act.
While waiting in the wings, his crutches slipped and he fell,
breaking his *other* leg in two places. "Could it be that I am destined to never leave this theater on my own two feet?" he complained as he was carried away on a stretcher.

• The same scene has caused problems before. In a 1965 production in Rome, the gunfire scorched the face of tenor Gianni
Raimonde. And, according to legend, another tenor in an early
production was killed in the same scene.

• However, *not* having the guns go off proved fatal to yet
another tenor. He was nonplussed when the guns failed to go

off as scheduled, and promptly died of a heart attack.

• Professionalism under pressure: During a production in Covent Garden, Maria Callas's hair caught on fire during a scene with Scarpia, a villain played by Tito Gobbi. Gobbi improvised a lecherous lunge, embracing her while patting out the fire. Callas responded in character by recoiling from from the villain, whispering, "Thank you, Tito," as her character followed the script and stabbed his character to death.

Composer of the cursed opera, Giacomo Puccini

• In the 1920s, another performance at the Metropolitan Opera in New York ended during the same scene. A trick blade failed to retract, and Tosca (Maria Jeritza) stabbed Scarpia (Antonio Scotti) for real. He survived and continued in the role for another decade.

• Not surprisingly, a scene where Tosca flings herself off a parapet is another one where mishaps can happen. In 1993, Elisabeth Knighton Printy jumped off the wrong side of the stage in St. Paul, Minnesota, and fell more than 30 feet, breaking both legs.

• Legend has it that stagehands were worried about one particularly hefty soprano and replaced the mattress below with a trampoline. When the time came to jump, Tosca dramatically sang her farewell and leaped into the darkness. An instant later, she bounced back into view two or three times, bringing down the house.

• Another incident, perhaps apocryphal, turned the same dramatic scene into an incident of mass suicide. In one rushed production, the "supers"—extras hired to stand around in costume on-stage—weren't in on the rehearsals, so the director gave them the opening night instructions to "exit with the principals." When Tosca leaped, the supers, seeing no other principal players on stage, shrugged and leaped after her.

SHUT UP AND DEAL
Do the math—there are 635,013,599,600 possible hands of bridge.

After You Flush

WHAT HAPPENS TO THE STUFF IN THE BOWL?

You flush. Waste and water whirlpool down the drain and out of your life. Where does it go? What happens to it? We sent one of our intrepid staff members—Oilville Goochland—to find out. Here's his report.

A S SOON AS YOU FLUSH THE TOILET, you start a process that is a modest miracle. One day, with the help of sewer and sanitation workers, I traced the path of waste from my home near Oakland, California. Its system is typical of that of most modern cities.

Flushing the toilet sends body waste surfing on several gallons of water down through an S-shaped stink trap and into a pipe that threads through the walls and under the floor. A small pipe beneath the house leads to a pipe under the street and eventually to an 18-inch-wide sewer main, headed on a 3-hour, 7-mile trip toward a sewage treatment plant near Oakland's Bay Bridge.

The sewer system here has 1,800 miles of sewer pipes serving more than 600,000 people in eight cities covering 83 square miles. After meandering through sewer mains for a few hours and about 5 miles, coaxed along by gravity and pumping stations, my flush reaches the interceptor main, so-called because it intercepts the waste that once flowed freely into the open waters. Until 1951, the sewage dumped right into the San Francisco Bay. It was so bad that health agencies in the 1930s prohibited all recreational water activities, and motorists driving along the shore made a habit of raising their windows and holding their noses at the stench. Finally, the East Bay Municipal Utility District (EBMUD) built huge "interceptor mains" paralleling the shoreline.

The mains are huge, 9 feet across—easily big enough to drive a car through. My flush has become completely indistinguishable from the rest of a fast-moving sewage river rolling and tumbling into the sewage treatment plant— urine, fecal matter, toilet paper, and waste water have dissolved into a brown, smelly soup.

An average of more than a million gallons of sewage arrive here every hour, about 80 million gallons a day. The river peaks at about 10 A.M. (when the morning showers and flushes arrive) and 10 P.M. (from the evening's baths, laundry, and dish washing). The plant can handle up to 320 million gallons a day, with temporary storage of another 95 million gallons, which sometimes becomes necessary during storms when rainwater seeps into ancient, broken pipes upstream.

STRAINING AT STOOL

At the plant, a walk down a flight of stairs lets you see and smell the river of sewage flowing in. Here treatment begins with a pipe spewing chlorine to kill bacteria.

Each step in the sewage treatment process removes a specific class of material from the water waste. The first step strains out what they call "rags," whether made of cloth or not, which just means the really big stuff. The sewage runs through two grates of vertical bars. The first has bars set 4 inches apart to catch the really big stuff: shoes, dead animals, rocks, ropes, and other large things that have inexplicably found their way into the pipes. The bars on the second grate are a half-inch apart to catch the smaller stuff. A long rake continually moves along the bars, pulling things like feminine hygiene products, baby wipes, condoms, string, dental floss, and unidentifiable

A tour group gets a glimpse and whiff of the incoming sewage.

clumps of paper onto a conveyor belt headed for a landfill truck.

An engineer tells me that sometimes they find paper money caught among the "rags." So what do you do, I ask? He pauses with a half-smile, choosing his words carefully. "We take it out, wash it off, and put it back into circulation."

SHOWING A LITTLE GRIT

The water moves next into one of the eight grit aeration tanks. "Grit" is used to mean anything that sinks. This includes sand, gravel, coffee grounds, eggshells, and much of the stuff that people grind up in kitchen garbage disposals. The method is simple: Air jets bubble up lighter stuff and allow heavier stuff to hit bottom. There's a giant screw in the bottom of the tank that constantly pushes the grit out of the tank for disposal in a landfill.

Bubbling in the air, explains my guide, also "keeps anaerobic bacteria from smelling up the place. It strips out gasoline, diesel fuel, and hydrogen sulfide, the gas that smells like rotten eggs. And it floats the scum—your basic oils and greases—so we can deal with it in the sed tanks."

SEDIMENTARY JOURNEY

After degritting and floating the scum, the sewage flows into one of sixteen sedimentation tanks. There it sits for about 2 hours, allowing sludge solids to settle to the bottom of the tank. What look like extra-long bicycle chains glide bars across the tank to skim off scum. A similar system is working unseen at the bottom of the tank, scraping sludge to a low spot on one end, where a pump sucks it out and sends it to the digesters (which we'll visit later).

AN INFUSION OF CULTURE

In the next tank, the wastewater gets dosed with tons of oxygen—about 140 tons a day. The plant manufactures its own supply, cooling compressed air down to –175° C until it becomes a liquid, and separating the oxygen out by distillation.

While a huge blender blade stirs the oxygenated mixture, the plant adds "activated sludge" enriched with microorganisms. It acts like yeast in bread dough, multiplying like microscopic rabbits in the oxygen-rich water and gobbling up most of the remaining pollutants.

Staff microbiologists have to

When an uncultured biomass takes over, it looks like "a huge chocolate mousse."

17 feet across and able to hold 1.5 million gallons of water.

As the water flows through, giant scrapers rotate constantly along the bottom, moving solids out of the tank. Most of those solids are microorganisms from the previous step, which are shipped back to the oxygenation tank to culture the next batch of wastewater.

The water—now clear and smelling like water—continues on through a flow control system that looks a lot like a large-scale decorative water sculpture in a hotel lobby.

Before the water leaves the plant, it's again dosed with chlorine to kill pathogens, then dosed with sulfur dioxide to neutralize the chlorine's negative effects on wildlife. The water travels 3 miles into the San Francisco Bay before being released. To minimize its impact on the bay, the water comes out of dozens of small holes, like a giant garden soaker hose, instead of one large opening. A little of the water is recycled for use on the grounds, but EBMUD has elaborate future plans for recycling this virtually clean waste water back to customers for irrigation, landscaping, and toilet-flushing.

watch this phase closely. "Certain troublesome microorganisms can take over if we don't constantly balance out the system," says my guide. What happens then? "With an unhealthy biomass, we see excessive flotation and foaming—sometimes enough to come right over the handrails. When that happens, it looks like a huge chocolate mousse."

SEEKING CLARIFICATION

After its 2 hours in the oxygenation tank, the water moves into a big round pool called a secondary clarifier,

SLUDGE FEST

As we wave good-bye to the reclaimed water, only the sludge remains.

After it was pumped out of the sedimentation tanks and clarifiers, the sludge traveled to one of twelve huge white silo-shaped tanks called digesters. As the name implies, a digester works like a stomach, holding the sludge with no air circulation at 95° F, allowing anaerobic bacteria to do its smelly thing. Much gas is produced in the process, and it's about 60 percent methane. It's piped to the plant's power station and burned, generating about 40 percent of the plant's electrical needs.

After 25 to 30 days, the sludge emerges as a wet, soil-like humus. It travels to one of three perpetually howling centrifuges to remove excess water. The sludge no longer smells like an outhouse, but sort of fishy, like the beach at low tide. The sludge flows in at a rate of a thousand gallons per minute, gets spun at 1,600 RPMs, and then flows out the other end.

Despite the days of digestion, there's still a lot of it. What do they do with it? Some sludge gets used by landfills to cover up the day's trash. Some is trucked into rural areas and spread on farmland as a soil conditioner for crops. And for a little irony, some is composted and sold to fertilizer companies that, in turn, sell it back to the same consumers who flushed it down the toilet months earlier.

WINGING IT

According to the Catholic Church, angels have ranks and hierarchies, just like the employees of a well-run utility company. Let's start from the bottom:

Third Choir

1. Angels: Your basic winged guardians who watch over us all.

2. Archangels: Angelic equivalent of foremen or sergeants.

3. Principalities: Supervisors of the archangels and angels.

Second Choir

4. Powers: Lower middle-management angels that report to Virtues.

5. Virtues: Middle middle managers that report to Dominions.

6. Dominions: Upper middle managers, not much more known about them.

First Choir

7. Thrones: Seem to be high-ranking administrative assistants to higher-ups.

8. Cherubim: Executive VPs with wings, human head, and an animal's body.

9. Seraphim: Notable by their six wings, Seraphim are the only beings allowed in the presence of God.

Secrets of '76

THINGS YOU DIDN'T KNOW ABOUT THE REVOLUTION

You know everything about the American Revolution, right? We thought so, too, but here are some things that might surprise you about that part of history.

THERE WERE TWO BOSTON TEA PARTIES
Well, okay, sequels never get the same attention as the original. Which is why we don't hear much about the second one. The first time the Sons of Liberty snuck aboard British ships and dumped tea in the harbor took place on December 16, 1773; the second one, on March 7, 1774. Both were meant to protest a tax of 3¢ per pound on tea; between the two parties, the little stunt cost British monopoly the equivalent of $3 million in modern money.

JOHN ADAMS DEFENDED THE BRITISH IN COURT ... AND WON
The Boston Massacre was used well by revolutionary propagandists, who portrayed the incident as a case of British soldiers killing four Americans with little provocation. In fact, the soldiers were under attack. One was being beaten with a board and pelted with rocks and ice when other British soldiers ran to his defense. They came under attack as well, and eventually they fired their guns at the crowd. Despite his sympathy for the rebels, John Adams figured they deserved a fair trial. He did a good job, too—two of the four defendants were found innocent, the other two guilty of manslaughter ... but that sentence was commuted to making penance (under the plea of "benefit of clergy") and having their thumbs branded with a C.

THE REVOLUTIONARY WAR SAW THE FIRST SUBMARINE ATTACK
This was in New York Harbor on September 6, 1776. A
Connecticut inventor named David Bushnel got his design
inspiration from a tortoise and created a one-man, hand-pro-
pelled submarine of two rounded shells that he called (sensibly
enough) the Turtle. Late that autumn night, the Turtle submerged and snuck up on the HMS *Eagle*, the flagship of the
British Navy. Alas, it had to surface before it could fulfill its
mission of securing a cask of gunpowder to the *Eagle's* hull. To
speed the retreat, the Turtle dropped its cask, which exploded
with a harmless 'though deafening explosion, and high tailed it
back to shore.

BENEDICT ARNOLD WAS A DAMNED FINE GENERAL
For the three years before he turned traitor, Benedict Arnold
was the best general the Continental Army had. He nearly captured Canada, fought the British Navy to a standstill on Lake
Champlain, and captured a large contingent of the British Army
at Saratoga. Ironically, this last victory convinced the French to
send troops to help the revolutionaries against their ancient
enemies, the British. It was an alliance that Arnold strongly
deplored—so much so, that he decided to switch sides, instead
of fight alongside the hated French. As a British officer, he led
expeditions that burned Richmond, Virginia, and New London,
Connecticut. After the war, he moved to London, England.

ONE IN SEVEN CONTINENTAL SOLDIERS WAS BLACK
It was an idea that made George Washington nervous—giving
arms to volunteer slaves and freemen. However, when a battal-
ion of African Americans distinguished themselves at the Battle
of Bunker Hill, he changed his mind. The much-decorated First
Rhode Island Regiment consisted of 33 freedmen and 92 slaves
who were promised freedom if they served. They distinguished
themselves in the Battle of Newport. However, not many of the
enslaved soldiers lived long enough to be freed—the regiment
was all but wiped out in a British attack.

MORE AMERICANS JOINED THE BRITISH SIDE
About a third of Americans supported the revolution. About a
third supported the king. The rest just wanted to be left alone.
The British recruiting efforts were better than the Continental

Army's. In a 1779 count, there were 6,500—8,000 Americans in the British Army, and only 3,468 with the revolutionaries.

IF IT WEREN'T FOR THE FRENCH, THE PATRIOTS WOULD'VE LOST
The French had reason to want to screw things up for the British in the New World, so they dived in to help the Americans. Their Navy blockaded much of the coastline, and their Army fortified the small American force. At the battle that won the war, Yorktown, there were nearly three French soldiers and sailors for every one American. Washington's Army had grown to 11,000, but it was the 29,000 French troops that turned the redcoated tide.

THE SITE OF THE BOSTON TEA PARTY IS NOW ON SOLID GROUND
The city has filled in so much of the Boston Harbor that the site is several hundred yards inland, near a freeway.

PAUL REVERE DIDN'T MAKE IT TO CONCORD AND LEXINGTON
If Paul Revere didn't make it to warn the Minutemen, then why is he famous? Maybe because "Listen my children and you shall hear/Of the midnight ride of Dr. Samuel Preston" doesn't rhyme. In fact, three men rode out on the journey. Revere and Richard Dawes got turned back by the British. Prescott, though, slipped around the enemy. He was the guy shouting, "The British are coming!" as he rode to Concord.

A SIGNER OF THE DECLARATION CHANGED HIS MIND ... TWICE
After signing the Declaration of Independence and agreeing to "mutually pledge to each other our Lives, our Fortunes and our sacred Honor," Richard Stockton of Princeton, New Jersey, changed his mind. He had had qualms in the first place, and when he got captured by the British during the war, he decided to sign an oath disavowing the document and swearing allegiance to the king. However, after the war ended, he changed his mind again and publicly supported the winning side.

KING GEORGE III NEARLY RESIGNED AFTER THE LOSS OF AMERICA
After Parliament refused to keep fighting after the British loss at Yorktown, George III drafted a letter of abdication, but didn't follow through. He did keep his hopes high, however, that the Americans would beg to have him as king again.

The Devil's Dictionary: K–L

More of *The Devil's Dictionary* by Ambrose Bierce (1842–1914?)

KILL, *v.t.* To create a vacancy without nominating a successor.

KILT, *n.* A costume sometimes worn by Scotchmen in America and Americans in Scotland.

KING, *n.* A male person commonly known in America as a "crowned head," although he never wears a crown and has usually no head to speak of.

KLEPTOMANIAC, *n.* A rich thief.

LABOR, *n.* One of the processes by which A acquires property for B.

LAP, *n.* One of the most important organs of the female system—an admirable provision of nature for the repose of infancy, but chiefly useful in rural festivities to support plates of cold chicken and heads of adult males.

LAUGHTER, *n.* An interior convulsion, producing a distortion of the features and accompanied by inarticulate noises. It is infectious and, though intermittent, incurable.

LAWFUL, *adj.* Compatible with the will of a judge having jurisdiction.

LAWYER, *n.* One skilled in circumvention of the law.

LAZINESS, *n.* Unwarranted repose of manner in a person of low degree.

LEXICOGRAPHER, *n.* A pestilent fellow who, under the pretense of recording some stage in the development of a language, does what he can to arrest its growth, stiffen its flexibility and mechanize its methods.

LIBERTY, *n.* One of Imagination's most precious possessions.

LIFE, *n.* A spiritual pickle preserving the body from decay. We live in daily apprehension of its loss; yet when lost it is not missed.

LINEN, *n.* A kind of cloth the making of which, when made of hemp, entails a great waste of hemp.

LITIGATION, *n.* A machine which you go into as a pig and come out of as a sausage.

LOQUACITY, *n.* A disorder which renders the sufferer unable to curb his tongue when you wish to talk.

LOVE, *n.* A temporary insanity curable by marriage.

LUMINARY, *n.* One who throws light upon a subject; as an editor by not writing about it.

Cold Comfort

HOW THE POPSICLE GOT ON THE STICK

It's a sugary, fruity drink, frozen on two sticks so you can split it with a friend. Here's the story behind this comforting childhood treat.

HOW MANY THINGS have been invented by eleven-year-old boys? Lots, no doubt. But how many of them would you want to stick in your mouth?

Eleven-year-old Frank Epperson, the story goes, accidentally left a glass of soda pop mix and water on his back porch. The stirring stick was still in it. That night the temperature got well below freezing. Absentminded Frank went out and found the stick emerging from a frozen block of soft drink. His friends and family were amazed. On that night in 1905, the Popsicle was invented.

You could question the details of the story. On a cold winter's day, after all, how many people take a cold drink outside to enjoy? How often do eleven-year-olds mix up a soft drink and then forget to drink it? Isn't it more likely that Epperson had figured out what would happen and left the glass outside on purpose? Or, even more likely, that he simply made up the story years later when his patent application came under question? Hmmm.

Well, regardless, a decade or two later, the very same Frank Epperson was running a lemonade stand at an amusement park in Oakland, California. When a man has to stand and squeeze lemons all day, he starts thinking philosophically. Epperson decided that when life hands you lemonade, you should make Popsicles. He remembered that cold winter night years earlier and decided to blow that lemonade stand and go into the business of selling fruity frozen confections.

Epperson started making his frozen drinks at home and transporting them each morning to the the amusement park to sell. He called them Epsicles, after his name and "icicles." Nobody seemed too excited by the name, including his own children, who took to calling them "Pop's cycles." Eventually, that name more or less stuck. Popsicles it was.

Epperson later admitted that he had heard about ice cream on a stick not long before he'd begun making Popsicles. A few years earlier, a man named Harry Burt had figured out a way to keep the ice cream from falling off. He called the product "Good Humor." However, Burt went into a decidedly bad humor when he heard that Epperson was trying to patent Popsicles, figuring the similarity was more than coincidental. Burt protested Epperson's patent in 1923. The two eventually reached a compromise: Epperson agreed to make only sherbet and water ice products and leave the dairy-

based concoctions to Burt. (Many years later the two companies merged.)

Popsicles grew very popular in outdoor summer events in the 1920s. When the Great Depression hit, however, the company's profits slipped fast. In response, the company designed the two-sticked Twin Popsicle we know today, so that two kids could share one nickel Popsicle.

At first, Epperson froze each Popsicle in a large test tube using a several-hour process. Nowadays, though, it takes only about eight minutes. The molds sit in a pool of supercooled brine, and the liquid formula is squirted into them. After a few minutes, the sticks are stuck in when the liquid is half-frozen and thick enough to hold them up. At the end, the mold is lifted out of the brine and heated slightly. Machines pull the hardened Popsicle out of the molds and dip them in water. A thin layer of the water freezes, smoothing the surface and giving the Popsicle a glossy sheen.

Millions of Popsicles are sold in about three dozen different flavors. But the top three best-selling flavors are the traditional orange, cherry, and grape.

Between Courses

TRICKS FOR THE DINNER TABLE

These are tricks that will endear you to everyone at the table ... except perhaps the person who owns the fine crystal that you're trying to flip spoons into.

L OOKING FOR A WAY TO AMUSE YOURSELF, your friends, or small children at a restaurant or between courses at a family dinner? Then we've got some amusing stunts for you. Just one word of caution: Try these tricks at home first ... with your own dishes.

WINE GLASS BALANCE

This one looks downright scary, but is mostly harmless. You pick up a wine glass and hold it on the top edge of the plate. Subtly adjusting it, like you're trying to find the balance point, you suddenly let go. It wobbles a little, but people are amazed when the wine glass stays put.

How you do it. As you're holding the dinner plate with your hand, you sneak your thumb up to support the glass.

TIDDLY SPOONS

Let's do launch! Whaddya say, best of 10 tries, or until we break the glass ... whichever comes first?

SUPPORTING THE MIDDLE GLASS

Place four glasses in a square pattern and challenge those present to suspend a fifth glass in the center of the pattern using just four dinner knives, with neither glass nor knives touching the table.

How you do it. Temporarily put the fifth glass in the center of the pattern as a support. Lay the knives down in the overlapping pattern below. If you do it right, you can move the middle glass to the top of the knife blades, where it will stay suspended in midair. Violà!

CHANGING SEASONS

You take a clear glass shaker, very obviously full of salt, and when you pour it, pepper comes out.

How you do it. Unscrew the cover of a clear glass salt shaker and lay a paper napkin over the top. Push the napkin into the shaker, creating a shallow pocket. Fill this pocket with pepper. Screw the cover back onto the shaker, being careful not to tear the napkin inside. If you don't see flecks of pepper falling into the salt, you're okay. Carefully tear away the excess paper from the napkin that's sticking out from around the edge of the cover. Now, when someone shakes the salt, pepper will come out. Now do the reverse to the pepper shaker.

A BIG JERK AT THE DINNER TABLE

What's the classic stunt that's infamous for disastrous results? Ah yes, the old jerk-the-tablecloth bit.

How to do it. We don't recommend start-ing with a full china set—maybe a napkin, a glass, and water-tolerant carpet. Grasp the napkin firmly, and slide it swiftly from under the glass. Don't jerk it hard, but don't pull too softly, either. If you do it right, the glass will remain on the table and not a drop will spill. If you do it wrong ... well, at least you have a napkin on hand.

UNIDENTIFIED FLYING SAUCERS

This is another stunt involving skill, dexterity, and jeopardy to place settings. We suggest trying it on a soft couch first.

How to do it. Place a saucer upside down

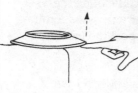 with its lip extending beyond the edge of the table. Point your index finger under the overhanging lip of the saucer. Now, flip the saucer into the air with your finger and catch it between your thumb and middle finger before it lands again on the table. Simple!

FRUIT ON THE REBOUND

You suddenly bounce an apple off the floor, nearly to the ceiling. You catch it nonchalantly and take a bite out of it.

 **How you do it.** Without warning, lift a fruit or baked potato above shoulder level and pitch it at the floor, as hard as you can. (Nobody can see that you didn't actually let go, because your hand has gone below table level.) At exactly the same time, tap your foot loudly against the floor and follow the apple's presumed path with your eyes. For the "rebound," flip the apple straight into the air with your hand and wrist only, without moving your arm.

A TIME FOR LEVITATION

There is no time like mealtime for revealing your awesome hidden powers of levitation. Please use these secrets only for good, not for evil.

ASSAULT ON GRAVITY

1. Hide a toothpick behind your middle finger and hold it there with your thumb.

2. Announce that the secrets of levitation have been taught you by your esteemed guru, A. Baba Reba. Place your middle finger on the top of the salt shaker. Craftily wedge your hidden toothpick into one of the shaker's holes.

3. Command the salt shaker to rise. Slowly lift your hand a few inches off the table as your hand and brow tremble with the psychokinetic effort.

4. Bring the shaker back to earth and dislodge the toothpick. Announce: "You have just witnessed a miracle!" Ditch the toothpick in your lap; don't repeat the trick.

SELF-RISING BREAD

This is an old trick; but if somebody claims to know it there's even a variation to confound them.

1. Hold a breadstick in your left fist. Turn your hand toward you and away from your companions.

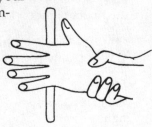

2. Grasp your wrist with your right hand. Sneak your unseen right index finger up into your hand and rest it on the breadstick to hold it in place. Slowly open your fist—the breadstick stays attached to your hand!

3. That's the trick. But since this is an old one, somebody may say they can do it, too. If so, challenge them to demonstrate. As they do, secretly slip a knife under your watchband, and when you do the trick again, wedge the breadstick under its blade.

4. Say: "One thing Guru Baba Reba taught me was to never take the other hand away." With that, you pull your right hand away from your wrist. The breadstick will stay in place. Ooh!

CORPORATE AMERICA SPEAKS

Protecting consumers is not something that comes naturally to the people who run corporations. Seat belts? Air pollution standards? What seems like common sense now was once derided as "radical" and "absurd." Here are some examples.

• *"Hell, there's more nitrates in a kiss than in a ton of bacon."* — Larry Lee, National Pork Producers' Council

• *"If no changes are made, either by Congress or the EPA, we will not be able to build cars after late 1974 because we will not be able to meet the standards."* — Henry Ford II, whining about clean air mandates

• *"All this concern about auto safety ... it's of the same order as the hula hoop — a fad. Six months from now, we'll probably be on another kick."* — W. B. Murphy, president of Campbell's Soup Company, commenting on fickle consumers and their concerns

• *"I find it difficult to believe that the seat belt can afford the driver any great amount of protection over and above that which is available to him through the medium of the safety-type steering wheel if he has his hands on the wheel and grips the rim sufficiently tight to take advantage of its energy absorption properties and also takes advantage of the shock-absorbing action which can be achieved by correct positioning of the feet and legs."* — Howard Gandelot, vehicle safety engineer for General Motors, 1954

• *"We should not fall prey to the beautification extremists who have no sense of economic reality."* — Fred L. Hartley, president of Union Oil

• *"Uninterrupted scenery, too, can get pretty monotonous. Billboards are only a way of humanizing what is still an overwhelming landscape."* — June Martino, McDonald's executive, 1959

A Name in Common?

It's easy, really—we'll give you a series of first or last names and you tell us what name goes with all of them. For example, number 1 is "Irving." Now try the rest.

1. Washington, Berlin, Julius.
2. Washington, Lloyd, Sand, Custer, Clooney.
3. Woody, Hesse, Melville, Wouk, Pee-wee.
4. Brooks, Laird, Harold, Ott, Gibson.
5. Patrick, Ford, O., John, VIII.
6. Kennedy, Billy, Pete, MacGowan, Bowl.
7. Kennedy, Jay, Adams, Elton.
8. Eddy, Palmer, Benedict, the Pig.
9. Bowie, Henry, Brown, P. D., Jesse.
10. Danny, Aquinas, Clarence, Jefferson.
11. George, Ness, T. S.
12. Hal, Camp, Garrick, Niven, Letterman.
13. James, Brothers, Kilmer, Oates.
14. Meredith, Henry, Spike, Jason, Oswald, Marvin.
15. King, Hardy, North, Cromwell, Twist.
16. Joe, St., Armstrong, L'Amour, XIV.
17. Mary, Van Buren, Dean, Luther, Purple.
18. Jones, John, Dizzy, Jimmy, James, Rusk.
19. Mrs., Simon, Peter, Les, Ru, Revere.
20. Ives, Ray, Prince, Nick & Nora, Schultz, Dickens.

ANSWERS: 1. Irving; 2. George; 3. Herman; 4. Melvin; 5. Henry; 6. Rose; 7. John; 8. Arnold; 9. James; 10. Thomas; 11. Eliot; 12. David; 13. Joyce; 14. Lee; 15. Oliver; 16. Louis; 17. Martin; 18. Dean; 19. Paul; 20. Charles.

Oscar Who?

THE NAMES BEHIND THE AWARDS AND PRIZES

Who is Nobel and could he have ever won a Peace Prize? Did Pulitzer embody excellence in journalism? For that matter, were Ryder, Heisman, and Stanley even athletes?

THE AWARD: NOBEL PEACE PRIZE
WHAT IT'S FOR: PEACEMAKERS
NAMED FOR: THE INVENTOR OF DYNAMITE

The Nobel Peace Prize is something of an irony, in that it was funded by the inventor of dynamite. It's said that Alfred Nobel was shocked when a newspaper mistakenly printed his obituary. It essentially called Nobel a merchant of death and said that his invention of high-powered explosives triggered an escalating arms race of mass destruction. To salvage his reputation and the family name, Nobel decided to will $9,000,000 to establish prizes for chemistry, literature, medicine, physics, and peace.

THE AWARD: PULITZER PRIZE
WHAT IT'S FOR: JOURNALISM
NAMED FOR: A TABLOID PUBLISHER

In the 1890s, Joseph Pulitzer became involved in an ugly newspaper war that inspired the term "yellow journalism." No headline was too tasteless, no crime too bloody in the battle for readers between Joseph Pulitzer's *New York World* and W. R. Hearst's *New York Journal*. When Pulitzer died in 1912, he willed money for an annual prize that would award excellence in journalism.

THE AWARD: OSCAR
WHAT IT'S FOR: MOVIE MAKERS
NAMED FOR: AN EMPLOYEE'S UNCLE

The Oscar statuette is meant to look like a knight holding a crusader's sword, standing on a reel of film. However, on first see-

ing it, an Academy employee named Margaret Herrick blurted out, "It looks like my Uncle Oscar!" Academy staffers began to informally refer to the award by that name, and Herrick's quip spread through the film community. In 1934, Walt Disney publicly called it an "Oscar" during an acceptance speech, but the Academy didn't officially use the nickname until 1939. Ms. Herrick later became executive director of the Academy. We don't know what became of her uncle.

THE PRIZE: NEWBERY MEDAL
WHAT IT'S FOR: CHILDREN'S BOOKS
NAMED FOR: A BRITISH BOOKSELLER
The foil medal embossed on the front of some kids' books indicates the book has won the Newbery Award. It was established in 1921 by Frederic G. Melcher, publisher of *Library Journal* and *Publishers Weekly*. The Newbery was named for John Newbery, who owned London's Bible & Sun bookstore in the 1700s. He was the first person to print and sell books specifically for chil-

dren. His titles included *A Little Pretty Pocket-Book* (1744) and *Goody-Two-Shoes* (1765).

THE PRIZE: MACARTHUR FELLOWSHIP
WHAT IT'S FOR: TALENTED, SMART "GENIUSES"
NAMED FOR: A COUPLE OF SKINFLINTS
The John D. and Catherine T. MacArthur Foundation gives grants of $500,000 paid out over five years to two dozen creative folks every year. Who were the MacArthurs? While they lived, John D. and wife Catherine T. were notoriously thrifty tycoons who lived in an apartment in a rundown motel that they'd bought in Florida, running their insurance and real estate holdings from a booth in the motel's coffee shop. John died in 1978 and Catherine in 1981, and their stinginess paid

off, in a way—the foundation they founded as a tax dodge is now the sixth largest in the United States, with $4.2 billion in assets.

THE PRIZE: EMMY
WHAT IT'S FOR: TELEVISION
NAMED FOR: A NOW-OBSOLETE TV TUBE

The Emmy Award statuette consists of a winged woman holding a globe over her head. However, Emmy has no human counterpart—the name's a garbled variation of "Immy,"a nickname for the *image orthicon*, a tube once used in television cameras until it was replaced by the more advanced *vidicon* in the 1960s.

THE PRIZE: CLIO
WHAT IT'S FOR: ADVERTISING
NAMED FOR: A GREEK MUSE

The Clio Awards are named after the Greek muse of history, whose name comes from the Greek *kleos* ("glory"). Why it's named for the muse of history instead of something more appropriate—for example, the Sirens, whose sweet songs led sailors to their doom—we don't know.

THE PRIZE: STANLEY CUP
WHAT IT'S FOR: HOCKEY
NAMED FOR: A BUREAUCRAT

Lord Stanley without his cup

Frederick Arthur, known officially as "Lord Stanley of Preston, England," was the governor-general of Canada in the late 1800s, when it was still a British colony. His son played a newly invented Canadian game called hockey, and Lord Stanley became a fan. Before Lord Stanley returned to England in 1893, he paid a silversmith $50 for a gold-plated silver bowl for the National Hockey Association's amateur hockey champions. When the NHA went pro and became the National Hockey League, the Stanley Cup went pro, too.

THE PRIZE: RYDER CUP
WHAT IT'S FOR: GOLF
NAMED FOR: A SEED MERCHANT
The Ryder Cup was started in 1926 by Samuel Ryder, a wealthy English businessman who made his fortune from selling penny packets of flower seeds. Samuel Ryder's idea of good prize money? "I'll give $5 to each of the winning players," he offered. "And I'll give a party afterwards, with champagne and chicken sandwiches." Eventually he was convinced to put up $250 for a gold trophy instead.

THE PRIZE: CY YOUNG AWARD
WHAT IT'S FOR: BASEBALL PITCHERS
NAMED FOR: EARLY PITCHER
Over twenty-two seasons, Denton True "Cy" Young won more games than any other pitcher in history: 511, almost 100 more than any other pitcher, out of a career total of 906. Young retired in 1911, and the award was established in 1956, the year after his death.

THE PRIZE: HEISMAN TROPHY
WHAT IT'S FOR: COLLEGE FOOTBALL
NAMED FOR: EARLY PLAYER & COACH
Football player and coach John W. Heisman wasn't just the inspiration for the Heisman trophy, he also invented the center snap in the game and coined the term "hike." He also invented the hand-off, the hidden ball trick, the double lateral, and the "flea flicker." Heisman coached at a number of colleges from 1892 to 1927, including Auburn, Clemson, Georgia Tech, and Rice. His most memorable game: a record-breaker in 1916 in which his Georgia Tech team squeaked past Cumberland University of Tennessee, 222 to 0.

THE PRIZE: DAVIS CUP
WHAT IT'S FOR: TENNIS
NAMED FOR: NE'ER-DO-WELL HARVARD BOY
In 1899, four members of the Harvard tennis team decided to challenge the best and brightest tennis players of Britain. One of

the four, Dwight Filley Davis, paid $700 for a trophy. By 1905, all available spaces on it were filled with names, so he shelled out $500 more for a silver tray to go with the cup. For that contribution, the award was named for Davis after he died in 1945.

The Latest Word In Sanitation

The name SY-CLO on a closet means health insurance for your home or any building in which the closet is placed; it means freedom from all those diseases which are usually traceable to noxious odors and poisonous gases arising from ordinary closets.

SY-CLO stands for more than mere flushing; it stands for a wonderful syphonic action of great power—an action which literally pulls the contents of the bowl into the drain, cleansing the non-reachable parts, instantly sealing the outlet channel with a water trap to an unusual depth, and absolutely preventing all danger of gas.

The SY-CLO Closet stands for an interior cleanliness and purity impossible in an iron closet, and unknown in any closet but one made of china—like the SY-CLO. Hand-moulded of china all into one solid piece like a vase, the SY-CLO is without crack, joint or rough surface to collect dirt or disease germs. It is as clean inside and out as a china pitcher, being made exactly the same way and of the same material.

The surface of the SY-CLO Closet cannot chip off, is not affected by acid, water or wear, and hence cannot rust or discolor as an iron closet does. The SY-CLO is strong, simple, durable; it cannot get out of order and, with ordinary care, will last as long as the house in which it is placed.

It costs but little more than the common closet, and when health and comfort are considered, it really costs less; in fact, *your doctor pays the bill.* Your plumber will tell you that SY-CLO is absolutely the latest word in perfect sanitation.

Send for booklet on "Household Health"— mailed free.

POTTERIES SELLING CO.
Trenton, N. J.

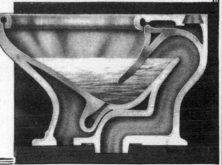

Get a Job!

CAREERS YOUR GUIDANCE COUNSELOR NEVER MENTIONED

Slapper: Prepares clay for potters.
Advertisement Conveyancer: Wears sandwich board.
Devil: Assists a printer.
Shrager: Prunes trees.
Wabster: Weavers cloth.
Intelligencer: Spies on people, armies, or governments.
Pricker: Makes clothes patterns.
Skinker: Bartender in an ale house.
Back Washer: Cleans wool before it's turned into yarn.
Dykeman: Digs ditches.
Jagger: Sells fish.
Pugger: Mixes clay for ceramics.
Bagniokeeper: Manages a brothel or bath house.
Dripping Man: Buys and sells secondhand fat.
Purefinder: Collects animal poop for use in making leather.
Jongler: Travels and entertains people.
Skelper: Sells bees.
Bal Maiden: Works surface mines (female).
Quister: Bleaches cloth.
Dry Stane Dyker: Builds stone walls.
Xylographer: Carves wooden blocks for printing.
Zincographer: Etches designs in zinc plates for printing.
Kisser: Makes helmets.
Wet Nurse: Suckles the infant of another.
Ratoner: Catches rodents.
Ant Catcher: Collects ants for ant farms.
Baller: Rolls balls of clay for potters.
Slaymaker: Carves wooden pegs for looms.
Palister: Maintains the grounds of parks.
Earth Stopper: Fills holes made by gophers and badgers.
Batman: Acts as personal assistant to a military officer.
Faggotter: Bundles sticks and firewood.

R$_x$: Drain His Blood!
How Doctors Killed George Washington

How did the best minds of medicine come up with the outlandish theory that draining your blood would be the best medicine?

THIS IS A STORY OF HOW DOCTORS started with a sore throat and ended up with a dead patient. It illustrates the dangers of trusting what "everyone knows is true" instead of learning from your own observations.

When George Washington retired from the presidency in 1797, he was sixty-five years old and as healthy as an ox. Although the former general complained to Thomas Jefferson that he felt he was "growing old" with "bodily health less firm," he was fit enough to ride on horseback for several hours on daily inspections of his farms and fields.

On December 12, 1799, Washington went out as usual, despite snow, wind, and freezing rain. Five hours later, he returned home with a sore throat. He was kept awake that night by a violent cough, and so he sent for his doctor, Dr. James Craik.

Craik did standard doctorly things of the time: he had Washington gargle with a mix of vinegar and sage tea. Then he wrapped the former president's throat with *cantharides* – now known as "Spanish fly," an extract of dried beetles that raises painful blisters on the skin – to "draw the inflammation to the surface." That treatment may have been painful and unnecessary, but at least it wasn't fatal. However, that was about to change: he next drained a half-pint of Washington's blood.

DOESN'T WORK? GIVE HIM MORE OF THE SAME
Hard to believe, but none of these things seemed to help. Washington still didn't feel any better. In fact, he was doing

worse—in pain and feeling weaker. Go figure.

Perhaps the doctor should have taken a cue that blistering and bleeding was not helping. Instead, he decided that the patient needed even more of the same. Craik took another half-pint of blood.

DISCREDITED THEORIES

How was it that doctors came to believe that draining a patient's blood would somehow help heal them? Well, blame it on the Greeks. They had a theory that went something like this: The body's essence is made up of the "Four Humours": blood, yellow bile, phlegm, and black bile. In order for your body, mind, and character to be healthy, these four fluids need to be in perfect balance. If something goes seriously wrong, you can take out some of the person's blood and the other fluids will magically adjust themselves back into balance, restoring health, sanity, and moral fiber.

It was a crazy idea … and it didn't work. Doctors in the more scientific parts of the world like the Far East and Middle East had abandoned bleeding as ineffective and dangerous centuries earlier, but doctors in Europe and America continued "balancing the humours" of their patients with knives and leeches well into the nineteenth century.

MEANWHILE, BACK AT MT. VERNON

After two bleedings in one morning, Washington was in anything but "good humour." The doctor waited for a few hours to see if Washington would perk up. He did not, so the afternoon Craik set about bleeding him again. Later that afternoon, his colleague Dr. Elisha Dick arrived, and the two bled Washington one more time. This time, the blood was thick and came slowly. No wonder—he was dehydrated and

George Washington's life draining away

anemic after losing two pints of blood in one day.

Martha Washington tried to intervene to have the bleeding stopped, according to an eyewitness account by Tobias Lear, Washington's secretary: "Mrs. Washington, not knowing whether bleeding was proper or not in the General's situation, begged that much might not be taken from him, lest it should be injurious, and desired me to stop it; but when I was about to untie the string the General put up his hand to prevent it, and as soon as he could speak, said—'More, more.'"

Washington's condition worsened even more. The former president sunk slowly into stupor and then death, killed by his doctors and a misplaced faith in their skills. During a millennium of medical malpractice, Washington was only one of the thousands of patients who were doctored to death.

More Pot Shots

Some favorite bathroom shots. Send us yours! (See page 478.)

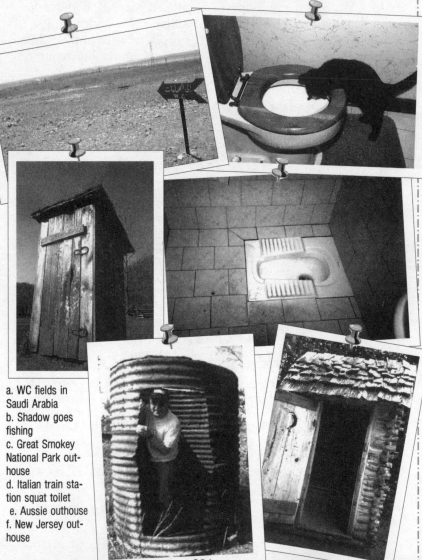

a. WC fields in Saudi Arabia
b. Shadow goes fishing
c. Great Smokey National Park outhouse
d. Italian train station squat toilet
  e. Aussie outhouse
f. New Jersey outhouse

I Curse Thee, Too!

And more of our favorite long-forgotten insults from
merrye old England.

BLOWMAUNGER: "A fat, blown-cheek'd person, as if blown up with fat by full feeding and juncketing: or perhaps it may be applied to one who puffs and blows while he is eating. Perhaps from the French blankmanger…a kind of flummery (a tasty but insubstantial dish)." — Frederick Elworthy's *Devonshire Glossary*, 1879

CRUMP: "One that helps solictors to affidavit men and swearers…who, for a small sum will be bound or swear for anybody, on that occasion putting on good cloaths to make a good appearance, that bail may be accepted." — B.E.'s *Dictionary of Canting Crew*, 1698–1699

FUSTILUGS: "A great foul creature. The foulness implies bad smelling. Used only in the plural." — Frederick Elworthy's *Devonshire Glossary*, 1879

GLOBSLOTCH: " A greedy, clownish person … apt to gobble his food." — William Holloway's *Dictionary of Provincialisms*, 1838

GONG-FARMER: "A night-man; a cleanser of privies or cesspools. From *gong*, a privy." — Robert Hunter's *Encyclopedic Dictionary*, 1894

GONGOOZLER:"An idle and inquisitive person who stands staring for prolonged periods at anything out of the common." — Joseph Wright's *English Dialect Dictionary*, 1896–1905

Barrymorisms II

The Barrymore family has a long relationship with Hollywood, from Lionel, John, and Ethel, down to Drew. Here are a few words of wisdom from the late, great actress, Ethel Barrymore.

ON THE AUDIENCE
"I never let them cough. They wouldn't dare."

ON SUCCESS
"For an actress to be a success, she must have the face of Venus, the brains of a Minerva, the grace of Terpsichore, the memory of a Macaulay, the figure of Juno, and the hide of a rhinoceros."

ON THE COMPETITION
"The face of Garbo is an Idea, that of Hepburn an Event."

ON LIVING
"You must learn day by day, year by year, to broaden your horizons. The more things you love, the more you are interested in, the more you enjoy, the more you are indignant about — the more you have left when anything happens."

ON LAUGHTER
"You grow up on the day you have your first real laugh at yourself."

ON FAILURES
"Our achievements speak for themselves. What we have to keep track of are our failures, discouragements, and doubts. We tend to forget the past difficulties, the many false starts, and the painful groping."

ON FAITH
"When life knocks you to your knees — and it will — why, get up! If it knocks you to your knees again, as it will, well, isn't that the best position from which to pray?"

HER DYING WORDS
"Is everybody happy? I want everybody to be happy. I know I'm happy."

Gatorade
INVENTING IT WAS NO SWEAT

This from a book we like called *How the Cadillac Got Its Fins*, which is—alas—currently out of print.

I S DRINKING A "SPORTS DRINK" any more effective than drinking water while exercising? Several studies have suggested that the answer is no, unless you're involved in an extraordinary level of exertion, like running an ultra-marathon. On the other hand, Gatorade and the research that spawned it did one undeniable service for the sports community: It broke down a lethally misguided notion held by old-style coaches about the detriments of drinking liquids while exercising.

Idle questions from a coach brought James Robert Cade, a kidney researcher at the University of Florida, into sports research. In 1965, Florida Gator assistant coach DeWayne Douglas asked Cade, "How come football players never have to pee during games? Since players lose as much as 15 pounds during a game, where does all that weight go? And why do they seem to run out of gas during the fourth quarter?"

Cade did some research and found that players playing hard in the Florida sun sweated at an amazing rate, losing water, sodium and potassium. As a result, the players' kidneys shut down to conserve liquid, so players didn't have to pee. On the other hand, the loss of liquid was potentially dangerous, and led to fourth-quarter sag.

Cade analyzed sweat and came up with a liquid of similar composition. He added a lime flavoring to make it more palatable, but kept the flavor light, figuring it would inspire players to drink more of it. He mixed up a huge quantity of the stuff and presented it to the coach.

"TASTES LIKE PEE"

When the Gators started drinking Cate's concoction during play, they discovered that they didn't sag midway during the game—and that the heat didn't leave them as exhausted as before. They dubbed it "Gatorade" and even got used to the taste after a while. One player had complained that the concoction "tastes like pee"; Cade, ever the scientist, went back to his lab, took a sample of his own urine, chilled and sampled it, and reported back to the player that "urine doesn't taste a bit like Gatorade."

The big jug of Gatorade on the sidelines engendered a mystique of invulnerability among the Gators and eventually among the teams they played. In 1967, when Florida beat Georgia Tech 27–12 in the Orange Bowl, Tech's coach claimed they lost because "we didn't have Gatorade."

That year, Cade licensed the rights to Stokely-Van Camp, which began paying him a royalty on every drink sold. Jugs of Gatorade began appearing on the sidelines at professional football games, and coaches all over the country began changing a deeply held but completely erroneous belief. For decades, most had denied their athletes liquid during games and practices, thinking it would cause debilitating muscle cramps and worse. Athletes were allowed only damp towels to suck on when they got thirsty. As a result, about 50 school athletes died every year from heat stroke. Cade's research—and that highly visible jug on the sidelines—convinced coaches to rethink. Heat stroke deaths dropped to nearly zero.

When royalty money began pouring in, the University of Florida sued Cade, saying that it should own the rights to Gatorade because he was an employee at the time of his development. Cade countered that he had worked on Gatorade on his own time. In fact, early in the process, he had asked his department administrators to help him develop and patent the liquid, which would have given the university full rights to the drink, but they turned him down.

The final court settlement gave Cade and his researchers 80 percent of the profits and the rest—about $2 million a year—to the university.

298

Mad Tea Party

A CLASSIC TALE FOR KIDS OF ALL AGES

If you've only seen the cartoon or the movie of Lewis Carroll's *Alice's Adventures in Wonderland*, you really must read the book. Let us get you started. Would you like some tea?

THERE WAS A TABLE SET OUT under a tree in front of the house, and the March Hare and the Hatter were having tea at it: a Dormouse was sitting between them, fast asleep, and the other two were using it as a cushion, resting their elbows on it. "Very uncomfortable for the Dormouse," thought Alice; "only, as it's asleep, I suppose it doesn't mind."

The table was a large one, but the three were all crowded together at one corner of it: "No room! No room!" they cried out when they saw Alice coming. "There's PLENTY of room!" said Alice indignantly, and she sat down at one end of the table.

"Have some wine," the March Hare said encouragingly.

Alice looked all round the table, but there was nothing on it but tea. "I don't see any wine," she remarked.

"There isn't any," said the March Hare.

"Then it wasn't very civil of you to offer it," said Alice.

"It wasn't very civil of you to sit down without being invited," said the March Hare.

"I didn't know it was YOUR table," said Alice; "it's laid for a great many more than three."

"Your hair wants cutting," said the Hatter. He had been looking at Alice with great curiosity, and this was his first speech.

"You should not make personal remarks," Alice said with severity; "it's very rude."

The Hatter opened his eyes very wide on hearing this; but all he SAID was, "Why is a raven like a writing-desk?"

"Come, we shall have some fun now!" thought Alice. "I'm glad they've begun asking riddles.—I believe I can guess that," she added aloud.

"Do you mean that you think you can find out the answer to it?" said the Hare.

"Exactly so," said Alice.

"Then you should say what you mean," the Hare said.

"I do," Alice hastily replied; "at least I mean what I say— that's the same thing."

"Not the same thing a bit!" said the Hatter. "You might just as well say that 'I see what I eat' is the same thing as 'I eat what I see'!"

"You might just as well say," added the Hare, "that 'I like what I get' is the same thing as 'I get what I like'!"

"You might just as well say," added the Dormouse, apparently talking in his sleep, "that 'I breathe when I sleep' is the same thing as 'I sleep when I breathe'!"

"It IS the same thing with you," said the Hatter, and here the conversation dropped. Alice thought over all she could remember about ravens and writing-desks, which wasn't much.

The Hatter was the first to break the silence. "What day of the month is it?" he said, turning to Alice: he had taken his watch out of his pocket, and was looking at it uneasily, shaking it every now and then, and holding it to his ear.

Alice considered a little, and then said, "The fourth."

"Two days wrong!" sighed the Hatter. "I told you butter wouldn't suit the works!" he added, looking angrily at the March Hare.

"It was the BEST butter," the Hare meekly replied.

"Yes, but some crumbs must have got in as well," the Hatter grumbled: "you shouldn't have put it in with the bread-knife."

The Hare took the watch and looked at it gloomily: then he dipped it into his cup of tea, and looked at it again: but he could think of nothing better to say than, "It was the BEST butter, you know."

Alice had been looking over his shoulder with some curiosity. "What a funny watch!" she remarked. "It tells the day of the month, and doesn't tell what o'clock it is!"

"The Dormouse is asleep again," said the Hatter, and he poured a little hot tea upon its nose. The Dormouse shook its head impatiently, and said, without opening its eyes, "Of course, of course; just what I was going to remark myself."

"Have you guessed the riddle yet?" the Hatter said, turning to Alice again.

"No, I give it up," Alice replied: "What's the answer?"

"I haven't the slightest idea," said the Hatter.

"Nor I," said the Hare.

Alice sighed. "I think you might do something better with the time," she said, "than waste it in asking riddles that have no answers."

"If you knew Time as well as I do," said the Hatter, "you wouldn't talk about wasting IT. It's HIM."

"I don't know what you mean," said Alice.

"Of course you don't!" the Hatter said contemptuously. "I dare say you never even spoke to Time!"

"Perhaps not," Alice cautiously replied: "but I know I have to beat time when I learn music."

"Ah! that accounts for it," said the Hatter. "He won't stand beating. Now, if you only kept on good terms with him, he'd do almost anything you liked with the clock. For instance, suppose it were nine o'clock in the morning, just time to begin lessons: you'd only have to whisper a hint to Time, and round goes the clock in a twinkling! Half-past one, time for dinner!"

("I only wish it was," the March Hare said to itself.)

"That would be grand, certainly," said Alice thoughtfully: "but then—I shouldn't be hungry for it, you know."

"Not at first, perhaps," said the Hatter: "but you could keep it to half-past one as long as you liked."

"Is that the way YOU manage?" Alice asked.

The Hatter shook his head mournfully. "Not I!' he replied. "We quarrelled last March—just before HE went mad, you know—" (pointing with his tea spoon at the March Hare) "—it was at the great concert given by the Queen of Hearts, and I had to sing 'Twinkle, twinkle, little bat! How I wonder what you're at!' You know the song, perhaps?"

"I've heard something like it," said Alice.

"It goes on, you know," the Hatter said, "'Up above the world you fly, Like a tea-tray in the sky. Twinkle, twinkle—'"

Here the Dormouse shook itself, and began singing in its sleep, "Twinkle, twinkle, twinkle, twinkle—" and went on so long that they had to pinch it to make it stop.

"Well, I'd hardly finished the first verse," said the Hatter, "when the Queen jumped up and bawled out, 'He's murdering the time! Off with his head!'"

"How dreadfully savage!" exclaimed Alice.

"And ever since that," the Hatter went on mournfully, "he won't do a thing I ask! It's always 6 o'clock now. It's always tea-time, and we've no time to wash the things between whiles."

"Then you keep moving round, I suppose?" said Alice.

"Exactly so," said the Hatter: "as things get used up."

"But what happens when you come to the beginning again?" Alice ventured to ask.

"Take some more tea," the March Hare said to Alice, very earnestly.

"I've had nothing yet," Alice replied in an offended tone, "so I can't take more."

"You mean you can't take LESS," said the Hatter: "it's very easy to take MORE than nothing."

"Nobody asked YOUR opinion," said Alice.

"Who's making personal remarks now?" the Hatter asked triumphantly.

This piece of rudeness was more than Alice could bear: she got up in great disgust, and walked off; the last time she saw them, they were trying to put the Dormouse into the teapot.

"At any rate I'll never go THERE again!" said Alice as she picked her way through the wood. "It's the stupidest tea-party I ever was at in all my life!"

Kicks, Spikes & Slapshots
INVENTING THE WILD WORLD OF SPORTS

Before sports became big business, games were just games, and people invented them and changed them as they saw fit. Here are the stories behind some of our favorite sports.

SOCCER

As early as 400 B.C., Chinese athletes played a soccer-like game. The Romans played a non-kick version in the third century. By the 1100s, London children played a form of soccer they called "football." Soccer moved into all English schools by the early 1800s, but each school interpreted the rules differently. In 1848, school representatives met at Trinity College in Cambridge and agreed upon a standardized set of soccer rules.

RUGBY

According to its legendary history, rugby was invented by a renegade schoolboy named William Webb Ellis at Rugby School in Warwickshire, England. One day in 1823, when his "football" (soccer) team was badly losing, Ellis picked up the ball and ran for the goal while onlookers watched in dumfounded amazement. He was heavily penalized on the field and forced to write a letter of apology afterward. However, his simple act of frustrated defiance inspired the idea of a game where you can kick, throw, or run with the ball, and "Rugby-styled football" eventually became just "rugby."

AMERICAN FOOTBALL

It's hard to believe, but football was once so deadly that it was nearly outlawed in the United States.

In 1874, a team from Montreal's McGill University visited Harvard and taught its soccer team how to play a variation of

Football in the good old days. Note the elbow in the face of the ball carrier.

rugby. Harvard then introduced it to other Eastern colleges. Walter Camp, who had played for Yale from 1876 to 1882 established a scoring system, downs, yards to gain, and the center's snap to the quarterback.

By 1900, football had become increasingly violent, but players still did not yet wear pads or helmets. In 1909 alone, 27 players died and hundreds more were perma-

nently injured. Gunfighter-turned-sportswriter Bat Masterson, no stranger to mayhem, wrote, "Football is not a sport in any sense. It is a brutal and savage slugging match between two reckless, opposing crowds. The rougher it is and the more killed and crippled, the more delighted are the spectators, who howl their heads off at the sight of a player stretched prone and unconscious on the hard and frozen ground."

Woodrow Wilson, then president of Princeton University, convened an intercollegiate football rules committee to see if the game should be changed, or even outlawed. After five months, the committee issued its recommendations, prohibiting some of the most dangerous practices, like diving tackles, blocking with linked arms,

Worst Shut-Out in Football History

The most uneven game in football history took place in 1916. Georgia Tech had been humiliated in an earlier athletic contest, so its football team demanded that Cumberland University meet them on the football field to settle the score. Unfortunately, Cumberland had canceled its football program that year, but the school cobbled together a team of volunteers, some of whom had never even played the game before.

Georgia Tech, using the excuse of an earlier defeat to act with poor sportsmanship, piled on the points. The final score? 222-0.

picking up and carrying ball carriers, and interfering with pass receivers. Deaths and injuries went way down, however, some hardcore fans complained that the changes ruined the game forever.

BASKETBALL

"Basketball" could've easily been called "box ball" or even "trashcan ball."

In 1891, James Naismith invented a dribble, pass, and shoot game for bored, snowbound students at a YMCA in Springfield, Massachusetts. In designing the court, he had intended to use wooden boxes for his targets. Unfortunately, when he asked the custodian for boxes, he said there were none in any of the club's back rooms. "But," he added, "I have two old peach baskets down in the store room, if they'll do you any good."

Naismith shrugged and nailed the peach baskets on the balconies at either end of the gym. They just happened to be ten feet off the floor,

which is why that came to be the regulation height for baskets. Later, when it became clear that the thin wood baskets weren't going to hold up for long, Naismith switched to wire trash cans, and then eventually to the hoop and netting combination we see today.

VOLLEYBALL, THE ALTERNATIVE

Volleyball was invented in Holyoke, Massachusetts by William Morgan in 1895 for sedentary businessmen who found the new sport of basketball too strenuous.

ULTIMATE FRISBEE

In 1967, high school student Joel Silver introduced his idea of a soccer-like Frisbee game to Columbia High School in Maplewood, New Jersey. In 1969, Silver formed a team at the school and they played in a parking lot.

The rules were revamped in 1970 by Silver and two friends. In 1975, Yale hosted the first organized tournament. That same year, World Frisbee Championships adopted Ultimate as a sanctioned game.

RODEO

Rodeo developed on ranches in the late 1800s. Cowboys

competed informally at bronco riding and steer roping. The first rodeo that offered prizes and attracted paying spectators was held in Prescott, Arizona, in 1888. Cowboys eventually formed the first professional rodeo organization in 1936.

HOCKEY

McGill University, which had an important role in the development of football, played an even more pivotal role in the invention of ice hockey. But the game itself was invented by unknown members of the British Army.

It's true that field hockey games — with balls and without the ice — were played by ancient Egyptians, Greeks, Arabs, Romans, and Persians. Irish played "hurley" more than 2000 years ago, and native South Americans had a similar game when Columbus arrived in 1492. However, the dubious genius of trying to play the basic game while sliding on ice skates took a special kind of crackpot genius you'd expect to find only among extremely bored soldiers in a wintry clime.

And so it was: British soldiers stationed in Canada in the mid-1850s came up with the basics of ice hockey. The rules were refined and set down by students at McGill University in Quebec in 1879.

The name comes from the French word for a shepherd's crook, *hoquet*. By the beginning of the twentieth century, the sport had spread into the U.S. and Europe. In late 1917, professional players formed the National Hockey League.

MUSICAL NOTES

• The difference between two notes that are an octave apart is that the higher note is vibrating twice as fast as the lower one.

• Our musical scale has twelve notes, of which we normally sing only seven (do-ra-mi-fa-so-la-ti). Chinese music uses five notes. Arabic uses seventeen. Indian, twenty-two. The Japanese use the same seven notes that we do, only "fa" is half a step higher.

Slogos 3!

It's pretty weird that beer companies use cute little forest creatures to hawk their alcoholic products. But hey, it makes a good Slogo quiz. We're going to give you slogans from well-known beers—past and present. Match the slogan to the right animal logo. Rated: Hard.

1. Which of the following animals was the logo for Molson—the beer company that claimed, "What beer's all about"?

A. Deer

B. A fox

C. A duck

D. An opossum

E. Horses

2. "Grab _____ by the neck!" suggested Weinhard's ads. Which animal was not only the company's logo, but the name of the beer, too?

A. A boar

B. An eagle

C. A goose

D. A moose

E. A bear

3. Which spokes-animal goofed off in Hamm beer ads that boasted, "Land of sky blue waters"?

A. An aardvark

B. A turtle

C. Rainbow trout

D. Frogs

E. A bear

4. This animal group sang back up for the "King of Beers," Budweiser.

A. Puppies

B. Raccoons

C. Deer

D. Bears

E. Frogs

5. "[Name] means great beer." This animal's decapitated head represents a beer by the same name.

A. A pig

B. A moose

C. A rhinoceros

D. A fox

E. A duck

6. "Follow your instincts," said this beer's slogan, but we wouldn't follow this red animal logo anywhere in the wild.

A. A wolf

B. A deer

C. An eagle

D. A mouse

E. A lion

7. In ads, this animal was featured with voice-overs claiming, "It's Miller time!"

A. An elephant

B. A beetle

C. A tiger

D. An eagle

E. A moose

Answers: *1. C: Three quacks for the Molson Duck. 2. A: Weinhard's Boar. 3. E: The Hamm bear skated on frozen lakes and otherwise goofed off and had a grand time in the old Hamm beer commercials. 4. E: The Budweiser Frogs—named Bud, Weis, and Er—proved to be Budweiser's most beloved ad campaign to date. 5. B: Consumers never have seemed bothered by drinking something named after a disembodied game animal. 6. A: Red Wolf beer. 7. D: The Miller Eagle, representing freedom and flight—two things made infinitely more difficult when intoxicated.*

Ripe Ol' Corn

"UNCLE JOSH PLAYS GOLF"

"Uncle Josh," Cal Stewart's country bumpkin, had problems figuring out modern city life (circa 1901). Here he tries out the fad sport that was sweeping the nation—golf.

WELL, ABOUT TWO WEEKS AGO the boys said to me, "Uncle we'd like to have you come out and play a game of golf?"

Well, they took me out behind the woodshed where mother couldn't see us and them durned boys dressed your uncle up in the doggondest suit of clothes I ever had on in my life. I had on a pair of socks that had more different colors in 'em than in Joseph's coat. I looked like a cross atween a monkey and a cirkus rider, and a-goin' across the medder our turkey gobbler took after me and I had an awful time with that fool bird. I calculate as how I'll git even with him 'bout Thanksgiving time.

Well, the boys took me into the pasture, and they had it all dug up into what they called a "T," and they had a wheelbarrow full of little Injun war clubs. They called one a nibbler, and another a brassie, and a lot of other fool names I never heerd afore, and can't remember now. Then they brought out a little wooden ball 'bout as big as a hen's egg, and they stuck it up on a little hunk of mud. Then they told me to take one of them thar war clubs and stand alongside of the ball and hit it.

Well, I jist peeled off my coat and got a good holt on that war club and I jist whaled away at that durned little ball, and by gum I missed it, and the boys all commenced to holler "foozle." Well, I got a little bit riled and I whaled away at it again, and I

hit it right whar I missed it the first time, and I whirled round and sot down so durned hard I set four back teeth to achin', and I pawed round in the air and knocked a lot of it out of place. I hit myself on the shin and on the pet corn at the same time, and them durned boys was jist a-rollin' round on the ground and a-hollerin' like Injuns.

Well, I begun to git madder 'n a wet hen, and I swore I'd knock that durned little ball way over into the next county. So I rolled up my sleeves and spit on my hands and got a good holt on that war club and I whaled away at that lit-

tle ball agin, and by chowder I hit it. I knocked it clear over into Deacon Witherspoon's paster, and hit his old muley cow, and she got skeered and run away, jumped the fence and went down the road, and the durned fool never stopped a-runnin' 'til she went slap dab into Ezra Hoskins' grocery store, upset four gallons of apple butter into a keg of soft soap, and set one foot into a tub of mackeral, and t'other foot into a box of window glass, and knocked over Jim Lawson who was settin' on a cracker barrel, and broke his durned old wooden leg, and then she went right out through the window and skeered Si Pettingill's hosses that was a-standin' thar, and they run away and smashed his wagon into kindlin' wood' and Silas has sued me for damages, and mother won't speak to me, and Jim he wants me to buy him a new wooden leg, and the neighbors all say as how I ought to be put away some place fer safe keepin', and Aunt Nancy Smith got so excited she lost her glass eye and didn't find it for three or four days, and when she did git it the boys was a-playin' marbles with it and it wuz all full of gaps, and Jim Lawson, he trimmed it up on the grindstane and it don't fit Nancy any more, and she has to sort of put it in with cotton round it to hold it, and the cotton works out at the corners and skeers the children and every time I see Nancy that durned eye seems to look at me sort of reproachful like, and all I know about playin' golf is, the feller what knocks the ball so durned far you can't find it or whar it does the most damage, wins the game.

Fore-Footed Friends

Uganda's Jinja Golf Course has some interesting house rules. For instance, if a ball lands near a crocodile and it's deemed unsafe to play it, you may drop another ball. If your ball lands in a hippopotamus footprint, you may lift and drop the ball without incurring penalty. (Don't try invoking these rules at most golf courses, however—we've tried and it doesn't seem to work.)

• Golfers in Australia report that crows and currawongs (an indigenous black bird) swoop down and steal balls. When one bird's nest was blasted with a water cannon, 40–50 golf balls came raining down.

• In 1994, a farmer in Germany sued because errant golfers were hooking balls into his field. After one of his cows suffered a sudden death, the vet discovered a golf ball lodged in its throat. Further investigation revealed that thirty cattle had a collective total of 2,000 balls lodged in their stomachs.

• At the Talamore Golf Course in Southern Pines, North Carolina, you have the option of renting an old-fashioned golf cart for $20 ... or a llama caddy for $100.

• How's this for a hole-in-one? In 1981, on a par-3 hole at Mountain View (California) Golf Course, amateur Ted Barnhouse hit a wayward ball over a fence into a cow pasture. The ball bounced off a grazing cow's head, ricocheted off a lawn mower, bounced off the flag and into the hole.

• Cattle's revenge? A herd of about fifty cattle invaded the eighteenth hole of the 1984 St. Andrews Trophy, menacing several golfers in their path. The stampede was driven back by officials and golfers waving 8-irons, averting cattle-clysm.

• While playing a tournament in South America, Sam Snead was once attacked by an ostrich. The birdie bit him on the hand, rendering him out of commission for two weeks.

• On a golf course in Natal, South Africa, Molly Whitaker was about to hit a shot from a bunker when a monkey leaped from a tree and wrapped its arms around her neck. Her caddie chased it away, and the game continued.

Knock, Knock!

WHO'S THERE?

Knock knock jokes became a fad in the 1930s among grownups, but quickly made their way down to the youngest set. Here are some favorites of all age groups....

Knock knock.
Who's there?
Yule.
Yule who?
Yule never know.

Knock knock.
Who's there?
Dwayne!
Dwayne who?
Dwayne the bathtub, I'm dwowning!

Knock knock.
Who's there?
Wendy.
Wendy who?
"Wendy red red robin comes bob, bob bobbin' along...."

Knock knock
Who's there?
Sara.
Sara who?
Sara doctor in the house?

Knock knock.
Who's there?
Atch.

Atch who?
Gesundheit.

Knock knock.
Who's there?
Owl.
Owl who?
Owl you know unless you open the door?

Knock knock.
Who's there?
Boo.
Boo who?
Oh, don't cry. It's only a knock-knock joke.

Knock knock.
Who's there?
Dishes.
Dishes who?
Dishes me. Who ish you?

Knock knock.
Who's there?
You.
You who?
Whaddya calling me for?

Presidential Trivia II
PRESIDENTS & THEIR VICES

From the question & answer books *Just Curious, Jeeves* and *Just Curious About History, Jeeves*, by Jack Mingo and Erin Barrett, we found some more juicy bits of gossip on some United States Presidents and Veeps.

How much older was Grover Cleveland than his wife Frances?

She was twenty-one and he was forty-nine. Cleveland was the first and only president to marry in the White House. The public went crazy over the couple. They saw her as the young gal who put the reins on an old codger, their bachelor president. However, the story has a twist: the couple had had a different type of relationship prior to their romance. She was his ward. When her father—Cleveland's former law partner, Oscar Folsom—died in a carriage accident when Frances was eleven, he left Cleveland his estate. Grover Cleveland spent the rest of Frances' childhood financially and emotionally supporting her and her mother.

Who was the first presidential candidate to be endorsed by TV Guide?

That prestigious honor goes to Ronald Reagan. *TV Guide* can also be remembered as the first print venue to publish the conservative Republican coalition's "Contract With America" that helped Newt Gingrich capture the House of Representatives in the 1996 campaign.

Who was the most unpopular president in history?

Probably John Tyler. After he vetoed key points of his own Whig Party's program, his entire cabinet resigned except one member, an armed mob stormed the White House and threw rocks through its windows, and members of his party introduced an impeachment resolution in the House of Representatives. (It failed 127 to 83.) Spurned by both parties, Tyler retired after finishing his one partial term. Teddy Roosevelt summed him up 75 years later: "Tyler has been called a mediocre man, but this is unwarranted flattery. He was a politician of monumental littleness."

What happened in the duel between Alexander Hamilton and Aaron Burr?

America's most infamous duel took place on July 11, 1804 in Weehawken, New Jersey. Burr and Hamilton had become political rivals when Burr won a Senate seat that had belonged to Hamilton's father-in-law. When Burr left the vice presidency and ran an unsuccessful campaign for New York governor, he was the victim of a vicious smear campaign that he thought Hamilton might've had a hand in. Afterward, when Hamilton made some negative statements about him in the press, Burr challenged him to a duel. Hamilton was killed, but Burr's "victory" made him a political and social pariah, and murder charges hung over his head in New York and New Jersey.

A few years later Burr got himself even further in disgrace when he was caught putting together a private army with the hope of conquering parts of Louisiana and Mexico and creating his own kingdom. He was tried for treason, but escaped conviction on a technicality. After hiding out in Europe for a few years and piling up debt, he had to leave quickly to escape debtors' prison. Returning to New York, Burr managed to get the old murder charges dropped and began practicing law again. Still, after personal setbacks including the death of his beloved daughter and a disastrous late-life marriage and divorce, he lived a life "severed from the human race" (as he put it) and died forgotten in 1833 at the age of 80.

What United States president slept through most of his term?

President David Rice Atcheson. He was president for one day on March 4, 1849. James Polk's term ended then, but Zachary Taylor refused to be sworn in on a Sunday so the job went automatically to the senate president pro tem. "I slept most of that Sunday," he admitted, and Taylor was sworn in the next day.

Who was on his knees playing marbles when told he had become president?

John Tyler. William Henry Harrison had died a month

into his term and on April 6, 1841, Tyler was found deep in a game of aggies and given the news that he was the first vice president to succeed a dead president. Two decades later, Tyler apparently lost those marbles. He renounced his citizenship and joined the Confederacy.

When in American history was it a crime to criticize the president?

During the second half of John Adams' administration, which has become known as the Federalist Reign of Terror. Under the Alien and Sedition Acts, it became a crime to criticize the president. It got so bad that his vice president, Thomas Jefferson, stopped signing his letters, correctly assuming that government agents were reading his mail. More than twenty newspaper editors and a member of Congress were jailed. (Representative Matthew Lyon got four months in jail and a $1,000 fine for writing an editorial in a Vermont newspaper; his constituents re-elected him while he was in jail and paid his fine.) The law finally expired after Jefferson became president.

Who was on Richard Nixon's "Enemies List?"

Literally hundreds of peo-ple and organizations. The list was given to government agencies like the IRS with quiet presidential orders to harass the people on it. He wanted payback.

Some of the more famous names on the list included movie stars, politicians and media folks, including Carol Channing, Jane Fonda, Dick Gregory, Judith Martin ("Miss Manners"), Steve McQueen, Joe Namath, Paul Newman, Gregory Peck, Edward Kennedy, Edmund Muskie, Harold Hughes, Walter Mondale, William Proxmire, Jack Anderson, Rowland Evans, Julian Goodman, Marvin Kalb, Joseph Kraft, Dan Rather, James Reston, and Daniel Schorr.

Nixon's list also targeted an odd assortment of groups like the National Education Association, the American Civil Liberties Union, the National Organization for Women, National Cleaning Contractors, Philip Morris, the Urban League, MIT (Massachusetts Institute of Technology), the World Bank, and Harvard Law School.

What did Vice President Martin Van Buren always have beside him when he presided over the Senate?

A pair of pistols.

Just 15 Minutes a Day

> But it will mean a tremendous difference in their positions and earning power fifteen years from now.

HERE are two men of equal position and business income. Which of them represents you?

They read about the same number of hours each week. But one has no plan for his reading; at the end of the year he has little or nothing to show.

The other talks like a man who has traveled widely, though he has never been outside of the United States.

He knows something of Science, though he had to stop school at fifteen. He is at home with History, and the best biographies, and the really great dramas and essays. Older men like to talk to him because he has somehow gained the rare gift of thinking clearly and talking interestingly.

What's the secret of his mental growth? How can a man in a few minutes of pleasant reading each day gain so much.

Dr. Charles W. Eliot, from his lifetime of reading, study and teaching, forty years of it as president of Harvard University, has answered that question in a free booklet that you can have for the asking. In it are described the contents, plan and purpose of

Dr. Eliot's
Five Foot Shelf of Books
The pleasant path to a liberal education

EVERY well-informed man and woman should at least know something about this famous library.

The free book tells about it—how Dr. Eliot has put into his Five Foot Shelf "the essentials of a liberal education," how he has so arranged it that even "fifteen minutes a day" is enough, how in pleasant moments of spare time, by using the reading courses Dr. Eliot has provided for you, you can get the knowledge of literature and life, the culture, the broad viewpoint that every University strives to give.

"For me," wrote one man who had sent in the coupon, "your little free book meant a big step forward, and it showed me besides the way to a vast new world of pleasure."

Think of it. The satisfaction of being a marked man or woman in any company. And all for a few minutes of pleasant reading each day.

This is the promise of the Five Foot Shelf. Two hundred thousand Americans have proved that promise; they have tested the value of Dr. Eliot's guidance.

Send for this free booklet that gives Dr. Eliot's own plan of reading

P. F. COLLIER & SON COMPANY
Publishers of Good Books Since 1875
Branches and Representatives Everywhere
New York

Stately Knowledge

12 REASONS WHY YA GOTTA LOVE WISCONSIN

We've searched the vaults and come up with some pretty impressive facts and stories about Wisconsin. Here are a dozen of our favorites.

1   Look out below! In 1962, a 21-pound fragment of the Soviet space satellite *Sputnik IV* landed at the intersection of Park and North 8th streets in Manitowoc, Wisconsin. Nobody was hurt.

2   From 1884 to 1918, Baraboo, Wisconsin, was the headquarters of the Ringling Brothers Circus and six other circuses. Circus World Museum is housed in the original Ringling building and features circus acts, elephants, calliopes, magic shows, and about 200 restored circus wagons. Every year in mid-July, bands, horses, elephants, and circus wagons star in the world's biggest circus parade, marching from Baraboo to Milwaukee.

3   Harry Houdini was the best and most famous magician of all time. His real name was Erich Weiss and he was born in Budapest, Hungary. A son of a rabbi, he was brought as an infant to Appleton, Wisconsin, where he was raised. (In later years he would claim that he had actually been born there.)

4   In 1902, Bill Harley and three Davidson brothers, all in their twenties, started building motorcycles in Milwaukee, creating the first American company to do so. In their first year of operation, they built only three motorcycles. Ole Evinrude helped them, and then decided that a similar motor with a propeller could move a rowboat. It worked like a charm, and he began selling his new invention, the Evinrude outboard motor.

5 Sayner, Wisconsin, lays claim to its own invention: the first snowmobile, invented by Carl Eliason in 1925. As far as we know, he wasn't affiliated at all with any of the Harleys, Davidsons, or the Evinrudes.

6 Milwaukee resident Christopher Sholes built the very first typewriter in 1873. Mark Twain bought one of the newfangled machines for $125 (a whole lot of money back then) and became the first author to submit a typewritten manuscript to a publisher (his book *Life on the Mississippi).*

7 In the capital of Madison, Wisconsin, there are more bicycles that people living in the city. In fact, bicycles outnumber citizens by a ratio of 3 to 2.

8 Luck, Wisconsin, home of The Duncan Yo-Yo Company, has long advertised itself as the "Yo-Yo Capital of the World." We guess that's why people always keep coming back ... and back ... and back....

9 An inventor named Ben Hirsch was walking along Turtle Creek in Beloit, Wisconsin, in the early 1940s when a name for his new car polish suddenly came to him: Turtle Wax.

10 In 1856, in Watertown, Wisconsin, Mrs. Carl Schurz opened the first American kindergarten. She had been a pupil of Friedrich Froebel, who started the kindergarten movement in 1837. *Kindergarten*, by the way, is German for "children's garden." Froebel's first choice for a name had been *kleinkenderbeschaftigungsanstalt*, which means "institution where small children are occupied," but even Germans had trouble saying it, so he settled for "kindergarten."

11 Wisconsin produces more milk than any other state, which may explain why milk is its Official State Beverage and the cow is its Official State Domestic Animal. It's a little harder to figure out, however, why its Official State Dance its the polka.

12 It's no wonder then, that many dairy "firsts" come from this state. In 1887, malted milk was invented by William Horlick in Racine, Wisconsin. And the ice cream sundae had first appeared six years earlier in Two Rivers.

Word Thieves 4

TERMS WE'VE BORROWED FROM THE SPANISH

Thanks to Spanish explorers, conquistadors to the New World, and Hispanic influences since then, more than 10,000 words have migrated from Spanish into American English.

alligator: From *el lagarto* meaning "the lizard."

bonanza: *Bonacia,* a Spanish word derived from Medieval Latin, meaning "calm sea."

breeze: From *brisa,* which translates to "northeast wind."

buffalo: When the Spanish saw American bison for the first time, they applied their name for a wild ox: *bufalo.*

cafeteria: It originally meant "coffee shop" as *café* means "coffee" in Spanish.

cockroach: From *cucaracha.*

Colorado: Meaning "rust-colored." It describes the red soil.

embargo: From the verb *embargar* ("arrest, impede").

Florida: Ponce de Leon landed in Florida on Easter in 1513. He named the land after the traditional Spanish Easter festival of the flower: *Pascua de Florida.*

mosquito: It means "little fly."

Nevada: Translates to "snow-capped."

patio: This is the Spanish word for "courtyard."

savvy: It's a derivation from the Spanish phrase *¿Sabe usted?,* meaning "do you know?"

serrated: This word comes from *serra* ("saw"). The name Sierra also comes from the same source, referring to peaks that are irregular and jagged.

tornado: An alteration of the Spanish word *tronada* meaning "thunderstorm."

vanilla: From *vainilla* ("little sheath"), describing the shape of vanilla pods. It descends from the Latin word *vagina* ("sheath").

Potty Pourri

RANDOM KINDS OF FACTNESS

• After snoozing through a screening of *Gone with the Wind* at the White House, President Franklin D. Roosevelt complained, "No movie has a right to be that long!"

• One of Walt Disney's favorite hobbies was planning train wrecks on his half-mile of miniature train tracks.

• Would you buy a car called the Pastelogram, Piluma, Mongoose Cigique, or Utopian Turtletop? All of these names were considered for a futuristic car model in the late 1950s, but the company decided to play it safe and name the car after the company founder's late son. It didn't help, and the funny-looking Ford Edsel became a marketing laughingstock.

• Which song had the highest sheet music sales in history? No, it's not "Happy Birthday," "The Star Spangled Banner," or "Yesterday." It was "Yes, We Have No Bananas" by Frank Silver and Irving Cohn. It sold over half a million copies in its first few weeks of sale in 1923.

• Being called a twit isn't technically so bad. It's the name breeders use for a pregnant goldfish.

• In the 1930s, when Pepsi first came on the market, it cost a nickel for a 12-ounce bottle. That sounds really cheap, but it's about the same as today's price if adjusted for inflation: 60¢.

• You would expect a law against lawyers accepting bribes, but in 240 B.C., Rome passed a law against lawyers accepting fees.

• Peter the Great, working to modernize Russia, passed a law that men with long whiskers had to pay a special tax.

• The term "vaccine" comes from the Latin *vacca*, meaning "cows." There's good reason for this. The first successful small-pox vaccine in 1796 was derived from cowpox.

• To hard-boil an ostrich egg, set your egg timer for 40 minutes.

Fox Tales

SOME FOXY FABLES FROM AESOP

The Greek slave Aesop may or may not have really existed, but his fables have stood the test of time. Here are some about those wily foxes.

THE FOX, THE COCK, AND THE DOG

One moonlight night a Fox was prowling about a farmer's hen-coop, and saw a Cock roosting high up beyond his reach. "Good news, good news!" he cried.

"Why, what is that?" said the Cock.

"King Lion has declared a universal truce. No beast may hurt a bird henceforth, but all shall dwell together in brotherly friendship."

"Why, that is good news," said the Cock; "and there I see some one coming, with whom we can share the good tidings." And so saying he craned his neck forward and looked afar off.

"What is it you see?" said the Fox.

"It is only my master's Dog that is coming toward us. What, going so soon?" he continued, as the Fox began to turn away as soon as he had heard the news. "Will you not stop and congratulate the Dog on the reign of universal peace?"

"I would gladly do so," said the Fox, "but I fear he may not have heard of King Lion's decree."

Cunning often outwits itself.

THE FOX AND THE CAT

A Fox was boasting to a Cat of its clever devices for escaping its enemies. "I have a whole bag of tricks," he said, "which contains a hundred ways of escaping my enemies."

"I have only one," said the Cat; "but I can generally manage with that." Just at that moment they heard the cry of

"Just the thing to quench my thirst."

a pack of hounds coming toward them, and the Cat immediately scampered up a tree and hid herself in the boughs. "This is my plan," said the Cat. "What are you going to do?" The Fox thought first of one way, then of another, and while he was debating the hounds came nearer and nearer, and at last the Fox in his confusion was caught up by the hounds and soon killed by the huntsmen. Miss Puss, who had been looking on, said:

"Better one safe way than a hundred on which you cannot reckon."

THE FOX AND THE GRAPES

One hot summer's day a Fox was strolling through an orchard till he came to a bunch of grapes just ripening on a vine which had been trained over a lofty branch. "Just the thing to quench my thirst," quoth he. Drawing back a few paces, he took a run and a jump, and just missed the bunch. Turning round again with a One, Two, Three, he jumped up, but with no greater success. Again and again he tried after the tempting morsel, but at last had to give it up, and walked away with his nose in the air, saying: "I am sure they are sour."

It is easy to despise what you cannot get.

THE FOX AND THE STORK

At one time the Fox and the Stork were on visiting terms and seemed very good friends. So the Fox invited the Stork to dinner, and for a joke put nothing before her but some soup in a very shallow dish.. This the Fox could easily lap up, but the Stork could only wet the end of her long bill in it, and left the meal as hungry as when she began. "I am sorry," said the Fox, "the soup is not to your liking."

"Pray do not apologize," said the Stork. "I hope you will return this visit, and dine with me soon." So a day was appointed when the Fox should visit the Stork; but when they were seated at table all that was for their dinner was contained in a very long-necked jar with a narrow mouth, in which the Fox could not insert his snout, so all he could manage to do was to lick the outside of the jar.

"I will not apologize for the dinner," said the Stork:

"One bad turn deserves another."

THE FOX WITHOUT A TAIL

It happened that a Fox caught its tail in a trap, and in struggling to release himself lost all of it but the stump. At first he was ashamed to show himself among his fellow foxes. But at last he determined to put a bolder face upon his misfortune, and summoned all the foxes to a general meeting to consider a proposal which he had to place before them. When they had assembled together the Fox proposed that they should all do away with their tails. He pointed out how inconvenient a tail was when they were pursued by their enemies, the dogs; how much it was in the way when they desired to sit down and hold a friendly conversation with one anoth-

er. He failed to see any advantage in carrying about such a useless encumbrance. "That is all very well," said one of the older foxes; "but I do not think you would have recommended us to dispense with our chief ornament if you had not happened to lose it yourself."

Distrust interested advice.

THE FOX AND THE GOAT

By an unlucky chance a Fox fell into a deep well from which he could not get out. A Goat passed by shortly afterward, and asked the Fox what he was doing down there. "Oh, have you not heard?" said the Fox; "there is going to be a great drought, so I jumped down here in order to be sure to have water by me. Why don't you come down, too?" The Goat thought well of this advice, and jumped

"How well you are looking today."

down into the well. But the Fox immediately jumped on her back, and by putting his foot on her long horns managed to jump up to the edge of the well. "Good-bye, friend," said the Fox, "and remember next time,

"Never trust the advice of a man in difficulties."

THE FOX AND THE CROW

A Fox once saw a Crow fly off with a piece of cheese in its beak and settle on a branch of a tree. "That's for me, as I am a Fox," said Master Reynard, and he walked up to the foot of the tree.

"Good-day, Mistress Crow," he cried. "How well you are looking today: how glossy your feathers; how bright your eye. I feel sure your voice must surpass that of other birds, just as your figure does; let me hear but one song from you that I may greet you as the Queen of Birds."

The Crow lifted up her head and began to caw her best, but the moment she opened her mouth the piece of cheese fell to the ground, only to be snapped up by Master Fox.

"That will do," said he. "That was all I wanted. In exchange for your cheese I will give you a piece of advice for the future:

"Do not trust flatterers."

THE FOX AND THE MASK

A Fox had by some means gotten into the storeroom of a theatre. Suddenly he observed a face glaring down on him and began to be very frightened; but looking more closely he found it was only a Mask such as actors use to put over their face. "Ah," said the Fox, "you look very fine; it is a pity you have not got any brains."

Outside show is a poor substitute for inner worth.

THE FOX AND THE LION

When first the Fox saw the Lion he was very frightened, and ran away and hid in the wood. Next time however he came near the King of Beasts he stopped at a safe distance and watched him pass by. The third time they came near one another the Fox went straight up to the Lion and passed the time of day with him, asking him how his family was, and when he should have the pleasure of seeing him again; then turning his tail, he parted from the Lion without much ceremony.

Familiarity breeds contempt.

Blue Jeans

FROM A MINER TO MAJOR FASHION

What's more essential than blue jeans? Everyone has at least one pair. But for most of their history, they were considered working class garments, frowned upon by parents, educators, and other members of the bourgeoisie.

BLUE JEANS STARTED with a man named Levi Strauss, born "Loeb" in Bavaria in 1829. After his father died of consumption in 1845, his mother decided that there was no future for her children growing up Jewish in anti-Semitic Bavaria. In 1847, Loeb moved with his mother and two sisters to the golden promise of America, where he changed his name to Levi because it "sounded more American."

Strauss's two older brothers had arrived a few years earlier and started a business selling dry goods in New York City. Strauss began learning the business, and in 1848 traveled to Kentucky to earn his living as a traveling peddler, schlepping fabrics, threads, pins, needles, hooks, buttons, ribbons, combs, and scissors from town to town.

Strauss carried his goods on his back with the hope of someday joining the more established peddlers who used a horse-drawn wagon and eventually progressed to owning a store somewhere. (Sometimes this last transition happened when their wagons broke down or their horses suddenly died.)

He peddled his wares on foot for several years. Then he succumbed to gold fever. It was 1849, and gold had been discovered in California. Tens of thousands of laborers, lawyers, teachers, clerks, and farmers trekked and tried getting rich in the gold fields. Twenty-four-year-old Levi Strauss thought he could get rich, too, but not by digging. He knew that the influx of people had created shortages of everyday things and jacked prices up. Apples that would cost a nickel in New York sold for 50¢ in California. A $15 dollar wagon could fetch over $100. Strauss loaded merchandise from his brothers' store onto a ship bound west around South America.

THE MAKING OF A BUSINESS

At the end of the five-month journey, Strauss arrived in San Francisco. He found a great demand for the sewing supplies he brought. One account has it that his ship was met by eager merchants in rowboats who bought everything but a roll of tent canvas before the ship had even docked. When he tried to sell the roll, somebody told him, "Canvas, hell. You shoulda' brought pants. Pants don't wear worth a hoot in the diggin's," so Strauss brought the canvas to a tailor and had stiff but sturdy pants sewn from the brown fabric. They sold out in a flash.

Strauss sent word back to New York to send more canvas. Meanwhile, he salvaged sails from among the 700 ships in the harbor that sailors had abandoned to dig for gold. (The city eventually sank them into the mud and built boardwalks over them.)

"Eureka!"

Levi and his brother-in-law, David, opened a dry goods shop, and Levi continued making work clothes out of whatever materials came in on the latest merchant ship. Levi peddled pants and other dry goods in mining camps and towns with names like Rough and Ready, Bedbug, Henpeck City, and Ground-hog's Glory. He saw firsthand how mining was particularly hard on trousers because of the miners' continuous squatting, kneeling, and stuffing pockets with ore. He learned from the miners that canvas chaffed unbearably (most miners didn't wear underwear); they preferred pants of a flexible yet sturdy cotton fabric from Nîme, France. It came in bundles labeled *serge de Nîme* which they read as "denim." Strauss also found that indigo was the most popular color because it hid dirt stains. In 1853, Strauss started Levi Strauss and Company to make denim pants.

A RIVETING STORY

But the company still hadn't licked the pocket problem. Complaints rolled in from miners that tools and ore samples ripped the seams too easily.

Strauss couldn't come up with a satisfactory solution, but a tailor in Reno, Nevada, did. Jacob Davis had been given an order for work clothes by a woman who complained that her husband's pockets always tore through. Davis had chosen his heaviest twill and then had an idea: Why not use rivets on the pockets to reinforce them? Sure enough, the rivets worked. Davis started making riveted work clothes, selling 200 pairs of pants in eighteen months.

Davis knew he had a good idea, and he wanted to file a patent on his idea. His wife, however, threatened to leave him if he spent $68 on a patent fee. So he wrote to the Levi Strauss Company and offered to share his idea if Strauss would finance the patent. He sent along two samples of his pants of duck and blue denim, with a letter explaining everything:

> The secratt of them pents is the rivits that I put in these Pockets and I found the demand so large that I cannot make them up fast enough. I charge for the Duck $3.00 and the Blue $2.50 a pear. My nabors are getting yalouse of these success and unless I secure it by Patent Papers it will soon become a general thing. Everybody will make them up and thare will be no money in it.
>
> Therefore Gentlemen, I wish to make you a Proposition that you should take out the Latters Patent in my name as I am the inventor of it, the expense of it will be about $68 all complit.... The investment for you is but a trifle compared with the improvement in all Coarse Clothing. I use it in all Blankit Clothing such as Coats, Vests and Pents, and you will find it a very salable article at a much advenst rate....

While the idea was simple, it had a huge effect on sales. In the first year, Levi sold 21,600 riveted pants and coats to miners, cowboys, lumberjacks, and farmers throughout the West.

The rivet on the fly, by the way, was eventually removed after the company received dozens of hot, testy letters complaining about hot testes. It turned out that the rivet was a painfully good conductor of heat when the wearer crouched in front of a campfire. Later, because of complaints about scratched saddles and furniture, the back-pocket rivets were replaced with reinforced stitching.

COOL AND BLUE

Before the 1950s, jeans were

just for farmers and workers. But in the 1950s, consumers began seeing jeans in a new light. Thanks to Western movies and James Dean, blue jeans became cool within the teen set. During the proletari-at-chic 1960s, groovy denims became a counterculture uniform (especially when worn, torn, and patched). The 1970s brought forth the oxymoron of "designer jeans" costing as much as dress slacks. Today, you'd be hard pressed to find anyone who owned fewer than two or three pairs of blue jeans.

Working Conditions

Levi Strauss grew into a large company with the reputation of good employee relations and moderately progressive social policies. But that wasn't always the case. In this country, demagoguery and hysteria seem to arise every few decades against immigrants. During an anti-Chinese frenzy of the 1800s, Levi Strauss advertised that "Our riveted goods are made up in our Factory, under our direct supervision, and by WHITE LABOR only."

The claim, used until the end of the century, was not only despicable, but untrue as well. While Levi's sewing was done by sixty white women working for $3.00 a day, the fabric cutting was done by a Chinese man. The company repeatedly tried to replace him, but could find no white laborer who was able to do the job.

But the company has improved on this score. During World War II, it was among the first to hire African American workers in its factories, and refused to keep black workers segregated or limited to low-paying jobs. The company has promoted women and minorities, and developed a reputation for treating employees better than most big corporations.

Potty Pourri
RANDOM KINDS OF FACTNESS

- If life hands you peanut plants, make peanut butter. You can make 30,000 peanut butter sandwiches from just one acre.

- Some researchers have claimed that green in office environments reduces headaches, stomach distress, and other stress symptoms.

- Cows, sheep, dogs, and goats are aplenty in the Bible, but cats are never even mentioned once.

- Never give up the dream. Why, even George Orwell faced rejection. A publisher turned down his future bestseller *Animal Farm* with, "It is impossible to sell animal stories in the U.S.A."

- Manhole covers aren't round because someone at city planning liked the shape. Nope, they're round because they're the only common shape that won't fall through the holes if they get tilted sideways.

- Although the stalk of the rhubarb is delicious, beware: Its leaves are toxic and can kill you.

- A cow consumes the equivalent of a bathtub full of water every day. Granted, some of the moisture comes from the grass it eats, but it all adds up to about 50 gallons.

- Pinball game designers kept this in mind when creating a new pinball game: An okay player should get an average of about 47 seconds of play per ball. Too much more time and the machine loses potential revenue; less, and players feel so defeated they'll likely stop playing.

- Lost childhood: It used to be that kids could use Silly Putty to lift pictures off newspapers and then stretch them this way and that for comical effect. Alas, that innocent pleasure is all gone now, a victim of advances in smear-proof ink and newsprint.

- Bovines are cattle, but what are ovines? Sheep.

The Eyes Have It

CAN YOU TRUST WHAT YOU SEE?

What's wrong with the legs on this pachyderm?

This picture was drawn in 1915 by W. E. Hill. It was titled *My Wife and My Mother-in-Law*. Can you tell why? (Hint: One is looking away. The other is looking down.)

Holey Food

HOW THE LIFE SAVER GOT ITS HOLE

Why put a hole in the middle just for a catchy name? Well, that's not exactly how it all came to be, as you'll see.

IN 1913, CLARENCE A. CRANE, a candy manufacturer in Cleveland, Ohio, was having trouble with his line. The chocolates he sold didn't travel well during the hot summer months. Candy stores would order almost nothing from him between June and September. To stay in business, he decided to develop a line of hard mints.

His factory, however, was only set up for chocolates, so he jobbed the mints out to a pill manufacturer. Unfortunately, the pill maker's machine was malfunctioning—despite all efforts, it kept punching a hole in each mint's center.

The pill manufacturer presented the first batch apologetically to Crane, and told him that they'd try to fix the problem for the next batch. Crane looked at the candy and said, "Don't bother. Keep it the way it is. They looked like little life savers!" Suddenly, he had an irresistible name for the mints.

Crane advertised his "Crane's Peppermint Life Savers" as way of saving yourself from "that stormy breath." He designed a round paperboard tube and printed a label showing a crusty old seaman tossing a life preserver to a young woman swimmer. Still, he considered the product to be just a summer sideline and didn't push the idea any further.

Enter Edward John Noble, who made a living selling ad space on streetcars in New York City. One day he saw Crane's Life

Savers in a candy store and bought a roll on impulse. He was so impressed with the product that he jumped on a train to Cleveland to convince Crane that he should buy streetcar ads. "If you'd spend a little money promoting these mints," Noble told Crane, "you'd make a fortune!"

Crane wasn't interested. He still saw the mints as a sideline to his real product—chocolates. Noble persisted. Crane, to get rid of him, suggested sarcastically that he buy the Life Saver brand. He'd even throw in the defective pill machine for free. When Noble asked, "How much?" Crane was caught completely unprepared. He blurted out, "$5,000."

Noble thought the price was a steal, but he didn't have that kind of money. He returned to New York and was able to raise only $3,800. He went back to Cleveland and talked Crane's price down to $2,900, leaving $900 for his operating expenses.

Noble immediately started running into problems. It turned out that the roll Noble had tried tasted so good because it was fresh. After a week or two on the shelves, the candy started tasting like the paperboard it came in. Noble came up with a tinfoil wrapper that kept the flavor fresh, but, unfortunately, there were thousands of the old rolls sitting stale and unsold on candy store shelves. Store owners refused to order any more unless Noble exchanged the old rolls for new ones.

He made the exchanges, but the candy still wasn't selling very well. Noble started giving away free samples on street corners, to no avail. Luckily, he had kept his day job, but more and more of his weekly salary was going to propping up his company. He then came up with a brilliant marketing idea: Why sell his candy only in candy stores? He started convincing owners of drug stores, smoke shops, barber shops, restaurants, and saloons to carry Life Savers. He told them: "Put the mints near the cash register with a big 5¢ card. Be sure that every customer gets a nickel with his change, and see what happens."

It worked. With change in hand, customers impulsively flipped a nickel back to the clerk and pocketed a pack. Noble finally began making money from his product.

Other candy manufacturers

quickly discovered the magic of counter displays for impulse sales. The space around cash registers started getting overcrowded. To make sure he kept his counter space, Noble designed a large, segmented candy bin for store owners, leaving space for all the other candy products—but putting his Life Savers in the best position across the top. Life Saver counter displays can still be found next to checkout lines in supermarkets and drug stores everywhere.

Meanwhile, the company began expanding its line from the original Pep-O-Mint. Life Savers became the world's bestselling candy. Since 1913, the company has sold more than 44 billion of the familiar little tubular rolls.

IS THAT A SPARK IN YOUR MOUTH OR ARE YOU JUST GLAD TO SEE ME?

One of the three best in-the-dark revelations of adolescence is that if you crack a Wint-O-Green Life Saver between your teeth, tiny blue and green lights will flash in your mouth.

If you've never seen it happen, pick up a pack of Wint-O-Greens and wait until after dark. Turn out the lights and crunch one between your teeth while standing in front of a mirror. Besides feeling silly for standing in the dark in front of a mirror, you'll probably see a blue-green spark.

But how does it happen? Nabisco claims to get three or four queries about this phenomenon per month—enough to have a canned answer: It's "Triboluminescence resulting from crystal fracture" at work.

Huh? Simply put, when crystalline molecules of the candy are crunched and crushed, the free electrons run into the plentiful molecules of nitrogen in the air. The nitrogen molecules become excited and vibrate. They emit this extra energy in the form of mostly ultraviolet light; however a small bit of visible light is emitted as well. This is the spark you see in the mirror.

All hard candies that contain sugar create triboluminescence when cracked, though. So why do Wint-O-Greens produce a visible result when other flavors don't? Because oil of wintergreen has the

special ability to take in light with short wavelengths (ultraviolet) and then spit out light with longer wavelengths (visible light). This is called fluorescence. That's right: Wintergreen oil is fluorescent. It takes in the ultraviolet rays from the vibrating nitrogen molecules and spits out visible light in a blueish-green shade.

Electrically speaking, *triboluminescence* is mini-lightning bolts in your mouth.

Bits to Fill in the Holes

• Francis Bacon was the first to seriously study triboluminescence reaction, some 400 years ago.

• Scotch tape also makes good fodder in the dark. Try ripping some tape quickly from the roll and see if you can see the glow.

• Seven hours and ten minutes is the record set for holding a Life Saver in the mouth, intact. It was set by Thomas Syta of Van Nuys, California.

• Pep-O-Mint is the most popular Life Saver flavor in the world.

• The top-selling flavors in the United States are orange, pineapple, cherry, lemon, lime, Wint-O-Green, Pep-O-Mint, and butter rum.

• There are fourteen candies in a roll of Wint-O-Green Life Savers.

• Life Savers come in twenty-five different flavors. The fruit flavor packs contain orange, lemon, lime, pineapple, and cherry flavored candies.

• Other roll varieties include Tropical Fruit, Tangy Flavors, Chill-O-Mint, and Wild Sour Berry.

• Besides Life Savers, RJR Nabisco (the tobacco/food company) also owns Bubble Yum, Trolli gummy candies, Bonkers, Carefree, and Terry's chocolates.

He Said/She Said

PART DEUX

All's fair use in love and war.

"I don't have any buried anger against men, because my anger is right on the surface." —Camille Paglia

"It's not the frivolity of women that makes them so intolerable. It's their ghastly enthusiasm." —Horace Rumpole, *Rumpole of the Bailey*

"If men can run the world, why can't they stop wearing neckties? How intelligent is it to start the day by tying a little noose around your neck?" —Linda Ellerbee

"Women are nothing but machines for producing children." —Napoleon Bonaparte

"Men get their opinions as boys learn to spell: By reiteration chiefly." —Elizabeth Barrett Browning

"My wife is the sort of woman who gives necrophilia a bad name." —Patrick Murray

"I know what men want. Men want to be really, really close to someone

who will leave them alone."
—Elayne Boosler

"Women should have labels on their foreheads saying, 'Government Health Warning: Women can seriously damage your brains, genitals, current account, confidence, razor blades, and good standing among your friends.'" —Jeffrey Bernard

"Men should be like Kleenex, soft, strong, and disposable."
—Cher

"Love is the delusion that one woman differs from another."
—H. L. Mencken

"If men were as great lovers as they think they are, we women wouldn't have time to do our hair." —Marlene Dietrich

"A woman is like an appendix ... she's something a man is better off without."
—Popeye

"Give a man a fish and he eats for a day. Teach him how to fish and you get rid of him for the whole weekend."
—Zenna Schaffer

"Men who don't understand women fall into two groups: Bachelors and Husbands."
—Jacques Languirand

"If you never want to see a man again say, 'I love you, I want to marry you, I want to have chil-

dren.' They leave skid marks."
—Rita Rudner

"Women should be obscene and not heard."
—Groucho Marx

"The difference between government bonds and men is that government bonds mature."
—Debbie Perry

"Here's to woman! Would that we could fold into her arms without falling into her hands." —Ambrose Bierce

"When I eventually met Mr. Right I had no idea that his first name was Always."
—Rita Rudner, again

"Perhaps crimefighting is better left to the men, Batgirl, perhaps not. But this isn't exactly women's work."
—Batman

"I'm not denyin' that women are foolish; God Almighty made 'em to match the men." —George Eliot (Mary Ann Evans)

"Despite my thirty years of research into the feminine soul, I have not yet been able to answer the great question that has never been answered: What does a woman want?"
—Sigmund Freud

"Ass, n.: The masculine of 'lass.'" —Unknown

Fables & Foibles
ODD LITTLE STORIES FROM R. L. STEVENSON

You probably know Robert Louis Stevenson for books like *Treasure Island* and *Dr. Jekyll and Mr. Hyde*. But he also wrote a series of "fables" with a dark take on humanity and its foibles.

THE TWO MATCHES

One day there was a traveler in the woods in California, in the dry season, when the Trades were blowing strong. He was tired and hungry, and dismounted from his horse to smoke a pipe. But when he felt in his pocket he found but two matches. He struck the first, and it would not light.

"Here is a pretty state of things!" said the traveler. "Dying for a smoke; only one match left; and that certain to miss fire! Was there ever a creature so unfortunate? And yet," thought the traveler, "suppose I light this match—the grass might catch on fire, for it is dry like tinder; and they might evade me, and seize upon yon bush of poison oak; before I could reach it, that would have blazed up; over the bush I see a pine tree hung with moss; that too would fly in fire; and the flame—how would the trade wind take that through the flammable forest! I hear the joint voice of wind and fire, I see myself gallop for my soul, and the flying conflagration chase me through the hills; I see this forest burn for days, and the cattle roasted, and the springs dried up, and the farmer ruined, and his children cast upon the world. What a world hangs upon this moment!"

With that he struck the match, and it missed fire.

"Thank God!" said the traveler, putting his pipe in his pocket.

THE SICK MAN AND THE FIREMAN

There was once a sick man in a burning house, to whom there

entered a fireman. "Do not save me," said the sick man. "Save those who are strong."

"Will you kindly tell me why?" inquired the fireman, for he was a civil fellow.

"Nothing could possibly be fairer," said the sick man. "The strong should be preferred in all cases, because they are of more service in the world."

The fireman pondered a while, for he was a man of some philosophy. "Granted," said he at last, as a part of the roof fell in; "but for the sake of conversation, what would you lay down as the proper service of the strong?"

"Nothing can possibly be easier," returned the sick man; "the proper service of the strong is to help the weak."

Again the fireman reflected, for there was nothing hasty about this excellent creature. "I could forgive you being sick," he said at last, as a portion of the wall fell out, "but I cannot bear your being such a fool." And with that he heaved up his fireman's axe, for he was eminently just, and clove the sick man to the bed.

THE DEVIL AND THE INNKEEPER

Once upon a time the devil stayed at an inn, where no one knew him, for they were people whose education had been neglected. He was bent on mischief, and for a time kept everybody by the ears. But at last the innkeeper set a watch upon the devil and took him in the fact.

The innkeeper got a rope's end.

"Now I am going to thrash you," said the innkeeper.

"You have no right to be angry with me," said the devil. "I am only the devil, and it is my nature to do wrong."

"Is that so?" asked the innkeeper.

"Fact, I assure you," said the devil.

"You really cannot help doing ill?" asked the innkeeper.

"Not in the smallest," said the devil; "it would be useless cruelty to thrash a thing like me."

"It would indeed," said the innkeeper. He made a noose and hanged the devil.

"There!" said the innkeeper.

THE MAN AND HIS FRIEND

A man quarreled with his friend.

"I have been much deceived in you," said the man.

And the friend made a face at him and went away.

A little after, they both died, and came together before the great Justice of the Peace. It began to look black for the friend, but the man who had a clear character was in good spirits.

"I find here some record of a quarrel," said the justice, looking in his notes. "Which of you was in the wrong?"

"He was," said the man. "He spoke ill of me behind my back."

"Did he so?" said the justice. "And pray how did he speak about your neighbors?"

"Oh, he had always a nasty tongue," said the man.

"And you chose him for your friend?" cried the justice. "My good fellow, we have no use here for fools."

So the man was cast in the pit, and the friend laughed out aloud in the dark and remained to be tried on other charges.

THE CITIZEN AND THE TRAVELER

"Look round you," said the citizen. "This is the largest market in the world."

"Oh, surely not," said the traveler.

"Well, perhaps not the largest," said the citizen, "but the best."

"You are certainly wrong there," said the traveler. "I can tell you...."

They buried the stranger at the dusk.

THE DISTINGUISHED STRANGER

Once upon a time there came to this earth a visitor from a neighboring planet. And he was met at the place of his descent by a great philosopher, who was to show him everything.

First of all they came through a wood, and the stranger looked upon the trees. "Whom have we here?" said he.

"These are only vegetables," said the philosopher. "They are alive, but not at all interesting."

"I don't know about that," said the stranger. "They seem to have very good manners. Do they never speak?"

"They lack the gift," said the philosopher.

"Yet I think I hear them sing," said the other.

"That is only the wind among the leaves," said the philosopher. "I will explain the theory of winds: it is very interesting."

"I wish I knew what they are thinking," said the stranger.

"They cannot think," said the philosopher.

"I don't know about that," returned the stranger: and then, laying his hand upon a trunk: "I like these people," said he.

"They are not people at all," said the philosopher. "Come along."

Next they came through a meadow where there were cows.

"These are very dirty people," said the stranger.

"They are not people at all," said the philosopher; and he explained cows in scientific words which I have forgotten.

"That is all one to me," said the stranger. "But why do they never look up?"

"Because they are graminivorous," said the philosopher; "and to live upon grass, which is not highly nutritious, requires so close an attention to business that they have no time to think, or speak, or look at the scenery, or keep themselves clean."

"Well," said the stranger, "that is one way to live, no doubt. But I prefer the people with the green heads."

Next they came into a city, and the streets were full of men and women.

"These are very odd people," said the stranger.

"They are the people of the greatest nation in the world," said the philosopher.

"Are they indeed?" said the stranger. "They scarcely look so."

Three Facts about Robert Louis Stevenson

• It took Robert Louis Stevenson only six days to write *Dr. Jekyll and Mr. Hyde*, which runs about 60,000 words. That's an especially surprising output, since he was suffering from the advanced stages of tuberculosis. On the other hand, he fortified his night-and-day writing with lavish doses of medicinal cocaine.

• He had trained for engineering and then law, but decided to write instead.

• Stevenson spent his last years in Samoa, where the natives called him *Tusitala* (Teller of Tales).

Cowboy Country

SMILE WHEN YOU SAY THAT, PARDNER

The heyday of the American cowboy really lasted only about twenty years—from the late 1860s until the 1880s, when settlers' barbed wire put an end to the open ranges.

buckaroo: The first cowboys were *vaqueros* from Mexico. (*Vaca* is Spanish for "cow.") "Buckaroo" was what happened as Anglos attempt to pronounce the Spanish term.

cowpokes and cowpunchers: Cowboys got the name because they often had to poke or prod the cattle to get them to go into railroad cars.

Stetson: The classic cowboy hat came not from Texas or Wyoming, but from the John B. Stetson Hat Company in Philadelphia, Pennsylvania.

ten-gallon hat: Despite the name, it held only about 3 quarts. One theory is that it got its name from being big enough for "ten *galions*." (Galions are braids that decorated the hat's crown.)

chaps: Short for *chaparegos*, a vaquero invention that pro-

tected the legs from spiny vegetation and rope burn.

cowboy boots: There were two good reasons why cowboys wore high heels: to keep their feet from slipping out of the stirrups, and put some extra distance above the mud, muck, and cattle excrement.

cowboy demographics: The average cowboy was twenty-four, and he could expect a working career of about seven years. About half were white; about a quarter Mexican, and another quarter black.

corral: Spanish for "enclosed yard."

Every Picture Tells a Story

Arrangement in Gray & Black #1: The Artist's Mother by James Whistler

• The painting we call *Whistler's Mother* by Massachusetts-born James Abbott Lowell Whistler is the only American painting hanging in the Louvre in Paris.

• It's also the only painting that Whistler did of his mother.

• On this occasion, he painted his reluctant mom in a straight-backed wooden chair only because his scheduled model hadn't shown up.

• The painting has given people the impression that he was a sentimental Norman Rockwell sort of guy, but this wasn't his normal style. Whistler usually created more abstract art. He loved seeing himself as a shocking rebel against the art establishment, and presented himself and his work in ways that kept that image alive.

• Despite being a Yankee, Whistler throughout his life pretended to be a southern gentleman.

• He was later bankrupted by legal fees when he sued an art critic. Despite winning the lawsuit, he was awarded no money.

Even More Lear

More rhymes and drawings from Edward Lear's classic children's book, *The Book of Nonsense* (published 1846).

There was an Old Man of the West,
Who never could get any rest;
So they set him to spin
On his nose and chin,
Which cured that Old Man of the West.

There was an Old Person of Anerley,
Whose conduct was strange and unmannerly;
He rushed down the Strand
With a pig in each hand,
But returned in the evening to Anerley.

There was a Young Lady of Troy,
Whom several large flies did annoy;
Some she killed with a thump,
Some she drowned at the pump,
And some she took with her to Troy.

There was an Old Person of Berlin,
Whose form was uncommonly thin;
Till he once, by mistake,
Was mixed up in a cake,
So they baked that Old Man of Berlin.

There was an Old Man who said, "Well!
Will nobody answer this bell?
I have pulled day and night,
Till my hair has grown white,
But nobody answers this bell!"

There was an Old Person of Cheadle,
Who was put in the stocks by the beadle
For stealing some pigs,
Some coats, and some wigs,
That horrible person of Cheadle.

There was an Old Person of Chester,
Whom several small children did pester;
They threw some large stones,
Which broke most of his bones,
And displeased that Old Person of Chester.

There was an Old Person from Gretna,
Who rushed down the crater of Etna;
When they said, "Is it hot?"
He replied, "No, it's not!"
That mendacious Old Person of Gretna.

There was an Old Man of the Cape,
Who possessed a large Barbary ape,
Till the ape one dark night
Set the house all alight,
Which burned that Old Man of the Cape.

There was an Old Person of Ems,
Who casually fell in the Thames;
And when he was found
They said he was drowned,
That unlucky Old Person of Ems.

There was an Old Person of Ewell,
Who chiefly subsisted on gruel;
But to make it more nice
He inserted some mice,
Which refreshed that Old Person of Ewell.

Bugs!

EVERYTHING YOU WANTED TO KNOW ABOUT INSECTS

...But were afraid to ask.

INSECTS, DRUGS, ROCK 'N' ROLL

What is the song "La Cucaracha" about, anyway? The song is beloved by children and hungry office workers waiting for the lunch truck, but few people have seen an accurate translation. There's a reason for that. Strike up the trumpets, guitars, and violins, because here are the lyrics, along with a singable translation.

> La cucaracha, la cucaracha
> Ya no puede caminar
> Porque no tiene, porque le falta
> Marijuana que fumar.
>
> Ya la murio la cucaracha
> Ya la lleven a enterrar
> Entre cuatro zopilotes
> Y un raton de sacristan.
>
> Oh, there's a cockroach, yes, there's a cockroach—
> His travel plans became a joke
> Because he's missing, yes he's lacking,
> Marijuana he can smoke.
>
> Oh, it killed the poor old cockroach—
> Brought him to the funeral house
> He was carried by four buzzards
> And the churchyard sexton's mouse.

¡Ole niños, magnifico! Yes, the song is about a pothead cockroach's wasted life, squalid death, and tawdry funeral.

FLY, FLY!

How fast can a fly fly? When you're trying to catch a housefly, it may seem like it can take off at supersonic speed. Really, though, you could easily outrun one, or even outwalk it.

Although its wings can flap 200 times a second, a housefly flies through the air at a speed of only about 4.5 miles per hour. That's nothing compared to the world's fastest insect. That would be the Australian dragonfly, which can blast through the air so fast the experts don't agree on its top speed: their estimates range from a remarkable 35 mph to an unbelievable 60 mph.

A TERRIBLE FINISH
In order to make shellac, you have to crush shellac beetles. A pound of shellac takes about 150,000 of them. The red dye called cochineal is also made from crushing beetles. In this case, a red-colored scale beetle that lives only on prickly pear cacti.

BEE FOR THE PILGRIMS
There were no honeybees in America before European settlers first brought hives to America in 1622. Over the fol-

lowing years, many bees fled human-made hives and sought freedom in their own colonies throughout the New Land. By the late 1700s, honeybees had settled along most of the eastern side of North America. During the 1800s, they spread across the continent.

OUTNUMBERED
Entomologists estimate that there are about 10,000 bugs for every human being on Earth, which is no surprise to anyone who has gone outside on a hot summer night. Over 1.5 million insect species are known to populate the world today, but there may be many more out there waiting to be discovered and classified.

BLOODSUCKERS
If you're an average-sized adult, it would take about 1,120,000 mosquitoes to completely drain your blood.

LADYBUG'S NOT FOR BURNING
Why do they call ladybugs ladybugs when half of the bugs ain't ladies? During the Middle Ages, these aphid-eaters were regarded by farmers as having been sent from heaven. French farmers called them *les betes du bon Dieu* ("creatures of the good God") and *les vaches de la Vierge*

("cows of the Virgin"). Germans called them *Marienkafer* or "Mary's beetles." And the English called them "Our Lady's beetles," which became shortened to "ladybugs."

Why did the farmer value them so? Well, an adult female can consume 75 aphids and scale bugs a day, while a male may consume 40. Even its larva, resembling tiny alligators, chomps about 350 aphids before becoming a ladybug.

YOU LIGHT UP MY LIFE

Glowworms are the larvae of fireflies (although in some species they are flightless females). Fireflies spend one or two years in the larval state, but only 5 to 30 days as adults. As larvae, they eat earthworms, snails, and the larvae of other insects, killing their prey by injecting poison into them. As adults, they eat nectar from flowers or, in some species, nothing at all. There are about 1,900 glowing members of the *Lampyridae* family — not a bad name for a bug that lights up the night.

HEY BIG BOY, GOT A LIGHT?

Why do fireflies glow? Sex, mostly. Males flash a pattern of dots and dashes that is specific to their species. Female

F is for Firefly
that shines in the dark
And lights up the woods
with its tiny white spark.

fireflies wait for the correct signal, then they flash back. They meet and make beautiful luminescence together.

Well, most of the time that's how it works. However, the females of some species prey on the males of other species, imitating their mating signals, and then eating the lovesick males that come close.

MULTIPLY BY DIVIDING?

If you cut an earthworm in half, will both halves live and grow back? Alas, no. While some worms can regrow a tail if they lose it, the tail part dies. True, the lopped-off tail end can wriggle around helplessly for a few hours, but that's just like a chicken running around with no head. Furthermore, the head end may well die from the injury,

"Bookworms" don't eat just book bindings and glue, but any number of things. There's not even a specific bug—"bookworm" is used to describe any moth or beetle larvae found infesting books.

Makes us wonder what eats audio books—"tapeworms," maybe?

but it has a chance of surviving if its intestines and other vital organs are still intact.

Too bad. If worms could multiply by dividing, they could dispense with that messy, slimy worm sex. Worms are hermaphrodites (both male and female), so they can mate with any other worm of their species. They do that in a slimy sodden mess, writhing, putting together their clitella and exchanging sperm. Each partner ends up pregnant, laying an egg capsule a week later. After 14–21 days, one to five little squirmers hatch.

NO EATING IN THE LIBRARY
What did bookworms eat before there were books? After centuries of clay tablets and scrolls did they stand up and cheer in the fourth century A.D. when somebody got the bright idea of sewing and binding parchment? Well, no.

LONG LIVE THE KING
Queen ants and queen bees live in a matriarchal society and mate with expendable male courtiers. However, not all social insects suffer from the tyranny of gender supremacy. Termites live up to our highest ideals of gender egalitarianism. Unlike ants and bees, their nests have workers of both sexes. Furthermore, they have a king and queen that are bound together in a monogamous relationship of a sort that's seldom seen in royalty of any species. The royals mate for life, and they do it lustfully and regularly, keeping a termite queen happily popping out an egg per second day after day.

Despite this, the termite is poisoned and maligned by a selfish human world unwilling to share its wood products with such a virtuous, family-values sort of bug.

Life Lessons

HOW TO CHARM A SNAKE

Just in case you fall on hard times, here's a career option you might not have ever considered. The tools are few, there's little competition, and the show is worth the price of admission. You'll have it made!

Charming a snake looks near-impossible, but the steps are pretty simple. Before you begin, you have to get your props in order. You'll need a basket, a cobra, and a pungi—an oboe-like Indian reed instrument. You also may want to acquire a turban, a loin cloth, and a certain panache to accompany your act.

1. Take the lid off the basket with much fanfare. The cobra will rise from the darkness of the basket into the light, with its hood flared defensively. The crowd will go, "Oooh!" and step back. This is your cue to also jump back slightly, and make a point of keeping your wide, wary eyes on your snake.

2. Play your pungi. Although having some basic knowledge of how to play the pungi may help in convincing your audience of the trick's authenticity, the snake has no ears and won't care if you can't tell a B-flat from an A-sharp.

3. Here's the key step: sway to your music, making sure the tip of the pungi is in front of the cobra. A cobra can't pivot its eyes, so will follow the tip of your instrument with its whole head and body. Practice this well in order to get down the movements that the snake can keep up with. If you keep swaying, there's a good chance the snake won't strike.

4. Keep your distance while you're moving to keep the cobra from lunging and biting you. If it does attack, let's hope you've done what the professionals do—had it defanged beforehand.

Flornithology 3
HOW TO TELL THE BIRDS FROM THE FLOWERS

Even more entries from the field guide by Robert Williams Wood (1868–1955) for those who may have trouble seeing the difference.

The Pecan   The Toucan

The Auk   The Orchid

The Catbird   The Catnip

The Ibis   The Ibiscus

The Pipe   The Snipe

The Roc   The Shamrock

Forbidden Bible Tales

MIGHTY STRANGE STORIES FROM THE GOOD BOOK

There are a lot of Bible verses you won't necessarily hear
your preacher using as a text. In fact, most believers
haven't even run across them.

NOAH'S SON HAM SEES HIS DRUNK DAD NAKED, SO HAM'S SON IS MADE A SLAVE (GENESIS 9:20–6)

And the sons of Noah, that went forth from the ark, were Shem,
and Ham, and Japheth: and Ham is the father of Canaan. These
three were the sons of Noah: and of these was the whole earth
overspread.

And Noah began to be a husbandman, and planted a vineyard: and he drank of the wine, and was drunken. And he was
uncovered within his tent.

And Ham, the father of Canaan, saw the nakedness of his
father, and told his two brethren without.

And Shem and Japheth took a garment, and laid it upon both
their shoulders, and went backward, and covered the nakedness of their father. And their faces were backward, and they
saw not their father's nakedness.

And Noah awoke from his wine, and knew what his youngest
son had done unto him. And he said, "Cursed be Canaan; a servant of servants shall he be unto his brethren."

And he said, "Blessed be Jehovah, the God of Shem; And let
Canaan be his servant. God enlarge Japheth, and let him dwell
in the tents of Shem; and let Canaan be his servant. "

HEY, YOU GALS—SHUT UP! (I CORINTHIANS 14:34–5)

Let the women keep silence in the churches: for it is not permitted unto them to speak; but let them be in subjection, as also

saith the law. And if they would learn anything, let them ask their own husbands at home: for it is shameful for a woman to speak in the church.

LOT OFFERS HIS VIRGIN DAUGHTERS FOR GANG RAPE, THEN GETS DRUNK & IMPREGNATES THEM WITHOUT PUNISHMENT ... BUT HIS WIFE LOOKS BACK AT THE WRONG TIME AND GETS TURNED TO SALT (GENESIS 19:1–38)

And the two angels came to Sodom in the evening as Lot was sitting at the gate and Lot saw them; and he bowed with his face to the earth; and he said, "My lords, turn aside into your servant's house tonight, and wash your feet, and then you may rise up early, and go on your way." And they said, "No; we will spend the night in the street."

Yet he urged them strongly and they entered into his house; and he made them a feast, and baked unleavened bread, and they ate.

But before they lay down, the men of the city surrounded the house, both young and old, all the people from every quarter; and they called to Lot, and said unto him, "Where are the men that came in to you this night? Bring them out unto us, that we may have sex with them."

And Lot went outside, and shut the door after him. And he said, "I pray you, my brethren, do not act so wickedly. Now behold, I have two daughters who are virgins; let me, I pray you, bring them out, and you can do to them whatever you like: only to these men do nothing, since they have come under the shelter of my roof."

And they said, "Stand back." And they said, "This one fellow came here as an outsider, yet he's acting like a judge: now will we deal worse with you than with them." And they pressed hard against Lot, nearly breaking down the door. But the angels reached out their hands and pulled Lot into the house with them, and shut the door.

And they struck the men at the door with blindness, both small and great, so that they tired of trying to find the door. And the men said unto Lot, "Whom do you have here? Sons-in-law, and your sons and daughters, and anyone else you have in the city, take them away, for Jehovah has heard the disturbance of this place and has sent us to destroy it."

But Lot hesitated; and the men told hold of him, and upon the hand of his wife, and upon the hand of his two daughters, Jehovah being merciful to him; and set him outside the city and said, "Escape for your life! Don't look behind you, don't stay in the valley—escape to the mountain, or you'll be consumed."

Then Jehovah rained upon Sodom and upon Gomorrah brimstone and fire from Jehovah out of heaven; and he overthrew those cities and all the valley, and all the inhabitants of the cities, and that grew upon the ground. And Lot's wife looked back from behind him, and she became a pillar of salt....

And Lot went up out of Zoar, and dwelt in a cave, he and his two daughters. And the firstborn said unto the younger, "Our father is old, and there is not a man in the earth to come in unto us after the manner of all the earth: let us make our father drink wine, and we will lie with him, that we may preserve the seed of our father." And they encouraged their father to drink wine that night: and the firstborn went in and lay with her father; and he knew not when she lay down, nor when she arose.

And it came to pass on the morrow, that the firstborn said unto the younger, "Behold, I lay last night with my father: let us make him drink wine this night also; and go in, and lie with him, that we may preserve seed of our father." And they encouraged their father to drink wine that night also: and the younger arose, and lay with him; and he knew not when she lay down, nor when she arose.

Thus were both the daughters of Lot with child by their father. And the firstborn bare a son, and called his name Moab: the same is the father of the Moabites unto this day. And the younger, she also bare a son, and called his name Ben-ammi: the same is the father of the children of Ammon unto this day.

JESUS CURSES A FIG TREE FOR NOT BEARING FRUIT OUT OF SEASON (MARK 11:13–4, 20–22)

And seeing a fig tree afar off having leaves, he went to see if it had anything on it: but when he came to it, he found nothing but leaves; for it was not the season of figs.

And Jesus answered and said unto it, "No man eat fruit of you hereafter forever!" And his disciples heard it.... And in the morning, as they passed by, they saw the fig tree dried up from the roots. And Peter said to him, "Master, behold, the fig tree which you cursed is withered away." And Jesus answered to them, "Have faith in God." (**Note:** In the Matthew version of this story, the fig tree withers instantly before their eyes.)

GOD COMMANDS THAT FARMERS LEAVE SOME CROPS IN FIELDS FOR TRAVELERS AND THE POOR (LEVITICUS 19:10–11)

"And when ye reap the harvest of your land, thou shalt not wholly reap the corners of thy field, neither shalt thou gather the gleanings of thy harvest. And thou shalt not glean thy vineyard, neither shalt thou gather every grape of thy vineyard; thou shalt leave them for the poor and stranger: I am the Lord your God."

GOD COMMANDS GENOCIDE, LOOTING, AND RAPE (NUMBERS 31:1–18)

And Jehovah spoke to Moses, saying, "Avenge the children of Israel of the Midianites: afterward you shall be gathered with your people."

And Moses spoke to the people, saying, "Arm yourselves for war, that you may go against Midian, to execute Jehovah's vengeance. Of every tribe a thousand, throughout all the tribes of Israel, shall you send to the war." So there were delivered, out of the thousands of Israel, a thousand of every tribe, twelve thousand armed for war....

And they warred against Midian, as Jehovah commanded Moses; and they killed every male.... And the children of Israel took captive the women of Midian and their little ones; and all their cattle, and all their flocks, and all their goods they looted. and they burned their cities.

And they brought the captives, and the prey, and the spoil, unto Moses....

And Moses said unto them, "Have ye saved all the women alive? ... Now therefore kill every male child, and kill every woman that hath known man by lying with him. But all the girl-children and virgins, keep alive for yourselves."

Now the prey, over and above the booty which the soldiers took, was 675,000 sheep, and 72,000 cattle, and 61,000 asses, and 32,000 women who were virgins.

The soldiers split an additional 337,500 sheep, 36,000 cattle, and 16,000 women.

Toaster Foods

THE BEST THING SINCE SLICED BREAD

Hey, if you've got a toaster, why not use it for everything?

WHO WOULD'VE THOUGHT that we'd have the crust to offer two different takes on the seemingly mundane subject of toasters? (If you missed the history of toast and toasters on page 167, you might want to go back and read it first. Or not.) Bear with us, though, because the subject of toaster foods—foods deliberately designed to be made in your toaster—is an amusing one, and their histories are more interesting than we even imagined possible.

So set the settings (not too dark!) and pull down the lever, here are the stories behind some of our most popular (and sometimes most disastrous) toaster foods.

POP-TARTS

Pop-Tarts are more than mere convenience food, they have become pure pop culture: an easy laugh for comedians, a cultural and general milestone for the rest of us. Sit down, have a Pop-Tart, and we'll tell you the story.

On September 14, 1964, Kellogg's first rolled out Pop-Tarts in Cleveland, Ohio with a stern admonition to retailers to put them in the baked goods, cookie, or cake mix section of their stores ... but nowhere near their cereals. The company's detailed display instructions spelled out, "IN NO WAY SHOULD THIS PRODUCT BE SOLD AS A SUBSTITUTE FOR CEREAL," capitalized and underlined for emphasis.

The funny thing is that Kellogg's did not invent the toaster pastry, arch-rival Post did. It's just that Kellogg's was the first to really do it right. After World War II, Post had put a team to work to come up with non-cereal products. Their first successful product was Tang, a powdered orange juice substitute that got launched into the stratosphere when astronauts drank it in space. Their next product was Gaines Burgers, a semi-moist dog food that didn't spoil quickly on the shelf. Using the same technology, they came up with a fruit-filled pastry that could be stored for months without refrigeration.

On February 16, 1964, Post unveiled its new toaster pastry to the press, sending the food industry into an uproar.

Post, however, made two fatal mistakes. The company announced the product too early, before it was ready for release. This gave their arch-rivals at Kellogg's time to come up with their own toaster pastry. Furthermore, Post named its toaster pastry "Country Squares." This was a time when "country" implied rural bumpkins and "square" was slang for com-pletely unhip. "Country Squares" didn't sound wholesome and homegrown, as Post intended, it sounded like Barney Fife or Gomer Pyle.

Kellogg's rushed their pastry to the market in a scant six months, and its name was a double pun on the hippest thing happening at the time: "Pop Art," which Andy Warhol had made a household word with his giant soup cans and Brillo boxes. Pop-Tarts took the market by storm, advertised by an animated toaster named Milton; the company literally could not keep shelves stocked.

The first Pop-Tarts came out in four flavors: strawberry, blueberry, brown sugar cinnamon, and apple currant. The first three are still with us.

Through the years, the company developed innovations of its own including no-melt frosting and sprinkles that wouldn't dislodge in the toaster. Not that there haven't been some missteps along the way: Who still remembers Danish Go Rounds and such wish-we-could forget flavors as Chocolate Peppermint, Frosted Peanut Butter and Jelly, and Chocolate and Cherry Chip? Despite such missteps, heavy competition from other brands, and the fact that they don't microwave well at all, Pop-Tarts continue to control the lion's share of the toaster-pastry market.

EGGOS: WAFFLEY GOOD

"Hey, leggo my Eggo!" The name alone is a tip-off that the brand has been around a lot longer than most people suspect—the corporate fad of putting an *O* at the end of a brand name peaked at a time that brought us Jell-O, Grain-O, Zippo, Drano, Cheerios, Harpo, Groucho, Chico and sometimes even Zeppo.

In Depression-era 1935, Frank, Tony, and Sam Dorsa borrowed money to buy a waffle iron. Their idea was to build a better batter, which they'd sell premixed to restaurants; all they needed was a name. A fourth brother, George, piped up

with a suggestion: It's got a lot of eggs in it, why not call it "Eggo"?

The Eggo batter started selling like hotcakes, and in 1937 the company opened a huge batter factory in San Jose, California.

After World War II, the brothers noticed that Americans were buying record amounts of pre-cooked frozen foods. They abandoned the batter business and switched over to ready-made waffles. Within a year, they were pouring out 10,000 waffles an hour to keep up with the demand.

In 1968, the brothers sold out to Kellogg's, which used the "Leggo my Eggo" slogan to

raise waffle-consciousness in a hungry nation. Today, the brand covers more than half of the $500 million annual frozen waffle market.

LENDER'S BAGELS

It's hard to imagine, but twenty-five years ago, most Americans had never even tried a bagel. If you weren't Jewish, bagels were exotic and pretty much unknown; even if you were Jewish, bagels were hard to find if you were outside a major metropolitan area.

In 1927, Harry Lender immigrated from Poland and opened the first American bagel bakery outside of New York City. In New Haven, Connecticut, Lender sold retail from his own bakery, and also distributed bagels to jewish delis and grocery stores. Being that New Haven was a relatively small place, his "roll with a hole" spread into Italian, Irish, and Russian neighborhoods, too. However, bagels go stale fast and don't travel well. Lender's market was limited geographically by the bagel's short shelf life.

Trying to solve that problem, Harry's sons Murray and Marvin discovered that flash-freezing would keep bagels from going stale for months. The Lenders also decided to try to make the bagel more acceptable to mainstream America, softening the crunchy crust and chewy center that is the essence of genuine bagelhood. The strategy worked. Lender's frozen bagels converted gentiles across North America to their holey roll, even if purists grumbled.

The Lender family sold the business to Kraft in 1986, which seemed a perfect mar-riage, what with their Phila-delphia Cream Cheese, but Kraft turned around and sold it to Kellogg's, making it the premiere player in toaster foods.

THOMAS' ENGLISH MUFFINS

There really was a guy named Thomas, and he really was born English. However, despite some hints that sug-gest otherwise from the com-pany's advertising, Mr. Thomas was never a baker in England.

Samuel Bath Thomas was born in Plymouth, England in 1855. Looking for adventure and opportunities, the 21-year-old traveled to New York in 1876 and worked a number of menial jobs until he could speak the language. (Okay, so we're lying about that last part.)

Young Sam saved his money and in 1880 opened his own business, a bakery at 163 Ninth Avenue in Manhattan.

Perhaps he adapted the crumpet to American tastes, or perhaps it was the "Bara Maen," a Welsh bread cake baked on hot stones. No mat-ter, he managed to create the prototype of the "English muffin" (still completely unknown in England) — a bread baked with a griddle instead of an oven.

His was just one of several thousand small bake shops in New York, but his muffin caught the fancy of hoteliers, in part because it was just as easy to prepare as toast (pop in toaster and butter), but it was a classy alternative to crunchy, browned bread. Thomas delivered his muffins in glass-domed cases with "S. B. Thomas" stenciled on them, which created enough brand awareness to allow him to begin selling his toaster crumpet through grocery stores, as well.

Thomas died in 1919 and the business was inherited by his daughter and nephews. It was bought by CPC, a food conglomerate that is also known as Bestfoods. Following British tradition, CPC expanded the yeast-meets-west empire, colonizing the United States and subjugating Third World breads (Thomas' Sahara Pita Bread, Thomas' Bagels) into the Thomas' commonwealth.

TOASTER LOSERS

Not every toaster food product has been a success. Here are some that weren't:

• **Downyflake Toaster Eggs**. It was just too strange an idea.

• **ReddiWip's Reddi Bacon**. Bacon grease tended to leak, creating a fire hazard.

• **Toaster Chicken Patties**. Different grease, same fire hazard.

• **Electric French Fries**. According to one critic, the toast-shaped slab of potatoes "looked like a picket fence; tasted like a picket fence."

• **Toaster Breaks**. You'd think a company as smart as the maker of Hot Pockets wouldn't coin a name that sounds like a prediction of doom for your toaster. When the product faltered, though, the Chef America company replaced the name with one that sounded just as ominous: "Toaster Melts." At this writing, the product line has dwindled down to just one flavor (ham and cheese).

Pop-Up Toaster-Food Facts

• Researching Toaster Strudel, Pillsbury studied the pop-ups of 2000 models of toasters. They determined that 1.8 ounces was most toaster-compatible.

• Toaster pastries don't microwave well. If your toaster breaks, you can toast a single layer on a cookie sheet at 400° F. for five minutes.

• Very few toaster pastries are consumed by people over fifty.

More H. L. Mencken

- "Say what you will about the ten commandments: you must always come back to the pleasant fact that there are only ten of them."

- "It is only doubt that creates. It is only the minority that counts."

- "School-days, I believe, are the unhappiest in the whole span of human existence. They are full of dull, unintelligible tasks, new and unpleasant ordinances, brutal violations of common sense and common decency. It doesn't take a reasonably bright boy long to discover that most of what is rammed into him is nonsense, and that no one really cares very much whether he learns it or not."

- "Any man who inflicts the human race with ideas must be prepared to see them misunderstood."

- "Criticism is prejudice made plausible."

- "Marriage is a wonderful institution, but who would want to live in an institution?"

- "Every decent man is ashamed of the government he lives under."

- "Injustice is relatively easy to bear; what stings is justice."

- "It is hard to believe that a man is telling the truth when you know that you would lie if you were in his place."

- "A jury is a group of twelve people who, having lied to the judge about their health, hearing, and business engagements, have failed to fool him."

- "Faith may be defined briefly as an illogical belief in the occurrence of the improbable."

- "A poet more than thirty years old is simply an overgrown child."

- "A man may be a fool and not know it—but not if he is married."

- "Truth would quickly cease to become stranger than fiction, once we got used to it."

- "A newspaper is a device for making the ignorant more ignorant and the crazy crazier."

- "A celebrity is one who is known by many people he is glad he doesn't know."

- "A misogynist is a man who hates women as much as women hate each other."

- "Love is the triumph of imagination over intelligence."

- "'Tis more blessed to give than to receive; for example, wedding presents."

Re: Ducks
THE WILD WORLD OF DUCKS IN THE NEWS

DOWNING THE DUCKS
One beautiful fall day in London, 10 Downing Street was besieged by a whole hoard of waddling ducks. A mother with her seventeen babes in tow left St. James's Park—their usual hangout—crossed at least one very busy road, and headed straight for the prime minister's house. They evaded police efforts to round them up until one bright officer used his helmet as a ducky scooper. They were returned to the park without further incident.

MUST BE DUCK SEASON
In 1992 in San Antonio, Texas, a forty-year-old man sat in a Bank One, listening to a loan officer explain why he'd been turned down on his application. In response, the man disrobed and began quacking like a duck. He continued to quack like a duck even as police came and hauled him away.

DADDY'S GONE A-HUNTIN', SON
In Des Moines, Iowa, Jay Knudsen offers an interesting service to the families of avid duck hunters. For a fee, Knudsen will take the ashes of the deceased, load them into duck decoys, and fire at them. He'll also put the ashes into shotgun shells along with the gunpowder and fire at whatever the deceased would've wanted to shoot at—loved ones excluded, of course.

MARRIAGE ... NOT ALL IT'S QUACKED UP TO BE
From a psychology journal comes the story of the woman in Oklahoma who was convinced Donald Duck was trying to marry her. After her neighbors installed a satellite television dish, she lingered around it for hours on end, until one day Donald's wooing worked: she disrobed and climbed into the

dish. It was, said Mrs. Donald Fauntleroy Duck, their official wedding night and she was consummating the union.

A FOWL RAIN

During a cool Arkansas thunderstorm in December 2001, ducks began falling on White's Mobile Home Supply in Hot Springs, Arkansas. A flock of ducks had been toasted by lightning in the storm, and like manna from heaven, they had the makings of an early Christmas dinner for the employees. Owner Ron White said of the incident, "It was like tennis shoes falling out of the sky and then they realized they were ducks."

RUBBER DUCKY, YOU JUST WON

Listen up, because there are now official rules in Connecticut regarding those artificial duck races where proceeds go to charity. To list a few:

1. Every entrant must receive a map of the faux duckies' race route.

2. The race must be conducted on a stream or river with a

 steady current.

3. The start and finish lines must be clearly marked.

4. Organizers must provide means to prevent cheating by contestants guiding their duckies through the course.

5. All duck entrants must be put in a holding tank for inspection prior to the race.

6. No "counterfeit" fake ducks will be allowed to participate. (Isn't that an oxymoron?)

I SAID "DUCK!"

In November 2001, a man testing a jet-ski on a lake in Deerfield Beach, Florida, was smacked in the head by a flying duck and died. Traveling a speed of up to 55 mph, Leon Resnick didn't stand a chance against the 10–15 pound duck. A bystander said that the duck "might as well have been a cinder block."

Duck Down and Cover

• Eider down is insulating feathers that get shed in the spring by eider ducks. People collect it from their nests for jackets and comforters.

• *Eider* is German or Dutch in origin. It's a derivation of the word "duck."

• Eider ducks are the fastest horizontal flyers on Earth, reaching speeds of up to sixty miles per hour.

• A single comforter takes up to 85 nests of eider feathers.

Eyewitness

I WAS THERE AT THE BOSTON TEA PARTY

George Hewes was one of hundreds who helped unload tea from the tea boats docked in Boston in 1773. Here's his retelling of the events.

THE TEA DESTROYED was contained in three ships, lying near each other at what was called at that time Griffin's wharf, and were surrounded by armed ships of war, the commanders of which had publicly declared that if the rebels, as they were pleased to style the Bostonians, should not withdraw their opposition to the landing of the tea before a certain day, the 17th day of December, 1773, they should on that day force it on shore, under the cover of their cannon's mouth.

THE DAY BEFORE

On the day preceding the seventeenth, there was a meeting of the citizens of the county of Suffolk, convened at one of the churches in Boston, for the purpose of consulting on what measures might be considered expedient to prevent the landing of the tea, or secure the people from the collection of the duty. At that meeting a committee was appointed to wait on Governor Hutchinson, and request him to inform them whether he would take any measures to satisfy the people on the object of the meeting.

To the first application of this committee, the Governor told them he would give them a definite answer by five o'clock in the afternoon. At the hour appointed, the committee again repaired to the Governor's house, and on inquiry found he had gone to his country seat at Milton, a distance of about six miles. When the committee

returned and informed the meeting of the absence of the Governor, there was a confused murmur among the members, and the meeting was immediately dissolved,

many of them crying out, "Let every man do his duty, and be true to his country"; and there was a general huzza for Griffin's wharf.

DRESSING LIKE INDIANS

It was now evening, and I immediately dressed myself in the costume of an Indian, equipped with a small hatchet, which I and my associates denominated the tomahawk, with which, and a club, after having painted my face and hands with coal dust in the shop of a blacksmith, I repaired to Griffin's wharf, where the ships lay that contained the tea. When I first appeared in the street after being thus disguised, I fell in with many who were dressed, equipped and painted as I was, and who fell in with me and marched in order to the place of our destination.

When we arrived at the wharf, there were three of our number who assumed an authority to direct our operations, to which we readily submitted. They divided us into three parties, for the purpose of boarding the three ships which contained the tea at the same time. The name of him who commanded the division to which I was assigned was Leonard Pitt. The names of the other commanders I never knew.

We were immediately ordered by the respective commanders to board all the ships at the same time, which we promptly obeyed. The commander of the division to which I belonged, as soon as we were on board the ship appointed me boatswain, and ordered me to go to the captain and demand of him the keys to the hatches and a dozen candles. I made the demand accordingly, and the captain promptly replied, and delivered the articles; but requested me at the same time to do no damage to the ship or rigging.

ORDERS GIVEN

We then were ordered by our commander to open the hatches and take out all the chests of tea and throw them overboard, and we immediately proceeded to execute his orders, first cutting and splitting the chests with our tomahawks, so as thoroughly to expose them to the effects of the water.

In about three hours from the time we went on board, we had thus broken and thrown overboard every tea chest to be found in the ship, while those in the other ships were disposing of the tea in the same way, at the same time. We were surrounded by British armed ships, but no attempt was made to resist us.

AFTERMATH

We then quietly retired to our several places of residence, without having any conversation with each other, or taking any measures to discover who were our associates; nor do I recollect of our having had the knowledge of the name of a single individual concerned in that affair, except that of Leonard Pitt, the commander of my division, whom I have mentioned. There appeared to be an understanding that each individual should volunteer his services, keep his own secret, and risk the consequence for himself. No disorder took place during that transaction, and it was observed at that time that the stillest night ensued that Boston had enjoyed for many months.

During the time we were throwing the tea overboard, there were several attempts made by some of the citizens of Boston and its vicinity to carry off small quantities of it for their family use. To effect that object, they would watch their opportunity to snatch up a handful from the deck, where it became plentifully scattered, and put it into their pockets.

One Captain O'Connor, whom I well knew, came on

board for that purpose, and when he supposed he was not noticed, filled his pockets, and also the lining of his coat. But I had detected him and gave information to the captain of what he was doing. We were ordered to take him into custody, and just as he was stepping from the vessel, I seized him by the skirt of his coat, and in attempting to pull him back, I tore it off; but, springing forward, by a rapid effort he made his escape. He had, however, to run a gauntlet through the crowd upon the wharf, each one, as he passed, giving him a kick or a stroke.

Another attempt was made to save a little tea from the ruins of the cargo by a tall, aged man who wore a large cocked hat and white wig, which was fashionable at that time. He had slightly slipped a little into his pocket, but being detected, they seized him and, taking his hat and wig from his head, threw them, together with the tea, of which they had emptied his pockets, into the water. In consideration of his advanced age, he was permitted to escape, with now and then a slight kick.

The next morning, after we had cleared the ships of the tea, it was discovered that very considerable quantities of it were floating upon the surface of the water; and to prevent the possibility of any of its being saved for use, a number of small boats were manned by sailors and citizens, who rowed them into those parts of the harbor wherever the tea was visible, and by beating it with oars and paddles so thoroughly drenched it as to render its entire destruction inevitable.

Ripe Ol' Corn

"UNCLE JOSH AT CONEY ISLAND"

"Uncle Josh," Cal Stewart's country bumpkin, had problems figuring out modern city life (circa 1901). Here he visits New York's famous amusement park.

I'D HEERD TELL A WHOLE LOT at various times 'bout that place what they call Coney Island, and while I was down in New York, I jist made up my mind I was a-goin' to see it, so one day I got on one of them cars what goes across the Brooklyn bridge, and I started out for Coney Island.

Settin' right along side of me in the car was an old lady, and she seemed sort of figity 'bout somethin' or other, and finally she said to me, "Mister, do these cars stop when we git on the other side of the bridge?" I said, "Well now, if they don't you'll git the durndest bump you ever got in your life."

Well, we got on the other side, and I got on one of them tra-la-lee cars what goes down to Coney Island. I give the car feller a dollar, and he put it in his pockit jist the same as if it belonged to him. Well, when I was gittin' purty near there I said, "Mister, don't I git any change?" He said, "Didn't you see that sign on the car?" I said, no sir. Well, he says, "You better go out and look at it." Well, I went out and looked at it, and that settled it. It said, "This car goes to Coney Island without change." Guess it did; I'll be durned if I got any.

Well, we got down there, and I must say of all the pandemonium and hubbub I ever heered in my life, Coney Island beats it all. 'Bout the fust thing I seen there was a place what they called "Shoot the Shoots." It looked like a big hoss trough stood on end, one end in a duck pond and t'other end up in the air, and they would haul a boat up to the top and all git in and then come scootin' down the hoss trough into the pond. Well, I allowed that it'd be right smart fun, so I got into one of the boats along with a lot of other folks I never seed afore and don't care if I never see agin. They yanked us up to the top of that trough and then turned us loose, and I jist felt as though the whole earth had run off and left us.

We went down that trough lickety-split, and a woman what was settin' alongside of me, got skeered and grabbed me round the neck; and I said, "You let go of me you brazen female critter!" But she jist hung on and hollered to beat thunder, and everybody was a yellin' all at once't, and that durned boat was a goin' faster'n greased lightnin' and I had one hand on my pocket book and the other on my hat, and we went "kerslap" dab into that duck pond.

That durned boat upset and we went into the water, and that durned female critter hung onto me and hollered, "Save me, I'm jist a drownin'!" Well, the water wasn't very deep and I jist started to wade out when along come another boat and run over us, and under we went. Well, I managed to get out to the bank, and that female woman said I was a base villain to not rescue a lady from a watery grave. And I jist told her if she had kept her mouth shut she wouldn't have swallered so much of the pond.

Well, they had one place what they called the Middle Way Plesumps, and another place what they called The Streets of Cairo, and they had a lot of shows a-goin' on along there. Well, I went into one of 'em and set down, and I guess if they hadn't shut up the show I'd be settin' there yet. I purty near busted my buttins a laughin'. They had a lot of gals a-dancin' some kind of a dance; I don't know what they called it, but it suited me first-rate.

When I got home, the more I thought about it the more I made up my mind I'd learn that dance. Well, I went out in the cornfield whar none of the neighbors could see me, and I'll be durned if I didn't knock down about four acres of corn, but I never got that dance right. I was the talk of the whole community; mother didn't speak to me fer about a week, and Aunt Nancy Smith said I was a burnin' shame and a disgrace to the village, but I notice Nancy has asked me a good many questions about jist how it was, and I wouldn't wonder if we didn't find Nancy out in the cornfield one of these days.

MOST POPULAR NAMES
BY YEAR OF BIRTH, ACCORDING TO THE SOCIAL SECURITY ADMINISTRATION

1900 Boys: John, William, James; Girls: Mary, Helen, Anna

1905 Boys: John, William, James; Girls: Mary, Helen, Margaret

1910 Boys: John, William, James; Girls: Mary, Helen, Margaret

1915 Boys: John, William, James; Girls: Mary, Helen, Dorothy

1920 Boys: John, William, James; Girls: Mary, Dorothy, Helen

1925 Boys: John, Robert, James; Girls: Mary, Dorothy, Betty

1930 Boys: Robert, James, John; Girls: Mary, Betty, Dorothy

1935 Boys: James, Robert, John; Girls: Mary, Shirley, Barbara

1940 Boys: James, Robert, John; Girls: Mary, Barbara, Patricia

1945 Boys: James, Robert, John; Girls: Mary, Linda, Barbara

1950 Boys: John, James, Robert; Girls: Linda, Mary, Patricia

1955 Boys: Michael, James, David/Robert (tie); Girls: Deborah, Mary, Linda

1960 Boys: David, Michael, John; Girls: Mary, Susan, Maria

1965 Boys: Michael, James, John; Girls: Lisa, Maria, Karen

1970 Boys: Michael, David, John; Girls: Jennifer, Lisa, Kimberly

1975 Boys: Michael, Christopher, Jason; Girls: Jennifer, Amy, Michelle

1980 Boys: Michael, Jason, Christopher; Girls: Jennifer, Jessica, Amanda

1985 Boys: Michael, Christopher, Matthew; Girls: Jessica, Ashley, Jennifer

1990 Boys: Michael, Christopher, Joshua; Girls: Jessica, Ashley, Brittany

1995 Boys: Michael, Jacob, Matthew; Girls: Emily, Ashley, Jessica

The Devil's Dictionary: P

More of *The Devil's Dictionary* by Ambrose Bierce (1842–1914?)

PAINTING, *n.* The art of protecting flat surfaces from the weather and exposing them to the critic.

PANTHEISM, *n.* The doctrine that everything is God, in contradistinction to the doctrine that God is everything.

PASSPORT, *n.* A document inflicted upon a citizen going abroad, exposing him as an alien and pointing him out for special reprobation and outrage.

PATIENCE, *n.* A minor form of despair, disguised as a virtue.

PATRIOT, *n.* The dupe of statesmen and the tool of conquerors.

PATRIOTISM, *n.* In Dr. Johnson's famous dictionary patriotism is defined as the last resort of a scoundrel. With all due respect to an inferior lexicographer I beg to submit that it is the first.

PERSEVERANCE, *n.* A lowly virtue whereby mediocrity achieves an inglorious success.

PESSIMISM, *n.* A philosophy forced by the disheartening prevalence of the optimist's scarecrow hope and unsightly smile.

PHILANTHROPIST, *n.* A rich old gentleman who has trained himself to grin while his conscience is picking his pocket.

PHILOSOPHY, *n.* A route of many roads leading from nowhere to nothing.

PIETY, *n.* Reverence for the Supreme Being, based upon His supposed resemblance to man.

PLAN, *v.t.* To bother about the best method of accomplishing an accidental result.

PLEASURE, *n.* The least hateful form of dejection.

POLITENESS, *n.* The most acceptable hypocrisy.

POLITICS, *n.* A strife of interests masquerading as a contest of principles. The conduct of public affairs for private advantage.

POSITIVE, *adj.* Mistaken at the top of one's voice.

PRAY, *v.* Ask that the laws of the universe be annulled in behalf of a single petitioner confessedly unworthy.

PREFERENCE, *n.* A sentiment, or frame of mind, induced by the erroneous belief that one thing is better than another.

PRESENTABLE, *adj.* Hideously appareled after the manner of the time and place.

PRESIDENCY, *n.* The greased pig in the field game of American politics.

Archetypal Blonde

THE QUIRKY, SAD LIFE OF MARILYN MONROE

Marilyn Monroe was more than a movie star. She was an icon who shook up the sexually repressed 1950s. We've sifted through her biographies to give you the juicy stuff.

• A star was born on June 1, 1926, with the unlikely name of Norma Jeane Mortenson. Her mother, Gladys Pearl Monroe Baker Mortenson, was an emotionally unstable film negative cutter. Marilyn spent her childhood carted around between foster homes.

• Norma Jeane vowed she would never get married—that she was going to become a schoolteacher and have lots of dogs. She concocted the idea that Clark Gable was her biological father.

• In high school, Norma Jeane wrote news features for the school paper, concluding in one that "53 percent of the gentlemen prefer blondes as their dream girl."

• Norma left school at sixteen to marry twenty-one-year-old Jim Dougherty. She tried unsuccessfully to negotiate an agreement that they would not have sex after marrying.

• In April 1944, Norma Jeane took a wartime job spraying varnish on fuselage fabric. She became a parachute inspector. Soon after, she was discovered by an Army camera crew doing a "girls of the war effort" spread for GI morale. Her career began to blossom.

• By spring of 1946 she had appeared on thirty-three magazine covers. She had an affair with at least one photographer, and in September was granted a divorce from Jim. She was signed by Fox Studio that same year.

- After one movie deal, Fox declined to renew her contract. Monroe spent her small income on acting classes, rent, and car maintenance. She filled the gaps by prostituting off Hollywood Boulevard.

- With roommate Shelley Winters, Monroe began compiling a list of men she wanted to have sexual relations with. At the top of the list was Albert Einstein. (Whether it happened, nobody knows for sure, but later Winters came across a photo of Einstein inscribed, "With respect and love and thanks.")

- The price of stardom was high: At Columbia Studios, her bleached hairline was permanently heightened. Her drama coach taught her an overexaggerated, breathy voice that became so habitual she would later have to go to another coach to get rid of it. Her voice teacher paid for the correction of an overbite and to have her teeth bleached. Her agent arranged plastic surgery to remove a small bump from the tip of her nose and insert a silicone implant into her jaw to give it a softer line. She lifted weights to improve her bustline, and jogged each morning—neither activity commonplace for women in 1950.

- Monroe had camera fright, often vomiting before going on the set.

- But she was tough: While filming in 1952, Marilyn was diagnosed with acute appendicitis. She asked them to give her antibiotics and delay the operation until after the movie was finished. She returned to work and didn't have her appendix removed until nearly two months later.

- She learned her seductive "swivel" while filming a movie where she had to walk down a cobblestone street in high heels. After she saw the reaction from onlookers, she used that walk from that day on. When asked if her walk was natural, she quipped, "I've been walking since I was six months old." The Tokyo press dubbed Marilyn "Honorable Buttocks-Swinging Actress."

- She didn't wear any underwear, a custom very rare in 1952. The dress she wore in *Gentlemen Prefer Blondes* was so tight that she had to be sewn into it.

- When she met Joe DiMaggio, she was 25; he was 37 and retired from baseball.

- At their wedding, Marilyn turned to Joe and asked him if she died before him, would he place flowers at her grave every week—just as William Powell had done at the grave of Jean Harlow? Joe promised, and even though they were divorced when she died, he did so for decades afterward.

• Marilyn told a friend that Joe didn't like her work on screen: "He didn't like the women I played—he thought they were sluts. He didn't like the actors kissing me, and he didn't like my costumes. He didn't like anything about my movies, and he hated all my clothes." The famous blowing skirt scene brought matters to a head, and Joe reportedly got violent, causing bruises on her shoulders that had to be covered up with makeup. Two weeks later, Marilyn filed for divorce.

• After returning from her honeymoon with Joe, Marilyn told a friend that she was next going to marry Arthur Miller, author of *The Crucible* and other plays.

• Monroe did marry the playwright in June 1956. At the last minute, Monroe told friends that she wan't sure she wanted to marry him, but that she would go through it because she didn't want to disappoint the already-assembled wedding guests.

• Miller had second thoughts as well. He wrote in his journal that he feared his writing would be threatened by her continuous emotional de-

Marilyn and wooly friend in April 1946—her very first national magazine cover

mands. Sure enough, after the wedding he immediately sunk into a case of writer's block. Monroe convinced him to write a movie script for *The Misfits* for her. As their relationship deteriorated, he rewrote drafts of the script, making her character more and more unsympathetic.

• After *Some Like It Hot*, Tony Curtis said that kissing her was like "kissing Hitler."

• According to biographer Donald Spoto, best evidence suggests that Monroe had only one sexual encounter with John F. Kennedy and that she never slept with Bobby Kennedy—she reportedly wasn't attracted to him. She did find him a sympathetic listener, though, and would called his office repeatedly. The attorney general eventually started avoiding her calls.

• She started seeing a psychotherapist named Ralph Greenson, who relied heavily on drug therapy, routinely prescribing barbiturates and tranquilizers. He told her to visit at his house instead of his office, and convinced her that she needed to see him every day. Right before her death, Greenson was injecting her with drugs at least once a day, and had given her pre-

scriptions for strong sedatives.

• Although there are a number of conspiracy theories about her death, biographer Spoto suggests that her psychiatrist, Ralph Greenson, administered barbiturates or chloral hydrate as an enema (evidenced by the coroner's report), which, combined with sedative she had taken earlier, killed her. Greenson and a housekeeper he had hired to keep an eye on her then tried to cover up his error, says Spoto, resulting in various contradictory accounts that have fed the conspiracy theories.

• Persistent stories had it that DiMaggio and Monroe had been planning to get remarried at the time she died.

Eyewitness
I Saw Lincoln Assassinated

History books are fine, but there's always a sense that they're leaving out the good parts, the parts that help us see the events vividly. For that, you've got to go to the real people who were actually there.

THERE ARE STORIES WE ALL KNOW, yet in a way, we really don't. Sometimes details get lost in the retelling. For example, after Lincoln's shooting, did you know that mobs reigned and federal troops chased innocent playgoers out of Ford's Theater with bayonets? That John Wilkes Booth thought he'd be lionized as a hero? Let's listen to some of the voices of people who lived through the time.

THEATERGOER PETER DOYLE'S EXPERIENCES, AS TOLD BY HIS GOOD FRIEND WALT WHITMAN: The day, April 14, 1865, seems to have been a pleasant one throughout the whole land....The popular afternoon paper, the little "Evening Star," had spatter'd all over its third page, divided among the advertisements in a sensational manner, in a hundred different places, "The President and his Lady will be at the Theatre this evening...."

On this occasion the theatre was crowded, many ladies in rich and gay costumes, officers in their uniforms, many well-known citizens, young folks, the usual clusters of gas-lights, the usual magnetism of so many people, cheerful, with perfumes, music of violins and flutes.... The President with his wife witness'd the play from the large stage-boxes of the second tier, two thrown into one, and profusely draped with the national flag....

There is a scene in the play representing a modern parlor, in which two unprecedented English ladies are inform'd by the impossible Yankee that he is not a man of fortune, and therefore undesirable for marriage-catching purposes; after which, the comments being finish'd, the dramatic trio make exit, leaving the stage clear for a moment. At this period came the murder of Abraham Lincoln.

Great as all its manifold train, circling round it, and stretching into the future for many a century, in the politics, history, art, etc., of the New World, in point of fact the main thing, the actual murder, transpired with the quiet and simplicity of any commonest occurrence—the bursting of a bud or pod in the growth of vegetation, for instance. Through the general hum following the stage pause, with the change of positions, came the muffled sound of a pistol-shot, which not one-hundredth part of the audience heard at the time—and yet a moment's hush—somehow, surely, a vague startled thrill—and then, through the ornamented, draperied, starr'd and striped space-way of the President's box, a sudden figure, a man, raises himself with hands and feet, stands a moment on the railing, leaps below to the stage (a distance of perhaps fourteen or fifteen feet), falls out of position, catching his

Another Eyewitness

"When the second scene of the third act was being performed, and while I was intently observing the proceedings upon the stage with my back toward the door, I heard the discharge of a pistol behind me, and, looking round, saw through the smoke a man between the door and the President. The distance from the door to where the President sat was about four feet. At the same time I heard the man shout some word which I thought was 'Freedom!' I instantly sprang toward him and seized him. He wrested himself from my grasp, and made a violent thrust at my breast with a large knife. I parried the blow by striking it up, and received a wound several inches deep in my left arm, below the elbow and the shoulder. The orifice of the wound was about an inch and a half in length, and extended upward toward the shoulder several inches. The man rushed to the front of the box, and I endeavored to seize him again, but only caught his clothes as he was leaping over the railing of the box....I then turned to the President; his position was not changed; his head was slightly bent forward, and his eyes were closed. I saw that he was unconscious and, supposing him mortally wounded, rushed to the door for the purpose of calling medical aid." —**Major Henry Rathbone, who sat in the Lincolns' box with his wife-to-be. An odd footnote: 19 years later Rathbone would end up in a mental institution after stabbing his wife to death.**

boot-heel in the copious drapery (the American flag), falls on one knee, quickly recovers himself, rises as if nothing had happen'd, (he really sprains his ankle, but unfelt then)—and so the figure, Booth, the murderer, dress'd in plain black broadcloth, bare-headed, with full, glossy, raven hair, and his eyes like some mad animal's flashing with light and resolution, yet with a certain strange calmness, holds aloft in one hand a large knife—walks along not much back from the footlights—turns fully toward the audience his face of statuesque beauty, lit by those basilisk eyes, flashing with desperation, perhaps insanity—launches out in a firm and steady voice the words "*Sic semper tyrannis*"—and then walks with neither slow nor very rapid pace diagonally across to the back of the stage, and disappears. (Had not all this terrible scene—making the mimic ones preposterous—had it not all been rehears'd, in blank, by Booth, beforehand?)

A moment's hush—a scream—the cry of murder—Mrs. Lincoln leaning out of the box, with ashy cheeks and lips, with involuntary cry,

pointing to the retreating figure, "*He has kill'd the President.*" And still a moment's strange, incredulous suspense—and then the deluge!—then that mixture of horror, noises, uncertainty—(the sound, somewhere back, of a horse's hoofs clattering with speed)—the people burst through chairs and railings, and break them up—there is inextricable confusion and terror—women faint—quite feeble persons fall, and are trampled on—many cries of agony are heard—the broad stage suddenly fills to suffocation with a dense and motley crowd, like some horrible carnival—the audience rush generally upon it, at least the strong men do—the actors and actresses are all there in their play-costumes and painted faces, with mortal fright showing through the rouge —the screams and calls, confused talk—redoubled, trebled —two or three manage to pass up water from the stage to the President's box—others try to clamber up—etc., etc.

In the midst of all this, the soldiers of the President's guard, with others suddenly drawn to the scene, burst in— (some two hundred altogether)—they storm the house, through all the tiers, especially the upper ones, inflamed

War Department, Washington, April 20, 1865.

$100,000 REWARD!

THE MURDERER

Of our late beloved President, Abraham Lincoln,

IS STILL AT LARGE.

$50,000 REWARD

$25,000 REWARD

$25,000 REWARD

EDWIN M. STANTON, Secretary of War.

with fury, literally charging the audience with fix'd bayonets, muskets and pistols, shouting *Clear out! clear out! you sons of bitches*! Such the wild scene, or a suggestion of it, inside the playhouse that night.

Outside, too, in the atmosphere of shock and craze, crowds of people, fill'd with frenzy, ready to seize any outlet for it, come near committing murder several times on innocent individuals. One such case was especially exciting. The infuriated crowd through some chance got started against one man, either for words he utter'd, or perhaps without

In His Own Words

"I struck boldly, and not as the papers say. I walked with a firm step through 1,000 of his friends, was stopped, but pushed on. A colonel was at his side. I shouted, 'Sic Semper' before I fired. In jumping, broke my leg. I passed all his pickets, rode 60 miles that night, with the bone of my leg tearing the flesh at every jump. I can never repent it, although we hated to kill. Our country owed all her troubles to him, and God simply made me the instrument of His punishment....I am here in despair. And why? For doing what Brutus was honored for—what made William Tell a hero. And yet I, for striking down a greater tyrant than they ever knew, am looked upon as a common cutthroat....I have too great a soul to die like a criminal. O may He spare me that, and let me die bravely!" —**John Wilkes Booth, 27-year-old actor, states rights fanatic, white supremist, and assassin, writing in his diary shortly before being killed in a Virginia tobacco barn**

any cause at all, and were proceeding at once to actually hang him on a neighboring lamppost, when he was rescued by a few heroic policemen, who placed him in their midst, and fought their way slowly and amid great peril toward the station house. It was a fitting episode of the whole affair. The crowd rushing and eddying to and fro — the night, the yells, the pale faces, many frighten'd people trying the vain to extricate themselves — the attack'd man, not yet freed from the jaws of death, looking like a corpse — the silent, resolute, half-dozen policemen, with no weapons but their little clubs, yet stern and steady through all those eddying swarms — made a fitting side-scene to the grand tragedy of the murder. They gain'd the

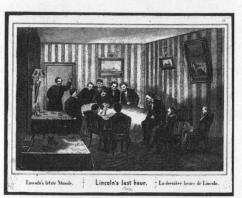

Lincoln's letzte Stunde. | Lincoln's last hour. | La dernière heure de Lincoln.

station house with the protected man, whom they placed in security for the night, and discharged him in the morning.

And in the midst of that pandemonium, infuriated soldiers, the audience and the crowd, the stage, and all its actors and actresses, its paint-pots, spangles, and gas-lights — the life blood from those veins, the best and sweetest of the land, drips slowly down, and death's ooze already begins its little bubbles on the lips.

We've Got Your Number

We'll give you a number, abbreviated words, and a clue. Tell us what the famous phrase is. Answers below. (Don't cheat!)

1. T F 2 & 2 F T (1920s song)

2. W I 64 (Fab 4 1920s-style song)

3. 3 S—L, M & C (Nyuk, nyuk, nyuk)

4. 50 S O T U (Last two were added in 1959)

5. 13 S & 50 S O T A F (Heavens to Betsy)

6. T 4 H O T A (Scary riders in the book of *Revelation*)

7. S W & T 7 D (Heigh-ho!)

8. H 57 V (Playing a catch-up game)

9. B & R 31 F (Rocky road, please)

10. 7 B F 7 B (Musical)

11. T 12 S O A A (Help yourself to a little self-help)

12. 5 G R, 4 C B, 3 F H, 2 T D & A P I A P T (Seasonal gifts)

13. R-A-D-D, 3 M I A T (One was a candlestick maker)

14. 1 L, 2 L, 3 L I (Kids' Native American census)

15. 3 B O G—L, E & J (Laws made, enforced, and interpreted)

16. T 9 P—M, V, E, M, J, S, U, N, P (Revolving and rotating)

17. 5 F 2, E O B (Another 1920s song)

18. P L I 1999 (1980s song)

19. G Y K O R 66 (1950s traveling music)

20. T 1812 O (Boom!)

Life Lessons
HOW TO WHITTLE A CHAIN

Whittlin' a chain out of a single block of wood seems like it should be near impossible, but it's not. You can do it, too. Here's how.

Whittling has long been a therapeutic method of relaxation. All it takes is time and patience, and it's fun in a slow, rural sort of way. Carve a chain from a single block of wood? It's impressive, and it can be done. Let's start with a three-link chain, knowing we can go for more next time.

1. Get a piece of basswood (or another soft wood) measuring $1\frac{1}{2}$ x $1\frac{1}{2}$ x 6 inches.

2. Take a pencil and draw guidelines as pictured above, on all six sides of the board.

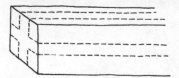

3. Begin cutting away the corner areas. Patiently slice a little at a time, or you'll split the wood. A good sharp knife and a meditative attitude will help a lot. You'll soon have a cross-shaped block that's 6 inches long.

4. Take your pencil and draw two end chain links butted together and 3 inches long as pictured below. Draw the middle link centered on the "arms" of the cross, also 3 inches long.

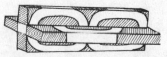

5. Start patiently whittling away the wood that doesn't belong to any of the links (dark areas, above).

6. Eventually the links will become individual pieces in a chain, linked but hanging free. Congrats! You did it!

Even More Pot Shots

Some more favorite bathroom shots. Send us yours! (See page 478.)

a. Toilet on beach
b. Ancient public toilets in Turkish ruins
c. Discarded toilets
d. Dawson City, Yukon Annual Outhouse Race
e. Abandoned western site
f. Mt. Kilamanjaro pit stop

Time Capsules

ADVICE AND SEX AIDS FROM THE PAST

If you wanted to give a sense of life in our time, what would you put in a time capsule? The people of the future plead: "No more newspapers and city council minutes!"

TO BE FRANK, the contents of time capsules are usually pretty unimaginative things: newspapers, books, maps, photos, census results, puffery from local governments, self-important letters from industry leaders and elected officials — that sort of thing. Occasionally, though, some quirky items find their way in. Here are some examples of such items:

MIAMI COUNTY COURTHOUSE, KANSAS: 1898
A bottle of 1890 "Old Rye" whisky.

BALTIMORE MEMORIAL STADIUM: 1954
Business cards, baseball cards, and 36¢ in nickels and pennies.

RENTON, WASHINGTON: 2001
A commemorative mug, T-shirt, "static cling decal," and deck of cards. Also, an IKEA furniture catalog.

LIVERMORE, CALIFORNIA: 1969
A letter from President Nixon, two beer steins, and a program from a local production of *Up with People*.

UNIVERSITY OF MASSACHUSETTS: 2000
A list of university parking regulations, a video of the U.M. marching band, and the text of 100 student e-mails selected randomly from the university's server.

AKRON, OHIO: 1950
A package of flower seeds from a local garden club, a "B.F. Goodrich Tubeless Tire Demonstration Kit," and a Sears-Roebuck catalog.

SAN FRANCISCO, CALIFORNIA: 2001
A piece of the AIDS Quilt, a pack of Pokemon cards, a bolt from the Golden Gate Bridge, and a box of Rice-A-Roni.

CURIE HIGH SCHOOL, CHICAGO, ILLINOIS: 1976
A list of the year's top ten records, a bus transfer, a program from *You're a Good Man, Charlie Brown,* and a full-color poster of the Sweathogs from TV's *Welcome Back, Kotter.*

MCKEESPORT, PENNSYLVANIA: 1964
A 1964 telephone book, a model of a 1964 Ford Mustang, and a can of Royal Crown Cola (which leaked and ruined some of the paper goods in the time capsule).

ROCHESTER, NEW YORK: 1873
Opened in 2000, this capsule included an envelope tucked into a book. It bore two contra-dictory messages: "For the Person Who Opens this Box" and (in a different hand) "Not to go in." Inside the envelope was a 127-year-old condom. As

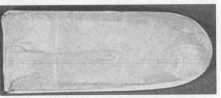
Uh, thanks, Great-great-great-granddad!

described by the modern-day Rochester Museum & Science Center, which displayed the condom with the rest of the contents: "This condom appears to be made from a segment of animal intestine, probably sheep or goat. Nearly 8" long and 3" in diameter, it has a light blue drawstring-type ribbon closure on the open end."

A CAVEAT
Whatever you decide to put in your own time capsule, heed this sobering observation from the International Time Capsule Society, which keeps track of such things: There are close to 10,000 time capsules that have been secreted around the world ... but most of them have already been lost or forgotten.

Month to Month
THE ROMAN ARTIFACT THAT RUNS OUR LIVES

Ever wonder where we got the names of our months? Blame the Romans. Legend has it that about 2,700 years ago, Numa Pompilius, the second emperor of Rome, invented the first Roman calendar. We're still stuck with it.

MARCH (MARTIUS)

"It's March 1—*Happy New Year!*" For centuries, Martius was the first month of the year, honoring the Roman god Mars. Although best known as the god of war, Mars was also the lord of agriculture and the mythical founder of Rome (thus making him first in war, first in peas, and first in the start of his countrymen).

APRIL (APRILIS)

The month of April takes its name from the Latin word *aperere*, meaning "opening," as the buds and leaves are all doing about that time of year. The Greeks associated the goddess Aphrodite with this month;

Mars needs women, but women need Juno.

she represented beauty, love, and fertility. In ancient Rome, Miss April was Venus, the goddess of vegetation and defender of feminine chastity.

MAY (MAIUS)

The Roman poet Ovid wrote that the name of this month came from *maiores*, the Latin word for "elderly." However, more credible sources credit Maia, the Greek goddess of fertility and mother of the god Mercury. Ritual sacrifices were made to Mercury on the first day of Maia's month. The Romans passed the day on to the Anglo-Saxons, who exchanged messy sacrifices for more festive things like May Day feasts, May queens, and May poles.

JUNE (JUNIUS)

Juno was Jupiter's sister, and the head Roman goddess. She was the goddess of marriage and happy females, and watched over women during events like marriage and childbirth. As a result, June weddings became a common custom. (However, poet Ovid swore that June actually came from the Latin word *juniores*, loosely meaning "young folk." But who you gonna believe — tradition or some unreliable poet?)

JULY (JULIUS)

Originally July was called *Quintilis Mensis* ("the fifth month" in Latin). That was until Julius Caesar came along and did a lot of fidgeting with the calendar. In honor of all his hard work on what became known as the Julian calendar, he named this month after himself.

AUGUST (AUGUSTUS)

Caesar Augustus decided to follow Julius's example and renamed *Sextilis Mensis* ("month number six") after himself. Augustus had tweaked Julius's calendar a little, so thought he deserved his own month, too.

SEPTEMBER (SEPTEMBER MENSIS)

Although it's now the ninth month, September comes from the Latin *septem* meaning "seven." (It got its name before January and February got moved to the beginning of the calendar.) According to record, several Roman emperors attempted to insert their names into the calendar on this month, but none of them really took, so it remains "September."

OCTOBER (OCTOBER MENSIS)

October, originally the eighth month in the calendar, comes from *octo*, Latin for "eight."

NOVEMBER (NOVEMBRIS MENSIS)

November comes from *nonus* ("nine").

DECEMBER (DECEMBER MENSIS)

Decimus means "ten" in Latin. In the early days of the calendar there were only ten months. The Romans were farmers and just stopped counting after December, since farming wasn't possible anyway and keeping track of the days was meaningless. The calendar would start up again on March 1 as it became clear that the spring equinox was approaching. In about 700 B.C., as Roman culture diversified, two months were tacked on after December.

JANUARY (JANUARIUS)

The new month of Januarius was made the first month of the year in 153 B.C. It was named for the two-headed Roman god Janus, the god who guarded beginnings.

Janus on the proverbial two-headed coin

January originally had 29 days, but Julius Caesar changed it to 31 in 45 B.C., because among the ancient Romans, 31 was considered luckier than 29.

FEBRUARY (FEBRUARIUS)

At the end of the year, February marked the festival of Lupercalia, a time of *februar* ("purification") in ancient Rome. (One of the activities included beating barren women with thongs of goat leather by holy priests in the hope of making them fertile.)

The month had either 28 or 29 days until 450 B.C. when it was shortened to 23 or 24 days. However, Julius Caesar's calendar lengthened it again, and he added a leap day at the end of the year every four years to keep the years even. It turned out to be a pretty good way of making up the extra time, even if it isn't at the end of the year any more.

MERCEDONIUS

Before Julius Caesar, Mercedonius was the thirteenth month. It lasted a varying number of days at the end of the year and functioned to fill in the gaps of the calendar. The name came from the Latin word *merces* ("wages"), because it was the traditional time for year-end wages to be paid. When Julius Caesar lengthened some of the months and created the leap year, he was able to eliminate Mercedonius from the calen-

More Beer!
IT'S GOOD FOR WHAT ALES YOU

"Those who drink beer will think beer," said Washington Irving. Have you ever wondered about the difference between an ale and a lager, or a porter and a pilsner? We can help.

ale: The main difference between beer and ale is that ale uses a yeast that floats to the top when it's done fermenting, and it isn't aged, which gives it a fruitier taste. Beer uses a yeast that sinks to the bottom and is aged.

lager beer: *Lager* means "storehouse" in German—in other words, aged beer. It's your basic, pale, highly carbonated standard American beer.

pilsner beer: The name comes from a beer made in the Bohemian town of Pilsen. It's any especially light, smooth beer.

stout: "Stout" once meant "strong" rather than fat, and that's why this dark, malty ale got the name in the nineteenth century.

porter: The name is short for "porter's ale," and supposedly came because produce carriers—or porters—of eighteenth century London preferred drinking it. In early America, this ale was served in what came to be known as "porterhouses"; one such tavern in New York City popularized the "porterhouse steak" in about 1814.

bock: A strong beer usually manufactured in fall or winter, bock may have as much as twice the alcohol as lager. The name comes from Einbeck (pronounced *Ine-bock*), Germany. In the United States, bock beer is sometimes made from the sediment left in beer-fermentation vats.

dark beer: It's dark only because brewers roast the malt before brewing with it.

malt liquor: For those who want to get wasted more efficiently, malt liquor is merely lager beer with a higher alcohol content, usually produced by adding sugar to the batch to give the yeast more to work with.

Another Little Latin Quiz

FOOD, LAW, OR AILMENT?

Here we go again! Circle the category that matches the meaning of the Latin word or phrase.

	Food	Law	Ailment
1. In ovis apalis	Food	Law	Ailment
2. Mutatis mutandis	Food	Law	Ailment
3. Isicia omentata	Food	Law	Ailment
4. Pro tempore	Food	Law	Ailment
5. Icterus gravis neonatrum	Food	Law	Ailment
6. Acanthosis nigricans	Food	Law	Ailment
7. Vignan unguiculata	Food	Law	Ailment
8. Non compos mentis	Food	Law	Ailment
9. Trismus nascentium	Food	Law	Ailment
10. Pepones et melones	Food	Law	Ailment
11. Minutal marinum	Food	Law	Ailment
12. Septicemia	Food	Law	Ailment
13. Morbi cutis	Food	Law	Ailment
14. Ova sfongia exlacte	Food	Law	Ailment
15. Lapsus calami	Food	Law	Ailment

Answers: 1. Food: Boiled eggs; 2. Law: "Change must be accounted for"; 3. Food: An ancient Roman burger patty; 4. Law: "For the time being"; 5. Ailment: Extreme jaundice in a newborn; 6. Ailment: A skin disorder; 7. Food: Black-eyed peas/beans; 8. Law: "Not mentally competent"; 9. Ailment: Infant tetanus; 10. Food: Ancient Roman melon dish; 11. Food: Seafood fricassee; 12. Ailment: Blood poisoning; 13. Ailment: Serious skin disease; 14. Food: Pancakes made with milk; 15. Law: "A slip of the pen"

Wisdom for Sale
BUSINESS ADVICE FROM THE SAGES OF THE AGES

"My rule always was to do the business of the day in the day." — The Duke of Wellington (1769–1852)

"No praying, it spoils business." — Thomas Otway (1652–1685)

"Who first invented Work — and tied the free
And holy-day rejoicing spirit down
To the ever-haunting importunity
Of business, in the green fields, and the town —
To plough-loom-anvil-spade-and, oh, most sad,
To this dry drudgery of the desk's dead wood?"
— Charles Lamb (1775–1834)

"No nation was ever ruined by trade." — Benjamin Franklin (1706–1790)

"He's happy who, far away from business, like the race of men of old, tills his ancestral fields with his own oxen, unbound by any interest to pay." — Horace (65–8 B.C.)

"Catch a man a fish, and you can sell it to him. Teach a man to fish, and you ruin a wonderful business opportunity." — Karl Marx (1818–1883)

"If a man can make a better mousetrap, though he builds his house in the woods the world will make a beaten path to his door." — Ralph Waldo Emerson (1803–1882)

"A financier is a pawnbroker with imagination." — A. W. Pinero (1855–1934)

"Finance is the art of passing currency from hand to hand until it finally disappears." — Robert W. Sarnoff (1918–1997)

"There is more credit and satisfaction in being a first-rate truck driver than a tenth-rate business executive." — Malcolm Forbes (1919–90)

Doctor Riots

THE MOBS THAT SMASHED MEDICAL SCHOOLS

One of the strangest chapters in the history of medicine are the mobs that rioted against doctors and medical schools. On the other hand, knowing the story, we might've rioted, too.

W HAT COULD CAUSE OTHERWISE NORMAL PEOPLE to riot against doctors and smash up medical schools? In 1788, eight people were killed and scores wounded in three days of rioting against doctors in New York City. The riot didn't end until a militia fired into the mob, resulting in most of the reported deaths and injuries.

LEND ME A HAND, WILL YOU?
Here's how it started. Medical students at the New York Hospital were dissecting bodies in a second-floor laboratory, and a boy playing nearby climbed a ladder to see what was going on. One of the medical students, startled and annoyed by the face at the window, waved a disembodied arm at the boy and told him it had belonged to his mother.

Unfortunately, the kid's mother had died recently. He ran to get his father, who was laying brick at a nearby construction site. The enraged dad and his co-workers rushed the laboratory and discovered the mutilated corpses. In response, they wrecked the place and took the bodies off for burial. When people saw the bodies and heard the stories, civil outrage spread from there. Mobs roamed the streets, breaking into hospitals and the homes of doctors and vandalizing them. The semiliterate mob even looted the house of a man named Sir John Temple when they misread his name as "Surgeon Temple."

Wisely, many doctors left town until it all cooled down; those who didn't were taken into custody by police for their own protection. Outside a jail that harbored four doctors, a mob gathered, intending to lynch them. When they began throwing paving stones at the state militia, the soldiers fired into the crowd, killing seven and injuring dozens more.

Remarkably, no doctors or med students were injured or killed in the New York riots.

THE "RESURRECTIONISTS"

Animosity toward the medical profession had been brewing for years. In those years, few bodies were legally available for dissecting—only those of executed criminals—so medical schools got bodies any way that they could. It made sense from their point of view. The dead person wasn't using the body anyway, and dissecting corpses would help doctors save lives of the living.

In some cases, doctors paid others to come up with bodies, but oftentimes, they took care of the grave robbing by themselves. The practice was tacitly encouraged by medical societies. Calling themselves "Resurrectionists," teacher-student teams would raid local graveyards by night.

Digging out dirt above one end of the coffin, they'd drill a dotted line of holes to weaken the lid and pry up the exposed end until it broke. Using a hook, they'd slide the body out of the coffin, strip it bare, and toss the clothes back in the coffin before covering with dirt again. (A quirk in the laws made stealing things—even clothes—from a coffin a much more serious crime than stealing the body itself.) A good grave-robbing team could do the whole operation in about an hour.

STUDENT BODIES

In response to the epidemic of grave robberies, it became the custom in university towns to place iron bars on graves and post an armed guard on the site for two weeks until the body rotted enough to be unsuitable for dissection.

You'd think you could shrug off the Doctors Riots as a bizarre exception, but that wouldn't be true. Until 1852, when laws were changed to make it easier for medical schools to get cadavers, there were at least thirteen similar anti-doctor riots in Illinois, Maryland, Massachusetts, New York, Ohio, Pennsylvania, and Vermont.

Ripe Ol' Corn

"UNCLE JOSH IN WALL STREET"

Early in the twentieth century, humorist Cal Stewart wrote hundreds of "Uncle Josh" stories, about a country bumpkin coming up against the modern world. Here's one of them.

I USED TO READ in our town paper down home at Punkin Centre a whole lot about Wall Street and them bulls and bears, and one thing and another, so I jist said to myself — now Joshua, when you git down to New York City, that's jist what you want to see.

Wall, when I got to New York, I got a feller to show me whar it was, and I'll be durned if I know why they call it Wall Street; it didn't have any wall round it. I walked up and down it 'bout an hour and a half, and I couldn't find any stock exchange or see any place fer waterin' any stock. I couldn't see a pig nor a cow, nor a sheep nor a calf, or anything else that looked like stock to me.

So finally I said to a gentleman, "Mister, whar do they keep the menagery down here?" He said, "What menagery?" I said the place whar they've got all them bulls and bears a fightin'. Well, he looked at me as though he thought I was crazy, and I guess he did, but he said, "You come along with me, I guess I can show you what you want to see."

Well, I went along with him, and he took me up to some public institushun, near as I could make out it was a loonytick asylum. Well, he took me into a room about two acres and a half square, and thar was about two thousand of the crazyest men in thar I ever seen in all my life. The minnit I set eyes on them I knowed they was all crazy, and I'd have to humor them if I got out of thar alive.

One feller was a-standin' on the top of a table with a lot of papers in his hand, and a-yellin' like a Comanche injin, and all the rest of them was tryin' to git at him. Finally I said to one of 'em, "Mister, what are you a-tryin' to do with that feller up thar on the table?" And he said, "Well, he's got 5,000 bushels of wheat and we are tryin' to git it away from him."

Well, the minnit he said that, I knowed for certain they was all crazy, 'cause nobody but a crazy man would ever think he had 5,000 bushels of wheat in his coat and pants pockits.

When they weren't a-looking I got out of thar, and I felt mighty thankful to git out.

LOOKED LIKE A LOONYTICK ASYLEM TO ME.

There was a feller standin' on the front steps; he had a sort of a unyform on; I guess he was Superintendent of the institushun; he talked purty sassy to me.

I said, "Mister, what time does the fust car go up town?" He said "The fust one went about twenty-five years ago."

I said to him, "Is that my car over thar?" He said "No sir, that car belongs to the street car company." I says, "Well, I guess I'll take it anyhow." He says "You'd better not, thar's bin a good many cars missin' around here lately."

I said, "Well now, I want to know, is thar anything round here any fresher than you be?" He said, "Yes, sir, that bench you're a sittin' on is a little fresher; they painted it about ten minnits ago."

Well, I got up and looked, and durned if he wasn't right.

The Fabled Frog
FROG TALES FROM AESOP

Clearly the frog played a role in ancient human life—the amphibian is the centerpiece for several of Aesop's fables. Here are but a few to keep you hopping.

THE FROGS WHO DESIRED A KING

The Frogs were living as happy as could be in a marshy swamp that just suited them; they went splashing about caring for nobody and nobody troubling with them. But some of them thought that this was not right, that they should have a king and a proper constitution, so they determined to send up a petition to Jove to give them what they wanted.

"Mighty Jove," they cried, "send unto us a king that will rule over us and keep us in order." Jove laughed at their croaking, and threw down into the swamp a huge Log, which came down splashing into the swamp.

The Frogs were frightened out of their minds by the commotion made in their midst, and all rushed to the bank to look at the horrible monster; but after a time, seeing that it did not move, one or two of the boldest of them ventured out towards the Log, and even dared to touch it; still it did not move. Then the greatest hero of the Frogs jumped upon the Log and commenced dancing up and down upon it, thereupon all the Frogs came and did the same; and for some time the Frogs went about their business every day without taking the slightest notice of their new King Log lying in their midst.

But this did not suit them, so they sent another petition to Jove, and said to him, "We want a real king; one that will really rule over us." Now this made Jove angry, so he sent among them a big Stork that soon set to work gobbling them all up. Then the Frogs repented when too late.

Better no rule than cruel rule.

THE HARES AND THE FROGS

The Hares were so persecuted by the other beasts, they did not know where to go. As soon as they saw a single animal approach them, off they used to run.

One day they saw a troop of wild Horses stampeding about, and in quite a panic all the Hares scuttled off to a lake hard by, determined to drown themselves rather than live in such a continual state of fear. But just as they got near the bank of the lake, a troop of Frogs, frightened in their turn by the approach of the Hares scuttled off, and jumped into the water.

"Truly," said one of the Hares, "things are not so bad as they seem:

"There is always someone worse off than yourself."

THE FROG AND THE OX

"Oh Father," said a little Frog to the big one sitting by the side of a pool, "I have seen such a terrible monster! It was as big as a mountain, with horns on its head, and a long tail, and it had hoofs divided in two."

"Tush, child, tush," said the old Frog, "that was only Farmer White's Ox. It isn't so big either; he may be a little

"Bigger, father, bigger."

bit taller than I, but I could easily make myself quite as broad; just you see." So he blew himself out, and blew himself out, and blew himself out. "Was he as big as that?" asked he.

"Oh, much bigger than that," said the young Frog.

Again the old one blew himself out, and asked the young one if the Ox was as big as that.

"Bigger, father, bigger," was the reply.

So the Frog took a deep breath, and blew and blew and blew, and swelled and swelled and swelled. And then he said: "I'm sure the Ox is not as big as this. But at this moment he burst.

Self-conceit may lead to self-destruction.

THE FROGS AND THE WELL

Two Frogs lived together in a marsh. But one hot summer the marsh dried up, and they left it to look for another place to live in: for frogs like damp places if they can get them. By and by they came to a deep well, and one of them looked down into it, and said to the other, "This looks a nice cool place. Let us jump in and settle here." But the other, who had a wiser head on his shoulders, replied, "Not so fast, my friend. Supposing this well dried up like the marsh, how should we get out again?"

Look before you leap.

THE BOYS AND THE FROGS

Some boys, playing near a pond, saw a number of Frogs in the water and began to pelt them with stones. They killed several of them, when one of the Frogs, lifting his head out of the water, cried out: "Pray stop, my boys: what is sport to you, is death to us."

One man's pleasure may be another's pain.

Who was Aesop?

Depending on who you ask, Aesop wrote between zero and several hundred fables in his lifetime. Some say that Aesop was a Greek slave who wrote down the folk tales that were popular at the time (620-525 B.C.), not unlike the Brothers Grimm. Tradition says that his owner finally freed him, but that he died at Delphi in 565 B.C.

It's a good story, but most now believe it to be just another story, that most of "Aesop's fables" came from two writers of the second century: Greek writer Valerius Babrius who mixed oral Greek tales with Indian ones, and the ancient Roman poet Phaedrus who translated them into Latin. This explains some the Roman influences in many of the popular fables from Aesop.

The word "Aesop" itself may very well have been invented by the ancient Greeks solely to denote this sort of tale with a moral from other kinds of stories. Regardless, it should be understood that Aesop was probably as mythical as the beasts in the stories.

Potty Pourri
RANDOM KINDS OF FACTNESS

- The stink of onion was once thought strong enough to scare off illness. Oniony folk remedies have included onion tea to stop a fever, rubbing an onion on your head if you have a headache, and mixing turpentine with fried onions to smear on your chest to choke out a cold.

- The Jolly Green Giant began his career as a scary-looking ogre wrapped in an animal skin. With the help of an artist, he was given a kinder and gentler touch that bean eaters everywhere continue to appreciate.

- The milk of a cow that's been eating onions tastes oniony.

- Larger Than Life: The Statue of Liberty is about twenty times bigger than an average American woman. From her toes to the top of her head, she measures a bit over 111 feet.

- Thank Thomas Jefferson for French fries. He brought back samples of fried potato sticks from France and dubbed them "Potatoes fried in the French manner." Americans shortened the name to "French fries."

- If you've got a new box of crayons, expect the black one to get used up first, then the red. Those are the two colors that see the most wear.

- Thomas More is the patron saint of lawyers.

- Experts claim that the common, everyday headache annually loses U.S. businesses $25 billion in productivity.

- Switzerland didn't allow women to vote until 1971.

- Luckily, his acting and inherited real estate paid well, because the most William Shakespeare earned for writing a play was £8 ($1,325 in today's money), never making more than an annual income of £20 ($3,313) from his writing.

- The father of pro golfer Lee Trevino was a grave digger.

Bad Trip

HOW TO DRIVE YOUR TOUR GUIDE CRAZY

A story in which Mark Twain and a group of fellow travelers get tired of the sights of Europe and decide to have some sadistic fun at the expense of their tour guides.

IN THIS PLACE I may as well jot down a chapter concerning those necessary nuisances, European guides. Many a man has wished in his heart he could do without his guide; but knowing he could not, has wished he could get some amusement out of him as a remuneration for the affliction of his society. We accomplished this latter matter, and if our experience can be made useful to others they are welcome to it.

All their lives long, tour guides are employed in showing strange things to foreigners and listening to their bursts of admiration. Think, then, what a passion it becomes with a guide, whose privilege it is, every day, to show to strangers wonders that throw them into perfect ecstasies of admiration! He gets so that he could not by any possibility live in a soberer atmosphere. After we discovered this, we never went into ecstasies any more—we never admired any thing—we never showed any but impassible faces and stupid indifference in the presence of the sublimest wonders a guide had to display. We had found their weak point. We have made good use of it ever since. We have made some of those people savage, at times, but we have never lost our own serenity.

The doctor asks the questions, generally, because he can keep his countenance, and look more like an inspired idiot, and throw more imbecility into the tone of his voice than any man that lives. It comes natural to him.

The guides in Genoa are delighted to secure an American party, because Americans so much wonder before any relic of Columbus. Our guide was full of animation—full of impatience. He said: "Come wis me, genteelmen!—come! I show you ze letter writing by Christopher Colombo!—write it himself!—write it wis his own hand!—come!"

He took us to the municipal palace. After much impressive fumbling of keys and opening of locks, the stained and aged document was spread before us. The guide's eyes sparkled. He danced about us and tapped the parchment with his finger: "What I tell you, genteelmen! Is it not so? See! handwriting Christopher Colombo!—write it himself!"

We looked indifferent. The doctor examined the document very deliberately, during a painful pause. Then he said, without any show of interest: "Ah, what did you say was the name of the party who wrote this?"

"Christopher Colombo! ze great Christopher Colombo!"

Another deliberate examination. "Ah, did he write it himself; or—or how?"

"He write it himself!—Christopher Colombo! He's own handwriting, write by himself!"

The doctor laid the document down and said: "Why, I have seen boys only 14 years old who can write better than that."

"But zis is ze great Christo—"

"I don't care who it is! It's the worst writing I ever saw. Now you musn't impose on us because we are strangers. We are not fools. If you have got any specimens of penmanship of real merit, trot them out! If you haven't, drive on!"

We drove on. The guide was considerably shaken up, but he made one more venture. He had something which he thought would overcome us. He said: "Ah, genteelmen, you come wis me! I show you beautiful, O, magnificent bust Christopher Colombo!—splendid, grand, magnificent!"

He brought us before the bust—it was beautiful—and sprang back and struck an attitude: "Ah, look, genteelmen! Christopher Colombo! Beautiful bust, beautiful pedestal!"

The doctor put up his eye-glass, procured for such occasions: "Ah—what did you say this gentleman's name was?"

"Christopher Colombo!—ze great Christopher Colombo!"

"Christopher Colombo—the great Christopher Colombo. Well, what did he do?"

"Discover America!—discover America, Oh, ze devil!"

"Discover America. No—that statement will hardly wash. We are just from America ourselves. We heard nothing about it. Christopher Colombo—pleasant name—is—is he dead?"

"Oh, corpo di Baccho!—three hundred year!"

"What did he die of?"

"I do not know!—I can not tell."

"Small-pox, you think?"

"I do not know, genteelmen!—I do not know what he die of!"

"Measles, likely?"

"May be—I do not know—I think he die of somethings."

"Parents living?"

"Im-poseeeble!"

"Ah—which is the bust and which is the pedestal?"

"Santa Maria!—zis ze bust!—zis ze pedestal!"

"Ah, I see, I see. Happy combination, very happy, indeed. Is this the first time the gentleman was ever 'on a bust'?"

That joke was lost on the foreigner—guides can not master the subtleties of the American joke.

We have made it interesting for this Roman guide. Yesterday we spent four hours in the Vatican, that wonderful world of curiosities. We came very near expressing admiration—it was very hard to keep from it. We succeeded though. Nobody else ever did, in the Vatican museums. The guide was bewildered—non-plussed. He nearly walked his legs off, hunting up extraordinary things, and exhausted all his ingenuity on us, but it was a failure; we never showed any interest in any thing. He had reserved what he considered to be his greatest wonder till the last—a royal Egyptian mummy, the best preserved in the world, perhaps. He took us there. He felt so sure this time, that some of his old enthusiasm came back to him: "See, genteelmen! — Mummy! Mummy!"

The eye-glass came up as calmly, as deliberately as ever. "Ah, what did I understand you to say the gentleman's name was?"

"Name? He got no name! Mummy! 'Gyptian mummy!"

"Yes, yes. Born here?"

"No! 'Gyptian mummy!"

"Ah, just so. Frenchman, I presume?"

"No! — not Frenchman, not Roman! — born in Egypta!"

"Born in Egypta. Never heard of Egypta before. Foreign locality, likely. How calm he is, how self-possessed. Is he dead?"

"Oh, sacre bleu, been dead three thousan' year!"

The doctor turned on him savagely: "Here, now, what do you mean by such conduct as this! Playing us for fools because we are strangers and trying to learn! Trying to impose your vile second-hand carcasses on us! — thunder and lightning, I've a notion to — to — if you've got a nice fresh corpse, fetch him out! — or by George we'll brain you!"

We make it exceedingly interesting for this Frenchman. However, he has paid us back, partly, without knowing it. He came to the hotel this morning to ask if we were up, and he endeavored as well as he could to describe us, so that the landlord would know which persons he meant. He finished with the casual remark that we were lunatics. The observation was so innocent and so honest that it amounted to a very good thing for a guide to say.

There is one remark (already mentioned) which never yet has failed to disgust these guides. We use it always, when we can think of nothing else to say. After they have exhausted their enthusiasm pointing out to us and praising the beauties of some ancient bronze image or broken-legged statue, we look at it stupidly and in silence for five, ten, fifteen minutes — as long as we can hold out, in fact — and then ask:

"Is — is he dead?" That conquers the serenest of them. It is not what they are looking for — especially a new guide. Our Roman guide is the most patient, unsuspecting, long-suffering subject we have had yet. We shall be sorry to part with him. We have enjoyed his society very much. We trust he has enjoyed ours, but we are harassed with doubts.

Cat Lovers

FROM THE AILUROPHILES

An ailurophile is someone very fond of cats. Here are a few examples from the book *Cats Don't Always Land on Their Feet* by Erin Barrett and Jack Mingo.

• Mohammed the prophet had a cat named Meuzza who, like most cats, had a favorite sleeping spot—on Mohammed's robe. It's said that one day Mohammed was trying to dress quickly to get to an urgent task, so simply he cut the sleeve off his robe rather than disturb Meuzza, who was sleeping peacefully on it. Lucky kitty.

• *"With the qualities of cleanliness, affection, patience, dignity, and courage that cats have, how many of us, I ask you, would be capable of becoming cats?"* —Fernand Mery

• Charles I, the King of England from 1600 to 1649, got the idea that if he lost his beloved black cat, disaster would befall him, so he had the cat guarded constantly. Unfortunately, the cat got sick and died. Strangely enough, Charles had been right—the day after, Charles was arrested for treason, and, a few days later, beheaded.

• Never give up: The February 1, 1991, edition of the *Albuquerque Journal* ran this classified ad: "Lost since March 1983, tortoise shell female cat, reward."

• The Pennsylvania Dutch have a tradition that harks back to an ancient belief in Europe: If you place a cat on a cradle in a new married couple's home, the couple will be blessed soon with children.

• *"I gave my cat a bath the other day. They love it. He just sat there; he enjoyed it, it was fun for me. Sure, the fur would stick to my tongue, but other than that...."* —Steve Martin

- The Ernest Hemingway house and museum on Key West still hosts a population of about sixty cats, half of which are polydactyls, or six-toed, felines. Hemingway was given a polydactyl by an old sea captain and many of the current cat population are descendants of this original.
- Actor Billy Crystal swears his cat, Mittens, likes "fishing and computer programming."
- Winston Churchill would refuse to eat until his cat, Jock, was also at the table. He called the beloved cat his "special assistant." Jock was reportedly resting alongside Churchill in his bed when the ill statesman died.

- Martha Stewart named her cats Mozart, Beethoven, Verdi, Vivaldi, Teeney, and Weeney.
- In her lifetime, life saver Florence Nightingale had more than sixty cat companions. She named most of her cats after famous men of her day. Some examples are cute little Disraeli, petulant Bismarck, and fuzzy Gladstone.
- Researchers say that stroking a cat reduces heart rate and blood pressure. (In the human, that is.)
- John F. Kennedy's daughter, Caroline, had a pet kitty during her stay in the White House. Its name was Tom Kitten. Tom was the first cat in the White House since Theodore Roosevelt's cat, Slippers.
- Amy Carter had a male Siamese named, of all things, Misty Malarky Ying Yang.
- King Henry I was tough on kitty killers. In ninth-century England he declared the penalty for ending a cat's life would be a whopping sixty bushels of corn.
- Sir Isaac Newton, while taking a break from his laws-of-gravity tests, invented the first cat door for his kitty, Spithead.
- Confucius, Chinese philosopher extraordinaire, believed his cat was sent to him from the heavens to impart inspired wisdom. Cats are good for that, you know.
- *"Be suspicious of anyone whose clothes are immaculate and completely free of cat hairs. It means they either don't like cats or don't hug the ones they have."* —Leigh W. Rutledge

From Lady to Cowboy
THE MARLBORO MAN GETS A SEX CHANGE

From "mild as May" cigarette aimed at addicting women, Marlboro switched to macho themes to reassure men that filters weren't "unmanly." Here's a case study of how well people can be manipulated by the right images.

D ID YOU KNOW that the idealized Marlboro smoker, now personified by rugged cowboys, was once a sophisticated woman? But it wasn't that the cowboys were transsexuals—it was the cigarettes.

Marlboro was born in 1924 as one of the first women's cigarette. In the decades before this, the idea of marketing cigarettes to women was more taboo than marketing them to twelve-year-olds is today (ask cartoony Joe Camel about the sticky problems with that one). But with the Suffragettes and the "Anything Goes" 1920s, women decided that there was no reason they couldn't develop the same filthy habits that men had (the health issues, although known to researchers, were not yet part of public consciousness).

Still, it was a tricky sell. Advertisers had to somehow convince women that stained teeth, foul breath, addictive cravings, and that dry, heaving morning cough were somehow genteel and ladylike. Philip Morris decided that their brand needed to have a classy, sophisticated name. Winston Churchill was in the news at the time, and it was being reported that he was related to the Earl of Marlborough. The marketers liked the sound of the Marlborough name, but didn't think it looked good on the pack. They lopped off the "ugh" and came up with "Marlboro."

In the 1920s, the Marlboro campaign was based around how "ladylike" the new cigarette was. The company printed a red band around the filter to hide those unattractive lipstick stains, calling them "Beauty Tips to Keep the Paper from Your Lips." They called Marlboro the "Mild as May" cigarette and added a tone of snobbishness: "Discerning feminine taste is now confirming the judgment of masculine connoisseurs in expressing unanimous preference for the Aristocrat of Cigarettes...." Marlboros developed a small following—enough to keep it alive, but not enough to be called a great success.

THE SWITCH

Two decades later, Philip Morris decided to "reposition" the brand to fit a new market niche—men who were afraid of lung cancer but who thought it unmanly to admit it. Here's what happened: In the early 1950s, scientists published a major, well-publicized study linking smoking to lung cancer. This was the "smoking gun" that the cigarette companies had been dreading for years. In 1953, for the first time ever, cigarette consumption dipped in the United States.

The cigarette companies moved fast. Then, like now, they pursued a contradictory strategy: claiming that the studies were "inconclusive" on cigarette safety, while simultaneously implying that their brands were somehow "safer" than other brands.

Unfiltered cigarettes suffered the biggest sales drop. Filtered cigarettes were perceived by smokers as "safer," but up to that point they had always been marketed to women. Men told marketers that they'd consider switching to a filtered brand, but were afraid they'd be subjected to ridicule if they smoked a "woman's cigarette."

Cigarette manufacturers had long resisted pushing filter cigarettes to men because filters implied that smoke was unpleasant or dangerous. Now, though, they started seeing some silver lining in doing so. Filtered cigarettes were more profitable because the filter material was cheaper than a comparable amount of tobacco. Besides, since filters screened out some of the smoke's harshness, manufacturers could use a cheaper grade of tobacco.

Philip Morris decided to give Marlboro a sex change

operation. The company hired Chicago advertising executive Leo Burnett to do the surgery.

Burnett's specialty was cute advertising characters like the Jolly Green Giant, the Keebler Elves, the lonely Maytag Repairman, Charlie the Tuna, Poppin' Fresh, and Morris the Cat. To defeminize Marlboros, he decided to use a series of the most testosterone-laced images he could think of.

He intended to present a lineup of muscled, sweaty sea captains, weight lifters, adventurers, war correspondents, construction workers, Marines, and the like. The cowboy was to be the first image of the series.

Philip Morris wasn't sure about the campaign. The company hired a research company that came back with the alarming report that there were only 3,000 full-time cowboys in the entire United States. How do you expect men working in a downtown office building to relate to an image like that? Burnett had to do some fast talking, but he eventually convinced the company to try the cowboy.

The campaign worked. In one year, Marlboro zoomed from a marginal presence with less than one percent of the market to the fourth best-selling brand. The company decided to forget the sea captains and soldiers and stick with cowboys.

MODEL COWBOYS

Burnett's first set of "cowboys" were professional models, some of whom had never been on a horse before. That led to a series of embarrassing gaffes that left cowpokes-in-the-know snickering. For example, an ad showed a cowboy's legs in close-up: his blue jeans were well worn, his hand-tooled boots were scuffed in all the right places ... but he had his spurs upside-down. After that, the agency started recruiting real cowboys from Texas and Montana for their ads.

In 1955, the agency added a trademark tattoo to their cowboy's hand. One model mused after a photo shoot that they had spent three minutes making up his face — and three hours painting the tattoo. In 1962, Burnett's agency bought the rights to *The Magnificent Seven* theme and added words ("Come to

where the flavor is, come to Marlboro Country").

The Marlboro Man has been one of the most successful advertising campaigns ever, keeping the cigarette at or near the top of the heap for years. When cigarette ads were banned from television in 1971, the cowboy made a smooth transition to print and billboards, since he never said anything anyway. He continued squinting off into the distance with that self-absorbed expression that addicts have when contemplating their next fix.

Everyone seems to love the cowboy. The image works as well at convincing women to smoke Marlboros as it does men. It also works well with blacks and Hispanics. (That's ironic, since even though many real cowboys were and are black or Hispanic, all the Marlboro Men have been Caucasian.) Best of all for the company (which has to replace all those dying customers), the cowboy has worked as a role model for kids and teens as well, making Marlboro the number one starter brand.

The popularity of the cowboy image has led to anti-smoking parodies as well. In France, Philip Morris sued an anti-smoking group that used a cowboy model to deliver an anti-smoking message, claiming trademark infringement. PM won a pyrrhic victory—a judgment of 1 franc instead of the $3 million they had asked for—but at least the company got the ads off the air.

The real cowboy models, meanwhile, periodically embarrass the company by dying like desperadoes from smoking-related diseases like lung cancer, emphysema, and strokes.

A Little Yiddish Quiz

KISS OR CURSE?

The Yiddish words below are either a compliment or an insult. Circle the nature of the meaning of each word.

1. Mensch	Kiss	Curse
2. Chazzer	Kiss	Curse
3. Chamoole	Kiss	Curse
4. Meiskeit	Kiss	Curse
5. Schmoe	Kiss	Curse
6. Haimish ponem	Kiss	Curse
7. Berye'h	Kiss	Curse
8. G'vir	Kiss	Curse
9. Noodge	Kiss	Curse
10. Shiker	Kiss	Curse
11. Maiven	Kiss	Curse
12. Zhlub	Kiss	Curse
13. Yente	Kiss	Curse
14. Chavver	Kiss	Curse
15. Shlump	Kiss	Curse

Answers: 1. Kiss: A nice guy; 2. Curse: A pig; 3. Curse: A jackass; 4. Curse: Ugly person; 5. Curse: A naive or goofy person; 6. Kiss: A friendly face; 7. Kiss: A good and competent housewife; 8. Kiss: A rich man; 9. Curse: A pest; 10. Curse: A drunk; 11. Kiss: An expert or connoisseur; 12. Curse: A crude person; 13. Curse: A gossip; 14. Kiss: A friend; 15. Curse: A slob.

Another Little Yiddish Quiz
ARE YOU A MENSCH OR A SCHMOE?

Can you tell which of these is an insult and which is a traditional Yiddish greeting? Match the phrase to its definition.

1. Mazel tov!   "Drop dead."

2. Kush meer in toches.   "Bless you."

3. Vee geyts?   "Hello, peace be with you."

4. Zay gezunt!   "Kiss my tushy."

5. Farshtinkener!   "Have a lousy life."

6. A shvarts yor!   "You rotten, stinky person!"

7. Sholem aleycham.   "How's it going?"

8. Ver derharget.   "Congratulations!"

9. A broch tsu dayn lebn.   "You deserve a lousy year!"

10. Le' chaim!   "To life!"

Answers: 1. *Mazel tov!* ("Congratulations!"); **2.** *Kush meer in toches.* ("Kiss my tushy."); **3.** *Vee geyts?* ("How's it going?"); **4.** *Zay gezunt!* ("Bless you."); **5.** *Farshtinkener!* ("You rotten, stinky person!"); **6.** *A shvarts yor!* ("You deserve a lousy year!"); **7.** *Sholem aleycham.* ("Hello, peace be with you."); **8.** *Ver derharget.* ("Drop dead."); **9.** *A broch tsu dayn lebn.* ("Have a lousy life."); **10.** *Le' chaim!* ("To life!")

More Fables & Foibles
ODD LITTLE STORIES FROM R. L. STEVENSON

You probably know Robert Louis Stevenson for books like *Treasure Island* and *Dr. Jekyll and Mr. Hyde*. But he also wrote a series of "fables" with a dark take on humanity and its foibles.

THE TADPOLE AND THE FROG
"Be ashamed of yourself," said the frog. "When I was a tadpole, I had no tail."

"Just what I thought!" said the tadpole. "You never were a tadpole."

THE PENITENT
A man met a lad weeping. "What do you weep for?" he asked.

"I am weeping for my sins," said the lad.

"You must have little to do," said the man.

The next day they met again. Once more the lad was weeping. "Why do you weep now?" asked the man.

"I am weeping because I have nothing to eat," said the lad.

"I thought it would come to that," said the man.

THE YELLOW PAINT
In a certain city there lived a physician who sold yellow paint. Those bedaubed with it from head to heel were set free from the dangers of life, and the bondage of sin, and the fear of death forever. So the physician said in his prospectus; and so said all the citizens in the city; who took care to be properly painted themselves, and took delight in seeing others painted.

There was in the same city a young man of a somewhat reckless life, who had reached the age of manhood, and would have nothing to do with the paint: "Tomorrow was soon enough," said he; and when the morrow came he would still put it off.

He might have continued to do until his death; only, he had a friend who, taking a walk with not one fleck of paint upon his body, was suddenly run down by a water-cart and cut off in his heyday. This shook the young man to the soul; and on the very same evening, in the presence of all his family, to appropriate music, and himself weeping aloud, he received three complete coats of paint and a touch of varnish on the top. The physician (who was himself affected even to tears) protested he had never done a job so thorough.

Some two months afterwards, the young man was carried on a stretcher to the physician's house.

"What is the meaning of this?" he cried, as soon as the door was opened. "I was to be set free from all the dangers of life; and here have I been run down by that self-same water-cart, and my leg is broken."

"Dear me!" said the physician. "This is very sad. But I must explain to you the action of my paint. A broken bone belongs to a class of accident to which my paint is quite inapplicable. It is against sin that I have fitted you out; and when you come to be tempted, you will give me news of my paint."

"Oh!" said the young man, "I did not understand that, and it seems rather disappointing. But I have no doubt all is for the best; and in the meanwhile, I shall be obliged to you if you will set my leg."

"That is none of my business," said the physician; "but if your bearers will carry you round the corner to the surgeon's, I feel sure he will afford relief."

Some three years later, the young man came running to the physician's house in a great perturbation. "What is the meaning of this?" he cried. "Here was I to be set free from the bondage of sin; and I have just committed forgery, arson, and murder."

"Dear me," said the physician. "This is very serious. Off with your clothes at once." And as soon as the young man had stripped, he examined him from head to foot. "No," he cried with great relief, "there is not a flake broken. Cheer up, my young friend, your paint is as good as new."

"Good God!" cried the young man, "and what then can be the use of it?"

"Why," said the physician, "My paint does not exactly prevent sin; it extenuates instead the painful consequences. It is not so much for this world, as for the next; it is not against life; in short, it is against death that I have fitted you out. And when you come to die, you will give me news of my paint."

"Oh!" cried the young man, "I had not understood that, and it seems a little disappointing. But there is no doubt all is for the best; and in the meanwhile, I shall be obliged if you will help me to undo the evil I have brought on innocent persons."

"That is none of my business," said the physician; "but if you will go round the corner to the police office, I feel sure it will afford you relief to give yourself up."

Six weeks later, the physician was called to the town jail.

"What is the meaning of this?" cried the young man. "Here am I literally crusted with your paint; and I have broken my leg, and committed all the crimes in the calendar, and must be hanged tomorrow; and am in the meanwhile in a fear so extreme that I lack words to picture it."

"Dear me," said the physician. "This is really amazing. Well, well; perhaps, if you had not been painted, you would have been more frightened still."

THE FOUR REFORMERS

Four reformers met under a bramble bush. They all agreed the world must change. "We must abolish property," said one.

"We must abolish marriage," said the second.

"We must abolish God," said the third.

"I wish we could abolish work," said the fourth.

"Do not let us get beyond practical politics," said the first. "The first thing is to reduce men to a common level."

"The first thing," said the second, "is to give freedom to the sexes."

"The first thing," said the third, "is to find out how to do it."

"The first step," said the first, "is to abolish the Bible."

"The first thing," said the second, "is to abolish the laws."

"The first thing," said the third, "is to abolish mankind."

Flornithology 4
HOW TO TELL THE BIRDS FROM THE FLOWERS

We bring you more of the field guide by Robert Williams Wood (1868–1955) for those who may have trouble seeing the difference.

| The Hawk | The Hollyhock | The Hen | The Lichen |

| The Butterball | The Buttercup | The Bay | The Jay |

| The Lark | The Larkspur | Puffin | Nuffin |

Family Feud

The Kellogg Brothers' Flaky Cereal War

"John Harvey Kellogg and W. K. Kellogg were like two fellows trying to climb up the same ladder at the same time," observed a man who knew them both. Like Jacob and Esau or Cain and Abel, it's a classic tale of a long-suffering younger brother conniving against his overbearing older brother.

YEAST-FREE DIETS? Megavitamins? Colon cleansing? If you think today's food faddists are eccentric, you should have been around during the last half of the 19th century. There were hundreds of health regimens, some sensible, some just plain crazy. It was from those roots that Kellogg's cereals grew and thrived.

One popular health guru of the time was Sylvester Graham, who inspired the whole wheat flour and cracker that still bear his name. He had a fanatical belief in the benefits of fresh air exercise in all weather, whole grain foods, and complete sexual abstinence to retain "vital bodily fluids." He believed that whole grains with bland flavorings suppressed sexual desire and that meat, salt, and spices are dangerous aphrodisiacs.

One of Graham's disciples was Ellen Harmon White, founder and head prophet of the Seventh Day Adventist Church. In 1855, she convinced her New England congregation to emigrate to west-

Dr. John Harvey Kellogg, the older brother

ern Michigan, where she established the world headquarters of her apocalyptic religious movement, and wrote books about diet and the evils of sex. Eleven years later, she decided to build the Western Health Reform Institute, a health spa to give the world a taste of her medicine.

ENTER THE FAMILY KELLOGG

John Harvey Kellogg's was two years old in 1852 when his family traveled to Michigan with the Adventists. Eight years later, William

Keith Kellogg was born. The two brothers, it turned out, were as different as could be: John was the golden boy who could do little wrong in his parents' eyes, while Will could do little right. While John was sent off to school, his parents figured a formal education for Will would be wasted since the Lord's apocalypse was still just around the corner. Besides, nearly everyone thought him a little dimwitted. (Actually, he was just nearsighted, but his health-faddist parents decided that a regimen of food and water cures would do more good than eyeglasses.) Will stayed home and worked in his father's broom factory.

DOCTOR AND CLERK

After graduating, John Harvey Kellogg became a school teacher in Ypsilanti, sixty miles away. Sister Ellen White offered to pay his tuition to Dr. Russell Trall's Hygeio-Therapeutic College in Florence Heights, New Jersey. A few years later, in 1876, the 24-year-old "Dr." Kellogg returned to Michigan to become the superintendent of the sanitarium. In a case of nepotism that he would live to regret, he hired his brother, Will, as his much put-upon chief clerk.

William would become embittered over the years as older brother John bullied him, took him for granted, and tried to hog full credit for mutual discoveries. Years later, Will would bite back.

Like White, John Kellogg was a believer in health food and complete sexual abstinence. He spent his honeymoon writing *Plain Facts for Old and Young,* a tract warning against the evils of sex. "Its effects upon the undeveloped person is to retard growth," he wrote, "weaken the constitution, and dwarf the intellect." Not surprisingly, Kellogg's marriage was apparently never consummated, which he believed made his wife very grateful. He wrote, "I should say that the majority of women, happily for them and for society, are not very much troubled with sexual feelings of any kind."

To suppress his patients' sexual desire, he used zwieback until a patient broke her dentures on it and demanded $10 to fix them. This prompted the notoriously tight-fisted doctor to begin looking for an alternative.

THE DREAM OF A FLAKE

John and Will decided a cold cereal would be the best thing. In 1885, John claimed that a dream showed him a way to make cereals into light and crispy flakes. Divinely inspired or not, his first attempts were failures. The brothers tried soaking wheat kernels and forcing them between steel rollers. The ker-

Will Keith Kellogg, the younger brother

nels were not flat enough for their purposes, so they began boiling them for longer and longer periods, trying to soften them enough to make an easily chewed flake. But even that didn't do the trick.

One night while they were boiling a batch, an emergency came up, so they left the kernels soaking and didn't come back to them for a day or two. By the time they returned, the kernels had grown moldy, but they decided to run them

The Battle Creek Sanitarium in its heyday

through the rollers anyway. It turned out that the extra time of soaking was just what the doctor ordered, resulting in very thin flakes that toasted up nicely, each individual kernel becoming a well-formed, albeit moldy, flake. After experimentation, they discovered that soaking the wheat in a tin container suppressed much of the moldiness, so they began rolling out wheat flakes.

John had intended to grind the flakes into a powder, but Will convinced him to keep the flakes whole instead. Unfortunately it didn't make much difference, since no one wanted to eat them. The unflavored wheat flakes tasted like sawdust.

Finally, in 1902, the brothers discovered that corn flakes tasted better than wheat flakes, especially when flavored with barley malt. Realizing that the flakes had commercial possibilities, the brothers set up their own private corporation, the Battle Creek Toasted Cornflake Company.

CEREAL DRAMAS

In their first year, the brothers sold 100,000 pounds of the new breakfast cereal. With success, however, they ran into problems. First of all, Sister White was furious that the Kellogg brothers had desecrated her divine institution with commercialism—and that she wasn't even getting a cut. Also, competitors and imitators began jumping onto the bandwagon (the company later changed its name to Kellogg's to distinguish it from its imitators).

Worst of all for the brothers' partnership, William Kellogg started adding sugar to the flakes to make them more palatable. When John Kellogg found out, he was livid. He believed that sugar would reverse the cereal's sex-suppressing effects. Will countered that sugar was necessary if they wanted people to eat the stuff.

Matters quickly worsened between the two brothers, culminating in a series of lawsuits over who owned the rights to the process and even the Kellogg's name. William eventually won the lawsuits and took full control of the Kellogg's Corn Flake Company, with Dr. John retaining shares. It became a huge success, in large part because of William's innovative advertising, promotion, giveaways, and sponsorships. One ad, considered positively risqué at the time, told women to wink at their grocers and see what they got (in most cases, by pre-arrangement with the company, a free sample box of Corn Flakes). The company also aimed advertising directly toward children, knowing that they had a disproportionate power over cereal purchases in a household.

THE END COMES

Will and John each separately lived to be ninety-one, but they after all the lawsuits were over, they met only a few times for quick business. John continued to preach his gospel, even after medical findings soundly disproved most of his theories. Not surprisingly, he and his wife Ellen had no children, but they adopted and fostered forty-two children over the years. In later years, his wife became a virtual recluse and Dr. Kellogg took to strolling the hospital grounds in white clothes, carrying a white cockatoo on his shoulder.

Shortly before John died in 1943, he sent a message of brotherly reconciliation to Will. Will's staff, however, withheld the message from him, figuring it would just stir up trouble. Someone finally told him about it in 1951 while he was on his own deathbed. "My God," he reportedly cried out, "why didn't anybody tell me before this?"

Every Picture Tells a Story

American Gothic **by Grant Wood**

• Grant Wood studied art in Europe before returning to Iowa to paint his friends and neighbors. *American Gothic* is a sly mixture of the two influences: the farm couple is portrayed in the naturalistic Gothic style of fifteenth-century Flemish and German art, in front of a house with Gothic windows.

• Built in an 1880s style called Carpenter Gothic, the house—which still exists—inspired the idea of the painting. Wood recognized the similarity to its European counterparts and visualized the Gothic-like painting. He quickly sketched his idea on scrap paper and had a friend take a photo of the house so he could use it in the studio.

• Wood, painting in 1930, wanted a timeless feel, so he researched nineteenth-century clothes before bringing in his models: his sister and his dentist. Each posed in separate sittings.

• Is this mean to portray a couple, or a farmer guarding his daughter from the world? No one knows for sure, but her far-away gaze and a loose strand of hair imply he's already lost her.

• The painting was controversial. Some locals, especially farm women, believed that Wood was mocking them.

The War Prayer

MARK TWAIN'S TAKE ON RELIGION & PATRIOTISM

Mark Twain wrote "The War Prayer" during the Philippine-American War and couldn't get it published then.
Unfortunately, it's still timely.

IT WAS A TIME of great and exalting excitement. The country was up in arms, the war was on, in every breast burned the holy fire of patriotism;

The drums were beating, the bands playing, the toy pistols popping, the bunched firecrackers hissing and spluttering;

On every hand and far down the receding and fading spread of roofs and balconies fluttering flags flashed in the sun;

Daily the young volunteers marched down the wide avenue gay and fine in their new uniforms, the proud fathers and mothers and sisters and sweethearts cheering them with voices choked with happy emotion as they swung by;

Nightly the packed mass meetings listened, panting, to patriot oratory which stirred the deepest deeps of their hearts and which they interrupted at briefest intervals with cyclones of applause, the tears running down their cheeks the while;

In the churches the pastors preached devotion to flag and country and invoked the God of Battles, beseeching His aid in

The Philippine-American War

What was the Philippine-American War about? After fighting the Spanish for Cuba and other colonies America wanted, Spain gave up and sold the Philippines for $20 million. The Filipinos who had helped fight believed they'd been promised independence, but the United States decided it wanted to keep the colony. After defeating the the Filipinos, America set up a colonial government, and American businesses bought up much of the country.

our good cause in outpouring of fervid eloquence which moved every listener.

It was indeed a glad and gracious time, and the half-dozen rash spirits that ventured to disapprove of the war and cast a doubt upon its righteousness straightway got such a stern and angry warning that for their personal safety's sake they quickly shrank out of sight and offended no more in that way.

Sunday morning came—next day the battalions would leave for the front; the church was filled;

The volunteers were there, their young faces alight with martial dreams—visions of the stern advance, the rushing charge, the flashing sabers, the flight of the foe, the tumult, the smoke, the fierce pursuit, the surrender!—then home from the war, bronzed heroes, welcomed, adored, submerged in glory!

With the volunteers sat their dear ones, proud, happy, and envied by the neighbors and friends who had no sons and brothers to send forth to the field of honor, there to win for the flag or failing, die the noblest of noble deaths. The service proceeded; a war chapter from the Old Testament was read; the first prayer was said; it was followed by an organ burst that shook the building, and with one impulse the house rose, with glowing eyes and beating hearts, and poured out that tremendous invocation—

"God the all-terrible! Thou who ordainest, Thunder thy clarion and Lightning thy sword!"

Then came the "long" prayer: that an ever-merciful and benig-

---

On Publishing "War Prayer"

To Dan Beard, who dropped in to see him, Clemens read the "War Prayer," stating that he had read it to his daughter, Jean, and others, who had told him he must not print it, for it would be regarded as sacrilege. He submitted it to his publisher, who rejected it as unsuitable for the times.

"Still, you are going to publish it, are you not?"

Clemens, pacing up and down the room in his dressing-gown and slippers, shook his head. "No," he said, "I have told the whole truth in that, and only dead men can tell the truth in this world."

"It can be published after I am dead."

—*Mark Twain, A Biography* by Albert Bigelow Paine, Harper & Brothers, 1912

nant Father would watch over our noble young soldiers and
aid, comfort, and encourage them in their patriotic work; bless
them, shield them in the day of battle, bear them in His mighty
hand, make them strong and confident, invincible in the bloody
onset; help them to crush the foe, grant to them and to their flag
and country imperishable honor and glory—

An aged stranger entered and moved with slow and noiseless
step up the main aisle, his eyes fixed upon the minister, his long
body clothed in a robe that reached to his feet, his head bare,
his white hair descending in a frothy cataract to his shoulders,
his seamy face unnaturally pale. With all eyes following him
and wondering, he made his silent way; without pausing, he
ascended to the preacher's side and stood there, waiting. With
shut lids the preacher, unconscious of his presence, continued
his moving prayer, and at last finished it with the words,
uttered in fervent appeal,

**"Bless our arms, grant us the victory, O Lord our God, Father
and Protector Of our land and flag!"**

The stranger touched his arm, motioned him to step aside—
which the startled minister did. During some moments he surveyed the spellbound audience with solemn eyes in which
burned an uncanny light; then in a deep voice he said:

"I come from the Throne, bearing a message from Almighty
God!" The words smote the house with a shock; if the stranger
perceived it he gave no attention. "He has heard the prayer of
His servant and will grant it if such shall be your desire after I,
His messenger, shall have explained to you its full import. For it

is like many of the prayers of men, in that it asks for more than he who utters it is aware of.

"God's servant and yours has prayed his prayer. Is it one prayer? No, it is two—one uttered, the other not. Both have reached the ear of Him Who heareth all supplications, the spoken and the unspoken. Ponder this—keep it in mind. If you would ask a blessing upon yourself, beware, lest without intent you invoke a curse upon a neighbor at the same time. If you pray for the blessing of rain upon your crop which needs it, by that act you are possibly praying for a curse upon some neighbor's crop which may not need rain and can be injured by it.

"You have heard your servant's prayer—the uttered part of it. I am commissioned by God to put into words the other part of it—that part which the pastor, and also in your hearts, fervently prayed silently. And ignorantly and unthinkingly? God grant that it was so! You heard these words: 'Grant us the victory, O Lord our God!' That is sufficient. The whole of the uttered prayer is compact into those pregnant words. When you have prayed for victory you have prayed for many unmentioned results which follow victory—must follow it, cannot help but follow it. God the Father commandeth me to put the unspoken part of the prayer into words. LISTEN!

"O Lord our Father, our young patriots, idols of our hearts, go forth to battle—be Thou near them! With them, in spirit, we also go forth from the sweet peace of our beloved firesides to smite the foe. O Lord our God, help us to tear their soldiers to bloody shreds with our shells; help us to cover their smiling fields with the pale forms of their patriot dead; help us to drown the thunder of the guns with the shrieks of their wounded writhing in pain; help us to lay waste their

humble homes with a hurricane of fire; help us to wring the hearts of their unoffending widows with unavailing grief; help us to turn them out roofless with their little children to wander unfriended the wastes of their desolated land in rags and hunger and thirst, broken in spirit, worn with

travail, imploring Thee for the refuge of the grave and denied it—for our sakes who adore Thee, Lord, blast their hopes, blight their lives, protract their bitter pilgrimage, make heavy their steps, water their way with their tears, stain the white snow with the blood of their wounded feet! We ask it, in the spirit of love, of Him Who is the Source of Love, and Who is the ever-faithful refuge and friend of all that are sore beset and seek His aid with humble and contrite hearts. Amen."

After a pause:

"Ye have prayed it; if ye still desire it, speak! The messenger of the Most High waits."

It was believed afterward that the man was a lunatic, because there was no sense in what he said.

Bathrooms through History

• In 1596, Queen Elizabeth I allowed her godson, Sir John Harrington, to install a flush toilet of his own invention in her living quarters. She lived to regret it when he published a small promotional booklet about it, making the queen's toilet the butt of many popular jokes.

• In 1775, Alexander Cumming improved Harrington's design by adding a "stink trap" to keep the sewer smells out of the house. Still, it would take another century before the toilet replaced the chamber pot and became a popular fixture in the house.

• In 1825, John Quincy Adams installed the first toilet in the White House, leading to much commentary, many jokes, and the adoption of "Quincy" as a slang word for toilet.

• In 1857, Joseph Gayetty invented the first packaged toilet paper—a packet of individual sheets—but the product sold poorly and Gayetty quickly discontinued it.

• For centuries, bathing was considered unnecessary, unhealthful, and even immoral. English diarist Samuel Pepys (1633–1703) noted with surprise that his wife had taken one bath in her life and was considering taking another!

• Benjamin Franklin started a lonely campaign to convince people that there were benefits to bathing. By the 1830s, the tradition of a once-a-week Saturday night bath started taking hold. By 1865, Vassar College required that all of its students bathe twice a week.

• By the 1880s, about 15 percent of all city dwellers in America had an indoor bathroom of one sort or another.

Foodonyms

A TOAST TO DRINK NAMES

What the heck is the Maxwell House, and why is Mary bloody? Here are some drink name origins that quenched our thirst for knowledge. Drink up!

Maxwell House: Joel Cheek, the grocer who invented this smooth blend of coffee in 1886, named it after a popular Nashville hotel. The Maxwell House was one of Cheek's big clients of the day.

Tom Collins: This drink's origin isn't exactly clear. Britain, the U.S., and Australia all lay claim to the bartender—one Tom Collins—who invented it sometime in the 1800s.

Bloody Mary: Named for Queen Mary I who ruled England from 1553 to 1558. Her violent repression of Protestants earned her the nickname "Bloody Mary."

Gimlet: Sir T. O. Gimlette, a British naval surgeon, developed this lime and gin drink in 1890 as a health beverage.

Grog: In 1749, British admiral Edward "Old Grog" Vernon ordered his sailors to drink rum and water daily to prevent scurvy. (It didn't.)

Martini: The martini is a variation of an earlier, sweeter drink named the Martinez after a mysterious stranger from Martinez, California, who ordered one in San Francisco's Occidental Hotel bar in the early 1860s.

Gibson: This martini variation is most likely named after the illustrator Charles Dana Gibson (creator of the "Gibson Girl"). He liked his martinis extra dry with an onion.

Rob Roy: This drink is named "Rob Roy" after the Scottish version of Robin Hood, since the Rob Roy is simply a Manhattan made with Scotch whiskey.

Tom & Jerry: Named after Jerry Hawthorne and his pal Tom, characters from an 1821 book by British sportswriter Pierce Egan. The two buddies liked to drink this mix of hot milk, egg, rum, and brandy.

Zen of the Clay Boy
THE MYSTICAL (BUT TRUE) ORIGIN OF GUMBY

He has a strange bump on his head, googly red eyes, and green skin.
He's not just a cartoon character, but also a Zen Buddhist
spiritual master. He's Gumby.

IN 1953, ART CLOKEY, a former seminary student, started playing with a movie camera and colorful plasticine clay. He
laboriously made a four minute animated art film he called
Gumbasia in honor of Disney's *Fantasia* which featured geomet-
ric shapes rolling and dancing to a jazz score. "Suddenly I saw
a kinetic force at work, what I call the Phi Phenomenon, which
is an impact on the nervous system brought about by images
and the way they're edited," says Clokey.

Sam Engel was a film producer at 20th Century-Fox who had
a teenage son that Clokey was
tutoring in English and Latin.
When Clokey showed him
Gumbasia, Engel said, "That's
the most fantastic thing I've
ever seen!" and asked if Clokey
could come up with some kid
films for the emerging medium
of TV.

FEATS OF CLAY
He went home and started
experimenting immediately,
molding hundreds of shapes in
different colors. He found that
clay characters didn't last very

long under constant handling or the heat of movie lights. Clokey came up with a simple character that could be cut out of clay with a homemade cookie cutter and be replaced every few hours.

He made his clay character with a protrusion on one side of his head, modeled after a photo he had of his father as a teenager with a huge cowlick hair lump. His friend, American Zen philosopher, Alan Watt, suggested that it was the "bump of wisdom that the Buddhists have." In that spirit, Clokey made the new character green with a touch of blue to suggest a field of grass under a blue sky. To provide *yin* for his character's *yang*, he created a down-to-earth horse sidekick colored an earthy orange-brown.

CHARACTERS UP THE YIN-YANG

Remembering that his father used to call the sticky, muddy clay around their farm in Michigan "gumbo," the Latin teacher in Clokey knew that the diminutive of *gumbo* would be *gumby*. "That was the first and last significant use I made of my seven years of Latin in school," he observed later. Based on Watts's observation that there are two kinds of people in the world, the prickly and the gooey, Clokey created two more characters, a dinosaur named Prickle and a tear-drop-shaped "what's-it" named Goo. Finally, for Gumby and sidekick Pokey, Clokey created a miniature hangout called the Zen Cafe.

Each character was moved a fraction of a millimeter per frame, again and again, 24 times for each second of cartoon. The series began as standalone, six-minute Gumby episodes, but they were eventually picked up by NBC to be shown during *The Howdy Doody Show*. Gumby proved so popular there he was spun off into his own show, which was hosted by comedian Pinky Lee.

WHERE'S THE MONEY?

Gumby started generating a lot of money. The problem was that Clokey wasn't getting much of it. He was paid a straight salary of $200 a week to write and produce the Gumby episodes. (That went up to $350 a week shortly before *The Gumby Show* was canceled in 1957.)

For eight years he refused to license the Gumby image for merchandising. "I was a very idealistic person," he says, "and I didn't want to exploit children." That attitude changed after Gumby's show left NBC and Clokey bought all rights back from the network. His Prema (Sanskrit for "universal love") Toy Corporation started manufacturing Gumby dolls and toys in 1964, the year that Gumby found new life in syndication and Clokey started getting rich.

THE SOUND OF ONE MAN FLOPPING

Not long afterward, however, Clokely's personal life fell apart, and so did his fortune. He went through a painful and expensive divorce with his wife of eighteen years in 1966, about the time that TV stations began dropping Gumby in favor of newer and slicker kid shows. Clokey invested his last dollars in a new venture—a flexy-faced doll called Moody Rudy—that bombed. His house went into foreclosure. In 1974, his daughter died in a car crash. Clokey went into heavy therapy and began "looking at various gurus" before adopting the teachings of Indian Swami Muktananda.

DEATH & REBIRTH

Clokey remarried in 1976, and three years later, he and his new wife Gloria traveled to Bangalore, India to visit a guru named Sathya Sai Baba, who supposedly had amazing magical powers. For some reason, Clokey brought a Gumby doll along to their audience with the guru. "I stood there with Gumby and he did this circular motion with his arms," Clokey says. "Out of nowhere he materialized this sacred ash. He plopped it right on top of Gumby. When we came home again, things started to happen." Gumby toy sales began to pick up, and then Eddie Murphy started doing a continuing Gumby skit on *Saturday Night Live*. The phone started ringing, and Gumby became hip again. Clokey received an $8 million contract with Lorimar for a new Gumby series. He started work on *Gumby – the Movie*.

Since then, the popularity of Gumby has been an ever-changing cycle of ebbs and flow. "Gumby is a symbol of the spark of divinity in each of us, the basis of the ultimate value of each person. Eddie Murphy instinctively picked up on this when he asserted, 'I'm Gumby, dammit!'" wrote Clokey in 1986. "When people watch Gumby, they get a blissful feeling. Gumby loves you. We love you. That's about all I can say."

Get a Job!

MORE JOBS YOUR GUIDANCE COUNSELOR NEVER MENTIONED

Knacker: Buys and sells animal carcasses and old horses.
Slubber: Operates a machine that prepares cotton for spinning.
Bead Piercer: Drills the holes in beads.
Faker: Hand-colors black and white photos.
Knocker-Up: Wakes up workers on the early shift.
Bellowfarmer: Maintains and repairs church organs.
Snobscat: Repairs shoes.
Feller: Cuts down trees.
Knoller: Rings bells.
Belly Builder: Puts together piano interiors.
Streaker: Mortician.
Tallow Chandler: Makes and sells candles.
Fewterer: Trains hounds and keeps them in hunting trim.
Linkerboy: Guides people through dark and unfamiliar streets.
Besom Maker: Makes brooms.
Ponderator: Inspects weights and measures.
Car Chaser: Controls movement of railway cars.
Flauner: Makes candy.
Loblolly Boy: Assists a ship's surgeon.
Birdboy: Scares crows away from crops.
Foot-Straightener: Assembles clock dials.
Scagiolaist: Makes imitation marble.
Blentonist: Finds water with a dousing rod.
Malster: Brews beer.
Trugger: Makes baskets.
Fripperer: Buys and sells old clothes.
Bodger: Carves chair legs.
Mudlark: Cleans out sewers.
Frobbisher: Polishes metal.
Topman: Sits as a lookout at the top of a sailing ship mast.
Bookholder: Prompts stage actors who have forgotten lines.
Muggler: Cares for pigs.

Dental Telepathy

A Magic Trick For Your Party

H ere's a card trick that has a surprise twist. "Oh, swell, another card trick," you say. But rest assured, this one  not only entertains small groups of people, but can reduce cavities by up to 23 percent. The card trick involves a toothbrush and its psychic friend, a very gifted tube of toothpaste. "Maybe you've heard of mental telepathy," you announce, "but this is a case of DENTAL telepathy." Your friend squeezes out a ribbon of toothpaste ... and imbedded in it, discovers the name of the chosen card!

THE SET-UP

• Before you do the trick, get a tube of gel toothpaste. We like Crest® for kids because the little sparkles make it seem more magical.

• Cut a tiny strip of clear plastic (clear plastic packing tape glued to itself will do) and write an 8 with a spade symbol on it with a waterproof marker. Push the strip into the toothpaste just inside the tube.

• Find the eight of spades and put it on the top of the deck. Now you're about ready to begin.

THE OPENER

Assemble your friends and tell them a breathless story about how you've always felt "incredibly aware" whenever you brush your teeth with this toothbrush and its spiritual guide, the Psychic Toothpaste Tube. "I want to demonstrate their incredible affinity," you say, mysteriously. "I'm sure you'll be as amazed as I was at their minty-fresh powers."

Have a volunteer step forward, and ask her to choose a number between ten and twenty. Get ready to do the next steps quickly, matter-of-factly, and without hesitation, because you don't want your audience to think too much about it.

THE "HELPER"

Let's say she chooses seventeen. Take the deck and start counting out loud, slapping the cards onto the table into a neat pile as fast as you can, until you get to seventeen.

Hand the pile to your volunteer and say, "Would you count these again to make sure I counted right?" Most likely she'll count exactly as she saw you do. If she doesn't, though, stop her and make sure she does—counting out loud and dealing the cards into a neat pile.

"Seventeen cards, right?" you say. "Great. Okay, now what I want you to do is gently brush the back of the top card with the Incredible Psychic Toothbrush. Gently! Now lay the toothbrush on top of the card to increase the psychic connection."

THE BIG SQUEEZE

Have her get the toothpaste tube from the bathroom. "Keep it away from the toothbrush, though—I don't want them whispering to each other." Ask her to open it and squeeze a ribbon of toothpaste onto her finger. "What does it say?" you ask.

Turn over the card. If you did the trick right, it's the eight of spades. If you have no shame, you might pun: "Careful not to drop the toothpaste or you'll be Crest-fallen."

Nothing But the Tooth

- Before the invention of the modern toothbrush, folks used twigs, leaves, sand, fingers, animal bristles, and quills—anything that would work to brush off plaque.
- Early versions of toothpaste were made from a mixture of abrasives and astringents, like wine and pumice or urine and burned bone ash.
- Before modern dentistry, people prized white teeth more than we do today. Before the twentieth century, "dentists" would often unwittingly cause dental decay in their wealthier patients. By filing away the enamel of the tooth, and applying a corrosive bleaching solution, they would allow decay to set in.
- George Washington's false teeth were made from hippopotamus bone and human teeth—but never from wood, as legend had it.
- The first toothbrush, as we know it, popped up in China and was made from coarse hog hair, set in bamboo or ivory.
- Crest was the first toothpaste to add flouride.Other toothpastes eventually followed suit.

Potty Pourri
RANDOM KINDS OF FACTNESS

• Ian Fleming was an avid birdwatcher. When he was casting around for "an ordinary-sounding name" for his new spy hero, his eyes landed on his favorite bird identification book: *Birds of the West Indies* by ornithologist James Bond.

• Watch for oranges in The Godfather. Whenever they appear on the screen, it's a signal that someone is about to die.

• Better do some studying between games: Only 8 percent of college baseball, basketball, and football players even make the draft for their pro sport. Only 2 percent actually make it onto a professional team.

• Cats have 32 muscles surrounding their ears, allowing them to turn each ear independently.

• When Pablo Picasso tried his hand at writing a play, he had all of his characters die at the end from inhaling the fumes from fried potatoes. The few friends who attended a performance of *Desire Caught by the Tail* had just one piece of advice: "Stick with painting, Pablo."

• Are you deathly afraid of a lawsuit? Then you're liticaphobic ... just like the rest of us.

• In case you were wondering, there are three good reasons why male walruses have those big, white tusks: (1) As weapons in fights with polar bears, (2) To give the big blubbery beasts some traction on ice when pulling themselves out of the water, and (3) Because lady walruses think they're sexy.

• Hoping to get a positive answer from your Magic 8-Ball? "CHANCES ARE GOOD." Of the twenty possible answers, only five are negative. Ten indicate "YES." The remaining five? They tell you to "ASK AGAIN."

• Don't age your rice wine. Unlike most other wines, sake is best when served fresh. Bonzai!

Silly Putty

BOUNCING BACK FROM OBLIVION

Bend me, shape me, bounce me off the wall. Silly Putty has been a fixture of childhood for fifty years. Here's how it happened.

SOMETHING FUNNY HAPPENED when the government began seeking an inexpensive rubber substitute during World War II. At General Electric's New Haven laboratory, chemical engineer James Wright was working on that problem. He combined silicone oil and boric acid into a gooey pink polymer. Excitedly, he tossed some down on the counter.

Boing! To his surprise, it bounced right back at him.

With high hopes, GE sent glops of the substance to scientists around the world, challenging them to find practical uses for it. They couldn't come up with any. Not that they didn't try. One scientist, noting that it retained its strange properties down to -70° F., tested it to see if it would work as an insulating or caulking material in Arctic climes. No such luck.

"Bouncing putty," as GE dubbed it, languished in limbo. Still, fun-loving GE scientists started mixing up small batches for parties. At one such affair in Connecticut in 1949, a chunk was passed to Peter Hodgson, Sr., high school dropout, advertising consultant, and bon vivant. As he fingered and massaged the chunk, the phrase "silly putty" suddenly came to him. Although he was already $12,000 in debt, he borrowed $147 more and bought 21 pounds of the polymer from GE at $7 a pound, which he packed into little plastic eggs and began selling as an adult toy at an incredible markup ($2 per half-ounce).

He was doing pretty well, selling as many as 300 eggs a day at a few outlets, when the *New Yorker* featured the putty in a small story. Within days, he received orders for 230,000 eggs.

Silly Putty, "the toy with one moving part," was on its way to becoming a national mania.

Originally, adults were the target market. Hodgson believed that kids wouldn't appreciate the putty's richness and subtlety: "It appeals to people of superior intellect," he told a reporter. "The inherent ridiculousness of the material acts as an emotional release to hard-pressed adults."

That marketing strategy worked initially, but, after about five years, the initial ratio of eighty percent adults to twenty percent children had inverted to twenty percent adults to eighty percent children.

Kids loved the stuff well, but not wisely—so much so that the manufacturer had to go back to the labs to reformulate it. The problem was complaints from parents about Silly Putty getting into hair, clothing, upholstery, and carpeting. The Silly Putty of today is less sticky than that made forty years ago, and the company now has a toll-free line that offers advice on how to get Silly Putty unstuck from things.

And, finally, the world has discovered practical uses for Silly Putty. It has been used by astronauts to hold tools in place while in zero-gravity, in physical therapy clinics to reduce stress and help people strengthen their hands and wrists, and at the Cincinnati Zoo to make casts of the hands and feet of its gorillas, and smoking cessation groups recommend Silly Putty to people trying to quit.

MORE NUTTY PUTTY FACTS

• American consumers buy more than 2 million eggs of Silly Putty every year.

• Silly Putty varieties include glitter, glow-in-the-dark, fluorescent colors and the original plain beige.

• When set on fire, Silly Putty produces a bright white flame. The charred remains crumble to bits.

• If Silly Putty is microwaved up to 3 minutes, it will begin to melt. If allowed to cool, it will return to its original consistency.

• Baked Silly Putty (450° oven for 15 minutes) not only stinks, it dries and gets gooey on the pan.

• Dropped from several stories up, a ball made of 100 pounds of Silly Putty will bounce about 8 feet. However, the ball will become somewhat misshapen upon impact.

Full Metal Lunch Jacket
THE BIRTH OF THE COOL LUNCH BOXES

There was a time not so long ago that, for school kids, the lunchbox was the ultimate in personal expression.

MORE THAN A MERE CARRYING CASE for peanut butter and bologna sandwiches, your lunchbox once showed who you were and who you aspired to be. The pretty-in-pink girls carried Barbie or the Monkees; tomboys brought Charlie's Angels; boys carried Roy Rogers; little kids carried Disney or the Jetsons ... and the completely clueless carried generic plaid. During the golden age (1950–1980), lunch boxes were a way to advertise your favorite band, TV show, movie star, or cartoon character.

Most people don't realize, though, that lunch boxes went through many stages of evolution. Let us tell you the story of how they came about.

WORKING-CLASS ROOTS

Before the popular lunch box, there was the working-class lunch pail. (And before the lunch pail, there were oiled goatskins, but let's not go *that* far back.) The lunch pail wasn't really a pail; it was a latching case of toolbox-grade metal that protected your noon-time meal from just about anything up to a small bomb. And they weren't chic; on the contrary, they showed that you didn't have the time, freedom, or money for a decent meal for lunch.

Still, working-class children in the 1880s wanted to emulate Daddy, so some created their own school "lunch pails" out of colorful tin boxes that once housed biscuits, cookies, or tobacco. From there, it was a small step to a box specifically made for

that purpose, and in 1902 the first true kids' lunch box came out. No, it didn't feature turn-of-the-century pop culture idols like P. T. Barnum, Buffalo Bill, or the Sousa Band—shaped like a picnic basket, it sported pictures of children playing.

BEYOND THE PAIL

True, there were forerunners, but it wasn't until 1950 that lunch boxes really entered their prime. It was an act of desperation by a company called Aladdin. Although the postwar market had created a demand for all kinds of consumer goods, metal lunch boxes were so durable that once a schoolkid bought one it could last until high school graduation.

Staring at charts of slumping sales, Aladdin execs started throwing around ideas:

"We've got these plain boxes—why don't we jazz them up with decals?" "Kids seem to like cowboys and Indians. How about using a TV cowboy? Maybe Hopalong Cassidy?"

And that's how Aladdin

stumbled into the ethos of "planned obsolescence" that drove the American economy for decades thereafter—convincing customers to habitually replace perfectly good products for the sake of novelty and style. Aladdin hired a designer to sketch the cowboy star onto decal material that they slapped onto the side of a red lunchbox. On the strength of that crude prototype, they convinced a big department store chain to

make an advance order of 50,000, and the box took off like bad guys hightailing it to their hideout.

Meanwhile, back at the ranch, another cowboy star became jealous. Roy Rogers wanted his own box, but Aladdin had turned him down with: "One cowboy is enough." So Roy saddled up and rode north to American Thermos in Connecticut. Like Aladdin, Thermos had seen sales slump in its sets of lunch boxes and thermos bottles, made even more acute by Aladdin's success. Thermos decided to do Aladdin's

cowboy box one better by using bright, full-color lithography on all sides of the box instead of a decal on just one face. It worked: the company sold 2.5 million Roy Rogers & Dale Evans boxes in 1953, increasing their total sales 20 percent in one year.

Aladdin retooled to also use full-box lithography for their 1954 line. So did newcomers ADCO Liberty and Universal, as well as another old-style lunch pail manufacturer, Ohio Art (which later diversified into making toys like

Etch-A-Sketch). In 1962, Aladdin added another trademark feature: designs stamped into the metal, giving a 3-D effect.

Lunchbox manufacturers began bidding for rights to hot new movies and TV shows. From 1950 until 1987, lunchbox manufacturers issued about 450 different designs.

The classic steel lunch boxes had a good run, selling about

The Disney Schoolbus was the biggest seller of all time—9 million total.

120 million between 1950 and 1970. Manufacturers in 1972 began switching to plastic to cut manufacturing costs. Meanwhile, concerned mothers and pandering state legislators banned metal lunch boxes as dangerous assault weapons. Ironically, the last metal lunch box of the classic era hailed the violent hero, Rambo, in 1987.

Life Lessons

SWIRLING & SNIFFING THROUGH A WINE TASTING

Follow these simple instructions and you'll be able to participate in a wine tasting without the least bit of embarrassment.

PEOPLE MAY LOOK PRETENTIOUS at a wine tasting, but there's a reason for everything they do. Step by step, here's what to do if you want to look like you belong there:

1. Hold the glass of wine up to your eyes and look at it. Enjoy the rich clear colors.

2. If you see anything suspicious, put it down and move on to another wine. What to look for: cloudiness (means wine isn't ready to drink), brownish hue (wine is too old), or pieces of glass or other residue. Pieces of cork won't hurt you.

3. Swirl your glass. Coat the inside edges with a thin layer of wine. The wine glass should be slightly curved inward at the top, to capture the smell of the wine (and decrease the chance of swirling the wine out of the glass), but you may also want to place your hand over the glass to capture the aroma.

4. Smell the wine. Place your nose deep into the glass to get a good whiff. A good wine should have a pleasant "bouquet." Wine that's going bad will smell like old sherry. Wine that's already gone bad will smell like vinegar. Other bad signs are wine that smells like rotten eggs (too much sulfur) or mildew (the cork has gone bad).

5. Swish the wine over your mouth and teeth. Clench your teeth and suck in air over your tongue and the wine to get the full aroma and taste at the same time.

6. If you're a "serious" taster, use the bucket provided to spit out the wine you've just tasted so you won't dull your senses. Otherwise swallow. Take notes of your observations about the wine. Eat a cracker to cleanse your palate and grab another glass.

Step Right Up!

HOW INCUBATOR BABIES BECAME A POPULAR SIDESHOW

Can't get funding to develop an invention that would save millions of babies? Well, how about doing what this doctor did—create a sideshow carnival exhibit? Here's the whole curious story.

CONEY ISLAND IN ITS HEYDAY: If early last century you joined the teeming crowds on the New York subway and traveled to the amusement parks on Coney Island, you'd experience things you couldn't do anywhere else. For example, you could ride one of the roller coasters, a thrill that was pretty much invented here in the ocean breezes off the tip of Brooklyn. You could gawk at sideshow freaks and a miniature town filled with 300 midgets, go on an elaborate trip "to the moon," or see a reenactment of the San Francisco earthquake or the Bible's Great Flood. If you were in search of racier stuff, you could see hoochy-koochy dancers or even visit an elephant-shaped hotel, where it was whispered you could find, for a price, an incredibly easy date.

However, in the center of Coney Island's crowds, noise, smells, lights, and excitement was perhaps the strangest exhibit of all was the Incubator Babies.

GIVING UP PREMATURELY

Until the 1940s, few maternity hospitals wanted to go to the expense of providing special facilities to handle premature babies. The thought was that such babies were too weak to survive anyway, so why bother going to any great effort beyond preparing the parents for the inevitable? The theory was a self-fulfilling prophecy: the death rate for preemies in most hospitals approached 85 percent.

In France, a doctor named Alexandre Lion thought this was a wasteful tragedy. In the 1890s, France's population was actually falling as birth rates fell and infant mortality remained high.

Because their bodies cannot yet regulate their temperature, premature babies often died from hypothermia. In 1891, Lion built a contraption with a cylindrical water boiler on the side to provide steady heat, and with a fan system that provided filtered air. The Lion incubator's effect on reducing mortality rates immediately proved remarkable, and the doctor sought hospital interest and funds to build more.

To his shocked surprise, neither funds nor interest were forthcoming. To try to drum up interest in his incubators with his limited funds, Lion decided to display them in exhibitions and international fairs. But simply showing them wasn't getting the idea across, so he took a bold step. He solicited premature infants from local hospitals. The hospitals, believing the preemies would die anyway, were happy to provide them. Lion hired medical personnel and wet nurses, and set up an exhibit behind glass of the preemie hospital of the future, with live babies.

The good doctor didn't anticipate that the medical establishment would continue its indifference to his invention. On the other hand, he was flabbergasted by how much interest ordinary citizens took in his exhibit. There were so many people who wanted to gawk through the glass at the tiny babies and the new-fangled machines that many of the fairgoers had to be turned away.

Lion came up with a way that he hoped would reduce the crowds and also help pay some of his expenses. He started charging admission. To his surprise, the crowds didn't diminish at all, and he finally started making money from his life-saving invention.

Lion's first exhibition success led to a flurry of invitations from other fairs. It also led to another pediatrician entering the field. Dr. Martin Couney also began exhibiting the life-saving devices at public expositions in Germany, then was invited to exhibitions in the United States.

He set up his first American exhibit in 1898 at the Trans-Mississippi Exposition in Omaha, Nebraska. After doing several incubator exhibitions, he decided to find a place where he could set up a permanent display, and where could be better than Coney Island? In 1904, Couney opened his first permanent exhibit in Luna Park under a sign announcing, "ALL THE WORLD LOVES A BABY." It was Coney Island's longest-running show, closing in 1943 when New York City hospitals finally opened their own preemie centers.

The exhibit at Coney Island was unusual in more ways than you'd expect. For one thing, the parents of the babies paid nothing for the extensive services provided. The 24-hour-a-day machines, nurses, and wet nurses were all paid for by the quarters of the curious spectators who stopped by. (Parents of the babies—as well as former patients as they grew up—got

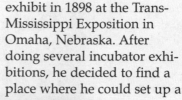

free passes to the exhibit.)

Also, the excellent care was open to babies of all economic classes and races, which was unusual at the time. Finally, the results Couney

"...dozens of faces peered at her curiously"

achieved were nothing short of a medical miracle. Reported the *Minneapolis Daily Star*: "It is a matter of statistical record that previous to the use of the incubator that only 15% of the prematurely born lived. By use of the incubator, 85% are saved." Of the 8,000 babies raised in the Coney Island incubators, more than 6,500 survived.

To the credit of the medical profession, they did eventually take note of Dr. Couney's success rate, and despite the carney atmosphere, began coming to see and learn from his experience. By the 1940s, hospitals around the country had finally caught up with the Coney Island sideshow exhibit by opening their own preemie wards. Couney, now quite old and modestly affluent, finally retired.

How Short Was Napoleon?

Despite his reputation as a puny guy, Napoleon Bonaparte wasn't really that short. True, he was only five-foot-two, but for a French person of the time, that was a pretty average height. True, in comparison to other leaders of the time he was short. And of course, *le Petite Corporal* was shorter than most men today. (Most women too, for that matter.)

Despite his shortcomings, Napoleon managed to conquer 720,000 square miles of territory during his years of making war, much more than any of the leaders who towered over him.

Still More H. L. Mencken

More quotes from H. L. Mencken, the controversial curmudgeon.

• "It is inaccurate to say I hate everything. I am strongly in favor of common sense, common honesty, and common decency. This makes me forever ineligible for public office."

• "A judge is a law student who marks his own examination papers."

• "Nature abhors a moron."

• "Conscience is a mother-in-law whose visit never ends."

• "The Christian Church, in its attitude toward science, shows the mind of a more or less enlightened man of the Thirteenth Century. It no longer believes that the earth is flat, but it is still convinced that prayer can cure after medicine fails."

• "It is often argued that religion is valuable because it makes men good, but even if this were true it would not be a proof that religion is true. Santa Claus makes children good in precisely the same way, and yet no one would argue seriously that the fact proves his existence."

• "The liberation of the human mind has been best furthered by fellow who heaved dead cats into sanctuaries and then went roister-ing down the highways of the world, proving to all men that doubt, after all, was safe — that the god in the sanctuary was a fraud."

• "Sunday: A day given over by Americans to wishing that they themselves were dead and in Heaven, and that their neighbors were dead and in Hell."

• "Suicide is a belated acquiescence in the opinion of one's wife's relatives."

• "Do not overestimate the decency of the human race."

• "A courtroom is a place where Jesus Christ and Judas Iscariot would be equals, with the betting odds favoring Judas."

• "A dachshund is a half-dog high and a dog-and-a-half long."

• "He marries best who puts it off until it is too late."

• "One horse-laugh is worth ten-thousand syllogisms."

• "I believe it is better to tell the truth than to lie. I believe that it is better to be free than to be a slave. and I believe that it is better to know than to be ignorant."

• "Life may not be exactly pleasant, but at least it's not dull."

We've Got Your Number

We'll give you a number, abbreviated words, and a clue. Tell us what the famous phrase is. Answers below. (Don't cheat!)

1. 7 W O T W (See the pyramids along the Nile)
2. T 3 F O E (Multiple-personality movie)
3. 5 G L — H O M E S (Water, water everywhere)
4. 7 D S (Gluttony's one of them)
5. 10 P O E (Locusts, boils, frogs, etc.)
6. F 451 (Bradbury book-burning book)
7. 12 K O T R T (The gal I had liked to lance a lot)
8. 3 PC — R, Y, B (Meet my colorful friend, Roy G. Biv)
9. Y 16, Y B, & Y M (1950s song)
10. 76 T I T B P (Friends, you've got trouble)
11. 666 — T M O T B (Another from *Revelation*)
12. 6 O O, H A D O T O (Either way's the same)
13. 50 W T L Y L (Paul Simon song)
14. A S I T S 9 (An old saying that's sew true)
15. A C H 9 L (Ask Morris, he'll tell you)
16. 30 D H S, A, J, & N (The rest have 28 or 31)
17. 2 I C, 3 A C (So says Jack Ritter)
18. 101 D (Disney doggies)
19. 10,000 L U T S (Disney dives)
20. 1-E ,1-H, F P P E (1950s novelty song)

Wicked Jim

MARK TWAIN'S SATIRE ABOUT KID STORIES

In Mark Twain's time, children's stories had heavyhanded morals at the end. It's a tradition that lamentably survives in kids' books even today, despite Twain's attempt to stomp it to death with this parody from 1865.

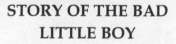

STORY OF THE BAD LITTLE BOY

ONCE there was a bad little boy whose name was Jim —though, if you will notice, you will find that bad little boys are nearly always called James in your Sunday-school books. It was strange, but still it was true that this one was called Jim.

He didn't have any sick mother either—a sick mother

who was pious and had the consumption, and would be glad to lie down in the grave and be at rest but for the strong love she bore her boy, and the anxiety she felt that the world might be harsh and cold towards him when she was gone. Most bad boys in the Sunday-books are named James, and have sick mothers, who teach them to say, "Now, I lay me down," etc., and sing them to sleep with sweet, plaintive voices, and then kiss them good-night, and kneel down by the bedside and weep. But it was different with this fellow. He was named Jim, and there wasn't anything the matter with his mother—no consumption, nor anything of that kind. She was rather stout than otherwise, and she was not pious; moreover, she was not anxious on Jim's account. She said if he were to break his neck it wouldn't be much loss. She always spanked Jim to sleep, and she never kissed him good-night; on the contrary, she boxed his ears when she was ready to leave him.

Once this little bad boy stole the key of the pantry, and slipped in there and helped himself to some jam, and filled up the vessel  with tar so that his mother would never know the difference; but all at once a terrible feeling didn't come over him, and something didn't seem to whisper to him, "Is it right to disobey my mother? Isn't in sinful to do this? Where do bad little boys go who gobble up their good kind mother's jam?" and then he didn't kneel down all alone and promise never to be wicked any more, and rise up with a light, happy heart, and go and tell his mother all about it and beg her forgiveness, and be blessed by her with tears of pride and thankfulness in her eyes. No; that is the way with all other bad boys in the books; but it happened otherwise with this Jim, strangely enough. He ate that jam, and said it was bully, in his sinful, vulgar way; and he put in the tar, and said that was bully also, and laughed, and observed "that the old woman would get up and snort" when she found it out; and when she did find it out, he denied knowing anything about it, and she whipped him severely, and he did the crying himself. Everything about this boy was curious—everything turned out differently with him from the way it does to the bad Jameses in the books.

Once he climbed up in Farmer Acorn's apple-tree to steal apples, and the limb didn't break, and he didn't fall and break his arm, and get torn by the farmer's great dog, and then languish on a sick bed for weeks, and repent and become good. Oh! no; he stole as many apples as he wanted and came down all right; and he was all ready for the dog too, and knocked him endways with a brick when he came to tear him. It was very strange—nothing like it ever happened in those mild little books with marbled backs, and with pictures in them of men with swallow-tailed coats and bell-crowned hats, and pantaloons that are short in the legs, and women with the waists of their dresses under their arms, and no hoops on. Nothing like it in any of the Sunday-school books.

Once he stole the teacher's pen-knife, and, when he was afraid it would be found out and he would get whipped, he slipped it into George Wilson's cap—poor Widow Wilson's son, the moral boy, the good little boy of the village, who always obeyed his mother, and never told an untruth, and was fond of his lessons, and infatuated with Sunday-school. And when the knife dropped from the cap, and poor George hung his head and blushed, as if in conscious guilt, and the grieved teacher charged the theft upon him, and was just in the very act of bringing the switch down upon his trembling shoulders, a white-haired, improbable justice of the peace did not suddenly appear in their midst, and strike an attitude and say, "Spare this noble boy—there stands the cowering culprit! I was passing the school-door at recess, and unseen myself, I saw the theft committed!" And then Jim didn't get whaled, and the venerable justice didn't read the tearful school a homily, and take George by the hand and say such a boy deserved to be exalted, and then tell him to come and make his home with him, and sweep out the office, and make fires, and run errands, and chop wood, and study law, and help his wife do household labors, and have all the balance of the time to play, and get forty cents a month, and be happy. No; it would have happened that way in the books, but it didn't happen that way to Jim. No meddling old clam of a justice dropped in to make trouble, and so the model boy George got thrashed, and

Jim was glad of it. Because, you know, Jim hated moral boys. Jim said he was "down on them milksops." Such was the coarse language of this bad, neglected boy.

But the strangest thing that ever happened to Jim was the time he went boating on Sunday, and didn't get drowned, and that other time that he got caught out in the storm when he was fishing on Sunday, and didn't get struck by lightning. Why, you might look, and look, and look, all through the Sunday-school books from now till next Christmas, and you would never come across anything like this. Oh no; you would find that all the bad boys who go boating on Sunday invariably get drowned, and all the bad boys who get caught out in storms, when they are fishing on Sunday, infallibly get struck by lightning. Boats with bad boys in them are always upset on Sunday, and it always storms when bad boys go fishing on the Sabbath. How this Jim ever escaped is a mystery to me.

This Jim bore a charmed life—that must have been the way of it. Nothing could hurt him. He even gave the elephant in the menagerie a plug of tobacco, and the elephant didn't knock the top of his head off with his trunk. He browsed around the cupboard after essence of peppermint, and didn't make a mistake and drink aqua fortis. He stole his father's gun and went hunting on the Sabbath, and didn't shoot three or four of his fingers off. He struck his little sister on the temple with his fist when he was angry, and yet she did not linger in pain through long summer days,

and die with sweet words of forgiveness upon her lips that redoubled the anguish of his breaking heart. No; she got over it. He ran off and went to sea at last, and didn't come back and find himself sad and alone in the world, his loved ones sleeping in the quiet church-yard, and the vine-embowered home of his boyhood tumbled down and gone to decay. Ah! no; he came home as drunk as a piper, and got into the station-house the first thing.

And he grew up, and married, and raised a large family, and brained them all with an axe one night, and got wealthy by all manner of cheating and rascality; and now he is the infernalest wickedest scoundrel in his native village, and is universally respected, and belongs to the Legislature.

So you see there never was a bad James in the Sunday-school books that had such a streak of luck as this sinful Jim with the charmed life.

The Origins of Snowball & Little Snookums

• Like dogs, bears, and raccoons, the entire cat family developed more than 50 million years ago from a small, weaselly animal called *Miacis.*

• Ancient Egyptians tamed an African wildcat called *Felis libyca* about 2500 B.C. Crusaders brought some back to Europe, and bred them with small European wildcats. That's how we got the modern shorthaired housecat.

• Longhaired cats, on the other hand, descended from the Asian wildcat *(Felis manul),* domesticated in India, also in about 2500 B.C.

• Unlike most domesticated animals, the size of cats has remained pretty much unchanged during its association with people.

• In ancient Egypt, the penalty for killing a cat was death, and cats were worshiped as gods. There was a practical reason: The Egyptians subsisted largely on grains in bread and beer, and cats kept rodents in check.

• Ancient Egyptian cat owners would shave their eyebrows in mourning and lovingly transport the cat carcass to one of the cities devoted to mummifying cats for their journey to the next world.

• The cats apparently didn't make it. In 1888, about 300,000 cat mummies were discovered still lounging around this world in a burial ground at the ancient city of Beni Hassan.

• The Jewish Talmud (about 500 B.C.) encourages people to adopt cats "to help keep their houses clean." On the other hand, the cat is the only domesticated animal not mentioned *even once* in the Bible.

The Devil's Dictionary: T–Z

More of The Devil's Dictionary by Ambrose Bierce (1842–1914?)

TAKE, *v.t.* To acquire, often by force but preferably by stealth.

TARIFF, *n.* A scale of taxes on imports, designed to protect the domestic producer against the greed of his consumer.

TELEPHONE, *n.* An invention of the devil which abrogates some of the advantages of making a disagreeable person keep his distance.

TELESCOPE, *n.* A device having a relation to the eye similar to that of the telephone to the ear, enabling distant objects to plague us with a multitude of needless details. Luckily it is unprovided with a bell.

TRICHINOSIS, *n.* The pig's reply to proponents of porcophagy.

TRUTHFUL, *adj.* Dumb and illiterate.

TSETSE FLY, *n.* An African insect (*Glossina morsitans*) whose bite is commonly regarded as nature's most efficacious remedy for insomnia, though some patients prefer that of the American novelist (*Mendax interminabilis*).

UGLINESS, *n.* A gift of the gods to certain women, entailing virtue without humility.

ULTIMATUM, *n.* In diplomacy, a last demand before resorting to concessions.

UN-AMERICAN, *adj.* Wicked, intolerable, heathenish.

VALOR, *n.* A soldierly compound of vanity, duty, and the gambler's hope.

VANITY, *n.* The tribute of a fool to the worth of the nearest ass.

VOTE, *n.* The instrument and symbol of a freeman's power to make a fool of himself and a wreck of his country.

WAR, *n.* A by-product of the arts of peace.

WHEAT, *n.* A cereal from which a tolerably good whisky can with some difficulty be made, and which is used also for bread.

WITCH, *n.* (1) Any ugly and repulsive old woman, in a wicked league with the devil. (2) A beautiful and attractive young woman, in wickedness a league beyond the devil.

YANKEE, *n.* In Europe, an American. In the Northern States of our Union, a New Englander. In the South the word is unknown. (See DAMNYANK.)

YEAR, *n.* A period of 365 disappointments.

ZEAL, *n.* A certain nervous disorder afflicting the young and inexperienced.

"BE MINE"

Sweet Tales of Candy Hearts

COAX ME, HUG ME, KISS ME ... you can say a mouthful with candy hearts, the Valentine's Day icon. There's a lot we learned about them. Be our Valentine, and we'll tell you more.

ABOUT 10 BILLION candy message hearts are sold each year. Eighty percent of those are made by the New England Confectionery Company (NECCO) of Cambridge, Massachusetts, founded in 1848.

• You can buy the hearts only from January 1 to Valentine's Day. Still, the company keeps three separate plants pumping them out, 18 hours a day, year-round, to keep up with the seasonal demand. Unless Valentine's Day falls on a Sunday, the machines keep making candy hearts for the next year even through the holiday.

• Every minute of the work day, each candy machine makes 12,640 hearts. That's about 45 bags a minute.

• Hearts with messages was the idea of Daniel Chase, brother of NECCO founder Oliver Chase, in the late 1860s. He first put messages *inside* heart-shaped candies that cracked open like fortune cookies. A new process in 1902 made it possible to imprint the messages on candy hearts with food dye.

• Not surprisingly, considering its name, the company also makes Neccos, those coin-sized chalky candies that come in rolls of many colors. The hearts use the Necco recipe rolled extra thick.

• Originally, NECCO Valentine's hearts (called Motto Hearts) were much bigger than today's version. They were big enough to feature sayings like "Oh my dear, do not squeal, you're safe with me in the automobile."

• The maximum inscription length for the small hearts nowadays is two lines, six letters per line.

• Today, dough for the hearts (sugar, corn syrup, corn starch, xanthan gum, pecan syrup, color, and flavor) is made in batches weighing 550 pounds. The dough is then rolled into yard-wide sheets, stamped with red sayings, and cut into heart shapes.

• Don't like the message you've gotten? There are 125 different phrases. Each year, the company replaces a handful of old phrases with new ones.

• Retired phrases over the years include HUBBA HUBBA, GROOVY, HANG TEN, DIG ME, BUZZ OFF, STOP, HOT STUFF, TRY ME, BAD BOY, SAY YES, and R-U GAY?

• NECCO rolls with the times, though. New phrases today include MEGABYTE, GO GIRL, YOU ROCK, BE MY ICON, FAX ME, TRES CHIC, WHAT'S UP, VOGUE, and URA QT. Spanish language hearts are also available (BELLIA, AMOR, ADIOS).

• The company gets requests from people year 'round, desperate to find a MARRY ME heart to propose marriage. They try to oblige, says a spokesperson—"How could we refuse?"

"My advice to you is get married: if you find a good wife you'll be happy; if not, you'll become a philosopher." —Socrates

"Only choose in marriage a woman whom you would choose as a friend if she were a man." —Joseph Joubert

Escape Artist

HOW TO ESCAPE AN ENCOUNTER WITH A BEAR

Bear encounters are on the rise. Bears would rather get a good meal from you than hunt one for themselves. So how do you survive an encounter with a bear? We'll show you.

FOLLOW THESE RULES, and you've got a good chance of coming out okay. First, it's best not to encounter bears at all. Black bears, brown bears, and grizzlies all love leftovers. No food should be stored in or near your tent. Food should be hung away from your sleeping area, high enough to keep bears from reaching it. Leftover scraps should always be burned.

1. If a bear comes into your camp, let it have anything you've got and get out of the way. Humans don't taste that good; the bears aren't looking to eat you.

2. If you're hiking alone, attach something loud to your pack. If you're with a group, talk loudly as you walk. This should keep most bears at bay.

3. If a grizzly approaches you, drop your pack and climb a tree, if possible—preferably one without branches for the bear to climb. If you encounter a black or brown bear, though, don't bother. They're both expert climbers.

5. Otherwise, drop your pack and back slowly away. Bears can outrun you—and will. Step well clear away from your pack, and drop to your knees. Curl up in a ball with your legs under you and your hands protecting your head and neck.

6. Play dead and stay completely inert if the bear sniffs you and checks you out. This has worked more often than not. Bears really aren't interested in eating you; they simply feel threatened easily and will fight.

Get a Job!

MORE JOBS YOUR GUIDANCE COUNSELOR NEVER MENTIONED

Funabulist: Walks tightropes.

Virginalist: Plays a virginal (harpsichord-like instrument).

Bowdler: Smelts iron ore.

Nagelschmiedmeister: Makes nails.

Gaffer: (1) Lights movie sets. (2) Shapes glass-blown bottles.

Brailler: Makes girdles.

Necker: Feeds cardboard into box machines.

Buddleboy: Maintains the vats for washing metal ores.

Vogler: Catches birds.

Rockman: Places explosives in mines.

Secret Springer: Makes watch mainsprings.

Egg Breaker: Separates yolks from whites for food industry.

Bullwhacker: Drives oxen.

Gatward: Keeps goats.

Busker: (1) Street entertainer. (2) Hair dresser.

Paling Man: Sells eels.

Gaunter: Makes gloves

Hacker: Makes hoes.

Carnifex: Butchers animals for meat.

Peruker: Makes wigs.

Gelder: Castrates animals.

Lingo Cleaner: Maintains looms.

Cod Placer: Puts pottery into a kiln.

Hoggard: Drives pigs.

Pigman: Sells crockery.

Lump Inspector: Monitors quality of bulk tobacco.

Honeydipper / Jakes Farmer: Cleans out port-a-potty sewage.

Deathsman: Executes prisoners.

Playderer: Weaves plaid cloths.

Masher: Runs mash tub in beer making.

Gandy Dancer: Tamps gravel between newly laid railroad ties.

Toe Puncher: Runs machine that flattens knitted sock seams.

Ben's Naughty Advice

Founding Father Fulminates on Flatulence

Some of Benjamin Franklin's writings were perfect for perusing in the privy, including this satire in which he uses farts to make a pungent point about scientific societies.

To the Royal Academy of Brussels

Gentlemen:

I have perused your late mathematical Prize Question, proposed in lieu of one in natural Philosophy for the ensuing Year. I was glad to find that you esteem *Utility* an essential point in your Enquiries, which has not always been the case with all Academies. Permit me then humbly to propose one of that sort for your Consideration, for the serious Enquiry of learned Physicians, Chemists, etc., of this enlightened Age.

It is universally well-known, that in digesting our common food, there is created in or produced in the Bowels of human Creatures a great quantity of Wind.

That the permitting this Air to escape and mix with Atmosphere, is usually offensive to the Company, from the fetid smell that accompanyes it.

That all well bred People therefore, to avoid giving such offense, forcibly restrain the Efforts of Nature to discharge that Wind.

That so retained contrary to Nature, it not only gives frequently great present pain, but occasions future Diseases such as habitual Cholics, Ruptures, Tympanies, etc., often destructive of the Constitution, and sometimes of Life itself.

Were it not for the odiously offensive smell accompanying such escapes, polite People would probably be under no more

Restraint in discharging such Wind in Company than they are in spitting or blowing their Noses.

My Prize Question therefore should be: To discover some Drug, wholesome and not disagreeable, to be mixed with our common food, or sauces, that shall render the natural discharges of Wind from our Bodies not only inoffensive, but agreeable as Perfumes.

That this is not a Chimerical Project & altogether impossible, may appear from these considerations: That we already have some knowledge of means capable of *varying* that smell. He that dines on stale Flesh, especially with much Addition of Onions, shall be able to afford a Stink that no Company can tolerate; while he that has lived for some time on Vegetables only, shall have that Breath so pure as to be insensible to the most delicate Noses; and if he can manage so as to avoid the Report, he may anywhere give vent to his Griefs, un-noticed. But as there are many to whom an entire Vegetable Diet would be inconvenient, & as a little quick Lime thrown into a Jakes will correct the amazing Quantity of fetid Air arising from the vast

"Musk, rose, or lily?"

Mass of putrid Matter contained in such Places, and render it rather pleasing to the Smell, who knows but that a little Powder of Lime (or some other thing equivalent) taken in our Food, or perhaps a Glass of Lime Water drank at Dinner, may have the same Effect on the Air produced in and issuing from our Bowels? This is worth the experiment. Certain it is also that we have the Power of changing by slight means the Smell of another Discharge, that of our Water. A few stems of Asparagus eaten, shall give our Urine a disagreeable Odour; and a Pill of Turpentine no bigger than a Pea, shall bestow on it the pleasing smell of Violets. And why should it be thought more impossible in Nature, to find means of making a Perfume of our *Wind* than of our *Water*?

For the encouragement of this Enquiry (from the immortal Honour to be reasonably expected by the Inventor) let it be considered of how small importance to Mankind, or how small a Part of Mankind have been useful those Discoveries in Science that have heretofore made Philosophers famous. Are there twenty men in Europe this day the happier, or even the easier for any knowledge they have pick'd out of Aristotle? What Comfort can the Vortices of Descartes give to a man who has Whirlwinds in his Bowels! The knowledge of Newton's mutual *Attraction* of the particles of matter, can it afford ease to him who is racked by their mutual *Repulsion,* and the cruel distentions it occasions? The Pleasure arising to a few Philosophers, from seeing, a few times in their lives, the threads of light untwisted, and separated by the Newtonian Prism into seven colours, can it be compared with the ease and comfort every man living might feel seven times a day, by discharging freely the wind from Bowels? Especially, if it be converted into a Perfume; for the pleasures of one Sense being little inferior to those of another, instead of pleasing the *Sight,* he might delight the *Smell* of those about him, and make numbers happy, which to a benevolent mind must afford infinite satisfaction. The generous Soul, who now endeavours to find out whether the friends he entertains like best Claret or Burgundy, Champagne or Madeira, would then enquire also whether they chose Musk or Lily, Rose or Bergamot, and provide accordingly. And surely such a Liberty of *expressing one's scent-iments, & pleasing one another,* is of infinitely more importance to human happiness than that Liberty of the Press, or of abasing one another, which the English are so ready to fight & die for.

In short, this Invention, if completed, would be, as Bacon expresses it, Bringing Philosophy home to Men's Business and Bosoms. And I cannot but conclude, that in comparison therewith for universal and continual Utility the Science of the Philosophers abovementioned, even with the addition, Gentlemen, of your mathematical prize, are, all together, scarcely worth a *Fart-hing.*

*Your most obedient
humble Servant

B Franklin*

Barrymorisms III

It can't be easy being the third generation of a great Hollywood family, but here's Drew, doing her best.

ON WISDOM

"I aspire to be a voice of reason one day."

ON HAPPINESS

"I don't want to be stinky poo-poo girl, I want to be happy flower child."

ON GOD'S WILL

"God made a very obvious choice when he made me voluptuous; why would I go against what he decided for me? My limbs work, so I'm not going to complain about the way my body is shaped."

ON FLORA

"Daisies are like sunshine to the ground."

ON FAUNA

"I've been a vegetarian for years and years. I'm not judgmental about others who aren't, I just feel I cannot eat or wear living creatures."

ON METAMORPHOSIS

"Everyone is like a butterfly, they start out ugly and awkward and then morph into beautiful graceful butterflies that everyone loves."

ON LIVING

"If you're going to be alive and on this planet, you have to, like, suck the marrow out of every day and get the most out of it."

ON FATE

"I've always said that one night, I'm going to find myself in some field somewhere, I'm standing on grass, and it's raining, and I'm with the person I love, and I know I'm at the very point I've been dreaming of getting to."

ON HOBBIES

"I am obsessed with ice cubes. Obsessed."

Anty Matters

How Uncle Milton Put the Ants in Ant Farm

Ants are maddening when running free in a quest for crumbs and butter. However, ants imprisoned in little prison farms allow us to relax and enjoy them again and again.

THE IDEA FOR THE ANT FARM struck Milton Levine in 1956, when Levine was at an Independence Day picnic at his sister's house. He was thirty-two at the time, and looking to expand his line of mail order novelties like spud guns and rubber shrunken heads. "The kids were more interested in lying around and watching ant hills than swimming in the pool. And it came to me. When I was a kid, we used to put ants in a Mason jar with a little dirt and watch 'em dig when they got to the sides. I thought, why not make one that was flatter, that people could see most of the tunnels?"

His first farms were 6 by 9 inches, the familiar solid-colored plastic frame holding a thin layer of sand between two sheets of transparent plastic. It featured a plastic farm scene—barn, silo, farmhouse, and windmill (about the same as they are now), and sold for $1.98.

Levine bought a 2-inch ad in the *Los Angeles Times*, inviting the curious to "watch the ants dig tunnels and build bridges" in their own Ant Farms. Levine got loads of orders, but that was just the beginning.

Not that selling ants was always a picnic. In the beginning, ants were dropping like flies—the result of either booze on the breath of the guy who assembled the kits (Levine's theory) or glue fumes (Levine's partner's theory). Whichever, the problem was eventually solved.

The Ant Farm has been an enduring product, to say the least. Sales began two years before the Hula-Hoop and are still going strong. More then 20 million Ant Farms have been sold, populated by more than 360 million ants. The company, now managed by Milton's son, Steven Levine, gets about 12,000 letters each year from Ant Farm owners (often former childhood owners reporting they had bought one for a child or grandchild). Not that there isn't an occasional complaint letter—one kid was mad that his ants weren't wearing top hats like some shown on the box.

Except for the price, the basic product is just about the same today as back then. You get a certificate that you have to mail in to get your ants,

Uncle Milton's Ant Farm Village

and the *Ant Watchers Manual*, which gives you information about your new livestock (Do ants talk? Yes. Do they take baths? Yes). One improvement from the early days: connectors for plastic tubes so you can string Ant Farms together and watch the ants crawl from one to another.

Why is he called "Uncle Milton"? "Everyone always said, 'You've got the ants, but where's the uncles?' So I became Uncle Milton."

INSECT ASIDES

• Coincidence? You decide: The Ant Farm was invented in the same year as Raid insecticide.

• All the ants supplied for the Ant Farm are female. In the ant world, there aren't many males, and all they do is mate and die (an anty-climax, if you will). Since the company can't legally ship queen ants, your colony can't reproduce and will eventually dwindle to nothing.

• Out of thousands of varieties of ants, the harvester ant was chosen to work on the Ant Farm because it's big and is one of the few varieties that will dig in daylight.

• The leading cause of death for ants is overfeeding. If you exceed the recommended ration of one birdseed or a single corn flake every two days, the food gets moldy, and your ants "buy the farm."

• The next leading danger is too much sunlight (baked ants). Shaking the farm has been known to cause mass death by shock (it's too darn frustrating to spend all those hours digging, only to have your work reduced to nothing in a few seconds).

• At a funeral, the ant grave-yard detail always carries the dead ant to the northeastern corner of the farm. If the farm is rotated to a new direction, the pallbearers march into action again, digging up the dead ants and reburying them in the northeast. Why? Nobody knows.

• The technical name for an ant farm (or any ant habitat) is *formicarium*.

• Every Ant Farm is com-pletely American-made. assembled and packaged in Southern California by dis-abled workers.

A Great Way to Start Your Day—with Cereal Trivia

• The original name for Cheerios was "Cheeri Oats" when it hit shelves in 1942. But Quaker Oats had a different Idea about the use of the term "oats" and tried to sue. Cheeri Oats quickly changed their name to Cheerios, the matter was dropped, and the cereal became a big hit.

• In the 1930s, it wasn't a baseball or football star, but a wild animal trainer named Maria Rasputin who appeared on a box of Wheaties.

• It happened to "Raisin Bran," "Shredded Wheat," and "Corn Flakes," but so far, the name "Grape Nuts" has not gone generic.

• Ah, the golden years of "free inside this box" cereal promotions: In the 1950s, Kellogg's offered a baking-powdered powered atomic submarine inside a box of cereal. General Mills gave away miniature license plates at around the same time. Quaker Oats, though, beat them both. It gave away a deed to a square inch of Yukon Territory.

• Cartoon geniuses Bill Scott and Jay Ward, of *Rocky and Bullwinkle* and *George of the Jungle* fame, were responsible for a cereal great, too. Ward and Scott were asked to come up with a fun ad campaign with animation, which they did with Captain Crunch. It wasn't until afterward that General Mills then designed the cereal to put in the boxes.

One More
Little Yiddish Quiz
ANIMAL, VEGETABLE, OR MINERAL?

Circle the correct category for each Yiddish term.

1. Shikse	Animal	Vegetable	Mineral
2. Kvetsh	Animal	Vegetable	Mineral
3. Shmutz	Animal	Vegetable	Mineral
4. Kishkes	Animal	Vegetable	Mineral
5. Shvitz	Animal	Vegetable	Mineral
6. Shnapps	Animal	Vegetable	Mineral
7. Gelt	Animal	Vegetable	Mineral
8. Smontzess	Animal	Vegetable	Mineral
9. Pupik	Animal	Vegetable	Mineral
10. Tsatske	Animal	Vegetable	Mineral
11. Knubble	Animal	Vegetable	Mineral
12. Latkes	Animal	Vegetable	Mineral
13. Fleyshik	Animal	Vegetable	Mineral
14. Knaiydleach	Animal	Vegetable	Mineral
15. Tsibele	Animal	Vegetable	Mineral

Answers: 1. Animal: A female gentile; 2. Animal: A complainer; 3. Mineral: Dirt—usually moral dirt; 4. Animal: Guts; intestines; 5. Mineral: A steam bath; 6. Vegetable: Liquor; 7. Mineral: Money; 8. Mineral: Gadgets; 9. Animal: A bellybutton; 10. Mineral: A knickknack; 11. Vegetable: Garlic; 12. Vegetable: Potato pancakes; 13. Animal: Meat products; 14. Vegetable: A matzo ball; 15. Vegetable: An onion

Ripe Ol' Corn

"Uncle Josh Rides a Bicycle"

"Uncle Josh," Cal Stewart's country bumpkin, had problems figuring out modern city life (circa 1901). Here he tries out yet another fad that was sweeping the nation—a big-wheeled bicycle.

A LONG LAST SUMMER Ruben Hoskins, that is Ezra Hoskins' boy, he come home from college and brought one of them new fangled bysickle machines home with him, and I think ever since that time the whole town of Punkin Centre has got the bysickle fever.

Old Deacon Witherspoon he's been a-ridin' a bysickle to Sunday school, and Jim Lawson he couldn't ride one of them 'cause he's got a wooden leg; but he jist calculated if he could git it hitched up to the mowin' machine, he could cut more hay with it than any man in Punkin Centre. Somebody said Si Pettingill wuz tryin' to pick apples with a bysickle.

Well, all our boys and girls are ridin' bysickles now, and nothin' would do but I must learn how to ride one of them. Well, I didn't think very favorably on it, but in order to keep peace in the family I told them I would learn.

Well, gee willikee, by gum. I wish you had been thar when I commenced. I took that machine by the horns and I led it out into the middle of the road, and I got on it sort of unconcerned like, and then I got off sort of unconcerned like. Well, I set down a minnit to think it over, and then the trouble commenced. I got on that durned machine and it jumped up in the front and kicked up behind, and bucked up in the middle, and shied and balked and jumped sideways, and carried on worse 'n a couple of steers the fust time they're yoked. Well, I managed to hang on fer a spell, and then I went up in the air and come down all over that bysickle. I fell on top of it and under it and on both sides of it; I fell in front of the front wheel and behind the hind wheel at the same time.

Durned if I know how I done it but I did. I run my foot through the spokes, and put about a hundred and fifty punctures in a hedge fence, and skeered a hoss and buggy clear off the highway. I done more different kinds of tumblin' than any circus performer I ever seen in my life, and I made more revolutions in a fifteen-foot circle than any buzz-saw that ever was invented. Well, I lost the lamp, I lost the clamp, I lost my patience, I lost my temper, I lost my self-respect, my last suspender button and my standin' in the community. I broke the handle bars, I broke the sprockets, I broke the 10 commandments, I broke my New Year's pledge and the law agin loud and abusive language, and Jim Lawson got so excited that he run his wooden leg through a knot-hole in the porch and couldn't git it out again.

Well, I'm through with it; once is enough fer me. You can all ride your durned old bysickles that you want to, but fer my part I'd jist as soon stand up and walk as to sit down and walk. No more bysickles fer your Uncle Josh, not if he knows it, and your Uncle Josh sort of calculates as how he do.

EZRA HOSKINS
GROWSERYS
&
POST OFFIS

French kings had a variety of colorful nicknames, including Louis the Fat (Louis IV), Louis the Indolent (Louis V), Philip the Amorous, Pepin the Short, Charles the Bald (Charles II), and Charles the Simple (Charles III).

Driving Passions

TALES ABOUT AUTOMOBILES

Buckle up, as *Bathroom Companion* correspondent Kathie Meyer maneuvers through some pretty weird car stories, as well as some interesting things you may not have known about the automobile.

NO TIP TO THE VALET NECESSARY

Going rate to buy a prime parking space in beautiful downtown Melbourne, Australia? Well, last time we checked, Jones Lang Wootton Company was offering them for fourteen thousand dollars. But that's nothing. The same properties company was offering spaces in Hong Kong for a half-million dollars each.

PAY YOUR PREMIUM TO ME NOW, MAKE YOUR CLAIMS TO ST. PETER

In 1994, Oklahoma City police discovered several credulous but sincere people had been sold an automobile liability insurance called "God's Insurance Policy." The policy was issued by "the Father, Son, and the Holy Ghost" and contained mostly text from the Bible. It cost $285 and stated that "God's policy" would lend better protection than the usual commercial variety. Purchasers said they'd been told that the policy complied with Oklahoma's mandatory-insurance law.

WHY VOLVO MEANS "I ROLL" IN LATIN

In April 2002, Irv Gordon proudly reached the 2 million mile mark on his 1966 Volvo P1800, a car he bought new when he was 25 years old. In the ensuing years, Mr. Gordon, 61, a retired school teacher, averaged 55,000 miles a year. He recorded his first million miles in 1987. Gordon has recovered the driver's seat twice, rebuilt the engine once

The 1898 Winton was the first car driven across America.

at 680,000 miles, and has changed its oil 660 times. He claims the car has never broken down or failed to start. Asked how he felt to reach 2 million miles, Gordon said, "I was so happy, I couldn't get out of the car."

SOMEONE FORGOT TO TELL VOLKSWAGEN

In 1891, Emile Levassor and Rene Panhard of France were the first to come up with the idea of putting the engine in the front end of automobiles. This design, known as the *Systeme Panhard*, was the forerunner of modern cars. The vehicle Levassor and Panhard designed had an upright Daimler engine, a pedal-operated clutch, a change-speed gear box which drove the rear axle, a front radiator, and wooden ladder-chassis.

THE EDSEL BREATHES A SILENT SIGH OF RELIEF

According to National Public Radio's *Car Talk* listeners, the ten worst cars of the millennium were: **10.** VW Bus. **9.** Renault Dauphine. **8.** Cadillac Cimarron. **7.** Dodge Aspen/ Plymouth Volare. **6.** Renault LeCar. **5.** Chevy Chevette. **4.** AMC Gremlin. **3.** Ford Pinto. **2.** Chevy Vega. **1.** Yugo!

BEATS SELLING LEMONADE

Road construction caused a traffic jam near the Jordan house in Corvallis, Oregon. Sean Jordan, out of school on summer vacation, organized his siblings and a cousin into a work crew to clear an old railroad line that ran parallel to the main road and through the Jordan property. The kids then created their own private toll road, manning the pike, and collecting 50¢ per vehicle. The kids earned $270 in an eleven-day period, despite the fact that someone stole their money the first night and some cars just sped by without paying.

WOMEN DRIVERS

After the first American automobile appeared in 1893, women contributed to its subsequent development more than people realize. In 1903, Mary Anderson invented a windshield wiper operated by using a handle inside the car. Anderson's goal was to improve safety while driving in poor weather conditions. In the next twenty years, women were granted more than 175 auto-related patents. These inventions included a carburetor, a clutch mechanism, an electric engine starter, turn signals, traffic lights, and a starting mechanism. And during the 1930s, geologist Helen Blair Bartlett used her knowledge of petrology and mineralogy to develop new insulation for spark plugs.

automobile service station (1899), the invention of the automobile self-starter (1911), and the site of the first pedestrian button for the control of a traffic light (1948). Akron is where Charles Goodyear developed the process of vulcanizing rubber in 1839, and it is widely recognized as the rubber capital of the world, thanks to the Goodrich and Goodyear plants located there.

Akron, Ohio: Rubber Capital of the World!

Ladies and cars have gone together since the beginning of car history.

TAKING THE CAR SERIOUSLY
Ohio can boast a number of firsts in U.S. transportation history. They claim the first ambulance service (1865), first automobile made by John Lambert (1891), first traffic light (1914), first full-time

DRIVING UP DAISIES
Robert James Thompson, attempted to avoid tickets by claiming it was his wife who was driving two of his vans when they were caught by speed cameras three different times in 2001. Police became suspicious when they attempted to ticket Mrs. Thompson and found a nota-

tion on her record that she had died in 1998. The fifty-nine-year-old Thompson, who runs a pest control business, exhibited a mastery of the obvious when he noted: "It's just because my wife's dead that I got caught."

AMERICA'S MOST STOLEN

According to the National Insurance Crime Bureau, the most frequently stolen automobiles in 2002 are: **10.** Ford F150. **9.** Ford Taurus. **8.** Chevy Caprice. **7.** Toyota Corolla. **6.** Chevy C/K Pickups. **5.** Jeep Cherokee. **4.** Honda Civic. **3.** Oldsmobile Cutlass. **2.** Honda Accord. **1.** Toyota Camry. Frequently stolen cars follow market trends and the list varies from location to location. For instance, the Oldsmobile Cutlass was 2002's number one stolen vehicle in New Orleans and Chicago; the Chevrolet full-size pickup topped the stolen list in Fresno, California; and the Accord was number one in New York state.

UP ON THE ROOFTOP, FOUR-WHEELS PAUSE

A friend of Dave Anthony's asked him to help tear down his house, so he began by knocking down the garage with his 1984 four-wheel-drive GMC pickup truck.

While ramming the garage and drinking liberally, a flash of genius struck Anthony: He decided to see if he could maneuver his truck up onto his friend's roof. He wanted a photograph of the truck to submit to a four-wheel-drive magazine. "It wouldn't be a good life without a challenge," he said. "If you don't break something, you aren't trying very hard."

Anthony's truck made it to the top, albeit with a great deal of damage. Police, called by neighbors, prevented the alcohol-besotted Anthony from driving the truck down, and so he was stuck with a hefty towing bill to add to his repair bill.

WHAT'S IN A NAME?

• The Edsel was named after Edsel Ford—Henry Ford's son, Henry Ford II's dad.

• "Diesel" means nothing in particular. It's the name of the fellow who invented the engine—Rudolph Diesel.

• The VW Bug was commissioned by Adolf Hitler, who wanted to call it *Kraft-durch-Freude Wagen* ("Strength Through Joy Car.") Luckily, marketers eventually convinced him that *Volkswagen* ("the People's Auto") sounded better.

Hog Wild!

A PIG IS WORTH A THOUSAND WORDS

If you're a pig lover (and who isn't?), you'll be in hog heaven with these pig facts submitted by *Bathroom Companion* correspondent Sue Shipman.

- Pigs don't sweat.
- A pig can run a 7-minute mile.
- Pigs have four toes to use on each foot, but only stand on two.
- Pigs are the source of more than forty drugs and pharmaceuticals, including insulin.
- Ben and Jerry's recycles waste from ice cream production by giving it to local Vermont hog farmers as pig slop. The farmers claim the animals enjoy all the flavors except Mint Oreo.
- Groundhogs have also been known as "whistle pigs."
- The words *hog* and *pig* are not interchangeable. It's all about poundage. A pig is a swine that weighs under 180 pounds. A hog is anything above that weight. Believe it or not, these weight class distinctions mean a lot if you're in the market for pigs.
- Some other pig terminology: *Piglet* is the name for a newborn pig until weaning (2 to 5 weeks). A *shoat* or *weaner* is a young pig; a *barrow* is a half-grown castrated male, and a *gilt* is a half-grown female. In the full-grown categories, *boars* are uncastrated males, *stags* are the castrated ones, and *sows* are all females. Remember this next time you're at a pig auction or you'll have bacon and egg on your face.

- In 1976 the swine flu vaccine caused more illness and death than did the disease itself.

- The phrase "pearls before swine" is from the Bible, Matthew 7:6 — "Give not that which is holy unto the dogs, neither cast ye your pearls before swine, lest they trample them under their feet."

No matter what your big brother told you, pigs don't fly: never have; never will.

- The upper part of a pig's haunch provides the best, and therefore most expensive, cuts of meat. Hence the term, "high on the hog."

- **THE INEFFECTIVE ROOTER** — an Aesopian story:

> A drunken Man was lying in the road with a bleeding nose, upon which he had fallen, when a Pig passed that way.
>
> "You wallow fairly well," said the Pig, "but, my fine fellow, you have much to learn about rooting."

- Large hog farms made it necessary for the North Carolina legislature to vote $170,000 to fund a swine odor task force in 1994. The task force declined to take their measurements using machines, stating, "The human nose is the primary element in most attempts to gauge odor."

- Burger King restaurants cook up about 500,000 pounds of bacon every month.

- Ever wonder why the piggy bank? It's yet another victim of faulty translation. The term probably comes from the obscure French word *pygg* — a certain type of clay used to make money jars in the fifteenth century.

- Hickory smoked bacon takes about twenty-one days to cure.

- About half of the domestic pigs in the world live in China.

- The largest pig ever was 2,552 pounds. His name was Big Bill.

- A piglet is born at about 3.5 pounds and can double its weight in a week.

- It took forty-eight little piggies to film the title role in the movie, *Babe*. Each pig could act only between the ages of 16 and 18 weeks, for consistency. Mechanical pigs also played roles in the movie and sequel. The studio swears that none of the pigs used in the movies were turned into ham or bacon—they all went to universities, ag colleges, or farms to live out their 15–20 year natural lives.

• Columbus introduced hogs to the Americas in 1493 on his second voyage.

• Pigs can get sunburned.

• Pigs are loud! The Concorde jet was banned from New York when its jets were louder than 112 decibels at take off. A university study measuring pig squeals found the squeals averaged between 100 and 115 decibels.

• Buying a "pig in a poke" means buying something sight unseen. Unscrupulous merchants in Medieval Europe would often put a runt pig or a stray cat in the small bag (which was called a "poke") instead of the promised young pig. So when wary buyers actually looked into the poke prior to their purchase, they would often "let the cat out of the bag."

• Calling a police officer a "pig" wasn't just from the 1960s; the term has been in used commonly among the criminal element for almost two hundred years before that.

• Since Muslims shun pork and devout Hindus do not eat beef, in New Delhi India you can get a "Maharaja Mac" at McDonald's. It is made of mutton.

• Pigs eat like, well, pigs. They're omnivores and eat anything from breads, fruits, and vegetables, to rodents, lizards, and even parts of other pigs. One of their favorite meals is rattlesnake.

• Pigs kill more people each year than sharks do. Pigs, however, are not really aggressive, they're just large and persistent—sometimes fatally so, especially to small children.

• Although pigs sound the same from country to country, how we interpret those sounds varies. Here's what a pig "says" in places around the world:

"Oink, oink"—America
"Crum, crum"—Poland
"Hulu, hulu"—China
"Groin, groin"—France
"Kryoo krool"—Russia
"Ood, ood"—Thailand
"Neff, neff"—Sweden
"Hrju, hrju"—Ukrainian
"Rok, rok"—Croatia/Serbia
"Buu, buu"—Japan
"Grunz"—Germany

W. C. Privy Wants You!

Join the Bᴀᴛʜʀᴏᴏᴍ Cᴏᴍᴘᴀɴɪᴏɴs ᴏғ Mʀ. Pʀɪᴠʏ (BCOMP)! Send an e-mail to *membership@bathroomcompanion.com* and we'll send you a printable free membership card, plus a "Go Away, I'm Reading the *Bathroom Companion*" door knob hanger for your bathroom. And don't forget to drop by our Web site at **www.bathroomcompanion.com** for bonus articles and more fun things.

Or if you prefer, write to us at Bathroom Companion, c/o St. Martin's Press, 175 Fifth Avenue, New York, NY 10010.

Send us your story ideas, photos, articles, Web links you like, or other cool stuff we'd want to know about for the next Bathroom Companion. If we use them, we'll thank you in the next book and maybe even send you cool stuff in return.

Last known photo of W. C. Privy in retirement, prematurely trying to invent the Rubik's Cube.

(For emergency use only)